EMPIRES OF EURASIA

EMPIRES OF EURASIA

How Imperial Legacies
Shape International Security

JEFFREY MANKOFF

Yale

UNIVERSITY PRESS

New Haven and London

CSIS | CENTER FOR STRATEGIC &
INTERNATIONAL STUDIES

Published with assistance from the Kingsley Trust Association
Publication Fund established by the Scroll and Key Society of Yale
College, and from the foundation established in memory of Calvin
Chapin of the Class of 1788, Yale College.

The views expressed in this work are those of the author and are not
an official policy or position of the National Defense University, the
Department of Defense, or the U.S. Government.

The Center for Strategic and International Studies (CSIS) is a
bipartisan, nonprofit policy research organization dedicated to
advancing practical ideas to address the world's greatest challenges.

Yale University Press books may be purchased in quantity for
educational, business, or promotional use. For information, please e-mail
sales.press@yale.edu (U.S. office) or sales@yaleup.co.uk (U.K. office).

Set in Janson type by Newgen North America.
Printed in the United States of America.

Library of Congress Control Number: 2021944485

ISBN 978-0-300-24825-8 (hardcover : alk. paper)

A catalogue record for this book is available from the British Library.

This paper meets the requirements of ANSI/NISO z39.48-1992
(Permanence of Paper).

10 9 8 7 6 5 4 3 2 1

Für Elise

Contents

Acknowledgments ix

A Note on Transliteration xi

Introduction 1

RUSSIA 16

1. Russian Identity Between Empire and Nation 23
2. Russia's Borderlands and the Territorialization of Identity 44
3. Russia's Near Abroad and the Geopolitics of Empire 60

TURKEY 81

4. Those Who Call Themselves Turks: Empire, Islam, and Nation 89
5. On the Margins of the Nation and the State: Turkey's Kurdish Borderland 107
6. The Geopolitics of the Post-Ottoman Space 123

IRAN 145

7. Iranian Identity and Iran's "Empire of the Mind" 153
8. Iran's Borderlands: The Non-Persian Periphery 169
9. Greater Iran (*Iranzamin*) and Iran's Imperial Imagination 189

CHINA   207

10. Civilization and Imperial Identity in China   213
11. China's Inner Asian Borderlands   231
12. Sinocentrism and the Geopolitics of *Tianxia*   251

Conclusion: A World Safe for Empire?   269

Notes   277
Index   343

Acknowledgments

WRITING A BOOK IS a mostly solitary process, but one that requires the support and collaboration of innumerable other people. Writing this particular book required me to learn an enormous amount about unfamiliar people and places, and I could not have managed it but for the generous aid, advice, and support provided by so many friends and colleagues.

At CSIS, I am grateful to the late Zbigniew Brzezinski for initially raising the topic, to John Hamre for suggesting I take it on, and to Josie Gabel, Mike Green, Victor Cha, and Rebecka Shirazi for their advice and insight. Heather Conley and Olga Oliker helped make sure I had time to finish the manuscript. Research associates Oliver Backes, Cyrus Newlin, and Roksana Gabidullina helped track down references and coordinated logistics for field research. Interns Amber Frankland, Robert Gill, Claire Haffner, and Kimberly Schuster provided research support. Emily Tiemeyer drew the maps. Bonnie Glaser assisted with contacts in China. Bülent Aliriza shared his knowledge of Turkish history and politics, and went out of his way to help arrange interviews in Turkey.

Dimitar Bechev, Paul Bushkovitch, Shannon Cassidy, Keith Darden, Andrey Ivanov, Robert Kaplan, Paul Kennedy, Sulmaan Khan, Michael Kimmage, Chris Miller, James Millward, Angela Stent, Farzin Vejdani, and Yang Zheng provided advice and encouragement. Isak Saaf assisted with translations from Old Russian. Special thanks are due to Eugene Mazo for acting as a de facto literary agent, not to mention, at times, as an armchair therapist. At Yale University Press, I am grateful to Jaya Chatterjee and Eva Skewes for their wisdom and guidance. Three anonymous reviewers suggested new sources and helped sharpen my thinking. The staff of Yale University libraries and the systems comprising the Washington Research

Library Consortium (WRLC) helped me track down obscure works, and were indulgent of missed due dates.

Research included meetings and interviews conducted on a nonattribution basis with approximately ninety scholars, journalists, NGO workers, businesspeople, officials, and diplomats in the United States, China, Russia, and Turkey. In Beijing, I am extremely grateful to Guan Guihai and Wang Jisi, who hosted me for a series of roundtables at Peking University. In Turkey, Meltem Ersoy put me in touch with several people from her network. Nebil İlseven organized a roundtable at the Progressive Thought Institute and a wonderful evening discussion of Ottoman history on a rooftop overlooking the Bosporus. Güven Sak hosted me for a seminar at TEPAV in Ankara. In Russia, I am particularly grateful to Aleksandr Abalov, Vladislav Inozemtsev, Ekaterina Kuznetsova, Sergey Markedonov, and Aleksey Miller for their time and their insights. Ekaterina Kuznetsova graciously shared some of her own unpublished work. I am also grateful to my new colleagues at National Defense University for their insights and for giving me the opportunity to complete revisions.

Bülent Aliriza, Jonathan Cristol, Bonnie Glaser, Lauren Hickok, Seçkin Köstem, Chris Miller, Olga Oliker, Ruslan Pukhov, Mahsa Rouhi, Michael Rubin, Rachel Salzman, Phillip Saunders, Alex Vatanka, and Joel Wuthnow provided feedback on drafts in various stages of completion. It goes without saying that none of them is responsible for any remaining shortcomings.

This project would not have been possible without the intellectual and financial support provided by the Smith Richardson Foundation (SRF). In our ahistorical age, SRF's support for the study of the historical roots of problems in international security is vital, and I am deeply grateful for SRF's interest in and support of my work.

The book is dedicated to my daughter Elise in the hope that she will inherit her father's curiosity about the world.

A Note on Transliteration

APART FROM DIRECT QUOTATIONS and the exceptions discussed below, Chinese names and words are rendered in the *pinyin* system. Turkish names from the Ottoman era are given their modern Turkish equivalents even when of Arabic or Persian origin (thus Adbülhamid rather than Abd al-Hamid). Russian and Persian transliterations are based on the Board of Geographic Names Romanization system. While I have kept diacritics in the references, I have left them out of the main text. I have avoided transliterating Russian hard (ъ) and soft (ь) signs in proper names, but designated them respectively as " and ' elsewhere.

People and places likely familiar to an English-speaking audience are provided in their most well-known form: Catherine II, Isfahan, Chiang Kai-shek, and Confucius rather than Yekaterina, Eşfahan, Jiang Jieshi, or Kongfuzi. Qing emperors are initially referred to by their era name (the Qianlong Emperor), though on subsequent mentions I use the era name as though it were a personal name (Qianlong). In line with prevailing usage in each country, I refer to inhabitants of the Republic of Azerbaijan as Azerbaijanis and to Oghuz Turkic-speaking Shi'as in northern Iran as Azeris. Names of cities are given in the form preferred by the states in which they are currently located (Kyiv, not Kiev)—without implying support for any particular state's claim.

Parenthetical dates next to the names of rulers designate regnal years.

Introduction

BENDER TODAY IS A small city in the Transnistrian Moldavian People's Republic, an unrecognized statelet that attempted to break away from the newly independent state of Moldova in the chaotic months following the collapse of the Soviet Union. The rather sleepy town is notable for two features: the large Ottoman-era fortress overlooking the city from a hill that rises up from the Dniester River, and the military base on its far side, housing Russian troops who belong to a peacekeeping force set up at the end of Transnistria's war for independence. Separated by half a mile and half a millennium, the fortress and the base testify to the enduring imperial competition that has shaped the history of not just this corner of southeastern Europe, but much of the Eurasian landmass.

Bender's fortress dates to the sixteenth century, when the town became an Ottoman frontier outpost during the reign of Süleyman the Magnificent (1520–66). Its construction came as the Ottoman Empire was tightening its grip on the Principality of Moldavia, whose Orthodox Christian rulers (*hospodars*) enjoyed substantial autonomy, but were appointed in Istanbul. The fortress later provided refuge for the Cossack hetman Ivan Mazeppa and the Swedish king Charles XII, whose defeat at the hands of Peter the Great (1696–1725) at Poltava in 1709 laid the foundation for the establishment of the Russian Empire. After passing back and forth between Ottoman and Russian control, Bender and its fortress were firmly incorporated into the Russian Empire when Alexander I (1801–25) annexed the surrounding region of Bessarabia in 1812, at the height of the Napoleonic Wars. Bender was then conquered and reconquered multiple times during the two world wars.

I

In the twenty-first century as in the sixteenth, Bender remains an outpost on the margins of empire. Just as Süleyman's architects built the fortress to ensure the Principality of Moldavia would remain within the Ottoman orbit, the base just below helps prevent the modern Republic of Moldova (of which Transnistria is legally part) from restoring its control of Transnistria, a prerequisite for securing membership in the European Union or NATO. The Moldovan government would prefer the troops leave, but, ruling over a small, weak state along Russia's postimperial frontier and constrained by the ceasefire it accepted to end the conflict, lacks full sovereignty over its territory and has little ability to force matters. Nor is this history unique. All across the Eurasian landmass, from Bender to Mosul and Sevastopol to Herat, cities and regions that were long objects of imperial expansion and rule are once again enmeshed in the geopolitics of empire.

The early twenty-first century is shaping up to be a new age of empire in Eurasia. This new imperial age is characterized by the willingness of the region's major powers—Russia, Turkey, Iran, and China—to intervene in the affairs of their smaller neighbors using military force, local proxies, economic dependence, and other tools of statecraft. Governments in Moscow, Ankara, Tehran, and Beijing project power and influence across their borders and into territories with which they are tied by bonds of history, culture, language, and religion. In Ukraine and Syria, as in Moldova, this pursuit of postimperial influence has brought military intervention and at least de facto territorial change. Elsewhere, the new imperial geopolitics takes the form of unequal economic relationships or bids to secure the loyalty of populations sharing cross-border religious, linguistic, or ethnic links. While different from the nation-states-as-billiard-balls model beloved of certain international relations theorists, this state of affairs would have looked familiar to an official of Süleyman's or Peter's court.

Russia, Turkey, Iran, and China, the four states driving this return to imperial geopolitics, are themselves heirs to long imperial traditions. The final iterations of the vast empires that ruled their territories, those of the Romanovs, Ottomans, Qajars, and Qing, respectively, all collapsed in the chaotic years between China's 1911 Xinhai Revolution and the coronation of Reza Khan as shah of Iran in 1925. Despite efforts by early postimperial rulers to replace these heterogeneous, territorially ambiguous empires with "modern" states, the transformation was only partial. Today, with the barriers that long kept Eurasia fragmented now eroding, connections dating to the imperial era are taking on new salience.

Seeking new sources of legitimacy as the post–Cold War lure of liberal democracy fades, contemporary politicians turn more to the imperial era as a reference point and source of inspiration. Russian president Vladimir Putin and Turkish president Recep Tayyip Erdoğan are particularly adept at portraying themselves as heirs to their respective countries' imperial traditions—a new tsar and a new sultan.[1] From the language of their speeches to the style of their buildings, they forge symbolic connections to the imperial past.[2] So in their own ways do Chinese president Xi Jinping and Iranian supreme leader Ayatollah Ali Khamenei. All portray continuity with an idealized past, in which they seek inspiration, a model of non-democratic politics, and status on the global stage. Imperial symbols like the Russian double eagle and the Ottoman *tuğra* (the sultan's stylized signature) adorn public buildings, many of which are themselves patterned on imperial models. The imperial capitals, Istanbul and St. Petersburg, have been given new prominence at the expense of Ankara and Moscow (both Putin and Erdoğan began their political careers in the municipal government of the old capitals). Meanwhile, Persepolis, capital of the Achaemenid empire, which the early Islamic Republic of Iran threatened to obliterate, is once again a prominent symbol of Iranian grandeur, and China debates rebuilding the Old Summer Palace, a symbol of imperial might destroyed by Anglo-French troops in 1860.

The central argument of this book is that these four states and their geopolitical ambitions remain indelibly shaped by their imperial pasts. Because they were once empires, Russia, Turkey, Iran, and China, I argue, are not—and are unlikely to ever become—nation-states inhabiting a sharply delineated territory and with a population sharing a common ethnic or linguistic identity. Like Britain and France, these four states transformed themselves after the end of formal empire into what Charles Tilly termed "national states," which "[govern] multiple contiguous regions and their cities by means of centralized, differentiated, and autonomous structures."[3] For historical and geographic reasons, however, they remain much closer to their imperial roots. As Geoffrey Hosking once observed, while "Britain *had* an empire, Russia *was* an empire—and perhaps still is."[4] So in their own ways are China, Iran, and Turkey (from the perspective of Ireland or Scotland, Britain is as well). Britain, France, and other former colonial metropoles have diverse populations and remain entangled to varying degrees with their former colonies through migration, military intervention, and institutions like the Commonwealth and *La Francophonie*. Yet they are territorially bounded: there is no ambiguity about the border between

Britain and India, or even between France and Algeria. Nor, with a few exceptions—like holders of British National (Overseas) passports in Hong Kong—is there ambiguity about who belongs to the national community. To a much greater degree, Russia, Turkey, Iran, and China remain internally diverse and territorially ambiguous, with elites who are cognizant of and at times eager to actively restore past greatness, including through the projection of power across their postimperial borders.

Most important, the recovery or reemergence of imperial legacies is one of the principal reasons China, Iran, Russia, and Turkey are all to varying degrees revisionist powers relative to a post–World War II global order that regards empire and imperialism as illegitimate. Since 1945, the principles of self-determination, states' sovereign equality, and right to territorial inviolability have served as the bedrock for claims of political legitimacy, and the foundation upon which the liberal norms and institutions underpinning the global order rest. Yet, in important ways, Russia, Turkey, Iran, and China have always posed a challenge to that order. Not only have all four failed to become liberal democracies, but as with Russian forces in Bender, they remain entangled with their onetime peripheries in ways that facilitate cross-border power projection and the disruption of smaller states' sovereignty and, in some cases, territorial integrity.

These four states also have increasingly difficult relations with the United States, which is the main designer and beneficiary of the current world order. Washington accuses China, Iran, and Russia—the three that are not U.S. allies—of pursuing "belligerent revisionism buoyed by dreams of restoring some lost glory" and failing to act like "normal states"—"normal" in this context implying being territorially satiated and strategically aligned with the United States.[5] Though a U.S. ally, Turkey's intervention in Syria and push for strategic autonomy (including deepening cooperation with Iran and Russia) are a source of tension for similar reasons. While relations between and among the four are complex, Russia, Turkey, Iran, and China are united by an aspiration to make the twenty-first-century world safe for empire.[6] That aspiration, in turn, underpins their increasing alignment with one another on major questions of international order, even when they remain at odds over specific territories and regions.

Relative to explanations emphasizing ideological (or political), structural, or civilizational causes, imperial legacies get surprisingly little attention in explaining China, Iran, Russia, and Turkey's revisionist turn. Ideological/political explanations suggest that China, Iran, Russia, and Turkey aim to dominate their neighbors and challenge an order built on sovereign equality because they have authoritarian leaders who embrace an ideological worldview that rejects the basic principles of liberalism and democracy.[7] While none of China, Iran, Russia, and Turkey is a liberal democracy, their political systems—from the Chinese Communist Party's (CCP) comprehensive domination to Erdoğan's electoral populism—differ substantially. Merely writing them all off as authoritarian sacrifices analytic precision, and risks overlooking the conditions that have produced their respective systems. It also ignores how other states with similar political systems remain status quo powers. Russia is hardly more authoritarian than, for instance, Belarus, and China's party-state closely resembles Vietnam's—but Moscow and Beijing are revisionist in a way that Minsk and Hanoi are not. To be sure, Russia and China—along with Iran and Turkey—are more ideological, in the sense of portraying their respective versions of "authoritarianism [as] more than an approach to governing or a means of enriching a corrupt ruling class" but also "a distinctive way of looking at the world" that they seek to legitimate at the global level.[8] Still, the diversity between these states' models suggests that authoritarianism by itself is too neat an explanation—and wrongly implies that a change of government alone would reconcile them to the existing order.

Structural explanations point less to these states' ideological rejection of that order than to their exclusion from it by the West—but overlook why these states were unable to join Western-led structures in the first place.[9] At the end of the Cold War, the United States assumed that liberal democracy was the only legitimate form of governance, and built or expanded institutions that prioritized liberal norms, excluding in the process states that did not measure up. Of course, the revolutionary clergy ruling the Islamic Republic of Iran was always going to be a poor fit for a political order based on international law. In Asia, the U.S.-led treaty alliance system left little space for an increasingly wealthy and confident but still autocratic China—though the U.S. sought to integrate China into a liberalized global economy through the World Trade Organization. By contrast, Russia and Turkey appeared in the early 1990s to be candidates for inclusion in an expanded trans-Atlantic West. Instead of integrating Russia, though, the West expanded NATO partly in response to a perception that Russia still threatened its neighbors. Meanwhile, the EU continued blocking Turkish membership because Turkey was insufficiently democratic—but also too big, too Muslim, and too poor, its borders too permeable—too different, in other words, from the would-be nation-states in Central and Eastern Europe that did achieve EU membership.

Civilizational arguments, in turn, emphasize the role of identity to suggest that Russia, Turkey, Iran, and China embrace values at odds with Western-style liberalism because they are, in essence, non-Western—and were not colonized by the West.[10] Politicians in all four have spoken of their states as embodying distinct civilizations with distinct political cultures, suggesting that the West's "universal values" are not so universal. Yet civilizations evolve and are composed of multiple strands. Is Iranian civilization Zoroastrian, Muslim, specifically Shi'ite, Persian, or some combination? Who decides—a Westernizing shah or revolutionary ayatollahs? Contrary to what Samuel Huntington posited, civilizational identity and its meaning are contested.[11] Moreover, multiple states can embody a particular civilization. What makes revisionist Russia a more "authentic" exponent of what Huntington termed Orthodox civilization than status quo–oriented Ukraine? Why is the People's Republic of China (PRC) more authentically "Chinese" than the Republic of China (ROC) on Taiwan, or more authentically Confucian than any number of East Asian states? Certainly, the claims of elites in Ankara, Beijing, Moscow, and Tehran that their states embody distinct civilizations matter, but primarily because they have the capability to mobilize that civilizational identity against the West's perceived hegemony. That capability, I argue is a consequence of the imperial legacies they inherited.

Empire

Thanks in part to the Cold War and the struggle for decolonization, which made it a term of opprobrium, the label "empire" remains politically fraught. To say a state is (or was) an empire is to imply that it is "wicked . . . anachronistic and doomed to disappear."[12] In part for this reason, Eurasia's postimperial states long attempted to patch over their imperial pasts. Until recently, much of the historiography also accepted a teleological view of empires' transitioning to nation-states or national states; or, as in some Western studies of the Soviet Union, pointed to the USSR's imperial elements to suggest it was on the way to following the Russian Empire onto the dust heap of history.

As a category of analysis, though, empire provides a useful lens for understanding how imperial successor states like China, Iran, Russia, and Turkey approach the political and security challenges they face in modern Eurasia. Of course, appreciating continuities with the imperial past does not imply that postimperial states are motivated solely by an atavistic urge to expand or dominate their neighbors. It suggests, rather, that the legacy of empire is one important reference point for making sense of these states' politics and foreign policy, and for understanding why they do not fit easily into an international system designed for a world that has turned its back on empire.

For such a ubiquitous term, "empire" has proven remarkably slippery.[13] Many Western analysts are quick to condemn any act of power projection, especially by rivals like Russia and China, as empire-building. Meanwhile, scholars have labeled entities ranging from Athens's Delian League to the European Union, and much in between, as empires.[14] Often "empire" and "imperialism" are used interchangeably, and sometimes are modified by qualifiers like "informal" or "free-trade."[15] Empires are often held to be the antithesis of nation-states that emerged in their wake, even though most European nation-states and national states began life as empires, their seeming homogeneity the result of a long process of subjection and domination that later generations had little interest in remembering.[16] So too the United States, whose westward expansion and attendant extermination of the Native American population that stood in its way, is the product of empire.[17]

In recent years, scholars have made great strides in the comparative study of empire, even if a precise definition remains elusive. At the bare minimum, an empire, as Dominic Lieven notes, is "a very great power that has left its mark on the international relations of an era" and "rules over wide territories and many peoples."[18] Beyond size and diversity, empire is also a distinct form of political organization, something between a unitary state and an international order comprised of multiple sovereign states.[19] According to Karen Barkey, empire is a "negotiated enterprise," where "the basic configuration of relationships between imperial authorities and peripheries is constructed piecemeal in a different fashion for each periphery, creating a patchwork pattern of relations with structural holes between peripheries such that "the direct and indirect vertical relations of imperial integration coexist with horizontal relations of segmentation."[20] An empire, in other words, is a center with many unconnected peripheries, a "'rimless' hub and spoke system." The territorial extent of an empire, defined only by subordination to a central authority, is ever-shifting, driven by the logic of perpetual expansion.[21]

Within this system, authority flows out from the center, while revenue, recruits, and other goods flow back from peripheries, which remain disconnected from one another. In contrast to an international system based on tribute or the power of a hegemon, however, imperial rule also shapes the internal structure of the peripheries, transforming more or less subtly their political institutions and social structures. Krishan Kumar suggests that metropoles "export their characteristic institutions to the periphery . . . creating a common culture that ensures that metropolitan institutions and ideas always have the upper hand."[22] Imperial legacies are visible therefore not only at the center of former empires, but around their peripheries too, where culture and institutions converge with those of the former center, which is often adept at manipulating them for its own ends.

The willingness and ability of imperial power to transform subject polities and peoples is, however, limited. Unlike the real or putative nation-states that emerged around their peripheries, Eurasia's empires did not seek ethnic, linguistic, religious, or institutional uniformity. Rather, they managed dependencies through a range of negotiated arrangements entailing varying degrees of autonomy, what Burbank and Cooper term the "politics of difference."[23] This approach involves either the use of viceroys or other agents of the center, or, conversely, the empowerment of local elites to collect tribute and marshal forces for war. Either way, distinct arrangements ensured that peripheries remained separate from the imperial "core" as well as from one another.[24] To say that modern Russia, Turkey, Iran, and China continue to bear traces of empire is to suggest that many of these characteristics still exist, from the preeminence of the state over the individual, to the "politics of difference" that allows Chechnya's Ramzan Kadyrov to build up a *sharia*-inflected statelet inside Russia, or the fluidity of borders between Turkey and Syria, Russia and Ukraine, or Iran and Iraq.

Empire, though, is not only a particular model of politics, but also what Ronald Grigor Suny terms a "discursive formation imbued with normative and subjective understandings," where the practice of imperial conquest and rule shapes expectations about the nature of the state.[25] In other words, empires behave a certain way by virtue of their elites regarding them as empires. The predecessors of today's Chinese, Iranian, Russian, and Turkish states aspired to expand their frontiers, encompassed multiple peoples, broadcast their legitimacy by coopting religious authorities, and claimed to owe allegiance to no higher authority. Imperial identities and the policies they inspired continue to resonate in Eurasia's postimperial states as well.[26] All claim a special destiny and elevated status relative to their neighbors, rejecting the suggestion that they should become "normal," territorially satiated, status quo powers.

Eurasia

Famously described by Mackinder as the "geographic pivot of history," Eurasia was for thousands of years an arena for exchange and geopolitical competition between empires, among them the predecessors of today's Chinese, Iranian, Russian, and Turkish states.[27] While Eurasia's empires engaged in the same processes of mapping, describing, categorizing, and manipulating communal identities as Europe's overseas colonial empires, their location at the center of the Eurasian landmass, "between the lower Danube River region in the west and the Yalu River region in the east, and between the sub-Arctic taïga forest zone in the north and the Himalayas in the south," set them on a distinct historical trajectory.[28]

That trajectory includes a shared political culture emerging from the nomadic steppes, which grounds legitimacy in military valor and territorial expansion.[29] Dating to a precapitalist age, such expansion had nothing to do with the search for markets or outlets for surplus capital, which Hobson, Lenin, and others blamed for Europe's imperialism.[30] It also produced states composed of contiguous territories, where the separation of center from periphery, colony from metropole is less clear-cut than between European metropoles and their overseas colonies. The territorial extent of Eurasia's empires was never fixed; throughout interimperial "shatter zones" in the Balkans, the Caucasus/eastern Anatolia, Mesopotamia, and Central Asia, sovereignty tended to be shifting, layered, and, at times, overlapping.[31] Administrative, much less cultural-linguistic uniformity was impossible to establish over such a large, constantly shifting territory. The lack of durable control in frontier regions meant that when imperial cores weakened, indigenous elites had an opportunity to pursue independence, or at least seek out other overlords. Connected to the imperial cores but never truly integrated, imperial peripheries like Ukraine, Iraq, or Afghanistan have again become sites of contestation in the twenty-first century.

Compared to the European colonial empires, boundaries between communities were also more permeable; the racial hierarchies at the heart of European colonialism were, if not absent, then much less clear-cut in Eurasia. While it would have been impossible to imagine an Indian or Jamaican dynasty on the British throne, ruling dynasties in Eurasia often came from a different ethno-linguistic background than the bulk of the people they ruled: Iran's Safavid and Qajar dynasties were Turkic-speaking Azeris, and the Qing was dominated by the originally Tungusic-speaking Manchus. The absence or irrelevance of ethno-linguistic identification between the dynasty and its subjects facilitated toleration of minority groups and the "politics of difference."

It complicated, however, nineteenth-century efforts at nation-building, undertaken in an effort to mobilize diverse populations behind the idea of maintaining the empire. These attempts to, in Benedict Anderson's famous phrase, stretch "the short, tight skin of the nation over the gigantic body of the empire" foundered on the paradox that building a nation within the empire required a degree of uniformity that made coexistence more difficult.[32] Thus because efforts to create an Ottoman civic nation, a policy eventually termed Ottomanism, "spoke" Turkish, Ottoman Greeks, Slavs, Arabs, and others perceived it as a form of Turkish rather than Ottoman nationalism, and sought their own futures outside of a Turkifying Ottoman Empire.[33]

Moreover, growing numbers of intellectuals and activists from the dominant ethnolinguistic group in all four empires also rejected these efforts to create a multiethnic, multireligious citizenry. They sought instead to make the multinational Russian (*rossiyskaya*) Empire more ethnically Russian (*russkiy*), the Manchu-dominated Qing more "Chinese," the Ottoman Empire more Turkish, and Qajar Iran more Persian. This emergence of ethnonationalism proved dangerous for "foreign" rulers like the Turkic Qajars and the Manchu Qing, portrayed by nineteenth-century nationalists as oppressors of the majority nation.

The collapse of all four empires was thus accompanied by communal violence targeting minorities alleged to have enjoyed unwonted privileges under imperial rule, as well as the emergence of separatist movements around the periphery. Some of these movements (such as those of the Hellenic Greeks, Poles, Afghans, and Outer Mongols) were successful, while others (those of the Kurds, Ukrainians, Azeris, or Tibetans) were not. Postimperial China, Iran, Russia, and Turkey all inherited unstable frontiers and borders that reflected political contingency more than clear geographic or cultural logic. Compared to Europe's colonial empires, Eurasia's terrestrial empires thus remained much more deeply entangled—ethnically, culturally, religiously, economically, and politically—with their postimperial peripheries.

And while attempts at nationalizing Eurasia's multiethnic empires largely failed, the effort itself helps explain one of the paradoxes of imperial nostalgia: many of the most ardent imperialists in modern China, Iran, Russia, and Turkey are also nationalists. A nationalist reading of history allows them to conflate the reality of the old empires with the modern idea of nation-states. Thus, the CCP claims the Qing as part of *Chinese* history, and sees the Qing's boundaries as the legitimate frontiers of the Chinese state—even as it demands that Manchus and other minority populations identify with "Chinese" culture. No comparable process of nationalization occurred, for instance, in the Cisleithanian—or "Austrian"—half of Austria-Hungary (where the dominant, pan-German strain of nationalism sought to abandon the multiethnic empire for a Greater Germany— an option foreclosed by Bismarck after the 1866 Austro-Prussian War). Today, few citizens of the Austrian Republic identify with the legacy of Habsburg Austria, or regard the Czech Republic, Slovenia, and other parts of Habsburg Cisleithania as part of Austria's "legitimate" patrimony.

Legacies

As shown by the polemics surrounding Britain's departure from the EU, empire and its loss continue to shape the politics and foreign policy of successor states in a variety of ways, in Eurasia as elsewhere.[34] The specific nature of empire in Eurasia, however, has left postimperial China, Iran, Russia, and Turkey facing a series of common challenges distinct from those of Britain and other onetime metropoles of overseas empires. Some of these legacies are physical or institutional relics of the past, such as ambiguity about the nature of national identity, borderlands trapped between the "politics of difference" and political integration, and the persistence of "near abroads" or postimperial spaces beyond the borders of the successor states. Others have to do with contemporary leaders' and publics' understanding of their own histories, in positing that China, Iran, Russia, and Turkey are the heirs of previous empires, and therefore retain the right to be "very great powers." The salience of imperial legacies for contemporary politics is thus the product of both path-dependence and conscious choices made by leaders on the basis of the political culture that produced them.[35] Collectively, the presence of these legacies suggests the existence of a kind of postimperial syndrome that shapes the behavior of Eurasia's postimperial states on the international stage in ways that fit poorly with post-1945 norms and institutions based on the principles of self-determination, sovereign equality, and territorial integrity.

Identity

As the "left-behind" rump of the old empires, China, Iran, Russia, and Turkey each has haphazard borders that do not necessarily align with the distribution of ethnic, linguistic, or religious communities. All four, in other words, face a mismatch between nation and state. All therefore promote a kind of supraethnic national identity, sometimes encapsulated in neologisms like *Rossiyskiy* or *Zhonghua minzu*, to emphasize the contrast with more ethnocentric conceptions of the nation like *Russkiy* or *Hanzu* (Han). These supraethnic, postimperial nations are heterogeneous, open to assimilation, and center more on culture than on ethnicity. They represent a strategy for maintaining the full extent of the territory inherited from the old empires in an age of nationalism, for stretching the nation's short, tight skin over the unwieldy geobody of the empire.

Yet because China, Iran, Russia, and Turkey have been exposed to the same nationalizing pressures as other modern states, ethnonationalism remains an important undercurrent, one that political leaders sometimes invoke as a tool for mobilization. Even adherents of the idea of a supraethnic, postimperial nation demand varying degrees of assimilation to the culture of the majority. Just as Ottomanism "spoke" Turkish, today's postimperial nations tend to "speak" the language of the dominant group. Among minorities, assimilation is rarely accepted without protest, and ethnic, linguistic, and religious minorities in all four states have pushed back, sometimes violently, while state authorities have, at times, adopted draconian measures in response. Especially in sensitive border regions, minority communities remain poorly integrated, and postimperial states approach them through a securitized prism.

Meanwhile, culturally focused approaches to identity allow Russia, Turkey, Iran, and China to maintain some connection to populations outside their state borders. While scholars usually focus on the distinction between civic and ethnic nationhood, China, Iran, Russia, and Turkey all maintain what Kumar and others have identified as an "imperial" approach to nationality, which identifies particular groups of noncitizens as real or potential members of the national community, thereby providing a justification for intervention in neighboring states' affairs.[36] Russia's policy of supporting "compatriots" and claims that Russians and Ukrainians comprise one people may be the clearest example, but Eurasia's other postimperial states behave similarly. Ankara not only portrays Turks and Azerbaijanis as "one nation, two states," but positions itself as a focus for the loyalty of (especially Sunni) peoples across the former Ottoman lands. Iran's revolutionary government similarly appeals to Shi'as across the Middle East. Even for China, which has been more cautious about appealing to populations in neighboring states, growing mobilization of overseas Chinese (*huaqiao huaren*) communities indicates a shift toward a more "imperial" articulation of Chinese nationality. This mismatch between the boundaries of the nation and the state thus provides a perpetual invitation for cross-border interventions, military and otherwise.

Borderlands

China, Iran, Russia, and Turkey all contain borderlands that remain loosely integrated into the fabric of the state, where they face a tension between the classical imperial tools of decentralization and indirect rule, and the more modern, "national" techniques of assimilation and integration. The volatility of these regions is the product of efforts dating back to the late imperial era to replace the segmented, negotiated arrangements tying the center to its peripheries with unified national states. At times, borderland regions like East Turkestan or the North Caucasus have experienced forms of indirect rule or been effectively beyond state control, while at others they have been subjected to harsh measures designed to homogenize and integrate them. Local inhabitants, many from different ethnoreligious communities than the one controlling the state, have occasionally rebelled, sometimes with support from related populations or governments in neighboring states. Russia, Turkey, Iran, and China have all experienced terrorism and insurgency emanating from their borderlands in recent decades, which in turn have both accelerated efforts to transform and integrate these regions and contributed to authoritarianism at home.

China's ongoing crackdown on the Uyghurs of Xinjiang, which aims at nothing less than the eradication of Xinjiang's difference and its incorporation into the Chinese "interior," is the most recent manifestation of a concern held by Eurasia's postempires about their ability to hold onto religiously and culturally distinct territories, many of which sought (and failed) to achieve independence in the wake of imperial collapse. In such borderlands, ethnic differentiation and cross-border linkages make it difficult for Eurasia's postimperial states to ensure security, much less complete integration of these regions into the fabric of the state and the nation.

As in contemporary Xinjiang, this struggle to assimilate borderlands has been a driver of authoritarian politics. From Mustafa Kemal Atatürk's (1923–38) adoption of one-party rule in response to the Kurdish revolt of Sheykh Said to Putin's use of the war in Chechnya to legitimate consolidation of a "power vertical" to Xi Jinping's elevation to "core leader" amid the crackdown in Xinjiang, securitization of borderlands provides an excuse to centralize power, crush dissent, and legitimate violence by state actors. Persistent volatility in borderlands is thus one of the main reasons for democracy's checkered history in all four of Eurasia's post-imperial states.

"Near Abroads"

The fluidity of Eurasia's postimperial borders cuts both ways, though. The geobodies of contemporary China, Iran, Russia, and Turkey are shrunken relative to the maps of the old empires at their heights. For many inhabitants of postimperial states, lost territories around the periphery remain objects of implicit or explicit desire. At the same time, onetime metropoles and peripheries remain economically, politically, and culturally linked in ways that make it impossible for the postimperial states to entirely disentangle their fates from those of smaller states that broke away as the old empires crumbled. Refugee flows, smuggling, insurgency, and other forms of instability around the margins of the state have a direct impact on China, Iran, Russia, and Turkey, which in turn have little choice but to remain engaged with their postimperial peripheries.[37] This interpenetration of center and periphery is one of the main reasons relations between the two is more volatile in Eurasia than, for instance, between metropolitan France and its former overseas colonies.

Even where they are not seeking to overturn the territorial status quo, many political and intellectual elites in China, Iran, Russia, and Turkey regard territories that broke away from the old empires as part of their "natural" sphere of influence. The Russian term "near abroad (*blizhnoe zarubezh'ye*)" encapsulates the view held by many officials, analysts, and ordinary people in Eurasia's postimperial states toward the former periphery. It implies "a new arrangement of sovereignty and an old familiarity, a long-standing spatial entanglement and a range of geopolitical emotions" that have left China, Iran, Russia, and Turkey deeply enmeshed in the affairs of their neighbors, even if the salience of these ties may vary over time.[38]

The entanglement can take the form of military power, as with the deployment of Russian forces to eastern Ukraine, Turkish forces to northern Syria, or Iranian proxies to Iraq. It also includes economic interdependence and cross-border family, tribal, and ethnocultural linkages, as well as visions for regional integration like China's Belt and Road Initiative (BRI) or Russia's Eurasian Economic Union. Above all it suggests that elites in the former metropole maintain a kind of proprietary view of the lands and peoples in the former periphery, regarding their sovereignty as limited and conditional.

Eurasia's Empires from Past to Future

By the start of the Cold War, empire had, according to Lieven, "disappeared from the contemporary political debate and became the property of historians."[39] Seven-plus decades later, it is returning. In the increasingly interconnected Eurasia of the twenty-first century, the interactions between large and small states, and between states and peoples (both within and without), bear a strong resemblance to the imperial geopolitics of an earlier age. Post–Cold War Eurasia is in the process turning into a continent less of states than of regions, where a handful of large, powerful polities contend with one another (and with outside powers like the European Union and the United States) for influence over the smaller states lying between them, in part by championing competing sets of norms and institutions.

Within this new Eurasia, power radiates out in something like concentric circles from Moscow, Ankara, Tehran, and Beijing, the cores of these large states. Within their borders are areas subject to direct control, and others, inhabited by ethnic or religious minorities, where central power is contested. Around the periphery of these large states, in places like Bender, is a kind of transition zone, where power balances are shifting and sometimes conditional, and where borders often matter less than the historical, familial, cultural, economic, and political relationships between peoples on either side of them. Meanwhile, memories of past greatness provide a reminder and an impetus for action that political leaders can invoke, knowing they will resonate with much of the population.

To the extent that it is driven by the personalities and calculations of figures like Putin or Erdoğan, then, it is tempting to believe that Eurasia's current imperial moment may prove contingent and perhaps will fade in different political circumstances. Yet these figures have not emerged in a vacuum. The resonance of their appeals to imperial legacies suggests that in important ways the imperial past is, to paraphrase William Faulkner, not dead and not even past. Alongside the structural legacies of empire, images of past glory will continue to provide a temptation for the kind of imperial geopolitics Russia, Turkey, Iran, and China pursue today. Even under more democratic leadership, these states may well continue to challenge an international order built out of the wreckage of—and that explicitly rejects—empire as a model of political organization.

RUSSIA

Russian Empire, ca. 1900 (© 2021, Center for Strategic and International Studies)

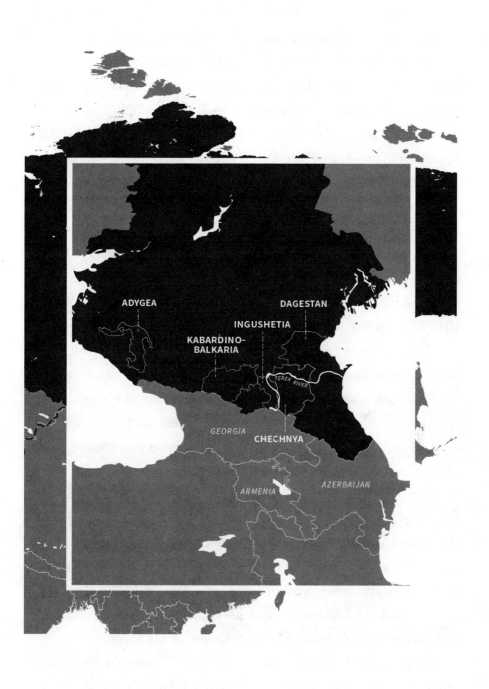

ADYGEA

DAGESTAN

INGUSHETIA

KABARDINO-
BALKARIA

TEREK RIVER

GEORGIA

CHECHNYA

ARMENIA

AZERBAIJAN

RUSSIA'S ANNEXATION OF THE Crimean Peninsula from Ukraine in March 2014 was the most brazen act of territorial aggrandizement the world had seen in decades. President Vladimir Putin justified it on the basis of Russia's imperial tie to the region. "Literally everything in Crimea," Putin claimed, "is suffused with our common history and pride," from the adoption of Orthodox Christianity by Grand Prince Vladimir of Kyiv in 988 to the Crimean War and the "Great Patriotic War" of 1941–45. Of course, Putin's reading of history was selective, and competing narratives, whether of the Turkic Crimean Khanate that dominated the peninsula until the eighteenth century or of post-Soviet Ukraine's legitimate sovereignty, hardly figured into it. Nonetheless, anticipating objections that Russian control would come at the expense of Crimea's inhabitants, Putin pointed to the long history of coexistence among "various peoples' cultures and traditions" within Russia, where "not a single ethnicity disappeared or dissolved in the course of centuries."[1]

Putin's claim to Crimea, in other words, rested on the idea that Russia—a former empire encompassing diverse peoples with their own histories and identities—embodied Crimea's history and civilization more authentically than a Ukrainian nation-state allegedly in thrall to extreme nationalism. The imperial imagery suffusing Russian media in the wake of the Crimea annexation reinforced this idea, summoning ordinary Russians to take pride in the restoration of Russia's imperial greatness following two-plus decades of geopolitical marginalization since the collapse of the Soviet Union, an event Putin earlier termed the "greatest geopolitical catastrophe of the [twentieth] century."[2] With the annexation of Crimea and subsequent occupation of eastern Ukraine, Putin staked his own legitimacy on Russia's imperial restoration—symbolized by the construction of a large statue of Grand Prince Vladimir outside the Kremlin.

From the Red Army's 1920 attack on Poland through the occupation of Eastern Europe after World War II and the invasion of Afghanistan in

1979, the successor states to the Russian Empire—first the Soviet Union and, since 1991, the Russian Federation—have continued projecting power across their formal borders. Though Putin has denied ambitions to restore the USSR or the Russian Empire, the 2008 occupation of the Georgian regions of South Ossetia and Abkhazia and pursuit of territorial revision toward Ukraine suggest that Russia remains something more than a territorially bounded state. Even after the recognition of Abkhazia and South Ossetia, the annexation of Crimea, and the failed attempt to incorporate eastern Ukraine, further expansion is not unthinkable, as ongoing intrigue over the future of Belarus suggests.[3]

The struggle for Ukraine and Belarus is the clearest manifestation of the dichotomy between cultural-national and imperial conceptions of Russian identity—between the mostly Orthodox East Slavic core centered on the medieval commonwealth of Kyivan Rus (*Kievskaya Rus'*) and the wider imperial formation known as Russia (*Rossiya*). With Moscow's annexation of the Belarusian and Ukrainian lands in the mid-seventeenth century, Muscovite officials increasingly portrayed Great, Little (Ukrainian), and White (Belarusian) Russians as branches of a tripartite "all-Russian" nation. This belief in the unity of the East Slavs remains influential in Russia—if less so in Belarus and Ukraine. Putin captured this understanding in his Crimea speech, when he claimed that the East Slavs' tenth-century conversion to Orthodoxy "predetermined the overall basis of the culture, civilization, and human values that unite the peoples of Russia, Ukraine, and Belarus," who collectively comprise "one people."[4] More extensively than Eurasia's other postimperial states, though, Russia also asserts a claim on the loyalties of populations living outside its borders. Putin's call to support not just Russians but also "Russian-speakers and compatriots" abroad suggests identification with a truly imperial nation whose geographic and cultural boundaries are themselves fuzzy, shifting along lines drawn by the state.[5]

Russia's imperial legacy also shapes Moscow's interactions with the roughly 19 percent of its population that does not identify as ethnically Russian.[6] Much of this population is concentrated in ethnic republics created by the USSR that dot Russia's eastern and southern peripheries. Since the collapse of the Soviet Union, these ethnic republics, above all in the North Caucasus, have experienced struggles between demands for local autonomy and the Kremlin's interest in strengthening the "power vertical (*vertikal vlasti*)." Russia held onto the North Caucasus thanks to two brutal wars in Chechnya and, more recently, a turn to consciously imperial forms of rule, where local notables—most prominently Chechnya's Ramzan Kadyrov—act as Russian vassals. Kadyrov's brutality, coupled with his infusion of Islamic (and pre-Islamic) elements to Chechen politics, is the starkest example of Moscow's continued reliance on the "politics of difference" in its postimperial borderlands.[7]

Unlike Belarus or Ukraine, the South Caucasus and Central Asia remained on the periphery of both the Russian Empire and the Soviet Union. Russia today has little interest in direct control or responsibility for states along its southern rim. Under President Boris Yeltsin (1991–99), Russia sought initially to cast them off. That approach proved unsustainable, given Russia's long, unstable southern borders. Instability throughout this mostly Muslim periphery threatened to spill across the border into Russia itself, especially following the outbreak of the First Chechen War in 1994. The waning of Russian influence also left a vacuum in the South Caucasus and Central Asia that other powers—including Iran, Turkey, the European Union, the United States, and, later, China—sought to fill.

Today, Moscow seeks to maintain the South Caucasus and Central Asia as a buffer zone against what it views as threats to its own security, ranging from drug trafficking to radical Islamists to NATO. Putin's Russia uses a range of tools to project influence in the region, including manipulation of conflicts on its neighbors' territory, control of infrastructure and media outlets, as well as, occasionally, military force. It also promotes schemes for regional integration designed to limit or slow the South Caucasus and Central Asian states' drift out of Russia's sphere of influence. As relations between Russia and the West have deteriorated since Putin's return to the Kremlin in 2012, these schemes have taken on new significance in Moscow's campaign to establish a Russocentric "Eurasia" as a counterweight to the Euro-Atlantic architecture and an alternative to Russia's now-stalled integration with the West.

This integration of the post-Soviet states into Russian-led multilateral organizations remains integral to Moscow's ambition to retain its standing as a major global power. Russia's claim to great power status centers not merely on possession of nuclear weapons, but more fundamentally, on the claim to be something greater than a normal country: a large state whose size and power ensure it a seat at the table on all major issues of international security. Despite its vast size and military capabilities, Russia's economy is sluggish and its political system under Putin, brittle. Its imperial hinterlands are increasingly the site of strategic competition not only with the West, but with Eurasia's other postimperial powers as well. Russia may have the most nakedly imperial aspirations of Eurasia's postimperial states, but they rest on a foundation that is receding in tandem with the Soviet past. Moscow's challenge therefore lies in either developing new sources of legitimacy for its claims to influence, or accommodating itself to the emergence of a multipolar Eurasia in which it is only one player among many.

CHAPTER ONE

Russian Identity Between Empire and Nation

 Putin's assertion that Russia retained a historically and culturally rooted responsibility to protect Ukrainian citizens in Crimea and Donbas was consistent with a long history of Russian rulers shaping the borders of communal identity for strategic ends. Geoffrey Hosking notes that in this process of molding Russian identity to suit the interests of an expanding state, "the political, economic, and cultural institutions of what might have become the Russian nation were destroyed or emasculated for the needs of the empire."[1] Yet that empire was one in which mostly Orthodox, Russian-speaking East Slavs were numerically dominant, and at times pressed demands for a privileged position incompatible with preservation of the empire. Imperial, Soviet, and post-Soviet rulers have therefore sought a balance between the diversity of empire and the overlapping religious, cultural, and ethnic claims of its largest population.

In founding the Russian Empire (*Rossiyskaya Imperiya*), Peter I promoted the idea of a common Russian (*rossiyskiy/rossiyskaya*) identity linked to the state and implying that political affiliation rather than ethnicity, language, or religion was the most important criterion for inclusion. While the Russian Empire's ruling elite "took for granted the predominance of Russian culture . . . and the Russian Orthodox religion," until the empire's final decades it tolerated a high degree of heterogeneity.[2] For the Russian Empire's cosmopolitan elite, Orthodoxy, Russian high culture (expressed during the nineteenth century mostly in French), and the Romanov dynasty (1613–1917) provided a common focus for loyalty and ensured the overall unity of the empire. As in Eurasia's other imperial formations, though, nineteenth-century political crises coincided with attempts to "nationalize" the empire by rooting its legitimacy in the largest ethno-religious community, ethnic Russians (*russkie*, sing. *russkiy/russkaya*). During the reigns of Alexander III (1881–94) and Nicholas II (1894–1917), appeals to Russian ethnonationalism were instrumental in the disorder and violence that preceded the 1917 Revolution.

Both Soviet and post-Soviet leaders similarly prioritized imperial preservation over valorization of ethnic claims. Unlike the rulers of Nationalist China, Kemalist Turkey, or Pahlavi Iran, they never portrayed their country as a nation-state, and allowed ethnic minorities varying degrees of cultural and political autonomy. From the Stalin period (1927–53) on, however, they assigned ethnic Russians a privileged, if still ambiguous, place within the multinational Soviet Union. Advancement within the Soviet (or post-Soviet) system required mastery of a Russian idiom among peoples of any ethnic and religious identity. At the same time, the Soviet Union tried to prevent Russian ethnonationalism from posing a threat to the USSR as a whole: unlike other Soviet peoples, ethnic Russians lacked their own Communist Party apparatus and ethnic homeland (the Russian Soviet Federative Socialist Republic, largest of the USSR's fifteen union republics, was itself a multiethnic patchwork).

Today's Russian Federation (*Rossiyskaya Federatsiya*) also maintains a balancing act between a multiethnic elite defined by its loyalty to the state and ethnic Russians' claims for special status. That state promotes the existence of a civic nation, but one defined largely in terms of the culture of the ethnic Russians who comprise close to 80 percent of its population. In the early 1990s, Yeltsin revived the term *rossiyskiy*, downplaying the salience of ethnicity as a category and disentangling Russia from its post-Soviet neighbors to reinforce the linkage between nation and state. Putin prioritizes maintenance of the postimperial state as well, but has gone beyond his predecessor in emphasizing the "state-forming [*gosudar-stvoobrazuyushchiy*]" role of ethnic Russians, even as he consistently rejects demands to slough off the non-Russian periphery in the North Caucasus.

And despite Yeltsin's efforts to separate Russia from its neighbors, political, economic, cultural, and other ties to the rest of the former Soviet Union persist. These ties are most developed with Belarus and Ukraine— majority Orthodox, East Slavic states with histories deeply entwined with Russia's own that, since coming under Muscovite control in the seventeenth century, Russian rulers have portrayed as part of their legitimate patrimony. Russia also maintains a series of overlapping and ambiguous relationships to peoples living in other parts of its postimperial periphery in the South Caucasus and Central Asia.

From the mid-1990s, reconsolidating influence across the former USSR has been a central pillar of Russian foreign policy.[3] That strategy entails efforts to encourage citizens of neighboring states to identify with the Russian Federation in its capacity as the successor to the USSR or the Russian Empire. Concepts like "compatriots (*sootechestvenniki*)," a "Russian World (*Russkiy Mir*)," or "Holy Rus (*Svyataya Rus'*)" embody the idea of a Russian imperial nation transcending the Russian Federation's borders. All of these concepts challenge neighboring states' efforts to construct their own civic nations and disentangle their histories from Russia. They also rest on enduring cultural and historical ties whose durability suggests the resonance of belief in this imperial identity not just in the Kremlin, but among ordinary people across the former Soviet Union who identify with a postimperial culture that still "speaks" Russian. While such ties are gradually waning, they remain an asset for Moscow's efforts to restore its authority throughout its postimperial space.

Empire, Religion, and Nation

In the premodern era, identity in the East Slavic lands known as Rus was primarily determined by religion. More than the state or the dynasty, the Orthodox Church acted as a focus for patriotic sentiment. The expansion of East Slavic principalities (including Moscow) was followed by colonization and conversion to Orthodoxy, which confirmed that conquered regions had become part of Rus and their inhabitants were no longer "foreigners" (*inovertsy*, lit. "of alien belief").[4] Ivan IV's (1533–84) conquest of the Kazan (1552) and Astrakhan (1556) khanates, however, raised the question of the relationship between mostly Orthodox Rus and the larger imperial formation known as *Rossiya*, or Russia, whose subjects now included large numbers of Turkic-speaking Muslim Tatars.[5] In varying forms, this tension between *Rus'* and *Rossiya* has remained at the heart of the contest over the nature and extent of Russian identity ever since.

While his troops destroyed mosques, Ivan IV allowed members of the Muslim Tatar elite to join the Muscovite service nobility (*dvoryanstvo*) and to own Orthodox serfs. For the Tatars and other conquered populations, loyalty and service, rather than religion, became the dominant basis

for inclusion in "Russia," which now was "delineated not by the nationality of its inhabitants but primarily by their subjection to the Orthodox
ruler of 'all Russia.'"[6] Members of the *dvoryanstvo* and educated society,
whatever their ethnic origin, thus developed a sense of "state patriotism,
that is, identification with the state and its ruler, rather than the nation."[7]
As Peter I, who proclaimed Muscovy's transformation into the Russian
Empire in 1721, wrote, a subject should think of himself as "an imperial
Russian and not [a member] of the Muscovite nation [*rossiyskim a ne mos-
kovskoy natsii*]."[8] Orthodoxy and Russian culture would remain important
determinants of status, but loyalty to the dynasty would become the dominant criterion for inclusion.[9]

Before the nineteenth century, the Russian Empire did not demand
religious, linguistic, or cultural assimilation among nonelites either. It did,
however, promote education, including native-language education, in its
colonial periphery as a tool of "enlightenment," which was held to include
linguistic Russification, conversion to Orthodoxy, and, among nomadic
populations, the adoption of settled farming. While this push for transformation was often disruptive, it also suggested that even members of Bashkir, Kazakh, Kyrgyz, or other nomadic societies could become members
of the imperial Russian nation.

As in the Eurasia's other empires, efforts to nationalize the Russian
Empire began in the nineteenth century as a response to political crises. In
the wake of the 1825 Decembrist uprising and the 1830–31 Polish revolt,
Nicholas I's (1825–55) minister of education, Sergey Uvarov, developed
the framework later called "Official Nationality," resting on the triad of
"Orthodoxy, Autocracy, Nationality (*Narodnost*)"—the last a term sufficiently imprecise for multiple interpretations. Official Nationality represented an attempt to mobilize nationalist ideas from the top down, and
to build something like a civic identity based on loyalty to the monarchy
and the Church.[10] It suggested that the dynasty ruled on behalf of the nation, without ceding its monopoly on defining membership in that nation.
Uvarov's views, however, were not dominant within the ruling elite, where
the older tradition of "dynastic cosmopolitanism" endured.[11]

Most calls for giving the empire a national coloring therefore came
from outside the elite. The Slavophiles, who became influential in the
1840s, "insisted the empire be defined in terms specific to the Russian, defined as Orthodox, core," rather than the empire as a whole.[12] The Slavophiles contrasted the traditions of the common Russian people with an
elite that aspired to live like European gentry. Their version of the nation

centered on culture rather than ethnicity, and therefore remained compatible with a multiethnic empire, albeit one where Russians held a privileged status. While Russian rulers worried about the populist, anti-elite implications of Slavophilism, the idea of ethnic Russians as the central or "state-forming" people would become an important element of later top-down approaches to nation-building.

By the end of Nicholas I's reign, political inertia, along with defeat in the Crimean War (1853–56), encouraged a new generation of thinkers to call for placing the well-being of ethnic Russians (among whom they included Belarusians and Ukrainians) at the center of the empire's concerns. The most influential spokesman for this agenda was the journalist Mikhail N. Katkov, who argued that the unity of the multiethnic Russian Empire could be maintained only by ensuring the Russian nation (*narodnost'*) was politically dominant. Katkov called for breaking the power of other national groups in the empire's borderlands, particularly that of the Poles in the Western Provinces (roughly modern Belarus, Lithuania, and western Ukraine), while imposing a normative version of Russian identity on peasants who spoke what would today be considered Belarusian and Ukrainian.[13]

This program of identifying the empire with the ethnic Russians gained new impetus in the reigns of Alexander III and his son Nicholas II, when nationality as a category (distinct from religion) took on increased salience. Alexander III's reign saw the popularization of the slogan "Russia for ethnic Russians (*Rossiya dlya russkikh*)." While "Russification" previously entailed measures to unify administrative procedures across the empire (*obruseniye* or *obrusevaniye*), Alexander III and Nicholas II pursued cultural Russification—aimed at "making Russians (*obrusiniye*)" through Russian-language schooling (some groups—Jews in particular—remained "foreign" even if they assimilated).[14] Alexander III and his circle, meanwhile, understood ethnic Russians not as the exclusive bearers of Russian imperial identity, but as a people that had voluntarily taken on the burden of building and managing the empire and the connective tissue holding it together.[15]

Russian ethnonationalism became a major source of the disorder that plagued the reigns of Alexander III and Nicholas II. It contributed to violence against Jews and other minorities at the hands of nationalist "Black Hundred" mobs organized by groups like the Union of Russian People (*Soyuz russkogo naroda*). It also fed separatist movements among non-Russians, including in previously tranquil regions like the Grand Duchy of Finland.[16] In June 1907, Nicholas II prorogued the liberal-dominated Duma and imposed a new electoral law aiming to "distill from Russia's chaos those elements in which lived a feeling for Russian statehood"— notably ethnic Russian landowners in the Western Provinces such as Petr Stolypin, whom Nicholas appointed premier.[17] Stolypin turned to the Duma's nationalist bloc to support his agrarian reform program—in the process legitimizing the nationalists' assault on Polish landowning and minority rights.[18]

The First World War further accelerated the process of "nationalizing" the Russian Empire. Expropriation of "alien" landowners—including previously privileged Baltic Germans—reflected a conceptual shift from thinking in terms of estates (*sosloviya*) to thinking in terms of nations.[19] Deportations from the front zone aimed at ethnic homogenization, even as large-scale movements of people undermined the regime's ability to maintain order. Critics looking for scapegoats for the failures of the war effort blamed "German domination (*nemetskoye zasil'ye*)" at court—often connected to the Hessian-born Empress Aleksandra Fedorovna.[20] This turn to ethnonationalism contributed to the development of separatist movements among non-Russians during the upheaval of the 1917 Revolution and Civil War, where support for non-Russians' self-determination proved crucial to the Bolsheviks' eventual victory.[21]

In 1922, Bolshevik leader Vladimir Lenin proclaimed "war to the death on Great Russian chauvinism." At his urging, the Bolshevik Party adopted resolutions compelling the "Russian proletariat . . . to help the less developed parts of the USSR."[22] However, the Bolsheviks' ability to appeal to Russian national sentiment, for instance over the 1920–21 war with Poland, anchored Russian nationalism to the "internationalist" cause of spreading the Revolution, mobilizing even anti-Communist Russians behind the war effort.[23] Meanwhile, Russian ethnonationalism became the preserve of White émigrés like the philosopher Ivan Ilyin. A supporter of Europe's fascist movements who experienced Hitler's rise from exile in Germany, Ilyin espoused the idea that "the world was corrupt; it needed redemption from a nation capable of total politics; that nation was un-soiled Russia" in its non-Communist guise.[24]

Emphasis on ethnic Russians as the foundation of the multinational Soviet Union became more pronounced under the Georgian Josef Stalin. In 1934, Stalin declared that the problem of Russian nationalism lay in the past. Textbooks were revised to emphasize that the Russian Empire's conquest of its neighbors was a "lesser evil" compared to the fate of other

colonized peoples. With the start of the Second World War, Moscow became more open to Russian ethnic and cultural themes, including the Orthodox Church and "imperialist" heroes such as Ivan IV and the Kyivan
grand prince Aleksandr Nevsky (1246–63), who were depicted in films by
well-known director Sergey Eisenstein. Stalin's toast celebrating the end
of the war in Europe—"to the health of our Soviet people, and in the first
place, the Russian people . . . because it is the most outstanding nation
of all the nations forming the Soviet Union"—reflected this view of the
USSR not as a Russian state, but as a multiethnic empire in the integration
of which the Russians were the dominant force.[25]

Postwar steps toward cultural and linguistic Russification reinforced
this trend. Nikita Khrushchev (1953–64) declared Russian the language
of interethnic communication, and oversaw educational reforms that
encouraged the teaching and learning of Russian. The concept of ethnic fusion (*sliyaniye*) was adopted as a solution to ethnic resentments, and
new emphasis placed on creating a multiethnic, but Russian-speaking, Soviet people (*sovetskiy narod*). While still internationalist in spirit, by the
Khrushchev era "socialism spoke Russian," as the Communist Party, and
the Soviet elite as a whole, came to resemble the ethnically diverse but
culturally Russified service elite of the imperial era.[26]

Russian ethnic nationalism—in both imperial and anti-imperial
forms—nonetheless remained influential, including within the Communist Party.[27] In response to growing separatism in the Baltic, Ukraine, and
the Caucasus during the era of *glasnost'* (openness) in the 1980s, ethnic
Russians across the USSR mobilized in "international movements" placing preservation of the empire ahead of ideological considerations.[28] Yet
Russian nationalism also existed in an anti-imperial guise. For figures like
the author Aleksandr Solzhenitsyn, inward-looking Russian nationalism
was an alternative to the burden of maintaining the Soviet empire, the loss
of Russia's distinct culture amid ethnic fusion, and the ecological devasta-
tion caused by socialist industrialization.[29]

Yeltsin mobilized this anti-imperial Russian nationalism to pursue
Russia's independence from the USSR. Under the guidance of his minister
of nationalities, Valery Tishkov, Yeltsin revived the term *rossiyskiy*, which
had long fallen out of use, anchoring it to a civic definition of Russian
identity and downplaying revisionist ambitions toward ethnic Russians
abroad.[30] The constitution Yeltsin forced through after shelling the Supreme Soviet in October 1993 emphasized Russia's "multinational people
(*mnogonatsional'nyy narod*)" and guaranteed equal rights to all Russian

citizens, making no reference to ethnic Russians.[31] Yeltsin's government also abolished the concept of "passport nationality," which permanently inscribed a person's nationality on their identity documents, and allowed Russian citizens to choose their own ethnonational designations.

Putin largely accepted the civic basis of Russian identity, but more than his predecessor infused it with both ethnic and imperial elements. Today, individuals of all ethnicities are allowed to be members of the civic nation; however, they are required to speak Russian and identify with Russian culture, which Putin portrays as an element in the overall unity of the state such that "the preservation of this country serves the interest of the Russian [*russkiy*] people."[32] Though acknowledging that Russia "for centuries developed as a multinational state" in a process characterized by "mutual accommodation, mutual penetration, [and] the intermixing of cultures," Putin also adopted the idea long prevalent in nationalist circles of ethnic Russians as Russia's "state-forming" people, with a mission "to unite, to bind together [Russia's] civilization . . . in a type of state-civilization where there are no 'national minorities,' . . . [because of our] common culture and common values."[33] The recognition of ethnic Russians' "state-forming" role was formalized with the July 2020 adoption of a constitutional amendment designating Russian the "state language of the Russian Federation . . . as the language of the state-forming [Russian] people."[34]

Portraying the Russian Federation as the embodiment of ethnic Russian identity is in part a strategy for opposing ethnonationalists' objections to the maintenance of a formal or informal empire.[35] Hostility to empire remains influential among Russian ethnonationalists demanding "Russia for ethnic Russians (*Rossiya dlya russkikh*)," and that the Kremlin should "stop feeding [i.e., subsidizing] the North Caucasus (*khvatit kormit' Kavkaz*")—a sentiment Aleksey Navalny, the face of Russia's democratic opposition, has also expressed. While Putin is critical of such demands—arguing they would eventually lead to calls to "stop feeding" Siberia, the Far East, or other regions—he is otherwise more willing than Yeltsin to promote not just the primacy of Russian culture but the political demands of Russian ethnonationalists.[36]

During his first two terms (2000–2008), Putin channeled ethnonationalist sentiment through patronage of "official" opposition parties, notably the Liberal Democratic Party of Russia (*Liberal'no-demokraticheskaya partiya Rossii*, LDPR), whose leader, the Jewish-born Vladimir Zhirinovsky, is notorious for extremist statements but backs Kremlin policy, and through support for ethnonationalist biker gangs, Cossack groups, and the pro-Kremlin youth movement *Nashi* (Ours). Putin also oversaw a rehabilitation of ethnonationalists from the White emigration, above all Ilyin, whose reburial in Russia he encouraged and whose works he encourages officials to read.[37] In embracing the language of ethnonationalism, the Kremlin aims, in the words of an activist from the ruling United Russia (*Yedinaya Rossiya*) Party, to "destroy the monopoly of extremists and scoundrels to speak on behalf of the Russian (*russkiy*) nation."[38]

Of course, toleration of ethnonationalist movements is instrumental, with officials seeking to rein it in when it risks spiraling out of control. Putin's government barred the nationalist Motherland (*Rodina*) Party from local elections and ousted its leader in 2004 when it appeared poised to gain large numbers of seats. Following a December 2010 nationalist riot outside the walls of the Kremlin, the government banned organizations like the Movement against Illegal Immigration (*Dvizheniye protiv nelegal'noy immigratsii*) and Slavic Union (*Slavyanskiy soyuz*) and arrested their leaders. The crackdown was a reminder that, as in Peter's day, the Kremlin seeks to define the balance between the multiple strands of Russian identity for its own ends.

"We Are All One Nation": Russia's Belarusian and Ukrainian Questions

The most visible manifestation of this top-down attempt to redefine the boundaries of Russian identity in recent years came with Putin's assertion that "Russians and Ukrainians are one people—a single whole" with a common history that provided a justification for the annexation of Crimea and occupation of eastern Ukraine.[39] This view has remained widespread among the Russian elite since the imperial era, when officials portrayed claims to Ukrainian and Belarusian nationhood as the product of foreign efforts to divide and weaken Russia. Today, belief in the fundamental unity of the East Slavs underpins Russia's aspiration to dominate modern Belarus and Ukraine, and ambiguities about the national and state borders between them.

The dispute over the nature of the Russian-Ukrainian-Belarusian relationship results from the diverging fates of the northeastern, northwestern, and southwestern regions of Kyivan Rus following the thirteenth-century Mongol conquest and the competition between successor states to claim the Kyivan legacy. Before Moscow's emergence as a major power under Ivan III (1440–1505), the rulers of the southwestern principality of Halych-Volyn (Latinized as Galicia-Volhynia) portrayed themselves as the legitimate heirs of Kyivan Rus. In 1253, Pope Innocent IV crowned the ruler of Halych-Volyn "King of Rus (*Rex Rusiae*)," and chroniclers called Prince Roman Danilovich "emperor of Rus."[40] Inhabitants of northwestern and southwestern Rus also maintained their own East Slavic literary languages and, until the creation of the Greek Catholic (Uniate) Church, a largely Orthodox identity.[41] Muscovite rulers, meanwhile, made "no assertion of ethnic affinity, nor [was] Kyiv treated as territory lost to Muscovy/Russia."[42]

By the late fourteenth century, though, much of southwestern Rus, including Kyiv and Halych-Volyn, had been conquered by Poland, while the northwest—later called Belarus—came under Lithuanian rule. Around the same time, Moscow began consolidating its own empire in the northeast. With the 1596 Union of Brest, which created the Greek Catholic Church and led to the persecution of Orthodox believers in Poland-Lithuania, some clerics begin pointing to ties of history, religion, dynasty, and identity between eastern and western Rus to seek support from the Russian tsar—the only independent Slavic, Orthodox sovereign—for a common "Slavic-Russian people [*slaveno-rossiyskiy narod*]" and a "*Slavia Orthodoxa*" uniting East Slavs in both Muscovy and Poland-Lithuania.[43] They portrayed conquest by Moscow as the only way to protect the true Orthodox identity of the southwestern Rus principalities from Polish domination and Counterreformation Catholicism.

These debates took on added significance in the mid-seventeenth century with the revolt of the East Slavic, Orthodox Zaporozhian Cossacks—whose seat was the fortified base or *sich* on the lower Dnieper River in the region "beyond the rapids (Ukrainian *za porohi*)"—against Polish-Lithuanian rule. Under the 1654 Peace of Pereyaslav, Cossack hetman Bohdan Khmelnitskiy accepted Muscovite protection. The 1667 Peace of Andrussovo then incorporated much of Ukraine east of the Dnieper, along with the cities of Kyiv and Smolensk, into the Muscovite realm. From the beginning, Muscovites argued that Pereyaslav signified the transfer of sovereignty from the hetman to the tsar, while the Zaporozhians (and later Ukrainian nationalists) viewed it as a military alliance that Moscow duplicitously invoked to justify imperial conquest.

The most influential proponent of the view that these agreements signified the historic reunification of Rus was the cleric and diplomat Innokenty Gizel, whose 1674 *Sinopsis* argued that the former Halych-Volyn, increasingly referred to as Little Russia (*Malaya Rossiya*), and its people—

Little Russians—comprised part of a larger Orthodox, all-Russian nation
that ought to be ruled by a single Slavic, Orthodox sovereign.[44] Gizel portrayed Kyiv as "the God-saved, glorious, and foremost among cities in
the Russian Empire [sic]," and Pereyaslav as the moment when Muscovite
Tsar Aleksey Mikhailovich (1645–76) "took the birthright of his progeni-
tors, the Royal city of [Kyiv], in his Royal hand as was his natural right."[45]
Gizel's work influenced, among others, Nikolay Ustryalov, author of the
Russian Empire's first official history textbook, which was instrumental in
making "the past of Ukrainian, Belorussian, Lithuanian, and even some
Polish ethnic territories as part of 'Russian' history," emphasizing the normative state of unity and advancing a claim to Belarus and Ukraine on the
basis of national, rather than dynastic principles.[46]

More than a century after Andrussovo, Russia annexed most of Belarus and Ukraine west of the Dnieper during the partitions of Poland-
Lithuania (1772, 1793, and 1795). As John LeDonne notes, the partitions
"terminated the historical justification of the Ukraine as a borderland,"
leading to the gradual elimination of the Cossack hosts as independent entities.[47] In their place, Catherine II (1762–96) established the Novorossiya
(New Russia) *guberniya* in eastern Ukraine, seeking to people it with colonists who would take up farming and secure the borders. While most of
the landowners came from the Russian Empire, Catherine was reluctant
to accept Russian peasants, who were likely to be escaped serfs, instead
preferring East Slavic refugees from Poland-Lithuania who, in modern
terms, would be called Ukrainians. Novorossiya—which would eventually
also include Crimea—was thus a mixed region where Russian high culture predominated. By the end of the empire, it was a densely populated
industrial zone, where Russian served as a lingua franca among the diverse
migrants who moved in to work in its factories.[48]

Farther west, the pre-partition elite was mainly Polish, while St. Petersburg perceived the peasant masses as merely "ethnographic material that
could be turned into either Poles or Russians," but not real or even in-
cipient nations in their own right.[49] Following the 1863 Polish uprising,
St. Petersburg sought to root out the influence of the Polish landowners
(*szlachta*) and the Catholic Church, which they believed was undermining
the Belarusian and Ukrainian inhabitants' identification with Russia and
threatening Russian control of the region.

Ukrainian political and cultural groups like the Brotherhood of
Sts. Cyril and Methodius (*Kirilo-Mefodyiyievs'ke Bratstvo*) were closed. A
July 1863 circular from Interior Minister Petr Valuyev banned publication
in Ukrainian (the ban lasted until Russia's 1905 Revolution).[50] Belief in the

existence of a Russo-Polish competition to shape the identity of border-land populations also led St. Petersburg to encourage Ukrainian-speakers on the opposite side of the border to adopt a pro-Russian ("Russophile") orientation, mobilizing them to support annexation during Russia's World War I–era occupation of Austrian Galicia.[51]

Despite the persecution of nationalist movements, Ukrainians and Belarusians who professed an all-Russian identity could be members of the imperial Russian elite.[52] As a Russian nationalist publicist wrote in 1912, "All Russians of different kinds should know how to speak, read, and write in Russian, but nobody can ever have anything against Little Russians knowing . . . their dialect, and Belorussians theirs."[53] The idea of Ukrainian (or Belarusian) as a language in its own right was, however, incomprehensible to Russian officials. World War I–era Foreign Minister Sergey Sazonov claimed, "As for Ukraine, it does not exist. . . . The peasants [in Ukraine] speak a language that the bourgeoisie does not understand, and . . . [literary Ukrainian] is a species of Volapük that no one understands."[54]

Unlike the Russian Empire, the USSR recognized Belarusians and Ukrainians as distinct nationalities (even though the Red Army suppressed the nascent Belarusian and Ukrainian states that emerged after the October Revolution). If anything, the USSR's model of ethnoterritorial federalism aided the consolidation of Belarusian and Ukrainian national identities within the territories of the Belarusian and Ukrainian Soviet Socialist Republics (SSRs), whose borders nevertheless reflected political expediency more than ethnographic or historic considerations. During the Russian Civil War (1917–22), factions in the Russian-speaking Donetsk Basin (Donbas), Odesa, and Crimea sought to set up their own Soviet republics. The Don Cossacks attempted to establish a state in southeastern Ukraine, with some claiming to represent a Cossack nation that was neither Russian nor Ukrainian.[55] At the end of the Civil War, the new Ukrainian SSR not only encompassed all these territories, it took in urban, industrial parts of the Donbas previously belonging to Russia and where Russian language and culture predominated—and which would be centers of pro-Russian sentiment in 2014.

Like other union republics, Soviet Belarus and Ukraine became incubators of national consciousness. During the era of *korenizatsiya*, or nativization, in the 1920s, Ukraine's political and educational systems underwent linguistic Ukrainianization.[56] Moscow nonetheless assigned ethnic Russians to the position of first secretary in Ukraine, suggesting both the continued importance of ethnic identities and Moscow's concern about centrifugal tendencies. These anxieties became more acute under Stalin. Ukrainian nationalist intellectuals were among the main targets of Stalin's Terror, charged with promoting separatism and counterrevolutionary ideas.[57]

While collectivization in the mid-1930s sparked famine throughout agricultural areas of the Soviet Union, it was particularly devastating in Ukraine, where as much as one-fifth of the total population died. Many Ukrainians came to regard the famine as an act of genocide, which they termed *Holodomor* (Soviet and Russian officials emphasized instead that collectivization affected all agricultural areas of the USSR). Despite the famine and persecution of nationalist intellectuals, Stalin supported the rehabilitation of Bohdan Khmelnitskiy and other "Ukrainian" heroes, who, in the official narrative, remained faithful to the all-Russian nation and contributed to Russo-Ukrainian unification.[58]

The Second World War saw numerous Ukrainians, especially those affiliated with prewar nationalist circles, fight for the Axis (though many more served in the Red Army). The radical fraction of the Organization of Ukrainian Nationalists (*Orhanizatsiya Ukrayins'kikh Natsionalistiv*, OUN) under Stepan Bandera set up a state in Nazi-occupied Ukraine and provided auxiliaries who served as police and concentration camp guards.[59] The OUN's armed wing, the Ukrainian Insurgent Army (*Ukrayins'ka Povstans'ka Armiya*, UPA), carried out anti-Soviet partisan warfare and participated in massacres of Poles, Jews, and Communists, in places holding out against the Red Army until the mid-1950s. These experiences confirmed many Russians' views of the radical, violent nature of Ukrainian nationalism and its association with Nazism.

Notwithstanding persecution of Ukrainian and Belarusian national activists, the Soviet leadership also accepted Russified Ukrainians and Belarusians as full members of the elite, including at the highest levels. Both Khrushchev and Leonid Brezhnev (1968–82) were Communist Party secretaries in Ukraine, and brought much of their entourage with them when they moved to Moscow; Brezhnev himself was from eastern Ukraine and identified as ethnic Ukrainian in some documents.[60] Belarusians and Ukrainians who accepted an all-Russian identity were often appointed to leading positions in other groups' autonomous areas. They also had among the highest rates of linguistic Russification, and the children of Belarusians and Ukrainians were the most likely of all non-Russian ethnicities to adopt a Russian identity.[61] The ambiguous position of Belarusians and Ukrainians became a major political problem during the last years of Soviet rule, when nationalist movements (especially in Ukraine) began mobilizing for independence.

In response, proponents of unity fell back on old paradigms to justify maintaining at least an East Slavic core from the crumbling Soviet empire. The most influential modern-era voice promoting East Slavic unification was novelist and philosopher Aleksandr Solzhenitsyn, who, more than Ilyin or the notorious Eurasianist Aleksandr Dugin, most Russian observers suggest, exerted a formative influence on Putin's own view of the nation. In his 1990 essay "How Should We Re-Build Russia? (*Kak nam obustroit' Rossiyu?*)," Solzhenitsyn argued that Russia's current borders were a product of the Soviet Union's disregard for the historic unity of the "Russian" people. With the USSR crumbling, Solzhenitsyn called for replacing it with a "Russian Union" comprising the East Slavic majorities of Russia, Belarus, Ukraine, and northern Kazakhstan.

Solzhenitsyn contrasted this Russian Union, based on what he saw as the historical and cultural bonds among the "Russian" people, with aspirations to recreate the Russian Empire—making clear that Russia should allow the Baltic states, the South Caucasus, and the bulk of Central Asia to go their own way. Russia must, he wrote, choose "between Empire, which destroys us ourselves first of all, and the spiritual and corporeal [*telesnyy*] salvation of our own people."[62] Solzhenitsyn's support for a Russian Union rested on the old distinction between Rus and Russia—between the Orthodox East Slavic "patrimony (*votchina*)" of Kyivan Rus, and the heterogeneous periphery acquired as Moscow became an empire. In the twenty-first century, this emphasis on a single Orthodox/East Slavic community underpins efforts to encourage citizens of Belarus, Moldova, and Ukraine to obtain Russian citizenship.[63]

Although Belarus and Ukraine acquired statehood in 1991, the nature of their identity remained contested within their borders. Belarus in particular struggled with the question of its relationship to the Russian state and Russian nation. In power since 1994, Belarusian president Aleksandr Lukashenko follows a Russocentric course that includes banning national symbols and restricting the use of the Belarusian language (spoken at home by slightly more than one-third of the population).[64] Belarus also maintains deep integration with Russia through the so-called Union State and through participation in the entire range of Russian-led multilateral integration projects.[65] Moscow has nonetheless sought to enhance its control over Belarus's economy and security policy, taking advantage of its economic dependence (especially for energy) and cultivating Russian sympathizers. These efforts culminated in late 2019 in an agreement to merge the countries' taxation, customs, and trade policies, and then in Moscow's efforts to consolidate its domination of the Belarusian state in exchange for keeping Lukashenko in power following the outbreak of large-scale protests in early 2020.[66]

While acceptance of a distinct national identity is more widespread in Ukraine, the presence of an ethnic Russian majority in Crimea and the persistence of Russian as a lingua franca outside the westernmost regions still feed Russian perceptions that, as Putin famously told George W. Bush, "Ukraine is not really a country."[67] Like Solzhenitsyn, Putin criticized the Bolsheviks' decision to expand Ukraine's borders to the east with little regard for ethnographic criteria or the preferences of the inhabitants.[68] The perception of Ukraine's borders as illegitimate contributed to Russian nationalists' support for the "return" of Crimea and revision of Ukraine's borders to bring Russian-speakers under Moscow's control. It also sustained Moscow's belief that the annexation of Crimea and attempt to restore an analogue to the imperial-era province of Novorossiya would find widespread support.[69]

Moscow consequently misread the development of Ukrainian civic nationalism, including among Ukraine's ethnic Russians and Russian-speakers. To the Kremlin's consternation, Ukrainians of all ethnic and linguistic backgrounds resisted the Russian invasion, which Moscow portrayed as a response to a "Banderite" emphasis on Ukrainian culture by the Ukrainian government that came to power in the wake of the 2013–14 "Revolution of Dignity." Yet especially in Crimea, the Russian attack was aided by the defection of members of the Ukrainian military and the thorough penetration of Ukraine's security services. This ability to suborn cooperation from Ukrainian officials and soldiers suggests that, if not ethnic identification with Russia, then at least a kind of imperial nostalgia does linger in certain quarters of Ukraine.

On the whole, though, the conflict failed to ignite widespread pro-Russian sympathy. Kremlin-backed uprisings in Dnepropetrovsk (Dnipro), Odesa, Kharkiv, and other cities failed; only in Donetsk and Luhansk were separatists able to secure control of local administration. Even in these *oblasts*, referenda on incorporation into Russia were abandoned when it became clear support was limited. The uprisings were followed by a conflict between the separatists and the Ukrainian army, as well as militias organized by local oligarchs. The willingness of Ukrainians, even from the east, to take up arms against Russia caught many in Moscow by surprise, contributing to the failure of the operation, which only direct Russian military intervention kept from collapsing.

The conflict also highlighted another ambiguity of Russian identity; some Russian ethnonationalists volunteered to fight for the Ukrainian side, which Russian propaganda was eager to tar as Nazis and "Banderites." Such pro-Ukrainian Russian nationalists argued that the "Banderites" in Kyiv were a more authentic manifestation of Slavic ethnicity than a Kremlin that preferred empire-building to racial purity.[70] Meanwhile, the inability of either Russia or Ukraine to establish secure control over Donbas—whose inhabitants remain ambivalent about both the Russian and Ukrainian nation-building projects—reflects the continued fluidity of borders and identity in what was long an imperial frontier.[71]

Russian Nations Beyond Russia

Efforts since 1991 to consolidate Russian identity—*rossiyskiy* or *russkiy*—within the borders of the Russian Federation remain at odds with a view of Russia as a civilizational state and the heir to a long imperial tradition. Not only do framings of identity that transcend borders have wide currency among the Russian public, the government cultivates them to a more explicit degree than in Eurasia's other postimperial states. Even beyond Belarus and Ukraine, Russian officials suggest that Moscow enjoys a claim on the loyalties of populations within and beyond the borders of the former Soviet Union with which it shares ties of history and culture. This imperial framing of Russian identity is partly a legacy of the Soviet collapse and the reality that families, businesses, and other groups are now divided by state borders. It also has a more ideological element linked to Russian geopolitical aspirations, with concepts like the "Russian World" providing a justification for efforts to reach into the domestic affairs of neighboring states, using the ambiguous nature of loyalty and belonging as a tool for empire-building.

Imperial articulations of Russian identity have a long pedigree, dating at least from the monk Filofey's portrayal of Moscow as the "Third Rome" and center of an Orthodox commonwealth following the 1453 fall of Constantinople. In the nineteenth century, ethnic affiliation supplemented religious ties, as pan-Slav thinkers like Nikolay Danilevsky emphasized a shared Slavic identity to justify Russian expansion in the Balkans by portraying Serbs, Bulgarians, and other Orthodox Slavs as victims of foreign oppression in danger of losing their identity. Pan-Slavs rallied behind their campaigns for independence from the Ottoman Empire in the (often frustrated) expectation that they would view Russia as a patron and protector.[72] Nor did the idea of Russia as a magnet for Slavic integration depend on the existence of the Romanov dynasty; it reemerged during the Cold War as a justification for the USSR's domination of Eastern Europe and continues to underpin Russian support for Serbian and other Balkan nationalist groups as part of Moscow's strategic competition with the West.

While the pan-Slavs and late-imperial Russian nationalists saw ethnoreligious minorities as, at best, second-class subjects, by the 1920s, thinkers associated with the so-called Eurasianist school, most of them anti-Bolshevik exiles like Petr Savitsky and Nikolay Trubetskoy, linked what they saw as Russia's special destiny to its multiethnic and multiconfessional nature. Eurasianism reemerged inside the Khrushchev-era Soviet Union in the writings of the historian Lev Gumilev, who argued that ethnic Russians and the other peoples of the USSR (plus Mongolia) shared a "common spirituality . . . psychological similarity and . . . mutual sympathy" that distinguished them from Western Europeans and, above all, Jews.[73] These views, in turn, influenced the sociologist Aleksandr Dugin, who in the 1980s pioneered a "neo-Eurasianism" combining emphasis on Russia's multiethnic identity, Cold War geopolitics, and the xenophobia of the European "New Right" to suggest that a restored Russian Empire should anchor a Eurasian alliance challenging the United States for global leadership.

Though the influence of neo-Eurasianism is often overstated, Dugin helped liberate the idea of empire from the grip of the (ethnic) nation. Dugin argued that ethnic Russians have always played a central role in the Russian state, but that Russia is "neither a multiethnic state, nor a state-nation [*gosudarstvo-natsiya*]," but was "practically from the beginning a potentially imperial state." He rejects both what he calls the "little nationalism" of ethnic Russians as well as the "ethnic imperialism" of Slavophiles and others seeking to assimilate ethnic minorities.[74] Despite some affinity with the idea of ethnic Russians as Russia's "state-forming" people, Dugin's outlook is more expansive in that it aspires to create a vast Eurasian empire in which Russia is only one—albeit dominant—component. Committed to fracturing the trans-Atlantic alliance and challenging the normative hegemony of liberalism, it is also an important element in Russian foreign policy debates.

Dugin's promotion of a Eurasian identity uniting Russians with their Finnic, Mongolian, and Turkic neighbors is one of several approaches to the question of Russian identity that has irredentist undertones. Other, sometimes overlapping groups emphasize different elements uniting Russians with people outside the Russian Federation's borders. They include advocates of the idea of "compatriots (*sootechestvenniki*), 'those with a common fatherland,'" the "Russian World," and "Holy Rus." Each in a different way suggests a mismatch between the borders of the Russian state and nation, and implies that Russia maintains an organic connection to populations outside its borders. Many proponents of these views also emphasize that Russia represents an alternative civilizational model based on its adherence to "traditional" values.

The idea of "compatriots" emerged with the collapse of the Soviet Union, which, as Putin noted, meant that "millions of people went to bed in one country and awoke in different ones, overnight becoming ethnic minorities in former Union republics."[75] As defined by a 1999 law, compatriots are "persons . . . possessing a common language, history, cultural traits, traditions, and customs" (later limited to members of ethnic groups "historically residing on the territory of the Russian Federation [and who have] made a free choice in favor of spiritual, cultural, and legal" ties with Russia).[76] Since 2008, Russia's Foreign Policy Concept has included protection of the "legitimate rights and interests of Russian citizens and compatriots residing abroad" as a foreign policy objective.[77] Before the war with Georgia, though, Moscow merely provided small grants and social services through organizations like the Russian World Foundation (*Fond Russkiy Mir*) and the Russian Agency for International Cooperation (*Rossotrudnichestvo*), largely to blunt calls by nationalist politicians like then-Moscow mayor Yury Luzhkov for more forceful support.[78]

The irredentist implications became clear with the wars in Georgia (2008) and Ukraine (2014–present). Then-President Dmitry Medvedev (2008–12) justified the invasion of Georgia on the basis of protecting "compatriots" living in the breakaway regions of South Ossetia and Abkhazia. While some South Ossetians and Abkhazians had received Russian passports (Russia has pursued such "passportization" in several places across the former Soviet Union), even the majority who had not were considered compatriots because of their past Soviet citizenship. Similarly, when Russia annexed Crimea in early 2014, Putin emphasized both ethnic Russians and other compatriots as targets for Russian protection. What mattered was not their citizenship or ethnicity, but the fact that they identified in some amorphous way with Russia (or the Soviet Union), because of their "culture, traditions, descent from ancestors [on the basis of which] they are ready to live in a unified state."[79]

In parallel with the category of compatriots, the late 1990s and early 2000s saw increased discussion around the Russian World, a more amorphous term suggesting "a fuzzy mental atlas on which different regions of the world and their different links to Russia can be articulated in a fluid way," but emphasizing Russian language and culture.[80] Developed by Kremlin "political technologists" Gleb Pavlovsky and Petr Shchedrovitsky, the Russian World became identified with the Russian Orthodox Church and the activity of Patriarch Kirill (who previously headed the church's external relations department).[81] It received official imprimatur in 2007, when Putin signed a decree creating the government-funded Russian World Foundation to support Russian communities abroad, promote Russian language and culture, and "improv[e] the image of Russia."[82]

The borders of the Russian World are defined by culture and political orientation more than by either geography or ethnicity. The foundation promotes a wide-ranging definition, which encompasses "not only ethnic Russians [*russkie*], not only Russian citizens [*rossiyane*], not only our compatriots [*sootechestvenniki*] . . . [but also] émigrés from Russia and their descendants. It is also foreign citizens who speak Russian, study or teach it, [and] all those who are sincerely interested in Russia and care about its future."[83] The foundation's activities include support for Russian-language and pro-Russian media outlets and NGOs, most visibly in Ukraine—efforts that Kyiv charges include funding separatist groups.[84]

While the Russian World is geographically fluid, "Holy Rus," a term first used by the sixteenth-century nobleman Andrey Kurbsky, is at once a geographic and a religious concept, stressing the shared values supposedly uniting the whole of the Russian Orthodox Church's "canonical territory" in Russia, Ukraine, Belarus, and Moldova.[85] Analogous to Solzhenitsyn's call for a Russian Union, the Holy Rus idea reflects a view of the nation that claims to be anti-imperial, in that it emphasizes the historic and cultural unity of the Orthodox East Slavs, even when they are divided by current borders.

The Holy Rus discourse also frames Russian identity around fealty to the church's view of Russia as a bastion of traditionalism under siege from modernity. This portrayal of Russia as the guardian of "traditional values" also underpins Russia's attempt to challenge Western influence on ideological grounds, by suggesting Western countries are "rejecting their roots, including the Christian values that constitute the basis of Western civilization."[86] Emphasis on "traditional values" provides a rationale for Russia to support populist, illiberal political forces in Europe and the United States—even if the emphasis on "traditional" values elides the reality of Russia's own political and confessional mosaic—and the eclecticism of its foreign proxies, who range from Communists to neo-Nazis. Moscow's identification with illiberal populists is less about fealty to the Orthodox Church's worldview than another example of the Kremlin defining inclusion in the "imperial" Russian nation on the basis of *raison d'état*.

Russia's Civilizational Empire

Of Eurasia's postimperial states, Russia is the most ambitious, and the most ambiguous, in cultivating the loyalties of noncitizens. Within the former Soviet Union, Moscow uses the idea of compatriots to reinforce demands for a postimperial *droite de regard*, and for limiting the sovereignty of its smaller neighbors. More generally, portrayal of Russia as a civilization-state and a bastion of "traditional" values in a changing world is part of the Kremlin's strategy for managing competition with the West, which, as Dugin and others recognized, is a target-rich environment for such appeals. The deliberately cultivated popularity of Putin and Russia among far-right movements in the United States and Europe is evidence of the Kremlin's success at anchoring this narrative in foreign societies, including in the West.[87]

Whether claiming Russians and Ukrainians comprise one people, suggesting Moscow has a duty to protect Russian-speakers abroad, or calling for a global coalition of supporters of "traditional" values, appeals for the loyalties of communities outside Russian borders are a powerful foreign policy instrument. They reflect a continued struggle over the nature of Russian identity that itself echoes debates dating to the imperial era about the role of the church, the place of ethnic Russians and their culture in the multiethnic state, and the relationship among the East Slavic peoples whose histories diverged after the fall of Kyivan Rus. They also suggest that attempts beginning under Yeltsin to build a civic *rossiyskiy* nation confined to the borders of the Russian Federation remain incomplete.

Of course, the efficacy of appeals to populations outside Russia implies that at least some peoples and communities are prepared to identify (at least in part) with an imperial Russian nation, whether because of a shared post-Soviet culture, because they accept the Kremlin's "traditional values" narrative, or for some other reason. A majority of Russian-speaking Ukrainians may not have lined up to support the Russian-backed insurgency, but enough of them (including military officers and officials) defected to suggest that Putin was not entirely wrong in thinking that Ukraine's position in the Russian national mosaic remained contested even within Ukraine.

The biggest obstacle to cultivation of a Russian imperial nation may lie within Russia itself. The popularity boost Putin received from the annexation of Crimea did not last. As in Iran, a growing share of Russians appears to resent the costs of empire-building at a time when living standards are stagnating. Even if the potency of calls to "stop feeding the Caucasus" have declined, a crisis of rising expectations means the Kremlin may have little choice but to focus more resources at home. More fundamentally, the passage of time ensures that the bonds of identity across the former Soviet Union that Russia relies on as a source of influence will fade, as they have in other postimperial spaces. Already, a younger generation with no memories of the USSR is growing up in much of the South Caucasus and Central Asia without ever learning Russian. Even if the Kremlin remains reluctant to give up on the idea of an imperial Russian nation, time and post-Soviet nation-building will chip away at its appeal across Russia's postimperial periphery.

CHAPTER TWO

Russia's Borderlands and the
Territorialization of Identity

ESPITE PUTIN'S commitment to consolidating a "power vertical," Russia remains a patchwork state with significant cultural, demographic, and political variation among regions. Compared to Eurasia's other postimperial states, it has a larger number of "borderlands"—some of which are actually in the interior. Along with major cities like Moscow and St. Petersburg, the largest concentrations of nonethnic Russians are in the twenty-one ethnic "republics" concentrated along the Volga, in Siberia, and the North Caucasus (since 2014, Russia has regarded Crimea and Sevastopol as a twenty-second ethnic republic). At once constituent elements of the Russian Federation as well as incubators of non-Russian identity, the ethnic republics—especially in the North Caucasus—represent a kind of liminal space, an "inner abroad" that the Kremlin worries could follow the union republics of the Soviet Union in seeking independence should power at the center weaken.

The relationship of these republics to the federal center is distinct from that of the remaining nonethnic provinces (*oblasts*) in that they are regarded as homelands for a particular ethnic population. Reflecting both imperial-era patterns of settlement and administration as well as the USSR's attempt to bring the Russian Empire's ethnoreligious patchwork under the unitary rule of the Communist Party, these ethnic autonomies played an important role in shaping, consolidating, and territorializing the boundaries of non-Russian identity. Though most now have ethnic-

Russian majority populations, ethnic minority power structures remain in place, leaving Moscow to pursue classically imperial strategies combining bargaining and coercion. Under Putin, seeking greater control over these borderlands has also provided a justification for enhancing the power of the state and embracing authoritarian rule.

Lacking the elements of statehood enjoyed by the USSR's fifteen union republics, the populations of Russia's ethnic autonomies underwent a high degree of linguistic Russification. Soviet-era in-migration further reduced the titular groups' share of the overall population (only Chechnya, Chuvashia, Ingushetia, Kabardino-Balkaria, Kalmykia, North Ossetia-Alania, Tatarstan, and Tuva had titular majorities in the 2010 census).[1] Yet like the union republics that became independent when the USSR collapsed, Russia's ethnic autonomies became incubators for local patriotism, as well as for ethnically based patronage networks dominating local politics. This process has been most pronounced and consequential in the seven republics of the North Caucasus, which retain the character of an imperial periphery, with strong ethnic and cultural identities and indirect rule that relies on a high degree of negotiation and accommodation of local elites.

The eastern North Caucasus—Chechnya, Dagestan, and Ingushetia—is the most volatile region and the most like a traditional borderland. With few ethnic Russians and strong religious, clan, and family structures still intact, the North Caucasus remains a site of political contestation, even if overt separatism has diminished since the 1990s. Chechnya, which went the furthest in the pursuit of independence, became the site of two bloody wars and a magnet for crime, radicalization, and terrorism that spread throughout the Russian Federation. Other republics, including Tatarstan, Bashkortostan, Sakha (Yakutia), and Tuva pushed less violently to assert their sovereignty vis-à-vis Moscow. Meanwhile, Ingushetia and North Ossetia battled each other over land and historical memory, while ethnic political entrepreneurs managed to carve out new republics of Adygea, Altai, and Khakassia amid the confusion and upheaval of the Soviet collapse. Putin's aspiration to create a stronger "power vertical" has entailed efforts to rein in the power of republican elites, who have responded with different combinations of accommodation and resistance. This reliance on the "politics of difference," above all in Chechnya, remains an obstacle to Russia's democratization and the creation of a civic state based on equal citizenship and uniform administration.

Imperial Expansion and Consolidation

The ethnic republics are a product of both the Russian Empire's emphasis on indirect rule over its periphery and the Soviet Union's model of ethno-territorial federalism. The Russian Empire's ability to consolidate and integrate new territories varied depending on distance, climatic and environmental conditions, and the proximity of rival empires. An inner core saw adoption of agriculture, linguistic Russification, conversion to Orthodoxy, and, often, an influx of Slavic peasant colonists.[2] In regions farther from the center, including the Volga, Siberia, the Far North, the Far East, and the North Caucasus, only some of these processes occurred. More distant peripheries in the South Caucasus and Central Asia, which only came under Russian rule in the nineteenth century, maintained greater differentiation and were ruled in a more colonial fashion.[3]

Distinctive forms of rule in the borderlands date to soon after Ivan IV's capture of Kazan and Astrakhan. A special *Kazanskiy prikaz* (Kazan Chancellery) was established following the conquest of Kazan in 1552 (a similar Siberian Chancellery was established in 1637). By the late seventeenth century, the *Kazanskiy prikaz* managed relations not just with the former khanates of Kazan and Astrakhan, but with most of the peoples living along the Volga, who were gradually transferred from the jurisdiction of the *Posol'skiy prikaz* (Ambassadorial Chancellery), signifying their progressive absorption into the Russian Empire. Volga Tatar elites were largely left alone, maintaining their religion and social organization under the loose oversight of a Muscovite *voyevoda*. The Volga and Siberia only came under more or less regular Russian administration in 1708, when Peter I's administrative reform abolished the Kazan and Siberian *prikazy*.

The integration of Russia's eastern and southern borderlands was further facilitated by the migration and settlement of agricultural colonists into the steppe, Siberia, and, in the nineteenth and early twentieth centuries, the Caucasus and Central Asia as "a force that underscored the inherent unity of the empire."[4] The influx of Russian peasants in search of land helped transform the social and political structure of the colonized regions, which, over time, became more firmly integrated into the political fabric of the empire. This process of frontier integration underpinned the view expressed by the nineteenth-century historian Sergey Solovyev of Russia as a "country that colonizes itself [*strana, kotoraya kolonizuyet-sya*]," even if, in reality, colonization meant indigenous populations were forcibly displaced.[5] Russian settlement sparked disputes over resources between settlers and natives that, at times, threatened the stability of the entire system. For instance, conflicts over land and water played a central role in a series of Bashkir revolts during the second half of the eighteenth century, and encouraged many Bashkirs to support the Cossack uprising led by Yemelyan Pugachev in 1773–75.[6]

All told, more than 9 million settlers (the vast majority Russians and Ukrainians) moved into Siberia, the Far East, the steppe, the North Caucasus, and, to a lesser degree, the South Caucasus and Central Asia by 1917.[7] Over a third of total migration occurred after 1871. Along with higher birth rates, migration contributed to faster population growth in the colonized regions that gradually shifted the Russian Empire's center of demographic gravity to the east and south, facilitating its consolidation as a single political space. A distinction remained, however, between areas of denser colonization and heavy Slavic settlement, and areas where colonization occurred late or in smaller numbers.[8] And though settlement played a central role in integrating the Russian Empire's frontier regions, even in the empire's final decades, the "vast majority of Russian peasants lived inside the borders of the pre-Petrine Russian state."[9] Many outlying areas, including some that stayed within the post-1991 Russian Federation, therefore remained culturally and linguistically distinct, often under various forms of indirect rule, in some cases until the very end of the empire.

Soviet Nationality Policy and the Territorialization of Ethnicity

The geography of Russia's borderlands is also the product of the Soviet Union's model of ethnoterritorial federalism, which assigned non-Russian populations specific territories as "homelands" within the multinational USSR, especially its largest component, the Russian Soviet Federative Socialist Republic (*Rossiyskaya Sovetskaya Federativnaya Sotsialisticheskaya Respublika*, RSFSR). The first ethnic autonomies emerged haphazardly amid the Russian Civil War, starting with the proclamation of a Tatar-Bashkir Republic on the Volga in March 1918. During the Twelfth Party Congress of 1923, the Bolsheviks transformed the Soviet Union into a complex web of ethnoterritorial autonomies. At the highest level were the, eventually, fifteen "union republics" that the Soviet Constitution guaranteed the—until 1991, theoretical—right to secede. The RSFSR and other union republics also contained lower-level autonomous entities, established as part of the Bolsheviks' plan to create "as many nation states with varying degrees of autonomy as there were nationalities."[10]

This approach aimed at the "territorialization of ethnicity," a compromise between the socialist internationalism of Rosa Luxemburg and the concept of deterritorialized ethnic autonomy advanced by Austrian Marxists. Associated above all with Josef Stalin, who headed the Commissariat for Nationality Affairs before taking power following Lenin's death in 1924, it rested on what Alfred Rieber terms Stalin's "borderland thesis," the idea that class consciousness across the Russian Empire's ethnic periphery was less developed than in its Russian core, and that attempts to impose a unitary, Russocentric model of administration would reinforce separatist tendencies.[11] The system was designed, according to Stalin, to "'take' autonomy away from [the national bourgeoisie], having first cleansed it of its bourgeois filth, and transformed it from bourgeois to Soviet autonomy."[12]

Moscow designated each autonomous area the homeland for a "titular" nationality—from Ukrainians with their own union republic to villages for small populations like Evenk reindeer herders in eastern Siberia. Russians, whom Lenin saw as the carriers of "great power chauvinism" that could threaten the entire project, did not receive their own ethnic homeland, leaving them in an ambivalent position within the larger Soviet system that would become increasingly problematic in the latter decades of the USSR. Autonomous areas maintained their own institutions that were to be "national in form, socialist in content." At the highest level, such institutions included schools, newspapers, and theaters in the titular language, which could also be used for administrative and judicial matters. In 1921, the Tenth Party Congress adopted the policy known as *korenizatsiya* (indigenization), which aimed to incorporate non-Russians into the local bureaucracies and higher education.

Each unit, meanwhile, had its own minorities; to grapple with this challenge, the USSR engaged in what Terry Martin calls "ethno-territorial proliferation," creating more and smaller territorial units down to the levels of individual villages, until the Soviet Union was a mosaic of overlapping and interlocking regions.[13] The RSFSR came to encompass both *oblasts* whose shape reflected historical and economic factors, as well as dozens of ethnic territorial units: Autonomous Soviet Socialist Republics (ASSRs), Autonomous *Oblasts*, and Autonomous *Okrugs*. The union republics had their own lower-level ethnic autonomies as well, including (after 1954) Ukraine's Crimean ASSR and Georgia's Abkhaz ASSR. This territorialization of ethnicity precipitated territorial conflicts, both between nationalities and, at times, between nationality groups and the state.

Unlike the union republics, the RSFSR's lower-level autonomies lacked most of the symbolic attributes of statehood and, at least by the era of high Stalinism, were regarded even by their leaders as more or less transitory. Moscow altered their borders, combined them with neighboring autonomies, and in some cases abolished them. During the Stalinist purges, some borderland populations—notably Chechens, Ingush, Karachay, Balkars, and Crimean Tatars—had their autonomous regions abolished and were expelled en masse for alleged collaboration with the Nazis. The postwar return of deported populations to Crimea and the North Caucasus would be a source of long-running conflicts over property and the restoration of territorial autonomies.

During the post-Stalin "Thaw," the remaining and restored ethnic autonomies underwent "an overt, publicized strategy of nativization (*korenizatsiya*) and a covert strategy of Russification" that produced an indigenous elite combining a non-Russian identity with full professional competency in—and, often, a preference for—speaking Russian.[14] Post-Stalin *korenizatsiya* was a response to non-Russians' exclusion from positions of power and influence in the center, but also a consequence of the power struggles that broke out after Stalin's death in 1953, and again following Khrushchev's ouster a decade later.[15] In the course of these struggles, senior officials made concessions to republican leaders in the Politburo and other institutions to cultivate their support. The result was to entrench ethnic power structures and patronage networks in many of the ethnic autonomies. Nevertheless, in contrast to the union republics, which controlled their own educational and cultural institutions, the RSFSR autonomies saw linguistic Russification accelerate, in part because Russian served as a prestige language, and because Khrushchev's 1958 educational reform entrenched it in middle and higher education.[16]

Russia's ethnic republics then engaged in a complex bargaining process with Moscow during the "parade of sovereignties" characterizing the Soviet Union's last years. In their struggle for control of the center, Soviet leader Mikhail Gorbachev (1985–91) and Russian president Boris Yeltsin competed for the loyalty of the republican leaders. Yeltsin encouraged them to take "as much sovereignty as you can swallow," and promised to restore the autonomies abolished by Stalin during the deportations of the 1940s. Gorbachev, meanwhile, supported the Russian republics' aspirations for equality with the union republics as a means of weakening Yeltsin's hand.[17] Local officials themselves came to recognize that appeals to national sentiment were a resource they could deploy to secure their own power against both the Kremlin and emerging grassroots nationalist movements.[18]

In most cases, republican leaders prioritized securing their territorial integrity against Moscow's attempts to redraw borders (or to regain territory lost under Stalin), and to assert judicial and fiscal autonomy from Moscow. The Kremlin opposed these efforts, but was hampered by its own political weakness—as well as its support for separatist movements in the former union republics, notably Georgia (South Ossetia and Abkhazia) and Moldova (Transnistria).[19] Yeltsin instead pushed for a federal treaty that would, according to his advisor on ethnic affairs Valery Tishkov, accept the republics' sovereign status in principle but "block their aspirations through the bureaucracy . . . and financial control."[20]

Yeltsin's 1993 constitution maintained the ethno-territorial framework inherited from Soviet times and defined the authority of the ethnic republics over cultural and economic issues quite broadly. The constitution and subsequent laws nonetheless retained several of the ambiguities of the Soviet system; for instance, maintaining ethnic autonomies for some, but not all non-Russians and confining the right to cultural development to specific territories (for instance, a Tatar living in Mari El does not have the same cultural rights as a Tatar living in Tatarstan).[21]

In 1994, Yeltsin agreed to establish relations with Tatarstan on the basis of a bilateral treaty. Tatarstan gained control over most revenue derived from its mineral wealth and taxation, along with the right to block federal laws that conflicted with its own, and to participate in international negotiations. The agreement reflected Yeltsin's limited options for reining in this pursuit of sovereignty, especially against leaders with strong local power bases like Tatarstan's Mintimer Shaymiyev.[22] Aside from war-torn Chechnya, the agreement with Tatarstan represented the largest concession to local nationalism in the Russian Federation, though Moscow accepted less extensive claims to autonomy on the part of forty-five other ethnic regions as well.[23] Similar to the dilemma faced by the Russian Empire in peripheries like the Grand Duchy of Finland, Moscow vacillated over how much integration of "loyal" regions like Tatarstan was necessary to prevent further fragmentation.

Coming to power amid an escalating crisis in the North Caucasus, Putin made restoring Moscow's authority the centerpiece of his approach to the ethnic autonomies. In 2000, Putin oversaw the creation of seven federal districts, each combining multiple ethnic and nonethnic regions and subject to a presidential representative likened by some observ-

ers to an imperial-era governor-general or viceroy. Putin also pressured
Shaymiyev and the other republican leaders to bring their laws and con-
stitutions in line with federal statutes and to abolish language asserting
the republics' sovereignty.[24] While most of the agreements between Moscow and the republics expired or were abolished during Putin's first two
terms in office (2000–2008), Chechnya only agreed to cede its claim to
sovereignty in 2010, and the bilateral treaty with Tatarstan lasted until
2017. Putin meanwhile pushed state corporations to take control of key
economic assets in the republics, such as Bashkortostan's Bashneft oil
company, acquired by the state in 2014. In Dagestan and elsewhere, local elites and their security services were purged for corruption and new
figures from outside the region brought in—and later rotated out to prevent their assimilation into local power structures. Shaymiyev and other
regional leaders with an independent power base were eventually persuaded to retire.

Despite this push for consolidation, the Kremlin has in practice recognized the limits of its authority and the need to work through local
elites, especially in the North Caucasus. Though Putin resisted calls from
some Russian nationalists and security officials to do away with ethnic
autonomies entirely, all the lower-level autonomies inherited from the
Soviet era (Autonomous *Oblast*s and Autonomous *Okrug*s) were abolished and their territory absorbed into larger non-national administrative
units—apart from the Jewish Autonomous Oblast, whose population is
less than 0.1 percent Jewish.[25] The status of the ethnic republics nonetheless remains a source of tension and an obstacle to Russia's political and
territorial consolidation.

One challenge is language. While many republican leaders sought to
enhance the status of the titular language in their republics, Putin's Kremlin enforced the status of Russian as the primary language for education
and administration. Under the auspices of the National Project for Education (*Natsional'nyy Proyekt 'Obrazovaniye'*), one of three national projects announced by Putin in 2018 as a fourth-term priority, the Ministry
of Education devoted increased resources to improving and expanding
the teaching of Russian in the republics.[26] Moscow also demanded an end
to compulsory courses in non-Russian languages, even sending inspec-
tors from the prosecutor general's office to schools to ensure that the use
of non-Russian languages was truly voluntary.[27] This crackdown sparked
protests in several republics, especially Tatarstan, but also heavily Russified and normally quiescent Komi.[28]

Nor has Moscow been able to disaggregate the ethnic power structures in all of the republics. It worries that in the event of a new political crisis at the center, leaders in regions with strong nationalist movements like Tatarstan and Sakha will come under pressure to demand restoration of their claims to sovereignty. Another concern is that republican leaders, like their federal counterparts, have been willing to countenance the existence of ethnic gangs that ensure titular control of important revenue sources and can be used to limit migration from outside the republic. When ethnic Yakut gangs attacked Central Asian labor migrants in Yakutsk in the spring of 2019, some Russian observers suggested that republican leaders' willingness to tolerate extreme nationalism contributed to the violence.[29] Moreover, the preservation of special status for the republics implies that Russia maintains different classes of citizenship, and that, in the eyes of many ethnic Russians, minorities receive preferences in the republics, which enjoy special subsidies for cultural production and where, in some cases, titular populations appear more likely to be hired for jobs with the republican administration.

Meanwhile, the conflict in Ukraine and Russia's annexation of Crimea created new incentives for the Kremlin to worry about the possibility of separatism, and coincided with a renewed effort at bringing the republics under direct control. Having inherited an ethnofederal patchwork, the Russian Federation continues struggling to balance aspirations for more unitary administration with the reality of entrenched local interests. Lacking the state capacity of the PRC and warier of provoking a backlash, Moscow has moved cautiously in the direction of consolidation. In the volatile North Caucasus, it has, at times, gone in the opposite direction, tolerating and even encouraging the "politics of difference" to maintain order.

The North Caucasus

The North Caucasus republics of Adygea, Dagestan, Ingushetia, Kabardino-Balkaria, Karachaevo-Cherkessia, North Ossetia-Alania, and, above all, Chechnya are in a category by themselves. In the 1990s, military conflict, ethnic violence, and terrorism frayed the bonds tying them to the Russian Federation. Ethnic Russians and others who had migrated to the region in the Soviet era departed en masse, leaving the North Caucasus by far the least "Russified" part of the country and reinforcing the ethno-territorial identity of the region's republics, especially the eastern republics of Chechnya, Dagestan, and Ingushetia. These developments accelerated the region's decoupling from Russia's political and social fabric, to the point that few Russian citizens from the rest of the country travel to Chechnya, Dagestan, or Ingushetia, and tend to regard migrants from the region as foreigners even though they hold Russian citizenship.

The liminal status of the North Caucasus is in part a result of the great difficulty the Russian Empire faced in conquering and incorporating it. During the eighteenth century, Russia began construction of what became the Caucasus Line, a string of forts running west from the Caspian along the Terek and Kuban Rivers, as it moved from indirect rule to "an aggressive expropriation of lands, deportation of local villagers, and harboring of native fugitives," coupled with efforts at "Christianizing the region . . . through settling Christians there and getting rid of Muslims."[30] By the time the conquest of the western North Caucasus was completed in 1865, Walter Richmond estimates that at least 625,000 Adyghes or Circassians (a group divided under Soviet rule into distinct Adyghe, Cherkess, Kabardian, and Shapsug nations) had died from violence, cold, hunger, or disease, while hundreds of thousands more fled to the Ottoman Empire.[31]

In the eastern North Caucasus, resistance was better organized and longer lasting, leaving the region more restive and more loosely integrated into the Russian Empire. The first major uprising began in 1785 under the Chechen Sheykh Mansur. His call for resistance united a broad front of Avars, Chechens, Kabardians, Kumyks, Nogays, and other Muslims in a struggle against Russian rule that continued in different forms until the defeat and capture of his successor Imam Shamil in 1859.[32] During the last decades of the struggle, the resistance created a unified political authority, subsequently known as the (North) Caucasus Imamate (*al-Imamat al-Qawqaz*, *Severo-Kavkazskiy Imamat*), that, at its height, extended over most of modern Chechnya and Dagestan, and maintained followers in the western North Caucasus as well. While Shamil was an Avar-speaker from Dagestan, he later wrote that "in those stormy and cruel times all the people of Daghestan and the other lands of the Caucasus were one family. . . . Dargins, Kumyks, Lezgins, Tabasaranis, Chechens, Ingush, Circassians and others all fought with me in this war."[33] Geography, strong communal bonds, and the ability to mobilize diverse populations under a charismatic religious authority made resistance in the North Caucasus particularly challenging, and has helped prevent the consolidation of Russian rule to the present.

Sheykh Mansur, Shamil, and other resistance leaders drew inspiration from the Naqshbandi Sufi *tariqa*, which had taken root in the North

Caucasus in the early nineteenth century.[34] The Naqshbandi *pir*s encouraged a return to orthodox Sunnism and, in some cases, support for the Sunni Ottomans, whose agents were also active in the region.[35] The targeting of Shamil's followers during and after the conflict decimated the *Naqshbandiyya*, allowing the rival *Qadiriyya tariqa* to expand its presence. Both the *Naqshbandiyya* and the *Qadiriyya* remained integral to resistance to Russian rule, including during the Russian Civil War, when the Caucasus was the site of a complex struggle among Reds, Whites, Cossack armies, and indigenous forces. The role of the Sufi orders was critical, since "only a mystical order could force the fiercely independent Mountaineers to submit to iron discipline in a hopelessly uneven struggle" with the Red Army.[36] This religious-ideological aspect gave the conflict a total character, and it was not until 1921 that the Bolsheviks put down the revolt nominally led by Shamil's great-grandson Said-Bek.

Chechnya then exploded in rebellion on three more occasions between 1921 and World War II, while a separate revolt broke out in Ingushetia in 1926. The 1928–30 Chechen revolt sparked by collectivization was especially widespread, eventually encompassing much of Dagestan, Ossetia, Kabarda, Balkaria, and Karachay as well. Insurgents declared *ghaza*, or holy war, massacred Soviet officials, and proclaimed a return to the autonomy promised by the 1923 Soviet Constitution. The revolt required large-scale military intervention and mass arrests by the security services to quell. Even then, guerrilla activity resumed after the start of World War II, to Moscow's dismay taking in the younger, Soviet-educated intelligentsia.[37]

This wartime insurrection helped prompt Stalin to order deportations of the entire Chechen, Ingush, Karachay, and Balkar populations, and significant numbers of Ossetians, Kabardians, Dagestanis, and Cherkess, to Central Asia. As in the late nineteenth century, these deportations were accompanied by large-scale destruction of cultural monuments and efforts to bring in European settlers to transform the landscape and integrate the region into the ethnic and territorial fabric of the Russian interior.[38] While imperial officials had refrained from carrying out mass deportations from the eastern North Caucasus, partly because its landlocked geography made the logistics too difficult, by the 1940s, the construction of railways allowed Stalin to complete the task of ethnic cleansing begun during the Caucasus Wars of the previous century.[39]

Although Khrushchev allowed the deported populations to return in the mid-1950s, for the remainder of the Soviet period, Moscow's control remained tenuous. The return of deportees sparked conflicts over land and resources with those who settled in the interim. Moscow's attempt to disentangle the region's ethnic mosaic, to make it fit the Soviet model of ethnically defined autonomies, led to the redrawing of administrative borders, for instance, moving some mixed districts from Ingushetia to North Ossetia and creating resentments that would come to the surface once Soviet power was gone.[40] Stalin's collectivization and antireligious campaigns, meanwhile, failed to root out the Sufi orders, which continued to provide a focal point for opposition, and remained linked ideologically to the legacy of resistance stretching back to Sheykh Mansur and Shamil.[41] Protests mushroomed during Gorbachev's *glasnost'*, initially over territorial issues, but soon encompassed a wider range of grievances.

Amid the anti-Gorbachev coup of August 1991, a Chechen National Congress headed by ex-Soviet air force general Dzhokhar Dudayev seized power in Grozny, and, in November, proclaimed independence from Russia. While Yeltsin encouraged the USSR's union republics to jettison the Soviet Union, he responded strongly to the Chechen declaration, fearing an independent Chechnya could accelerate Russia's own disintegration, become a toehold for Turkish influence, and jeopardize control of pipelines from the Caspian Sea. Dudayev's proclamation of independence set in motion the two Chechen wars (1994–96 and 1999–2006), which helped wreck Yeltsin's presidency and pave the way for Vladimir Putin's ascension.

The First Chechen War was an utter fiasco for the Russian military, whose largely conscript forces were unable to defeat the troops loyal to Dudayev, or to the increasingly independent field commanders such as Shamil Basayev, who emerged as Chechnya's main power brokers.[42] In August 1996, Chechen fighters seized Grozny itself, which the Russian air force subsequently leveled. The conflict was also accompanied by a growth of crime and terrorism. Militants loyal to Basayev and other field commanders carried out brazen attacks on civilian targets throughout the North Caucasus and in Russian cities. Despite the military and political disaster of the First Chechen War, Yeltsin mostly managed to keep the rest of the North Caucasus quiet and prevented intervention by sympathetic leaders in the South Caucasus like Georgia's Zviad Gamsakhurdia and Azerbaijan's Abulfaz Elchibey—both of whom were ousted by Russian-backed coups—or by outside powers like Turkey and the United States.[43]

Unable to eliminate the separatists, in 1996, Yeltsin accepted the Khasavyurt Accord, which conferred effective independence on the Chechen

Republic of Ichkeria. This de facto state remained a hotbed of kidnapping and smuggling, while militants continued their depredations against Russian civilians, aided by the absence of an effective border with the Russian "mainland." The dangers of leaving Chechnya outside the bounds of the Russian state came to a head in 1999 when, like his nineteenth-century namesake, Shamil Basayev and the Saudi-born half-Circassian commander known as Ibn al-Khattab launched an invasion of Dagestan aiming to set up a Caucasus-wide Islamic emirate.[44] The invasion of Dagestan and a wider upsurge in militant activity were indications that a conflict begun as a quest for independence was taking on an Islamist coloring, which culminated in the 2006 establishment of a Caucasus Emirate (*Imarat Kavkaz*) that pledged allegiance to al-Qaeda.

The invasion of Dagestan and upsurge of attacks in Russian cities prompted Yeltsin to appoint as his prime minister and heir presumptive Vladimir Putin, who almost immediately launched the Second Chechen War. Given the centrality of Chechnya to his rise and legitimation, Putin staked much of his presidency on the ability to solve the Chechen problem, even at the cost of political compromises unthinkable in other parts of Russia. While Chechen fighters loyal to Basayev and Khattab continued to carry out large-scale terrorist attacks, including the 2002 Dubrovka Theater siege in Moscow and the seizure of a school in the North Ossetian town of Beslan in September 2004, Moscow learned some lessons from its earlier failure. Rather than capture territory in the mountains, Russian infantry largely confined its operations to the lowlands north of the Terek River and outsourced the bulk of the fighting to Chechen groups loyal to the Kremlin.

In the political sphere, attempts to subordinate the North Caucasus to the "power vertical" gave way to large-scale subsidies for reconstruction in Chechnya and the development of a system of indirect rule under local proxies across much of the region. The most important Kremlin proxy was a former mufti named Akhmad Kadyrov, whose elevation to the position of president of Chechnya consciously echoed the Russian Empire's attempts to coopt the religious establishment.[45] A similar, if less extensive, system of indirect rule also prevailed elsewhere in the North Caucasus, where Putin's United Russia Party incorporated existing clan and family networks (as in Kabardino-Balkaria, where the Kokov family has provided three governors since 1991).[46] Further reinforcing the region's unique position within the Russian Federation, Putin created an eighth federal district for the North Caucasus in 2010 (excluding the Russian-majority

Republic of Adygea); when Moscow subsequently reintroduced gubernatorial elections across the country, most of the North Caucasus retained appointed leaders.

Following Akhmad Kadyrov's assassination in 2004, the Kremlin groomed his son Ramzan to take his place. Since becoming president three years later, the younger Kadyrov has ruled Chechnya as an autonomous fiefdom under a special deal with the Kremlin, enjoying tens of billions of dollars in subsidies and a degree of independence no other regional leader can match. Ramzan Kadyrov maintains his own armed units, known as *Kadyrovtsy*, who number upward of 20,000 well-armed soldiers. Besides battling militant groups, eliminating Kadyrov's foes, and maintaining a fear-based peace inside Chechnya, these forces act as a kind of praetorian guard in Russia as a whole. They also participate in military operations supporting Russian foreign policy in Ukraine, Syria, and elsewhere—at times clashing with armed groups of anti-Kremlin Chechens and other North Caucasians driven out by Kadyrov's iron-fisted rule.[47]

Kadyrov's perceived indispensability in keeping Chechnya pacified and ability to further Russian foreign policy objectives have convinced the Kremlin to maintain this form of special rule despite the cost and concerns about the unintended consequences. Such consequences reportedly include the assassination of agents of the Russian security services and non-Chechen dissidents, activists, and journalists in Russia and abroad, among them the journalist Anna Politkovskaya and opposition politician Boris Nemtsov.[48] Apart from maintaining his own armed forces, Kadyrov has been able to press various economic and political demands, such as subsidized gas deliveries and the transfer of mineral-rich territory from Ingushetia to Chechnya over the opposition of the (mostly non-Chechen) inhabitants.

The Kremlin also tolerated Kadyrov's introduction of an Islamist-inflected vocabulary to Chechen politics that, on the one hand, undercut the appeal of Salafist and jihadist groups (whose toehold remains stronger in Dagestan and Ingushetia), but also legitimated appeals to both *sharia* and the traditional law code, or *adat*, within the Russian political order. Kadyrov's invocations of *sharia* also provided justification for various abuses, notably the widespread roundup and murder of homosexuals. Even though the killing of oppositionists like Nemtsov and persecution of homosexuals likely never received Kremlin imprimatur, Moscow remains reluctant to move away from this system of indirect rule, even as it tightens central control throughout the rest of the Russian periphery. In part, this reluctance stems from concern about Chechnya's potential to again descend into anarchy; it also, however, rests on a recognition of the power Kadyrov has amassed over the Russian political system as a whole. As former Putin adviser Gleb Pavlovsky noted after the assassination of Nemtsov on a bridge across from the Kremlin, "If you can do something like this just outside [the Kremlin's] Spassky gate . . . then maybe you could do this *inside* Spassky gate as well."[49]

Russia's Asymmetric Federation

Every Russian government from the time of Ivan IV has struggled to balance regional interests and central control in a vast country with limited administrative capacity. Continued reliance on the politics of difference across its ethnic autonomies has left Russia something of a patchwork state. Unlike its postimperial peers, Russia never went through a phase of aggressive nationalization; even Stalin accepted the idea of national "forms" as a means of reconciling non-Russians to the Soviet experiment. Today, Russia offers inhabitants of its "borderlands" (both true borderlands and internal autonomies like Tatarstan) greater opportunities for communal self-administration than do China, Iran, or Turkey.

Meanwhile, the imperial-era pattern of Russian settlers transforming the physical and cultural landscape of the borderlands is reversing. Hinterlands across Russia are being depopulated, as far-flung residents of all ethnicities move in larger numbers to Moscow, St. Petersburg, and other cities. On the one hand, this development reinforces the ties binding the autonomous borderlands to the Russian state, as the presence of large numbers of Chechens and other North Caucasians in Moscow creates a community of interest between center and periphery that did not exist in earlier eras. At the same time, the depopulation of remote areas reinforces their peripheral status, exacerbated by an economic model where proceeds from natural resources flow to Moscow before being redistributed. This new periphery is thus not limited to the ethnic autonomies inherited from the Soviet period, but also includes Russian-majority regions of Siberia, the Far East, and Far North. Even as the Kremlin attempts to tighten its authority over the ethnic autonomies through creation of federal districts, emphasis on the role of the Russian language, or what in Soviet times was called "rotation of cadres," it risks finding itself in charge of a country whose "center" becomes ever smaller.

Nor is the Kremlin's ability to bring the ethnic autonomies under uniform administration guaranteed. Economic disparities between center and periphery remain serious and contribute to the spread of protests, many of them emphasizing local concerns. The push to expand central control, including the emphasis on Russian in local schools, remains unpopular. Despite the passage of a constitutional reform package allowing Putin to stay in power more or less indefinitely, the succession question has not gone away; when it does reemerge, bargaining between center and periphery is likely to be an important element in the quest for legitimacy, as it was following the Stalin and Khrushchev eras.

Meanwhile, Chechnya's experiment of indirect rule remains an outlier, and is for that reason unpopular with much of the Kremlin elite. Any attempt to change the status quo in Chechnya, however, will be fraught, given Kadyrov's ability to mobilize large numbers of armed, loyal, and ruthless followers. As long as Chechnya retains its special status, though, influential voices in Moscow will chafe at its defiance of the "power vertical," while local elites elsewhere invoke it as a model—or a warning—in their own push for greater autonomy. As much as Putin's legacy rests on restoring centralized authority after the "chaotic 1990s (*likhiye 1990e*)," his acknowledgment of the need for some degree of compromise with the borderlands is an underappreciated asset, one that his Chinese, Iranian, and Turkish counterparts do not necessarily share. The important question for Russia's future, then, is the extent to which this acceptance of the "politics of difference" will endure in a post-Putin Russia.

CHAPTER THREE

Russia's Near Abroad and the
Geopolitics of Empire

A S WITH EURASIA'S other great empires, the shrinkage of
Russia's borders left behind successor states locked in a web of
political, economic, and cultural ties to their former metropole.
Today, the relatively weak states of the South Caucasus and
Central Asia remain bound to Russia through varying degrees of economic,
cultural, and political ties, even as Moscow continues to regard them as
a "near abroad" lacking the full complement of sovereignty reserved for
Russia itself and other states in the "far abroad" and where it maintains
what then-President Medvedev called "privileged interests [*privilegiro-
vannye interesy*]."[1] Demand for recognition of Russia's privileged interests
does not imply a desire for imperial restoration so much as a demand that
outside powers, notably the United States, EU, and NATO, respect what
Moscow considers to be red lines in a region where Russian influence
predominates. Russia also seeks through political, economic, and military
levers to prevent (or at least slow) the drift of its post-Soviet neighbors
out of the Russian orbit, maintaining post-Soviet political systems that
resemble Russia's own, limiting or excluding any foreign military presence, and controlling its neighbors' economic ties with the outside world.

The aspiration to maintain the post-Soviet region as a zone of "privileged interests" is also linked with Russia's larger geopolitical objectives
and sense of itself as a great power.[2] After a brief flirtation with integration
with the West, by the mid-1990s, Russia's political class had reembraced

the idea of Russia as an independent global actor controlling a sphere of influence in Eurasia, an approach many Russians compared to the United States' Monroe Doctrine. It was shared across the political spectrum—from the economist Anatoly Chubais's call for a Russian "liberal empire" to the atavistic nostalgia of the "red-brown" coalition opposing Yeltsin's efforts to tie Russia to the West.[3]

The geography of Russia's postimperial longings is multifaceted. Strategic documents list the post-Soviet space as Russia's top regional priority.[4] In practice, the East Slavic realms of Belarus and Ukraine (plus, arguably, northern Kazakhstan) occupy a different space in Russian mental maps than do postcolonial areas of the South Caucasus and Central Asia. The Baltic states, which enjoyed an anomalous position in the Russian Empire and were independent for a generation during the interwar years, exist on the outer periphery of such imperial imaginings. Finland and Poland, which the Russian Empire controlled until the 1917 Revolution, are seen as potential security challenges, but not objects of desire or domination—though Moscow remains opposed to Finland's NATO membership or the deployment of U.S. forces to Poland. Russia also maintains a more limited postimperial regard toward much of the old Warsaw Pact, not to mention the Orthodox Balkans, which have longstanding political and security ties to Russia.

In the South Caucasus and, even more, Central Asia, Russian rule had a more colonial aspect than in its western peripheries. Even in the eighteenth and nineteenth centuries, Russia's limited administrative capacity meant that these regions were governed "at arm's length" by viceroys or governors-general, whose vast powers in principle were limited by distance and the small size of their staffs.[5] These regions also lacked *zemstva* (local councils) and other forms of self-administration prevailing in the interior, while Central Asia also lacked an indigenous Muslim spiritual administration. Only in the empire's last decades was mass colonization promoted to encourage "progress" and political consolidation. Outside northern Kazakhstan, though, colonization never reached the scale it took in the steppe or Siberia, and the South Caucasus and Central Asia retained their cultural and institutional distinctiveness up to and beyond 1917.

Soviet rule also had a colonial aspect, even as it shaped and consolidated new forms of identity in the South Caucasus and Central Asia.[6] Moscow used its southern borderlands to cultivate cross-border influence and, at times, facilitate further expansion. During and after World War II, Stalin used Soviet Azerbaijan to press claims to Iranian Azerbaijan.

Similarly, efforts to bring parts of eastern Anatolia under Russian rule were justified in terms of expanding the ethnic homelands of Soviet Armenians and Georgians. And when Soviet forces invaded Afghanistan in 1979, Moscow emphasized ties between Tajik and Uzbek communities on either side of the Soviet-Afghan border and deployed special "Muslim battalions" comprising soldiers from Central Asia (ironically, the invasion allowed the Islamism of the *mujahedeen* to make its way to the USSR with the returning troops).[7]

Russia's independence from the Soviet Union represented an attempt to disentangle Moscow from these imperial peripheries. Yeltsin made common cause with nationalist leaders and movements in the other republics, whose independence he promoted. With the new Russian Federation in dire economic straits, Yeltsin came to view maintaining the empire as a burden Russia could not afford, cutting military spending—lest the army try to remove him as it had Gorbachev—dismantling the KGB, and in 1993, ejecting the other post-Soviet states from the ruble zone. The attempt to build a territorially based *rossiyskiy* identity also entailed severing the links between Russia and the other republics.

While both the LDPR's Vladimir Zhirinovsky and the Communist Party's Gennady Zyuganov called for some version of imperial restoration, the figure most associated with the return to imperial geopolitics was Yevgeny Primakov, who served as Yeltsin's foreign minister from 1996 to 1998 and as prime minister from 1998 to 1999. An academic and former intelligence officer, Primakov argued that Russia ought to pursue its own course in international affairs rather than seek approbation from the West, and that the former Soviet Union represented a natural sphere of influence where Moscow should focus on "ruling out possibilities for any external forces to drive wedges between Russia and the other [post-Soviet] countries."[8] Though Primakov was a political rival of Vladimir Putin, as president, Putin embraced much of Primakov's worldview, especially with regard to maintaining Russia's dominant role and preventing the establishment of NATO or other hostile forces across the former Soviet Union.[9]

While Yeltsin's anti-imperial Russian nationalism helped bring down the USSR, a web of unequal relationships continued to bind the Russian Federation to the other republics and provide Moscow a source of leverage. Since the boundaries of the Soviet-era union republics were never intended to be international borders, the Soviet collapse left families, towns, and supply chains divided across multiple states. Some of these ties had security implications, notably the presence of ethnic Russian minorities in several new states, including northern Kazakhstan and Kyrgyzstan. In the Caucasus, ethnic communities like Ossetians, Lezgins, and Chechens lived on both sides of Russia's new international border as well. Instability on one side of the new border could therefore easily spread to the other.

Moreover, most political elites in the Caucasus and Central Asia are still Russian-speaking products of the Soviet education system. They preside over political systems themselves sharing a common post-Soviet heritage with Russia. Based on conditional property rights, informal rules, patronage networks, and the strategic manipulation of corruption, these systems provide numerous levers for Russian influence. Preserving this post-Soviet political model—sometimes dubbed "*Sistema* (The System)"—has been a principal objective of Russian policy toward its post-Soviet neighbors.[10] Moscow is therefore wary of mass mobilization calling for free elections or changes in government, like those which sparked "colored revolutions" in Georgia (2003), Ukraine (2004 and 2014), Kyrgyzstan (2005, 2010, and 2020), and Armenia (2018)—and which Russian officials blame U.S. and European democracy-promotion efforts for inspiring.

Although Moscow emphasizes maintenance of its leading role, both the South Caucasus and Central Asia have become contested zones as the United States, EU, Turkey, Iran, and, especially, China all adopt more active postures, even as Russia pulls back from regions (especially in Central Asia) viewed as less integral to its own security. Russia has largely failed to develop new relationships and tools to perpetuate or expand the influence it inherited from the Soviet era, especially among younger generations lacking cultural and familial connections to Russia. During three decades of independence, the states of the South Caucasus and Central Asia have grown more self-sufficient, with a stronger sense of their own identity and place in the world. As they seek security and development in today's more fluid and multipolar Eurasia, they try to hedge against excessive Russian influence. New forms of multilateral integration aim to reverse this erosion, but face similar questions about resources and how Eurasia fits into Russia's larger strategic calculus.

The South Caucasus

As a classic imperial shatter zone, the South Caucasus sits at the interstice of Russian, Turkish, and Iranian influence. The region's fragmentation also provides multiple opportunities for outside powers to intervene. Many of Russia's tools, including manipulation of ethnic conflicts, shifting of borders, deployment of peacekeepers, and control of critical economic assets (including pipelines), developed out of instruments employed by both the Russian Empire and the Soviet Union. Today, Moscow's interests in the South Caucasus are linked to the persistence of cross-border ties with the North Caucasus, the region's strategic location at the crossroads of Europe and Asia, and its continued fragmentation and volatility.[11]

Russia was drawn into the South Caucasus in the eighteenth century in support of the Christian Georgians against their Muslim neighbors. Facing continued Iranian onslaughts, King Erekle II of the east Georgian Kingdom of Kartli-Kakheti made repeated appeals to Catherine II for protection. In 1783, Catherine finally assented to the Treaty of Georgievsk, which established a Russian protectorate—but then failed to intervene to save Kartli-Kakheti from a devastating invasion at the hands of the Iranian Qajars. In response to this humiliation, Catherine's son Paul I (1796–1801) abrogated the treaty and annexed Kartli-Kakheti to the Russian Empire. In 1801, Alexander I deposed the Bagratid dynasty and abolished the kingdom.[12] In 1813, the Treaty of Golestan (Gülistan) ending the war with Iran affirmed Russian control of western Georgia, plus a series of Muslim-ruled khanates comprising modern Azerbaijan and Dagestan.[13] The Yerevan and Nakhjavan (Nakhichevan) khanates, with their large Armenian populations, remained outside Russian control until the 1828 Treaty of Torkamanchay (Türkmenchay), imposed following another victory over the Qajars.

The South Caucasus later came under the authority of Russian supreme administrators (*glavnoupravlyayushchiye*) or viceroys (*namestniki*), who acted as "de facto ambassadors . . . commanders in chief . . . and the supreme regional authority."[14] As early as 1812, Russia's Holy Synod abolished the Georgian Orthodox Church's autocephaly, transforming it into an exarchy of the Russian church, administered from 1817 by a Russian bishop. St. Petersburg also abolished the *mouravis*, governorships held by Georgian nobility, and replaced them with Russian administrators. The Muslim population, though, "remained essentially outside the Caucasian administration" until the 1820s, when supreme administrator Mikhail Yermolov attempted to abolish the khanal structures and impose Russian provincial administration.[15] For a time, St. Petersburg created a new Armenian province (*Armyanskaya oblast'*) from the former Yerevan and Nakhichevan khanates—an early example of territorializing ethnicity—in which Armenians from neighboring regions and across the Ottoman and Iranian frontiers were encouraged to settle.[16]

Administrative consolidation accelerated under Nicholas I and his first supreme administrator, Ivan Paskevich, who sought to "compel the inhabitants to speak, think, and feel in Russian," while recouping the costs of conquest by transforming the Caucasus into a source of raw materials and a protected market for Russian goods.[17] Though political centralization continued, Russian settlement was limited, helping preserve the peripheral nature of the South Caucasus and allowing it to maintain much of its indigenous culture. Soon after the annexation of Georgia, Russian officials began confiscating land for redistribution to Russian settlers. As late as the 1890s, however, a large majority of Russians in the region were religious nonconformists (Dukhobors, Molokans, and Subbotniks), many exiled from the Russian interior to the former khanates where they could not tempt Orthodox peasants to heresy.[18] Alexander III attempted to bring the Caucasus under regular provincial rule, but the viceroyalty was reestablished during the 1905 Revolution.

By the end of the nineteenth century, the South Caucasus was increasingly restive. Economic development, including the discovery of oil at Baku, created an industrial proletariat whose grievances mirrored those of workers throughout the Russian Empire, but also overlay ethnic and religious tensions between natives and migrant workers from outside the region. The South Caucasus thus saw some of the Russian Empire's worst violence during the revolutionary upheaval of 1905, and was on the front lines of the vicious Russo-Ottoman conflict in the First World War. In response to the attempted Ottoman invasion of December 1914, Russian commanders expelled and massacred thousands of Muslims and supported an Armenian uprising that briefly seized Van. While St. Petersburg viewed the Christian Armenians as allies against the Ottomans and indigenous Muslim groups, some officials saw the Ottomans' cleansing of Armenians from eastern Anatolia as an opportunity to move in Russian colonists.[19] The legacy of mistrust toward the Russian authorities, and between Armenians and Muslims, contributed to the fragmentation of the South Caucasus during the war and to the region's eventual reconquest by the Red Army.

The post–World War I settlements between the USSR and Turkey left the South Caucasus under Soviet control, but established special status for the regions of Abkhazia, Ajaria, Nagorno-Karabakh, and Nakhichevan. They also confirmed the bifurcation of the Armenian Highlands between the USSR and Turkey (whose Armenian population had been all but eliminated during the war), making the Yerevan-based Armenian SSR into a focal point for identification among Armenians inside and outside the USSR. Soviet rule was also instrumental in consolidating a distinct "Azerbaijani" identity among the Oghuz Turkic-speaking, mostly Shi'ite Muslim population living in the former khanates north of the Aras River, which Stalin, in particular, encouraged as a means of advancing a claim to neighboring Iranian Azerbaijan.

Stalinist industrialization and the Terror, which targeted members of the native intelligentsia and political elites, as well as groups like Kurds with cross-border ties, helped solidify Soviet rule and integrate the South Caucasus with the rest of the Soviet empire.[20] Yet old perceptions endured; Soviet leaders classified Armenians and Georgians as "advanced," while Azerbaijanis remained lower down the hierarchy and were underrepresented in the Soviet elite (especially the military and security services). In the 1940s, many were displaced as Stalin welcomed an influx of Armenian migrants from the Middle East. Meanwhile, local Party organizations were taken over by members of the republics' titular ethnic groups, who in the post–World War II era oversaw the increased homogenization of once-multinational cities like Tbilisi and Baku.[21] This ethnicization of politics complicated the management of the layered autonomies (such as South Ossetia) within the South Caucasus republics, where ethnic tensions, often overlain by territorial disputes, continued to simmer and at times spilled over into violence.[22]

The Soviet collapse then established independent states in the South Caucasus without disentangling the region from the neighboring North Caucasus, creating a zone of instability that, once the immediate impact of the collapse had passed, Moscow sought to contain. Chechens, Lezgins, Ossetians, and other ethnic communities now lived on both sides of Russia's undemarcated and poorly guarded borders. New governments in Azerbaijan and Georgia pursued a path of state-building that emphasized loosening postimperial ties to Russia while at times seeking to assimilate or displace their own minorities—who turned to Moscow for support.

The salience of these divisions mounted with the outbreak of ethnoterritorial conflicts in both the North and South Caucasus in the early 1990s.[23] Conflicts in Georgia's breakaway regions of Abkhazia and South Ossetia, and between Armenia and Azerbaijan over Nagorno-Karabakh, drew in Russian forces.[24] The conflict in Chechnya, meanwhile, encouraged the Russian military to intervene across the border to prevent separatists from establishing a foothold in remote regions of Georgia like the Kodori Gorge. Moscow also supported Lezgin separatists in Azerbaijan to deter Baku from aiding Chechnya's rebels. In each case, fighting ended with the breakaway regions outside the control of the state (Georgia and Azerbaijan, respectively) whose sovereignty was internationally recognized, resulting in "frozen conflicts" that have remained among the most important sources of Russian leverage.

These unresolved conflicts in the South Caucasus impose costs on all three states, which cannot consolidate their territorial integrity or achieve Euro-Atlantic integration and remain vulnerable to Russian coercion.[25] Russian peacekeepers patrolled the ceasefires between Georgia and its breakaway regions, which in turn depended on Russia for access to global markets. Armenia also found itself dependent on Russia in the wake of the First Nagorno-Karabakh War, as Azerbaijan and Turkey closed their borders and vowed revenge for Yerevan's seizure of Nagorno-Karabakh and seven surrounding regions of Azerbaijan. Though Russia guarantees Armenia's security, it remains the main weapons supplier to both sides in the conflict, as well as the principal mediator between them. It was Russia that imposed a ceasefire when renewed fighting broke out in April 2016, and at the end of the Second Nagorno-Karabakh War (2020), Moscow not only brokered an end to the fighting, but deployed peacekeepers to enforce it.

Russia has also sought to prevent the establishment of what it views as hostile foreign influence in the South Caucasus. Concern about foreign penetration emerged with the signing in 1994 of the first contract between Azerbaijan and Western energy companies aiming to build new east-west pipelines from the Caspian Sea bypassing Russian territory.[26] By weakening the imperial-era hub-and-spoke economic model tying the South Caucasus to Russia, projects like the Baku-Tbilisi-Ceyhan oil pipeline and the parallel Baku-Tbilisi-Erzurum gas pipeline allowed Azerbaijan and Georgia to reduce their dependence on Russia and pursue stronger ties with outside powers, including Turkey, the EU, and the United States. Moscow attempted to block such projects by limiting foreign access to the Caspian Sea, offering to buy Azerbaijan's gas, building its own pipelines to Turkey, and targeting pipelines with cyber and, likely, kinetic attacks.[27]

Concerns about foreign influence in Georgia grew following the 2003–04 Rose Revolution, which brought to power the pro-Western Mikheil Saakashvili. Among Saakashvili's top priorities were restoring control over Abkhazia and South Ossetia and bringing Georgia into NATO. The first of the so-called colored revolutions, the upheaval in Georgia reinforced Russia's perception that the United States and its allies were intent on using the rhetoric of democratization to weaken Russian influence across its postimperial periphery, a perception reinforced by subsequent "colored revolutions" in Ukraine and Kyrgyzstan and the Bush Administration's broader "freedom agenda."

After a series of crises between Moscow and Tbilisi and Saakashvili's heavy-handed attempt to assert control over South Ossetia, Russian troops invaded Georgia in August 2008. They soon pushed Georgian forces out of both South Ossetia and Abkhazia, which Moscow then recognized as independent states. Both the separation of Abkhazia and South Ossetia, and the creeping process of "borderization," in which Russian forces push the de facto line further into unoccupied Georgian territory, suggest the extent to which Russia continues to view the South Caucasus states as an imperial periphery to be reshaped and reconfigured by Russian power. The war also accelerated ethnic unmixing begun during the conflicts of the 1990s, as Ossetian militias expelled most of South Ossetia's remaining ethnic Georgians (most Georgian residents were expelled from Abkhazia in the early 1990s). Thus, while Russian intervention left Georgia territorially fragmented, it helped unify most inhabitants of the rump Georgian state around a European identity and Western-leaning foreign policy.

Central Asia

With the collapse of Afghanistan and spread of Islamism into Central Asia in the 1990s, Russia focused on maintaining the region's secular post-Communist governments as a buffer against the spread of extremism and terrorism into Russia itself. Russia also sought to maintain the dominant economic position it inherited from the Soviet Union (though it has more recently been overtaken by China as a source of trade and investment). Above all, Moscow prioritized ensuring that Central Asia did not become an outpost of hostile influence by preventing anti-Russian governments from coming to power and checking the expansion of U.S. and NATO influence. With the "loss" of Ukraine and the announcement of China's Belt and Road Initiative, moreover, Russia's plans for post-Soviet political and economic integration have come to focus on Central Asia, where it aims to, if not limit, then at least channel Chinese influence and maintain its own access to resources and markets.

Unlike its conquests in Europe or even the South Caucasus, Russian officials regarded Central Asia as a "colony" from the very beginning, comparing it to the overseas conquests of the European empires.[28] Like Britain and France, Russia proclaimed a *mission civilisatrice* emphasizing the eradication of "backward" practices like slavery and torture. Outside of Kazakhstan, Central Asian elites were not incorporated into the *dvoryanstvo*—though among nomadic populations, traditional elites maintained their role as interlocutors and executors of Russian rule.[29] Most of the population fell into the category of "aliens (*inorodtsy*)," possessing neither the privileges nor the duties of taxation and military service expected of other Russian subjects, while the small number of Russian settlers were regarded as the foundation for Russian rule.[30]

Incorporation into the Russian Empire transformed the region's economy, with cotton displacing grain as the agricultural staple in Transoxiana (the region between the Amu Darya and Syr Darya Rivers) to supply textile factories in the western part of the empire, and underpinning what would become an increasingly dependent economic relationship. Above all, Russian rule in Central Asia was imperial in that it depended on conquest and domination. As Foreign Minister Aleksandr Gorchakov wrote in 1864:

> The position of Russia in Central Asia is that of all civilized states which are brought into contact with half-savage nomad populations possessing no fixed social organization. . . .
> It is a peculiarity of Asiatics to respect nothing but visible and palpable force. The moral force of reasoning has no hold on them.[31]

By 1882, Russian Central Asia was divided between a Steppe General Government covering Western Siberia and the north of modern Kazakhstan and a Turkestan General Government based in Tashkent, while the Caucasus Viceroyalty directed the conquest and incorporation of the Turkmen east of the Caspian Sea.[32] The boundaries between these territories and the provisions for ruling them were frequently adjusted in line with the political winds in St. Petersburg and the priorities of Russian proconsuls on the ground. When its armies conquered Khiva and Bukhara, St. Petersburg left their native rulers on the throne: both the Khanate of Khiva and the Emirate of Bukhara outlasted the Russian Empire, though St. Petersburg abolished the Khanate of Khoqand in 1876 following an abortive rebellion against Russian rule.

While most of Central Asia remained under distinct forms of administration, Russian settlement resulted in the gradual and partial integration of the Kazakh steppe, which in turn has complicated the process of

disentangling northern Kazakhstan from neighboring southwestern Siberia.[33] Over a million Russian agriculturalists settled in the Steppe General
Government between 1897 and 1917, aided by legislation appropriating
nomads' land for the state and allowing peasant settlement on lands the
Ministry of Internal Affairs deemed in excess of their needs.[34] Russian
colonization, which disrupted nomadic migration and trade, helped spark
a Kazakh national movement and was a central grievance behind the uprising among Kazakhs and Kyrgyz that broke out in 1916 over attempts
to conscript Central Asians for compulsory labor during World War I.[35]
These revolts resulted in the death or flight of hundreds of Russians—and
hundreds of thousands of Central Asians—while further loosening Russia's political grip.[36]

Settlement and administrative consolidation in Transoxiana, conversely, remained nascent when the Russian Empire collapsed. Turkestan had been closed to further settlement amid difficulty finding land for
colonists and local resistance, including a major uprising in the Ferghana
Valley town of Andijon in 1898. Yet land hunger and St. Petersburg's interest in political integration overrode concerns about the disruption to
native life. In 1910, St. Petersburg drafted new rules allowing expropriation of "excess" land from local inhabitants, with the goal of bringing in
1.5 million new Russian settlers. By 1911 though, only around 6 percent
of the Turkestan General Government's population was Slavic, much of
it in Tashkent and fortified cities like Verny (Almaty) and Pishpek (Bishkek).[37] During and after the Civil War, Red Army troops put down native
uprisings, during which they conquered and abolished the Khivan and
Bukharan khanates. Native resistance (which Russians termed *Basmachi*,
or "bandits") nevertheless continued into the 1930s.[38]

The general absence of nationalist movements (outside the Kazakh
Alash Orda), the vigor of tribal and clan ties, and the lack of clear boundaries between spoken languages complicated the Bolsheviks' task of national delimitation, which proceeded primarily on tribal lines.[39] By the
mid-1930s, the former Steppe and Turkestan General Governments and
the territory of the former Khiva Khanate and Bukhara Emirate had been
refashioned into five union republics, a process that reshaped the geographic and social bases of power, elevating the role of Russian-dominated
cities like Almaty, Tashkent, and Bishkek at the expense of traditional
power centers like Bukhara.[40] To defuse the potential for separatism and
accelerate modernization, the Soviet government also included several
Russian-majority cities, including Akmolinsk (Nur-Sultan) in the new

Kazakh SSR. Dividing up the Ferghana Valley, center of the old Khoqand Khanate, proved particularly difficult given the interlocking tribal and linguistic ties among its populations, resulting in convoluted borders between the Soviet republics of Kyrgyzstan, Tajikistan, and Uzbekistan.[41] Deliberately or not, this spatial fragmentation inhibited cooperation between the Central Asian republics and allowed Moscow to maintain a divide-and-rule posture.

Perceptions of Central Asia's "backwardness (*otstalost'*)" encouraged Soviet planners to undertake extensive campaigns of cultural transformation, including the forced unveiling of women, which often prompted a fierce backlash.[42] The imperial nature of Soviet rule in Central Asia was further reinforced by patterns of development assigning Central Asia a role as a producer of natural resources, notably oil and cotton, and as a backwater where undesirable people and pollutants could be dispatched. In Kazakhstan, Stalinist development encompassed "denomadization" that reflected imperial-era perceptions—now imbued with a Marxist overlay—of nomadism as a "backward" mode of life destined to give way to more rational exploitation of resources. "Denomadization," accompanied by efforts to collectivize agriculture, sparked a devastating famine that may have killed as much as one-third of the Kazakh population in the 1930s.[43] Central Asia also suffered extensive ecological damage from Soviet rule, including the diversion of the Amu Darya and Syr Darya Rivers to feed Uzbekistan's cotton monoculture, which led to the shriveling of the Aral Sea, and the use of Kazakhstan's Semipalatinsk for nuclear testing. Populations deported from the Caucasus, Crimea, and the Far East during World War II were also sent to Central Asia, as were many dissidents in the late Soviet era.

As the Central Asian SSRs did not see much grassroots nationalist mobilization, independence came mostly unbidden. Yeltsin had little interest in propping up Central Asia. Yet turmoil in Afghanistan and the weakness of the new states posed a significant security challenge. Seeking to maintain the region as a buffer zone, Moscow focused on securing the old Soviet-Afghan border, maintaining troops, security service personnel, and border guards in Central Asia, and organized joint exercises focused on stopping extremist incursions.[44] Given the long, virtually unguardable border, Kazakhstan is Russia's most important partner in Central Asia and a member of all Russian-led multilateral initiatives, even though many Kazakhs worry about the potential for irredentism toward regions with large Slavic populations in the north.

Elsewhere, Moscow's concerns center on state weakness, which could allow the emergence of cross-border extremism and crime, as well as the growth of foreign influence. Russian forces intervened in Tajikistan's post-Soviet civil war on the side of the secular post-Communist ruler Emomali Rakhmon(ov), while Moscow (along with Tehran) was instrumental in brokering a 1997 ceasefire. After the end of the conflict, as many as 7,000 Russian troops remained behind. Russian border guards also patrolled the Tajik-Afghan border until 2005, seeking to prevent the spread of radicalism, violence, and narcotics from Afghanistan. Russia maintains several hundred additional troops in Kyrgyzstan and a small number in Kazakhstan as well. Though Russia supports Turkmenistan's official neutrality, when the situation on the Afghan-Turkmen border deteriorated in the mid-2010s, Moscow offered—or threatened—to dispatch its own forces to guard the border.[45]

The emphasis on maintaining a buffer against extremism, as well as limited historical and emotional connection to the region, has meant that, in contrast to its other postimperial peripheries, Russia has not been uniformly hostile to foreign political and military influence in Central Asia. Following the September 11, 2001 terrorist attacks, Putin consented to the establishment of U.S. bases in Kyrgyzstan and Uzbekistan. Only when U.S. attention shifted to Iraq did Putin press Bishkek and Tashkent to set a date for the departure of U.S. forces, and to amend the charter of the Collective Security Treaty Organization (CSTO) to ensure itself a veto over future deployments. Russia has more recently tolerated an expanding Chinese security presence in Tajikistan in the context of its strategic rapprochement with Beijing and overlapping concerns about state weakness and extremism.[46] Despite the collapse of relations, some Russian analysts also suggest that preventing the return of Central Asians who departed to fight in the ranks of the so-called Islamic State of Iraq and Syria (ISIS) represents a possible avenue for further cooperation with the United States.[47]

Moscow nevertheless continues to regard Central Asia as belonging to a Russian sphere of influence. It emphasizes institutional and other linkages held over from the Soviet era, including the dominance of Russian media outlets and the role of Russian-speaking, often Russian-educated elites, many of whom still look to Moscow to sort out their disputes.[48] Despite the rapid expansion of Chinese trade and investment, Russia also maintains numerous levers of economic influence. In particular, it remains the principal destination for Central Asian labor migrants, who, before the Covid-19 pandemic shut down travel, contributed a disproportionate

share of GDP in Kyrgyzstan (33.2 percent) and Tajikistan (29.0 percent)—
though its ability to manipulate the flow of migrants and remittances for
political ends remains uncertain.[49] As in Ukraine, Russia has also reportedly penetrated the security services of at least some of the Central Asian
states, giving it an important lever in the event of a crisis.

From the Russian Empire to Greater Eurasia

Along with military intervention and manipulation of frozen conflicts,
Russia maintains less overt tools of postimperial domination. The most
ambitious centers on efforts to use multilateral integration to consolidate
a Russian-dominated bloc in the center of Eurasia as a counterweight
to the Euro-Atlantic and Asia-Pacific regional orders, while binding the
South Caucasus and Central Asian states more tightly to Moscow. As
Putin remarked in 2013, "Eurasian integration is an opportunity for the
entire post-Soviet space to become an independent center of global development, rather than a periphery of Europe or Asia."[50] Russia thus aspires
to "the formation of a common economic and humanitarian space from
the Atlantic to the Pacific based on the harmonization and convergence of
the processes of European and Eurasian integration."[51]

Since the Soviet collapse, Moscow has promoted various schemes for
regional integration. Starting with the Commonwealth of Independent
States (CIS), established in 1991 to facilitate a "civilized divorce" among
the former Soviet republics, integration schemes have become more ambitious over time, linked to Moscow's interest in maintaining its leading
role throughout the former Soviet Union and consolidating a bloc of
states to support its global aspirations.[52] Initially synonymous with the
territory of the former Soviet Union or Russian Empire, "Eurasia" has in
Russian usage become a shorthand for aspirations to create a geopolitical
bloc centered on Moscow and apart from, if not necessarily hostile to, the
Euro-Atlantic West.[53] Initial plans for Eurasian integration emphasized
an East Slavic (Belarusian-Russian-Ukrainian) core; since the war with
Ukraine and Kyiv's embrace of a European rather than Eurasian identity,
Russia has focused increasingly on the Caucasus and Central Asia, and
on building a "Greater Eurasia (*Bol'shaya Yevraziya*)" encompassing states
both within and beyond the former USSR, but sharing elements of Moscow's political and economic outlook.

If in the 1990s, the Kremlin viewed integration as a tool for managing trade and investment, under Putin, Eurasian integration took on a

more explicitly geopolitical cast, reflecting Russia's renewed commitment to acting as a great power and the belief that "great powers do not dissolve in some other integration projects but forge their own."[54] Today, the Kremlin seeks to restore political and economic influence over the smaller post-Soviet states, while establishing the idea of "Eurasia" as a (Russian-dominated) geopolitical construct separate from the liberal West and defined by opposition to the liberal values associated with it. This approach is in keeping with the ideology of Eurasianist thinkers from Gumilev to Dugin about building a pan-Eurasian bloc centered on Russia. Even if the institutional forms of Russia's integration projects appear less ideological and more pragmatic, contemporary neo-Eurasianists are supportive, viewing them as contributing to the creation of the Russocentric regional order they envision.[55]

The 2008 global economic crisis was a major stimulus for accelerating the push for Eurasian integration. Medvedev made his first foreign visit as president to Kazakhstan in May 2008, when he announced the creation of a new Russian agency for CIS affairs outside the Ministry of Foreign Affairs, suggesting that the CIS countries continued to occupy a distinct place in the mental map of Russian officials. These efforts culminated in the establishment of a new Customs Union in 2010 and calls for progressive deepening of integration, as Moscow announced plans for a so-called Eurasian Economic Union as a platform for "mutually beneficial cooperation" with the EU and other multilateral organizations.[56]

During his 2011 presidential campaign, Putin called for establishing what he now termed a "Eurasian Union" as "a powerful supranational association capable of becoming one of the poles in the modern world and serving as an efficient bridge between Europe and the dynamic Asia-Pacific region.... and establishing a full-fledged economic union."[57] Putin's emphasis on the Eurasian Union as a geopolitical pole and dropping of the word "economic" from its name raised concern in other post-Soviet states, and in the West, about the project's neoimperial ambitions. Analyses from pro-Kremlin think-tanks reinforced the impression that Eurasian integration was more about recreating a simulacrum of empire and advancing Russia's geopolitical interests than promoting trade.[58]

This organization, once again called the Eurasian *Economic* Union (EAEU), came into being at the start of 2015, with Russia, Belarus, Armenia, and Kazakhstan as members. While its development stalled over a backlash to the invasion of Ukraine, Moscow still regards "deepening and expanding integration within the Eurasian Economic Union" as a "key objective."[59] Russia's dominant position within the EAEU and tendency to see it as a vehicle for setting the agenda for post-Soviet cooperation have limited other states' appetite for deeper integration.[60]

The EAEU has reoriented trade flows among member states toward Russia, reinforcing the hub-and-spoke pattern inherited from the past. Since Russia accounts for close to 85 percent of the EAEU's total GDP and its smaller neighbors depend on access to the Russian market, Moscow has been able to play favorites and bypass rules designed to ensure formal equality.[61] The EAEU also strengthened Russia's control over migration, with Moscow imposing additional barriers to migration from its non-EAEU neighbors (the threat of restrictions on migration was a major consideration in Kyrgyzstan's decision to join in mid-2015). Like China's Belt and Road Initiative, the EAEU also plays a role in setting and reinforcing norms of governance, legitimizing nontransparent, patronage-based models of political economy, and muting pressure for reform. Russia also seeks to build ties between the EAEU and other multilateral organizations, including the European Union and the Belt and Road Initiative, and with countries including Serbia, Israel, and Vietnam.

Similarly, Russia supports the CSTO, a multilateral security bloc that parallels and, in some ways, overlaps with the EAEU. Established on the basis of the 1992 Tashkent Treaty, the CSTO allows Russia to preserve influence over the military and security affairs of its neighbors by providing a platform for training, weapons sales, and joint exercises. With essentially the same membership as the EAEU (plus non-EAEU member Tajikistan), the CSTO plays a similar role as the kernel of a Russocentric bloc and a framework for keeping a subset of post-Soviet states under Moscow's security umbrella. Amid Russia's worsening relationship with the West, Moscow sought to expand the CSTO's capabilities, including establishing multilateral peacekeeping and rapid-reaction forces that could be deployed in response to crises and would provide multilateral cover for Russian-led intervention.

The CSTO also allows Russia to maintain a security presence outside its borders. Moscow took advantage of the creation of the CSTO Collective Rapid Response Force in 2009 to establish a new military base at Kyrgyzstan's Kant airfield under the CSTO banner. A December 2010 amendment to the organization's charter, meanwhile, allowed members to veto the presence of foreign military bases anywhere in the CSTO.[62] Adopted in the wake of the ouster of Kyrgyzstan's President Kurmanbek Bakiyev, who had gone back on a promise to eject U.S. forces deployed after 9/11 (and in whose overthrow Moscow may have had a hand), the amendment was perceived as a Russian effort to guard against the possible redeployment of U.S. troops in the region. As the framework for a Russocentric security bloc, though, the CSTO suffers from the hub-and-spoke model that has long characterized Russia's relationship with its post-Soviet neighbors. Kazakhstan largely supports fellow Turkic state Azerbaijan rather than CSTO member Armenia over Nagorno-Karabakh, while Belarusian president Lukashenko has suggested he would not deploy troops to Central Asia under CSTO auspices.[63]

The idea of Eurasian integration with an emphasis on Central Asia and as an alternative to deepening ties with the West is also at the heart of the Greater Eurasia initiative, rolled out by thinkers affiliated with the Valdai Discussion Club, and announced by Putin in his 2016 speech to the St. Petersburg Economic Forum. This Greater Eurasia is based on the "great potential for cooperation between the EAEU and other countries and integration projects," notably China, but also Iran, India, Pakistan, as well as multilateral groupings like ASEAN, the Shanghai Cooperation Organization (SCO), the EU, and the BRI.[64]

Among the declared goals of the Greater Eurasia project is creating a community of interest between the Russocentric EAEU and a Chinese-led East Asia to "create a continental order free from the dominance of the United States."[65] In that sense, Greater Eurasia represents an alternative to the longstanding assumption that an isolated Russia would have no choice but to adopt liberal democracy and seek to "join" the West. Even if Russia by itself is too weak to act as a motor for regional integration, a larger Eurasia that includes China and some subset of Europe offers an alternative to Russia's smaller neighbors trying to balance between East and West. By promoting non-Western governance norms, Moscow views Greater Eurasia as a mechanism for decoupling itself from the West, while consolidating its influence throughout its postimperial space.

The Greater Eurasia vision also provides a theoretical basis for linking the EAEU with China's BRI, a process that began with the signing of a joint communiqué in May 2015. Apart from challenging the normative hegemony of the West, this "integration of integrations" allows Moscow to influence China's growing ties with the post-Soviet states of the Caucasus and Central Asia.[66] Already, Chinese trade and investment—around $98 billion as of 2018—has overtaken Russian in much of the former Soviet Union.[67] Without a strategy for channeling Chinese investment and decision-making, Moscow fears it could both lose its privileged position and see the bulk of new infrastructure connecting Asia and Europe bypass Russian territory. And by opening the door to countries like India, Iran, and Pakistan, Greater Eurasia also aims to hedge against Chinese dominance of an emerging Eurasian order.[68] The Greater Eurasia vision thus aims to ameliorate the prospect of Sino-Russian competition over Central Asia, while allowing Moscow to manage the challenge that massive Chinese economic expansion poses to its own interests.

While the content and scope of Greater Eurasia remains vague, it is, like the EAEU and other post-Soviet integration projects, in part about perpetuating Russia's postimperial domination in Eurasia, while providing a mechanism for extending Russian influence outward. Yet the growing influence of China, as well as the smaller post-Soviet states' resistance to Russian domination, suggest that prospects for Greater Eurasia to restore Russian power and influence in its postimperial space are limited, particularly among countries (like Ukraine and Georgia already) whose own nation-building projects entail rejection of the Russian imperial legacy.

The Persistence of Russia's Near Abroad

Russia's influence in its postimperial hinterlands in the Caucasus and Central Asia is largely an inheritance from the past. Since the Soviet collapse was more recent than the loss of the Ottoman, Qajar, or Qing empires, the concrete links between Russia and its postimperial periphery are more robust. Much of Moscow's post-1991 approach has centered on reinforcing these links rather than creating a new basis for relations with its neighbors. With both the Caucasus and Central Asia becoming arenas for strategic competition with the West and Eurasia's other postimperial powers, Russia faces an increasingly complex landscape. The success or failure of its postimperial aspirations will depend on its ability to navigate between the competing interests of these other players.

In part because of its long history as the dominant power in both the Caucasus and Central Asia, Russia has struggled with the increasingly contested nature of regional geopolitics. From opposition to east-west energy pipelines to promotion of exclusive multilateral organizations, Russia's strategy has long been defensive, trying to prevent its smaller neighbors from abandoning their post-Soviet identities to seek integration with the West. This strategy has been effective both because Russia is more amenable to dealing with the corrupt, authoritarian governments in many of these states and because Russia is the devil the current generation of elites in the Caucasus and Central Asia knows. These leaders came of age in the USSR, speak Russian, and look instinctively to Moscow as a mediator. They may be zealous about their own sovereignty, for instance in preventing the EAEU from taking on supranational elements like a common currency, but still participate in such organizations in part because they know how to manage them for their own ends.

The challenge for Russia will become greater as this last Soviet generation yields to a younger cohort lacking the same knowledge of and affinity toward Russia. Knowledge of Russian in much of the Caucasus and Central Asia is sharply lower among the generation born after the Soviet collapse. While many young men, in particular, spend time in Russia as migrant workers, their experiences on the margins of Russian society tend not to be the kind that promote affection for or identification with Russian interests. Nor has Russia devoted substantial resources to renewing its cultural capital in these states. Where Turkey offers academic scholarships to students from the "Turkic World" and China operates Confucius Institutes throughout the region, Russia mostly relies on links inherited from the Soviet period. Putin's 2019 call to open more Russian schools in Central Asia represented a belated recognition of Russia's eroding influence with the younger generation.[69]

The growing multipolarity of regional geopolitics represents a different kind of challenge. While the West encouraged transformations that would erode the political and institutional legacies tying these states to Russia, the growth of Chinese (as well as Turkish and Iranian) influence is less disruptive, and, for that reason, more difficult for Russia to oppose. Since the start of the Ukraine conflict, moreover, Russia's embrace of strategic competition with the West has forced it into a greater accommodation with its postimperial peers in both the Caucasus and Central Asia—above all China, whose BRI represents a more ambitious vision for transforming Eurasia than anything put forward by the United States or Europe—but, especially since the Second Nagorno-Karabakh War, with Turkey as well.

While the BRI does not challenge the political status quo within the Caucasus or Central Asia (thus preserving political systems tractable to Russian influence), it does augur a longer-term challenge to Russia's inherited position as the regional pivot. Even before the announcement of the BRI, China was on its way to displacing Russia as Central Asia's main trading partner and source of investment. Though Beijing has remained deferential to Moscow's security interests, a growing Chinese economic stake will inevitably have consequences for security as well. Along with plans to tie the EAEU to the BRI, Russia's "Greater Eurasia" vision represents an attempt to manage this transformation toward a regional order in which Russia itself is just one player among many, balancing against Chinese domination while guarding its own equities. Until or unless Moscow can offer its neighbors a positive vision of the future and incentives to remain within Russia's sphere of influence, the erosion of Russia's post-imperial space is likely to continue.

TURKEY

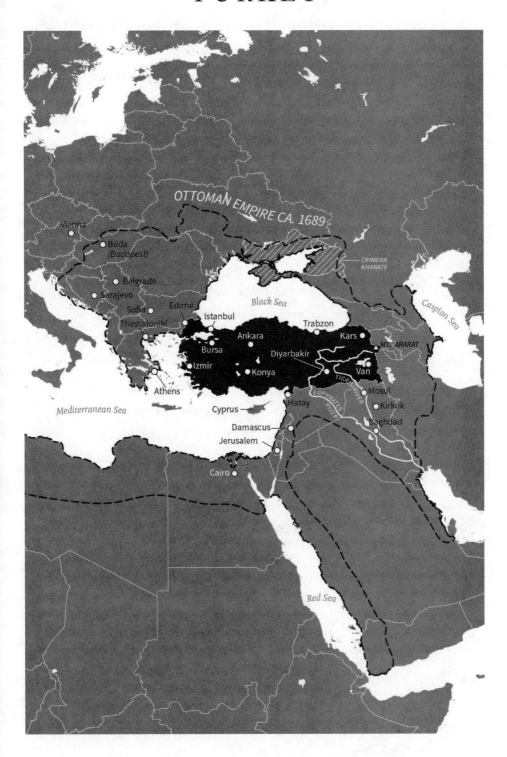

OTTOMAN EMPIRE CA. 1689

CRIMEAN KHANATE

Vienna

Buda
(Budapest)

Belgrade

Sarajevo

Sofia

Edirne

Thessaloniki

Istanbul

Black Sea

Trabzon

Kars

Ankara

MT. ARARAT

Bursa

Diyarbakir

Van

Izmir

Konya

TIGRIS RIVER

Athens

Mosul

EUPHRATES RIVER

Kirkuk

Mediterranean Sea

Cyprus

Hatay

Damascus

Baghdad

Jerusalem

Cairo

Caspian Sea

Red Sea

FOR MONTHS IN THE SPRING and summer of 2013, tens of thousands of Istanbul residents demonstrated against plans to build a shopping center on the site of Gezi Park, one of the city's last remaining green spaces. The demonstrators saw the planned development as an example of the corruption and creeping authoritarianism characterizing the rule of Prime Minister Recep Tayyip Erdoğan and his Justice and Development Party (*Adalet ve Kalkınma Partisi*, AKP). Yet for Erdoğan as well as for the demonstrators, the fight over Gezi Park was about more than a construction project. The planned shopping center was modeled on an Ottoman-era barracks that had once stood on the site. In 1909, military units loyal to the Young Turks, the reformist movement that had forced Sultan Abdülhamid II (1876-1909) to reinstate constitutional rule the year before, suppressed an Islamist counterrevolution seeking to restore Abdülhamid's autocracy, damaging the barracks that had served as the counterrevolution's headquarters in the process. The plan for a replica of the barracks was part of a wider effort under the AKP to reclaim Turkey's Ottoman heritage, overcoming what Erdoğan portrays as the rupture in Turkey's history lasting from the Young Turk revolution to the AKP's ascension in 2002.

More than its postimperial peers, Turkey embodies a paradox: a state whose founding ideology implied a rejection of the recent past, but whose elites, institutions, and mindsets were themselves products of the Ottoman system. The Turkish Republic's founder, Mustafa Kemal (Atatürk), had himself been an Ottoman officer and prominent figure in the Committee of Union and Progress (CUP), the Young Turk faction that dominated post-1909 governments and was responsible for bringing the Ottoman Empire into the First World War. Even after Sultan Mehmed VI (1918–22) fled on a British warship from Kemal's advancing Nationalists, much of the state structure—from the army to the civil bureaucracy—remained

(preceeding page) Ottoman Empire, ca. 1689 (© 2021,
Center for Strategic and International Studies)

in place, while the Treaty of Lausanne, signed with the Allies in 1923, established the Turkish Republic (*Türkiye Cumhuriyeti*) as the Ottoman Empire's legal successor.[1] Atatürk's efforts to subordinate religious institutions to the secular state grew out of the Ottoman-era struggle between bureaucratic modernizers and the religious establishment.[2] So too did the development of a statist system subject to periods of personalistic rule, military coups as "illiberal checks and balances," and the concentration of power in the center, not to mention a focus on gaining admittance to the club of "civilized" Western powers as a foreign policy beacon.[3]

Yet in other ways, the Turkish Republic represented a break with the Ottoman past. Atatürk and his followers viewed the Ottoman Empire's diversity as a source of weakness that contributed to its demise. They established in its place a new state centered on a Turkish nation, whose origins and traditions they sought in an idealized pre-Ottoman and, sometimes, pre-Islamic past. That nation was confined to people living within the borders ratified by the Treaty of Lausanne. Its members were required to subsume alternate identities and embrace Turkish language and culture. Atatürk's dictum, inscribed on his mausoleum in Ankara, "Happy is the person who says 'I am a Turk' [*ne mutlu Türküm diyene*]," emphasized the ascriptive nature of Turkish identity, which allowed any citizen of the Republic, regardless of ethnicity or religion, to say "I am a Turk," by identifying with Turkish culture and abandoning other forms of identification. This state-focused, culturally Turkish identity was part of a deliberate, defensive strategy to guard the new Republic against the nexus of communal mobilization and foreign intervention that led to the Ottoman Empire's loss of its non-Turkish peripheries in the Balkans, the Middle East, and the Caucasus.

Atatürk also created a modern, centralized republic in place of the heterogeneous collection of territories that swore fealty and paid tribute to the sultan, the "Divinely Protected Well-Flourishing Absolute

Domain of the House of Osman."[4] Such centralization posed particular difficulties in the heavily Kurdish areas of Southeastern Anatolia, where Kurdish tribal emirates were instrumental in securing the Ottoman Empire's frontier with Iran and, later, Russia, until an abortive late-Ottoman centralization effort fractured them, sparking widespread instability and violence between Kurds and their Christian Armenian and Assyrian neighbors. The Republic sought to secure this borderland by curtailing tribal autonomy, suppressing religious orders, and imposing cultural and linguistic assimilation. When all else failed, Ankara fell back on large-scale violence against Kurdish populations. Southeastern Anatolia nevertheless remained a postimperial borderland where the state lacked a monopoly on the use of force. Since the mid-1980s, it has been the site of a bloody insurgency waged by the Kurdistan Workers Party (*Partiya Karkerên Kurdistanê*, PKK) that has left 30,000–40,000 dead.[5] Throughout the conflict, the PKK's ability to find support and refuge across Turkey's borders with Iraq and Syria has impeded attempts to resolve the conflict militarily.

Turkey's Kemalist foreign policy, meanwhile, emphasized disentangling the Republic from its post-Ottoman periphery. With few exceptions, the Republic adopted an inward-looking strategic orientation, turning its back on formerly Ottoman territories outside Turkey's Anatolian heartland. Atatürk's aspiration to build a modern, secular state entailed downplaying Turkey's Islamic heritage, and with it, its historical links to the Arabian Peninsula, the Caucasus, and the Balkans, all of which had longstanding ties to Ottoman Anatolia. Another of Atatürk's dictums, "Peace at Home, Peace in the World [*Yurtta sulh, cihanda sulh*]," became the basis for Turkish foreign policy in the aftermath of the War of Independence. During the twentieth century, Turkey eschewed foreign interventions (apart from those, like the Korean War, conducted under UN auspices). Accession to NATO in 1952 and an aspiration to join the precursors to the European Union aimed at deflecting the Soviet threat and asserting Turkey's identity as a European rather than a postimperial Eurasian state.

Despite these efforts to subsume the imperial past, aspects of it continued to hang over the Turkish Republic. These imperial legacies would become more pronounced with the rise of the AKP, which looked to the Ottoman era as a source of inspiration. Drawing on Ottoman nostalgia that lingered among the Islamist and nationalist opposition throughout the Republican era, the AKP embraces a narrative of continuity between the empire and the Republic to criticize the secularist reforms of the Kemalists as ahistorical and alien to the wellsprings of Turkish identity. In its efforts to redefine the boundaries of the Turkish nation, manage its Kurdish borderland, and position itself at the center of regional order, the AKP aspires to overcome what it sees as the artificial divide in Turkish history represented by the collapse of the empire and the foundation of the Republic, while encouraging the cultural, economic, and, to some degree, political reintegration of a wider "post-Ottoman space."

Part of the AKP's Ottoman revivalism involves widening the aperture of the nation to encompass multiple layers of belonging. Drawing on a longstanding Islamist critique of the Republic, the AKP emphasizes the Ottoman Empire's Islamic identity, where "the religious could express itself in secular terms, just as the secular could use religious motifs."[6] The party argues that Kemalist secularization severed Turks not only from their authentic identity, but also from organic ties to other post-Ottoman peoples. By reembracing its Islamic essence, Erdoğan and his supporters suggest, Turkey can exert a claim on the loyalties and sympathies of foreign, especially post-Ottoman, Muslims. The AKP has also adopted a less extensive and less systematic interest in the fate of Turkic-speakers dispersed across Eurasia from the Balkans to East Turkestan (Xinjiang)—most in regions never subject to Ottoman rule—

which helps cement its alliance with the Nationalist Movement Party (*Milliyetçi Hareket Partisi*, MHP) and reconciled nationalists of various stripes to AKP rule.

Emphasis on an Ottoman-Islamic core to Turkish identity also allows the AKP to supplement previous governments' efforts to solve the Kurdish problem through hardening borders and seeking administrative uniformity with aspects of a classically imperial approach to frontier management. Invoking the example of Abdülhamid II, appeals to a common Ottoman-Islamic heritage suggest that Kurds—at least the majority who are Sunnis—can be full members of the Turkish nation without ceasing to be Kurds. This approach is central to the AKP's strategy for integrating the Kurdish borderland and ending the conflict with the PKK. So too though are efforts to secure the frontier through cross-border military operations—notably large-scale interventions in northern Syria—and the development of vassal-like relations with the Kurdistan Regional Government (KRG) in northern Iraq.

The AKP's turn to Ottoman themes also has wider implications for Turkish foreign policy. As Erdoğan and the AKP consolidated their grip on power, Turkish foreign policy became less Western-centric, with Ankara aspiring to the role of regional leader and pivot state, encapsulated in the notion of "strategic depth (*stratejik derinlik*)," popularized by former Foreign Minister and Prime Minister Ahmet Davutoğlu.[7] Pointing to the impact of instability around its borders for Turkey's own security, Davutoğlu called for restoring ties with Turkey's post-Ottoman periphery in the Balkans, the Caucasus, and, in particular, the Middle East. During Davutoğlu's tenure as foreign minister, Ankara attempted to mediate regional conflicts while building direct ties with (especially Sunni) populations in neighboring states. Since the onset of the Arab Spring in 2011, Turkey has also attempted to export aspects of its own political model, while intervening militarily in Syria, Libya, and the South Caucasus. Yet with unstable politics, a heavily indebted economy, and tetchy neighbors, intervention in these conflicts forced Ankara to confront questions about the limits of its capabilities and the risks of imperial overstretch in a region where imperial rivals Iran and, especially, Russia are pursuing their own ambitions.

CHAPTER FOUR

Those Who Call Themselves Turks

Empire, Islam, and Nation

A S THE CENTENNIAL of the Turkish Republic approaches, Atatürk's aspiration to weld a civic nation to the territory of the state remains incomplete. That nation, where all inhabitants of the Republic are encouraged to assimilate to a hegemonic Turkish culture and focus their loyalty on the territory of the Republic itself, was designed to guard against the fragmentation that overtook the late Ottoman Empire, culminating in the partition and occupation of Anatolia by the Allied powers under the terms of the Treaty of Sèvres (1920). Though Mustafa Kemal's Nationalists ended the occupation and overturned the treaty, Turkish strategic culture remains dominated by a "Sèvres Syndrome" linked to this nexus of separatism and foreign intervention.[1]

In response, the early Republic fostered "a Jacobin mentality [and] . . . an official, monolithic, absolute Turkish identity" that suppressed or ignored "the multiple identities that came to be imprisoned in the periphery."[2] For populations like Kurds or Muslim refugees from the Balkans, saying "I am a Turk" thus meant prioritizing loyalty to the state and its territorial integrity over wider religious or ethnic consciousness. Coupled with the early Republic's ardent secularism, this territorial vision of the nation eschewed post-Ottoman irredentism, as well as pan-Islamist and pan-Turkic ideals, in favor of a territorially bounded community comprising, in theory, all inhabitants of Anatolia irrespective of religion, language, or ethnicity.[3]

Yet tension between civic, religious, and ethnic approaches to identity—what the Russian Tatar émigré Yusuf Akçura characterized in 1904 as the Ottoman Empire's "three types of politics"—did not fade with the establishment of the Republic.[4] Alternate conceptions portraying and Islamic core to Turkish identity and the position of Turks at the center of a wider Islamic community, or as the kernel of a "Turkic World" stretching from the Balkans to East Turkestan, continued to exist around the margins of Turkish politics, challenging the official understanding of a Turkish nation "clearly but passionately delimited to Anatolia."[5] These alternative views of Turkish identity became integral to political debates after both the restoration of multiparty politics in 1950 and the return to democratic rule after the 1980 coup.[6] Today, the AKP takes advantage of the Islamic and, to a lesser degree, pan-Turkic framings of Turkish identity to appeal to populations living outside the Republic.

In seeking to connect the Republic to the centuries of imperial history that preceded it, the AKP has sought to widen the aperture of the Turkish nation by supplementing the category of citizenship (*vatandaşlık*) with what Davutoğlu called *tarihdaşlık*, a neologism implying those sharing a common history (*tarih*).[7] More comfortable than their predecessors with the idea that Turkish identity is capacious enough to include more than just those who "call themselves Turks," the AKP has encouraged connections between Turkey and its neighbors on the basis of ties—historical, religious, and ethnic—that Kemalist nation-building sought to subsume. Like the Russian notion of "compatriots," invocations of a community united by a shared history suggest less an effort at territorial revision than one aimed at establishing Turkey at the center of its own regional order, with populations outside the Republic identifying in some capacity with a "Greater Turkey (*Büyük Türkiye*)."

For the AKP, this idea of a Greater Turkey is colored by Ottoman nostalgia wrapped in the language and symbolism of Islam. It encompasses a deliberate effort to "Islamize" historical memory of the Ottomans and elide the actual heterodoxy and heterogeneity of the Ottoman elite, as well as the Ottoman government's efforts to manage religion for secular ends. Domestically, it means greater opportunity to articulate identities beyond Kemalism's "Jacobin" Turkishness—for groups historically resident in Anatolia like the Kurds as well as for the descendants of the millions of non-Turkish migrants who made their way to Anatolia as the Ottoman Empire's grip on Crimea, the Balkans, and the Caucasus slipped. It also entails a transborder geographic imagination that emphasizes the unity of the post-Ottoman space as an organic whole united by a shared Ottoman-Islamic heritage. As Davutoğlu noted in a 2009 speech in Sarajevo:

> Turkey is a small Balkans, a small Middle East and a small Caucasia. There are more Bosnians living in Turkey than those living in Bosnia; more Albanians living in Turkey than those in Albania; more Chechens living in Turkey than in Chechnya; more Abkhazians than those in Abkhazia. . . . For all these Muslim nationalities . . . Turkey is a safe haven and a homeland. You are most welcome as well, because Anatolia belongs to you; and make sure that Sarajevo is ours.[8]

Alongside the emphasis on Islam, the AKP also pays tribute to the idea of what former Prime Minister and President (1993–2000) Süleyman Demirel termed a "Greater Turkic World (*Büyük Türk Dünyası*)" encompassing the Turks of Anatolia as well as the Turkic-speaking peoples of Europe, the Caucasus, Russia, Central Asia, and Xinjiang, and, in some cases, the "Turanian" Hungarians, Finns, and others.[9] "Turkism (*Türkçülük*)" and identification with the "Outer Turks (*Dış Türkler*)" have been staples of a small but vocal right-wing opposition since the late Ottoman era, associated since the 1960s especially with the MHP. Since the Soviet collapse, emphasis on the "Turkic World," especially the Caucasus and Central Asia, has become something of an implicit assumption among parties across the political spectrum—even if it is not a first-order priority for any individual party or movement.[10] More recently, the role of the MHP as a bulwark and, since 2018, a coalition partner of the AKP has brought this view of the nation mainstream acceptance. It represents an "imperial" articulation of the nation, but one in which Ottoman nostalgia plays little part, since little of the "Turkic World," outside southeastern Europe, was ever under Ottoman rule.

Erdoğan and his associates maintain a deliberately ambiguous balance between these contending identity discourses. The AKP inherited and maintains Atatürk's commitment to a civic nation limned by the borders of the Republic, promoting what Erdoğan sometimes calls *Türkiyelilik* (emphasizing the state—*Türkiye*).[11] It is also, though, a product of the "Turkish-Islamic Synthesis," which emerged in the mid-twentieth century as a critique of Kemalist secularism, emphasizing the centrality of Islam to Turkish national identity, and looking back to the Ottoman period as the authentic embodiment of Turkish Islamism. This nexus of Islam and nationalism is instrumental to the AKP's ambition to reassemble a kind of Turkey-centric post-Ottoman space and position itself as a source of influence and inspiration for Sunnis across Eurasia and the Middle East, and coexists with a muted but increasingly visible portrayal of Turkey as the nucleus of a Greater Turkic World.

From Ottoman *Millet*s to Turkish Nation

Prior to the *Tanzimat* era (1839–76), individual status in the Ottoman Empire was mostly a product of religion. Though the expanding Ottoman *beylik* (emirate) Islamized the landscape of Istanbul and other conquered cities, it did not pursue a policy of forcible conversion. Islamization in Anatolia and the Balkans mainly came through compulsory resettlement (*sürgün*) of Turkish tribes and proselytization by dervish orders. Many Byzantine Christians, meanwhile, held positions in Ottoman service; even after the fall of Byzantium in 1453, a disproportionate share of Ottoman officials was of Christian origin. Conscripted through the levy of Balkan Christian children (*devşirme*) or taken as slaves, they included around one-third of the Ottoman Empire's grand viziers (*vizir-i azam*). The mothers of several sultans were Christian-born as well.

With Selim I's (1512–20) conquest of the Mamluks in 1517, the Ottoman Empire's population became majority Muslim. The sultan was now the preeminent ruler in the Sunni world, controlling the caliphate and the Two Holy Mosques, but still depicted himself as a pious ruler looking out for justice and the welfare of his subjects—Muslim and non-Muslim.[12] Despite subsequent efforts to construct an "institutional Sunnism," to provide a legal and a moral justification for Ottoman rule, Ottoman Islam never entirely broke with the legacy of the nomadic Turks who provided the nucleus of the Ottoman polity, notably the importance of Sufi and dervish orders—many of them quite heterodox from the perspective of Sunni clerics in Baghdad or Cairo.[13] Dynastic patronage for these orders was a means of channeling and controlling folk Islam, which retained a strongly syncretic character and could at times manifest itself in opposition to Ottoman rule. The importance of Sufi and dervish orders like the Mevlevi, Halveti, Bektashi, and, in the nineteenth century, the Naqshbandi has, however, always posed a challenge to Ottoman and Turkish claims of leadership in the Islamic world.[14]

While the multiethnic class of "professional Ottomans" who administered the empire were generally required to be Muslims, multiple local, religious, and tribal communities (known as *ta'ife* or, especially from the nineteenth century, *millet*s) were integrated into the fabric of the state as self-administering corporate entities.[15] Religious minorities were permitted to follow their own practices, rely on their own legal institutions, and remain exempt from military service in exchange for payment of a poll-tax (*cizye*), while the heads of the *millet* served as interlocutors with the authorities. This arrangement "allowed the ruled to feel confident as a recognized community with tangible autonomy in the religious and legal realms no matter where they resided in the empire."[16]

Non-Muslims, nevertheless, occupied an inferior social and legal position. Along with the *cizye*, sumptuary laws restricted what clothing they could wear. Sporadic state-approved violence also occurred, especially during periods of Islamic revivalism such as the seventeenth-century Islamic reform movement known as Kadızadeli.[17] Nor did the protections of the *millet* framework extend in full to Yazidis, Druze, or nonorthodox Muslims such as Qizilbash-Alevis or Ismailis.[18] The position of non-Muslims became more contentious during the nineteenth century, as many Christian peripheries rebelled against Ottoman rule with the backing of one or more of the European great powers. These rebellions resulted in enormous territorial losses and widespread communal violence between Muslims and Christians, sending millions of Muslim refugees streaming into Anatolia from Crimea, the Balkans, and the Caucasus.

Mid-nineteenth-century statesmen and intellectuals responded with calls to create a common identity transcending ethnic and sectarian differences.[19] In place of segmented communities, the 1839 Gülhane Rescript spoke of reviving "religion, state, country, and nation [*millet*]."[20] The use of *millet* to mean "nation" suggested a religious basis to Ottoman identity. Yet being Ottoman in the *Tanzimat* era meant more than just being Muslim. As the statesman Ahmed Cevdet Paşa recognized in 1858, "the ruler is Ottoman, the government is Turkish, the religion is Islam, and the capital is Istanbul. If any one of these four principles were to be weakened, this would mean a weakening of one of the pillars of the state structure."[21] It was the combination that allowed different communities to coexist and made the empire's cohesion possible.

The *Tanzimat* reforms provided the foundation for an approach eventually termed "Ottomanism (*Osmanlılık*)" that would, in different forms, animate subsequent efforts at restoring and reviving the Ottoman Empire. Ottomanism represented an attempt "to create a new concept of a political entity and to locate the source of its legitimacy within an imperial framework," in other words, to reconcile imperial and national visions of legitimacy by creating a nation encompassing all inhabitants of the empire regardless of ethnicity or religion.[22] Yet this approach remained shadowed by both existing assumptions and the continued loss of the Ottoman Empire's non-Muslim periphery. While early proponents of Ottomanism had rejected religion as a criterion for membership in the nation, their successors in the 1860s and 1870s, known as Young Ottomans, objected to what they perceived to be a policy that favored the non-Muslim minority over the Muslim majority.[23] Though they continued seeking to unite Ottoman subjects of all ethnicities and religions behind the empire's territorial integrity, Young Ottomans like the intellectual and playwright Namık Kemal emphasized an "Islamic nationalism (*İslam milliyetçiliği*)" and the use of Ottoman Turkish as a lingua franca.[24]

The European powers' support for Christian nationalist movements and extension of consular protection to Ottoman Christians, meanwhile, raised questions about the loyalty of non-Muslims. In the face of continued territorial losses stemming from the 1877–78 Russo-Ottoman War, Abdülhamid II embraced Islam more openly as the cornerstone of an Ottoman identity that would unite Turks, Balkan Muslims, Kurds, and Arabs—both those who were Ottoman subjects and those who were not—to resist the encroachment of European imperialism. Abdülhamid's invocation of Islam and Islamic symbolism was a "[national] integrationist project based on Islam," designed to create a new foundation for Ottoman legitimacy in an age of nationalism and European imperialism.[25] Abdülhamid placed renewed emphasis on the office of the Caliphate to seek "a new basis for solidarity among [his] Islamic subjects" and appealed for the loyalty of Muslims living under colonial rule in the British, French, and Russian Empires.[26] He also at least tolerated widespread violence against Ottoman Christians, including the "Hamidian massacres" of Armenians in the 1890s.

If Abdülhamid believed Islam to be the mortar that would hold his crumbling empire together, Akçura argued that Ottomanism failed because the empire's non-Turkish inhabitants rejected it—and that Abdülhamid's Islamism would only provoke further uprisings and European intervention. The only alternative, he suggested, was Turkic unity and the gradual assimilation of non-Turkic Muslims to a Turkish identity. According to Akçura, this approach would allow the Turks to "constitute a great political nation able to defend its existence among other great nations"— even if it meant giving up the non-Turkish parts of the Ottoman Empire.[27] Akçura's uncle (by marriage), the Crimean Tatar İsmail Gaspıralı (Gasprinsky), similarly pursued Turkic unity both within and beyond the Ottoman Empire, calling for a common Turkic language stripped of the Ottoman tongue's Arabic and Persian borrowings and emphasizing the principle of "unity in faith, thought, and action [*Dilde, fikirde, işte birlik*]" among Turkic peoples throughout Eurasia.[28]

These ideas became more prominent under the Young Turks who displaced Abdülhamid in 1908-09. Throughout the Second Constitutional Era (1908–13), intellectuals like Ziya Gökalp sought to inculcate Ottoman patriotism with a Turkish core. The Young Turk CUP supported an Ottoman renewal, but one expressed in the language of Turkish nationalism, having "accepted the reality of an Empire in which members of Christian minorities had developed their own nationalisms, and put forth a Turkish nationalism to take its place among them."[29] As İsmail Enver, a leading CUP figure who served as minister of war, remarked, "While I am primarily Ottoman, I do not forget that I am a Turk, and nothing can shake my belief that the Turkish race is the foundation of the Ottoman Empire."[30] Over time, the CUP's openness to multiple nationalisms gave way to a deliberate campaign to assimilate Muslim migrants to a Turkish identity, and, during the Balkan Wars (1912–13) and World War I, to the wholesale expulsion and killing of Christian Greeks, Armenians, and Assyrians.[31]

At the conclusion of the First World War, the Allied powers occupied Istanbul and much of Anatolia. Desperate to hold together what remained of the empire, the last Ottoman parliament voted to establish new borders via the so-called National Oath (*Mısak-i Milli*), which declared territories under Ottoman control at the time of the 1920 Mudros Armistice and inhabited by "a Muslim Ottoman majority" united by "religion, descent, and common aims" to be "an indivisible whole."[32] Reflecting Gökalp's understanding of a nation as comprised of multiple "tribes" but "connected by a bond which consisted of a shared moral education . . . [and] feelings," the *Mısak-i Milli* implied that while Turkish identity in the new state would have a territorial basis, Turkish culture would provide the mortar needed to hold together the empire's rump in Anatolia and integrate the large numbers of Muslim refugees from Russia and the Balkans.[33]

Consequently, Turkish nationalism came to emphasize the territory of the Republic, which replaced the territorially fluid "Divinely Protected Well-Flourishing Absolute Domain of the House of Osman."[34] A Turk henceforth was any person who resided in the borders of the Republic and professed loyalty to it. Atatürk himself emphasized that "Turk" had neither an ethnic nor a religious meaning: he claimed it was adopted as the name of the new state and its people merely because "at the time it was the most well-known term," and criticized the alleged pan-Islamic and pan-Turkic reveries of his predecessors.[35] The new nation remained grounded, however, in Turkish culture, and governments throughout the Republican period perceived efforts at defining alternative identities, especially among the Kurdish population concentrated in Turkey's southeastern periphery, through the prism of separatism and possible foreign intervention.

This civic-territorial version of Turkishness is ethnically inclusive—at least among Muslims, who comprise close to 99 percent of Turkey's population (including 10–15 percent who are Alevi). It has been more problematic for the relatively small Armenian, Greek, and Jewish communities who remained in Turkey following the mass expulsions of the decade between the Balkan Wars and the establishment of the Republic.[36] While these communities faced violence and discrimination, many politicians and the media invoked the combination of foreign intervention and Christian separatism that proved fatal to the Ottoman Empire to paint them as a threat to Turkey's territorial integrity and as outsiders to the nation.[37]

Among the most sensitive issues was the nature of and responsibility for the mass killing of Armenians (and other Christians) during World War I. Narratives implicating the CUP or suggesting these events constituted genocide were censored, and scholars who challenged this consensus faced harassment and persecution, including criminal charges for "insulting Turkishness."[38] Instead, the official narrative argued, as Ronald Grigor Suny puts it, that "there was no genocide and the Armenians were to blame for it."[39] The Greek community, meanwhile, was caught up in the geopolitical rivalry between Ankara and Athens. Greeks endured both discrimination and violence—including a 1955 pogrom that elements in the government and security services helped provoke—before most of Istanbul's Greeks were expelled in 1964 amid tensions over Cyprus.[40] Despite the AKP's periodic calls for reconciliation, these minorities still face sporadic violence today. The most notorious incident in the AKP era was the 2007 assassination of the Armenian journalist Hrant Dink, who had earlier been convicted of "insulting Turkishness" for his work on wartime violence against Armenians.

Nor did the "Jacobin" assimilation the Republic long pursued efface the subnational identities of the late-Ottoman refugees from the Balkans, the Caucasus, or the Middle East. Descendants of refugees were at the forefront of Turkish businesses' investment in these regions in the period following the mid-1980s economic liberalization, and later took the lead in pushing for a more assertive approach to the conflicts in Chechnya and Abkhazia.[41] Refugees and their descendants remain influential in nationalist associations, including the MHP. Many also serve in the security services—to the extent that the Circassian policeman is something of a stereotype. Even Atatürk's Republican People's Party (*Cumhuriyet Halk Partisi*, CHP) now pays tribute to the idea of a Turkish identity encompassing the multitudes who brought their culture to Anatolia and "despite years of oppression never abandoned their cultures and beliefs."[42] While this stance would have been anathema to Atatürk himself, its acceptance within the modern CHP testifies to the distance Turkey has traveled during the two decades of AKP ascendancy.

Ottoman Nostalgia and Islamic Nationalism

Part of the Kemalist project of building a territorially bounded state included building a territorially bounded form of Islam. In 1924, the Grand National Assembly abolished the office of caliph, and the following year required pronouncing the call to prayer (*ezan*) in Turkish, while a 1928 orthographic reform constrained the teaching of Arabic script. Atatürk also replaced the Ottoman *şeyhülislam* with a Directorate of Spiritual Affairs (*Diyanet İşleri Başkanlığı*, or just *Diyanet*). *Diyanet* provided guidance for Friday sermons, becoming a vehicle for promoting an official "enlightened" Islam (based on the heterodox approach of groups like the Bektashis), at odds with the more puritanical strains prominent in the Arab world.[43]

While *Diyanet* promoted an officially sanctioned form of Islam, the Sufi orders, which Atatürk sought to ban, provided a language for articulating opposition in religious terms. Most of the major Islamist movements and figures in Republican Turkey, including the AKP itself, emerged directly or indirectly out of the Naqshbandi order. The key figure in transforming this critique of Kemalism into a "semipolitical movement" was Mehmed Zahid Kotku, an influential Naqshbandi sheykh and head of the İskenderpaşa Naqshbandi lodge in Istanbul, who in 1969 gave his blessing to the establishment of what would long be Turkey's most influential Islamist movement, *Milli Görüş* (National Vision or Outlook).[44]

Islamist thinkers were also at the forefront of efforts to reevaluate the imperial past, contrasting the pluralistic and religiously infused rule of the Ottomans with the Kemalists' centralizing, nationalizing, and secularizing approach.[45] Embracing a late-Ottoman view of the West as a source of both technological modernization and spiritual emptiness, the Naqshbandi writer Necip Fazıl Kısakürek called for a global Islamic Renaissance that would begin in Turkey. *Milli Görüş* founder and future prime minister Necmettin Erbakan (1996–97), meanwhile, sought to return Turkey to its Islamic origins—both to reconnect with the majority of the population that, he suggested, had been alienated by Kemalist modernization, and to restore Turkey's standing as a leader of the Muslim world.[46] This Ottoman-inflected critique would influence generations of Islamist politicians; Erdoğan—like Erbakan a member of the İskenderpaşa lodge— cites Kısakürek as an inspiration and got his start in politics in *Milli Görüş*.[47]

Even as they were aware of and participated to some degree in global trends, including the rise of Salafism, Turkish Islamists largely remained committed to the concept of "Islamic nationalism," a term used in Erbakan's campaign platform suggesting a correspondence between religious and "national" values. Kısakürek wrote that "a Turk is only a Turk after he becomes a Muslim," and depicted Turkey as a Muslim nation-state that should be ethnically as well as religiously homogeneous.[48] Many Turkish Islamists, including Erbakan and Kısakürek, maintained a geopolitical outlook at odds with the Western-oriented approach Turkey had adopted during the Cold War, one that helped pave the way for the more expansive vision of the nation adopted by their intellectual heirs in the AKP. Erbakan called for a Turkish-led Islamic Union, as well as a common Islamic currency and other forms of institutional cooperation among Muslim states that would allow Turkey to expand its global influence while organizing the Muslim world into an independent pillar of the global order.[49]

It would be Turgut Özal, an İskenderpaşa member who served as prime minister from 1983 to 1989 and as president from 1989 to 1993, who placed the Ottoman legacy at the foundation of attempts to devise a new model of "imperial governance" centered on Islam.[50] Unlike Erbakan, Özal was influenced by what he understood to be the flexible, tolerant Ottoman model of Islam, rather than the narrower, intolerant version becoming influential in the Arab world. Özal saw this tolerant Islam as a remedy for communal strife within Turkey as well as a platform for promoting Turkish influence among both its Muslim neighbors and, in the 1990s, the new Turkic states of the Caucasus and Central Asia.

Özal's focus on the Ottoman legacy for governance represented a break from—or, according to his secularist critics, an effort to "camouflage"—

the anti-Western, antisecular elements of the Ottoman revivalism associated with Erbakan's *Milli Görüş*.[51] In liberalizing the economy and creating space for religion in the public sphere, Özal contributed to the emergence of a "tolerant Islamic vocabulary" that encouraged expressions of ethnic and religious diversity within the framework of Turkish identity, and which provided a basis for extending Turkish influence in the newly independent states of the Balkans, the Caucasus, and Central Asia.[52] In a 1992 interview, Özal argued:

> In the imperial era as today, I believe Islam is the most important factor in the formation of [our] identity. It is religion that unites the Muslim societies of Anatolia and the Balkans. . . . It is true that today the Bosniaks and Albanians coming here are [among] those who say "I am a Turk." Turkishness together with Islam . . . provides a second basis for [creating] a common cultural identity for Muslims in the Ottoman territory [*Osmanlı mülkündeki müsülmanlar*].[53]

The AKP inherited much of this legacy when it emerged from the split within *Milli Görüş* following Erbakan's ouster and banishment from politics in a 1997 "soft coup." That legacy included an understanding of the link between Turkish national identity and Islam—which encompassed a view of Turkey as a homeland, patron, or model for Muslims elsewhere, what Erdoğan called "the hope of the Islamic world."[54] Erdoğan thus portrays the AKP era, which began in 2002, as reasserting an inherently Islamic "national will (*milli irade*)" disrupted by the CUP's coup against Abdülhamid and the founding of the Republic. Reconnecting Turkey to its Ottoman past is thus a central preoccupation for Erdoğan, who argues that "we should stop seeing the Ottoman and the Republic as two eras that conflict with one another."[55]

Ottoman themes are also a shorthand for Ankara's new geopolitical vision, in particular the aspiration to influence developments in the post-Ottoman space of the Middle East, the Balkans, and the Caucasus, and to position Turkey as an independent center of power. If Erbakan conceived of Turkey as an Islamic state among other states, Erdoğan and Davutoğlu are wont to identify Turkey as a civilizational state, one not confined to its borders, and that by virtue of its history and culture should become the center of a regional system operating on the basis of a shared Islamic-Ottoman heritage.[56] According to Davutoğlu, Islam was not only central to Turkish identity, but also a bond that united it with other post-Ottoman states, some of which had been similarly lured away by the West.[57] Only by reembracing that Islamic essence, he argues, can Turkey return to its rightful place as a "pivot state" at the center of its own regional order, rather than as an appendage of the West. As Michael Reynolds notes, "It is not a principally illiberal vision, although its historical and geographical dimensions clash with the nation-state, arguably the essential arena for liberal politics."[58]

The centrality of Islam to Davutoğlu and Erdoğan's understanding of Turkish and Ottoman identity has led them to support Islamist movements they saw, like the AKP itself, seeking to displace illegitimate secular rulers propped up by foreign powers. They thus reversed Ankara's longstanding aversion to the influence of *Milli Görüş* among Turkish migrants in Europe.[59] They also positioned Turkey as a major patron of Islamist movements seeking power in the Middle East during and after the Arab Spring. Support for groups like the Egyptian Muslim Brotherhood, Hamas, and other Islamist groups reflected Erdoğan and Davutoğlu's idea of Turkey as the nucleus of a new regional order in which Islam provided a foundation for democratic legitimacy as, they suggested, it had already done in Turkey since the rise of the AKP.[60] Noting that the Arab Spring was also a "Turkish Spring," Davutoğlu portrayed the uprisings as an opportunity for the Arab states to pursue "normalization" by returning to their Islamic roots, and to regain the consciousness of sharing a common destiny with one another and with Turkey.[61]

Similarly, the identification of Ottoman Islam as a bond tying Turkey to its neighbors contributed to Ankara's decision to accept millions of refugees from the Syrian conflict. Some Turkish officials were hopeful that refugees who stayed could, like migrants from the Balkans and Caucasus a century earlier, learn to call themselves (or at least their children) Turks, while those who returned could be sufficiently acculturated to act as a vehicle for Turkish soft power in a post-Assad Syria. Erdoğan was consequently caught off-guard by the emergence of an antimigrant backlash and even violence, with some AKP officials adopting nativist rhetoric at odds with the party's previous emphasis on welcoming refugees. At the same time, Davutoğlu noted that "we did not see [only] one sect, one ethnic group, or one religion" among the protestors of the Arab Spring, and hoped that the wave sweeping over the region would allow its inhabitants to overcome the fragmentation from which the Middle East had suffered since the collapse of the Ottoman Empire.[62]

This pluralistic outlook, seemingly at odds with Ankara's support for Islamists like the Muslim Brotherhood and *Milli Görüş*—not to mention Sunni militant groups like Hayat Tahrir al-Sham, which benefited from Ankara's decision to open its Syrian border to foreign fighters, and then coordinated operations in northern Syria with Turkish forces—suggests the central dilemma in Erdoğan and Davutoğlu's post-Ottoman vision.[63] On the one hand, the AKP recognizes and embraces the idea of Ottoman tolerance, which also provides a framework for addressing ethnic and religious tensions inside Turkey. On the other, by placing (Sunni) Islam at the center of its Ottoman memory, it makes common cause in Syria and beyond with Sunni militants implicated in widespread abuses; at home it risks alienating communities like Turkish Alevis who, a century after the Ottoman collapse, reject the implication that sultanic benevolence is more reliable as a source of dignity and security than equal, democratic rights. It has also complicated Ankara's efforts to promote regional integration, since many regional governments see Ankara's simultaneous push for integration and Islamization as a form of imperial domination.[64]

Turkism and the "Outer Turks"

Beyond the religious and the civic, the third conception of the Turkish nation Akçura identified emphasizes racial or ethnic criteria. Belief in a Turkish race became an important component of "Turkism (*Türkçülük*)," Gökalp's idea that the state should embody the aspirations of the Turkish nation. Though Gökalp—like Atatürk—emphasized culture as a basis for assimilation, many Turkists clung to a narrowly ethnic conception of Turkish identity while promoting solidarity and, in the extreme, political unification among the Turkic peoples across Eurasia. Writing in 1904, Akçura argued

> [Turkishness] will serve to unite the Turks who share a common language, common traditions, and to a certain extent a common religion, and who have spread themselves over the greater part of Asia and the eastern part of Europe and thus constitute a great political nation able to defend its existence among other great nations. In this great community, the Ottoman State—which is the most powerful and most civilized of the Turkish communities— would play the most important role."[65]

In the late Ottoman era, support for pan-Turkism was concentrated among émigrés from the Russian Empire, and thus had an intellectual pedigree distinct from the Turkish ethnonationalism developing among Ottoman Turks, even if the two eventually blurred.[66] These ideas influenced the CUP leadership, which disseminated pan-Turkic propaganda among Muslims in the Russian Caucasus and Crimea before the First World War, and whose identification of Turks as the only reliable constituency for holding the empire together underpinned their wartime campaigns to cleanse Anatolia of non-Turks.[67]

By the mid-1920s, Atatürk's government was actively curbing the activities of the émigré intellectuals and pan-Turkic organizations, fearing they could drag Turkey into a confrontation with the new Soviet Union, which was then reasserting control over the Turkic-speaking peoples of the Caucasus and Central Asia. Pan-Turkic organizations for their part were wary of the Kemalists' radical secularism and disinterest in the Turkic peoples outside Anatolia. Nonetheless, the combination of ethnonationalism and pan-Turkism remained part of the debate among scholars and journalists even during the period of one-party rule by Atatürk's CHP (1925–50). One of the most prominent nationalist intellectuals was Nihal Atsız, who wrote allegorical novels about pre-Islamic Turks and argued that the Ottoman Empire represented the apogee of the Turks' historical accomplishments.[68] Migrants from Russia and their descendants, meanwhile, continued calling for solidarity with the Turkic peoples who had fallen under Soviet rule; partially in consequence, ethnonationalist/pan-Turkic groups tended to adopt a strongly anti-Communist inclination that made them attractive partners for the military regimes that ruled Turkey following the coups of 1960 and 1971.

As with the Islamist opposition, the end of one-party rule created an opening for groups emphasizing *Türkçülük*. Most notable was the MHP, headed from 1969 until his death in 1994 by Alparslan Türkeş—a native of Cyprus and follower of Atsız.[69] Though later more accepting of Islam as a pillar of Turkic identity, the early MHP embraced a definition of the nation that stressed ethnic factors and invoked symbols linked to pre-Islamic Turkic mythology such as the grey wolf.[70] Never the largest party in parliament, the MHP nevertheless "succeeded in introducing Pan-Turkism into the mainstream of Turkish politics."[71]

Türkçülük has remained an influential strand in Turkish politics up to the present. Contemporary proponents, such as the academic, columnist, and former parliamentarian Ümit Özdağ, aim to "ethnicize" the definition of the nation to resist what they see as the domination of Turkey by "antinational" forces such as global capitalism and, especially, the European Union, and are critical of the assimilationist basis of Republican nationalism.[72] While earlier Turkists like Atsız were hostile to Islam, the generation that has become influential since the 1970s has sought a reconciliation by "Turkifying" Islam, paving the way for the "Turkish-Islamic Synthesis" and accommodation between the MHP and Islamist parties, including the AKP.

From early in its history, *Türkçülük* has had irredentist undertones, since the Anatolian Turks comprise less than half of the total speakers of Turkic languages worldwide. Both the Russian émigrés who brought knowledge of the situation in Crimea, the Caucasus, and Central Asia to the attention of the late Ottomans and their successors in the Turkish Republic encouraged the Turks of Anatolia to take an interest in the fate of their ethnic kin abroad. As Jacob Landau notes, though, the irredentist elements of Turkish ethnonationalism as espoused by figures like Akçura, Gökalp, and Atsız were initially implicit, only becoming prominent in the early 1970s with the emergence of the MHP and the crisis over Cyprus.[73]

With the Soviet collapse, Turkey sought to position itself as the patron and model for the newly independent states of the Caucasus and Central Asia. Ankara offered to speak for the new Turkic states at the United Nations. Özal and his successor Demirel made frequent visits to Central Asia and provided moral and material support to Azerbaijan during the 1993–94 war with Armenia over Nagorno-Karabakh. They also backed the establishment of Turkic organizations such as the Organization of Turkic States (*Türk Devletleri Teşkilatı*) and the engagement of the Turkish Cooperation and Coordination Agency (*Türk İşbirliği ve Koordinasyon İdaresi Başkanlığı*, TİKA), which argues that "Turkey and the countries in Central Asia consider themselves as one nation containing different countries."[74] Before falling out with the AKP, followers of the theologian Fethullah Gülen also played a prominent role in these efforts, sponsoring the establishment of schools throughout the Caucasus and Central Asia to provide a modern, high-quality education, along with instruction in the Turkish language.

While Erdoğan criticizes *Türkçülük* in principle as racist and contrary to Islam, the AKP takes advantage of the ambiguous nature of Turkish identity and sympathy for the "Outer Turks" to support Turkic parties and organizations throughout Eurasia and the Middle East.[75] Ankara thus supports Turkmen militias in both Iraq and Syria, though the most consequential manifestation of this commitment to Turkic solidarity may be Turkey's strategic alignment with Azerbaijan. Adopting a formula first employed by former Azerbaijani president Heydar Aliyev, Turkish officials and commentators often describe the relationship as "one nation, two states." While Ankara supported Baku in the First Nagorno-Karabakh War, the partnership grew closer with the AKP's renewed pursuit of strategic autonomy and regional preeminence following the 2016 coup attempt. By 2019, Turkey was Azerbaijan's main partner, providing both arms and proxy fighters instrumental to Baku's victory in the Second Nagorno-Karabakh War. The war was thus a strategic triumph not just for Baku, but also for Ankara, which cemented its position as a major player in a region where Russian influence had long prevailed.

Nonetheless, power imbalances with its postimperial rivals limit Ankara's ability to act as a patron for the "Outer Turks." While Istanbul has been a center for the Uyghur diaspora since Chinese forces defeated the Second East Turkestan Republic in 1949, and pro-Uyghur sympathy in Turkey is widespread, Ankara's response to the Chinese crackdown in Xinjiang has been measured.[76] After previously criticizing Beijing's persecution of Uyghurs, Erdoğan during a July 2019 visit went so far as to say that "the inhabitants of Xinjiang [not East Turkestan, the term preferred by most Uyghurs] are happy in prosperity," which his office later attempted to explain as a mistranslation.[77] Uyghur exiles worry that Ankara is unable to protect them from Chinese security forces even on Turkish soil—a fear reinforced by a 2017 extradition treaty critics worried Turkey would ratify in order to access Chinese Covid-19 vaccines.[78]

Erdoğan and other leaders have been more vocal on behalf of the Crimean Tatars, who have since 2014 suffered under Russian occupation, just as their ancestors were driven in large numbers to the Ottoman Empire by Russia's 1783 conquest of the Crimean Khanate. Today, Turkey hosts exiled Crimean Tatar activists and maintains extensive ties with Crimean Tatar diaspora groups abroad (including in Ukraine). Turkish officials claim to raise the conditions facing the Crimean Tatars in meetings with the Kremlin, and frequently emphasize that Ankara will never recognize the annexation of Crimea.[79] Given its dependence on Russian energy and a larger strategic context that includes conflicts in Syria, Libya, the Caucasus, and elsewhere, though, Turkey has refrained from joining EU sanctions over the annexation—even as it develops an increasingly close defense and security partnership with Ukraine.[80]

Is There a Greater Turkey?

The idea that Turkey sits at the center of a wider Islamic or Turkic community appeals to a sense of postimperial greatness and longing for status within Turkey itself. Yet even more than with Russia's appeals to compatriots or a Russian World, the idea of a Greater Turkey has struggled to gain traction outside the country's borders—whether in an Ottoman-Islamic or a pan-Turkic guise. Both approaches suffer from their artificiality, not to mention Turkey's limited capabilities as a medium-sized state with a volatile and heavily indebted economy, and which remains dependent on the United States for much of its security.

While the Ottoman Empire's physical legacies are visible throughout the Balkans and parts of the Middle East, the end of the Ottoman era is too long ago to be part of living memory, unlike the existence of a shared Russian-speaking, post-Soviet culture underpinning the idea of a Russian World. The Ottoman collapse was also exceptionally chaotic and bloody, with millions of people uprooted or killed as Ottoman rule crumbled. The large-scale violence of the final Ottoman century and its aftermath precipitated a vast un-mixing of peoples who increasingly sorted themselves along communal lines. The cosmopolitan Ottoman culture that once characterized places like Thessaloniki (Salonica)—Atatürk's birthplace—is largely a thing of the past. Even if affection for the Ottoman era in places like Greece were greater, the bonds that held the Ottoman world together have frayed significantly over the past century, a process that Turkey's own nation-building process encouraged.

The centrality of Islam to the AKP's understanding of the Ottoman past represents a particular challenge to aspirations to consolidate a shared post-Ottoman identity. Turkish Islam—dominated by the Hanafi *madhab* and with strong heterodox and Sufi influences that date back to the nomadic Ottomans—has long been distinct from versions practiced in the Arabian Peninsula, where the Hanbali and Shaf'i schools and, more recently, Salafism have had a greater impact. Few Arab Muslims take seriously claims about Turkish Islam as a model or Turkey as a leader of the Muslim world (if anything, Ankara worries about the spread of Salafism at home). In the Balkans and the Caucasus, where local Islam is closer to the Turkish variety, secular governments and populations are wary of Ankara's state-backed Islamic outreach. Local officials and clerics see Turkey's efforts to promote a shared Islamic identity as a threat to both secularism and state patriotism by encouraging Albanians, Bosniaks, Bulgarians, and Kosovars to prioritize their identity as Muslims, and to look to Turkey as

the defender of their faith. Nationalist backlash and accusations of disloy-
alty have followed.[81]

The attractiveness of a common post-Ottoman identity outside of
Turkey is also limited by the fact that nation-building projects in the post-
Ottoman Balkans and Middle East are largely built on a rejection of the
Ottoman past. The notion of *tarihdaşlık* has little resonance among populations schooled to see the Ottoman period as a time of oppression, even
in majority-Muslim states. Tellingly, Davutoğlu's comment that "Sarajevo
is ours" was criticized not only by Serbs, but also by many Muslim Bosniaks, whose Serbian/Croatian persecutors targeted them as representatives of the "foreign" and "Turkish" Ottoman Empire during the Bosnian
War of the 1990s.[82] Nor has Turkey been able to give much substance to
the idea of a Greater Turkic World. While Turkey is an important trade
partner and destination for students and migrants from Central Asia,
Turkic solidarity is largely confined to the realm of soft power. Solidarity with Crimean Tatars and Uyghurs is popular at home, and underpins
the MHP's continued support for the government, but is constrained by
Ankara's need to stay on good terms with Moscow and Beijing.

While Erdoğan (and Davutoğlu) brought Ottoman nostalgia and the
belief that Turkey is destined to be a major independent power to the
political mainstream, they were drawing from a deep well of conservative
opposition to Atatürk's Republic that looked to the Ottoman period for
inspiration. Political change, setbacks in the Middle East, and alienation
from its Western allies may eventually force Turkey to pursue a more re-
strained foreign policy, but the idea of a Greater Turkey will likely retain
its attraction for politicians seeking a larger role for a twenty-first-century
Turkish Republic no longer defined by its association with the West.

CHAPTER FIVE

On the Margins of the Nation and the State

Turkey's Kurdish Borderland

W
HEN NORTHERN Syria's Kurdish-majority town of
Kobani came under siege by ISIS in the fall of 2014,
neighboring Turkey refused repeated requests for assistance—despite Turkey's own recent history of ISIS-inspired
terrorism and the likelihood that Kobani's fall would result in a wholesale
massacre of its population.[1] The main force protecting Kobani from the
jihadist onslaught was the People's Protection Units (*Yekîneyên Parastina
Gel*, YPG), the armed wing of the PKK's Syrian affiliate. Concerned lest
the defense of Kobani reinforce the YPG's control of northern Syria and
its image as a legitimate representative of the Kurdish people, the Turkish government attempted to seal the border and stem the flow of aid.
Under enormous pressure from the United States and its European allies,
Erdoğan eventually relented. Rather than arming the YPG or sending in
its own troops, though, Ankara turned to a different Kurdish entity to
break the siege, allowing *peshmerga* fighters loyal to northern Iraq's Kurdistan Regional Government (KRG) to cross Turkish territory to reach
the front lines.

Turkey's response to the Kobani siege reflected the complexity underlying its long struggle to pacify, control, and integrate its Kurdish borderlands, whose liminal position is a product of the Ottoman Empire's
collapse and the partition of Ottoman Kurdistan between the new states
of Turkey, Iraq, and Syria.[2] While formerly Ottoman Kurdistan had been

a broad frontier region where tribes enjoyed free movement and substantial autonomy, post–World War I borders partitioned it with little regard for geographic or ethnic considerations, leaving restive Kurdish populations on the margins of what would become the Iraqi, Syrian, and Turkish states. All three would go to great efforts to integrate and transform their respective Kurdish borderlands and to attenuate the ties between Kurdish populations living across the new border. In Turkey, Atatürk's embrace of a "Jacobin" approach to nation-building aimed at guarding against the threat of Kurdish separatism; Kurds were required to "call themselves Turks," subsuming their separate tribal, linguistic, and ethnic identities within the territorially and culturally defined Turkish nation. Ankara, meanwhile, devoted substantial financial and military resources to consolidate its political, cultural, and demographic presence in heavily Kurdish areas of Southeastern Anatolia.

Success was at best partial. Cross-border tribal, family, and religious ties endured, sustaining a series of Kurdish revolts that, in turn, prompted some of the worst human rights abuses perpetrated by the Turkish state and contributed to the military's long-time domination of Turkish politics. By the mid-1980s, such discrimination helped spark the PKK's insurgency, whose very durability suggests the limits of the Kemalist effort to establish a uniform nation based on Turkish culture and the territory of the Republic. Exacerbating the danger posed by Kurdish revolts is the continued porousness of Turkey's postimperial borders. Not only have Kurdish insurgents been able to find refuge in remote regions of northern Iraq and Syria, governments in Baghdad and Damascus (not to mention Moscow) were more than willing to leverage the PKK presence for their own ends.

As the current entente between Turkey and the KRG suggests, though, Ankara's approach to the Kurds has always been multilayered— hostile to Kurdish nationalism or even cultural distinctiveness, but open to cooperation with Kurdish elements whose identities and aspirations align with the Turkish state's interests. Throughout the Republican period, Kurdish elites from the rural, tribal milieu remained aloof from mostly urban-based nationalist circles (including the PKK). Instead, they became pillars of Turkish administration in Southeastern Anatolia—just as the domination of conservative, tribal Kurds in northern Iraq would later be instrumental in Turkey's partnership with the KRG. Meanwhile, Kurds who consciously assimilated and adopted a Turkish identity found opportunities more extensive than those available to Uyghurs in China or

North Caucasians in Russia to become part of the political, cultural, and intellectual elite. Prime ministers and Presidents İsmet İnönü (1938–50) and Turgut Özal are among Turkey's many senior officials and military commanders with Kurdish ancestry. Many Turks therefore argue that being Kurdish—espousing a Kurdish identity in public—is a conscious political choice.

Opportunities for Kurdish inclusion have, if anything, become more accessible in the AKP era—especially for Sunni Kurds who prioritize a religious rather than a national identity. During the 2009–15 "Kurdish Opening (*Kürt açılımı*)," Ankara conducted peace talks with the PKK's imprisoned leader Abdullah Öcalan and adopted amendments allowing greater cultural expression in Kurdish. The opening depended, however, on Kurds themselves accepting a framing of Kurdish identity that prioritized Sunnism and Davutoğlu's notion of shared history over distinct national claims. It was also vulnerable to shifting political winds; when an upsurge in violence and Kurdish political mobilization in Turkey, along with the YPG's insurgency in Syria, posed a threat to its grip on power, the AKP reembraced the securitized approach of its predecessors.

The end of the Kurdish Opening also coincided with a new effort to contain the PKK threat on the territory of neighboring states. With the borders dividing Turkey from Iraq and Syria under increasing pressure from the flow of refugees, migrants, and militants, Ankara turned to economic levers, military incursions, cultivation of local partners like the Erbil-based KRG, and other familiar tools of imperial frontier management. If the region's borders are artificial, in other words, Ankara's goal became to extend its influence across those borders to position itself as the regional center of gravity and export the struggle against the PKK to its neighbors' territory.

The AKP not only projects political and military power into Iraq and Syria, it also appeals to Iraqi and Syrian Kurds (at least those who, unlike the mostly Yazidi inhabitants of Kobani, are Sunni) to identify Davutoğlu's "Greater Turkey" as their guardian against secular Arab despots like Saddam Hussein and Bashar al-Assad—as well as against the PKK's siren song of Kurdish independence. As Davutoğlu noted, when Saddam was massacring Iraqi Kurds, "our Kurdish brothers did not flee Iraq to return east or west; they returned to the north," to Turkey.[3] Whether this outward-facing strategy succeeds will depend on the extent to which Kurds—in Syria and Iraq as well as Turkey—are willing to see the Turkish Republic as the embodiment of their own political and cultural aspirations. If

Ankara's reluctance to save Kobani and retreat from the Kurdish Opening at home are any indication, Kurds have reason for skepticism.

Origins of Turkey's Kurdish Dilemma

The presence of Kurdish-speakers in eastern Anatolia and upper Mesopotamia seems to predate the arrival of the Turks. Kurdish tribes participated in medieval Seljuk campaigns against Byzantium, for which they received land in exchange for their support. More Kurds arrived in the wake of the Mongol and Timurid invasions, settling in regions where Armenian and Assyrian inhabitants had been uprooted by the violence of the era.[4] The Kurdish population also extended into the southern reaches of the Caucasus, a region that would in the nineteenth century fall under Russian control (a high percentage of Kurdish-speakers in the Caucasus are Yazidis who remain aloof from both Islamic and nationalist movements).[5]

Lacking their own state, Kurds never underwent a process of nation-building and linguistic standardization comparable to what Atatürk imposed in Turkey. Despite a shared cultural identity (*Kurdewati*), Kurds remain separated not only by borders, but also by religious, tribal, and linguistic divisions.[6] Most Kurds are Sunni, though in contrast to the Hanafi Turks, they tend to follow the Shaf'i *madhab*. A significant minority are what is today known as Alevi and in the sixteenth and seventeenth centuries would have been considered Qizilbash (*Kızılbaş*)—that is, heterodox, Shi'a-inspired Muslims susceptible to Safavid influence. A smaller number, especially outside Turkey, are Assyrian (Nestorian) Christian, Druze, Yazidi, or other religions. Kurds are also divided along linguistic and tribal lines; the Kurmanji dialect spoken by most Kurdish inhabitants of southeastern Turkey, northwestern Iran, northern Iraq, and northern Syria is not mutually intelligible with the Sorani dialect spoken by Kurds elsewhere in Iraq and Iran, or with the Zaza language spoken by many Kurds in central Anatolia. Those divisions aid Turkey's (and its neighbors') efforts to inhibit the formation of a unified Kurdish movement.

The Kurds of eastern Anatolia and upper Mesopotamia first came within the Ottoman sphere of influence in the course of Selim I's campaign against the Safavids, which culminated in his crushing victory at Chaldiran in 1514. The Peace of Amasya (1555) then established a broad frontier region between the two empires, leaving the bulk of Kurdistan within the Ottoman zone.[7] The Ottomans divided their Kurdish region into the three *eyalet*s of Diyarbakır, Raqqa, and Mosul (roughly corresponding to the modern Turkish, Syrian, and Iraqi Kurdish regions, respectively), each headed by a *vali* appointed by the court, while a centrally appointed *beylerbeyi* represented the sultan's power over Kurdistan as a whole. Kurdish emirs were appointed as Ottoman officials (*sancakbeyi*s) on their traditional lands, and invested with a drum and flag conferred by the sultan as symbols of office. In exchange, they were obliged to ensure security and stability along the Iranian frontier, collect tribute, and fight in the sultan's wars.

Recognizing the limits of their authority in this distant borderland, Selim and his successors allowed the nomadic Kurds (and their Turkmen neighbors) to maintain autonomy of varying degrees, in line with the Ottoman practice of recognizing specific communities (*millet*s) as separate administrative entities.[8] At the urging of his Kurdish adviser Idris-i Bitlisi, Selim agreed to make the power of the Kurdish emirs (all of them from established elite families) hereditary, a break with the usual Ottoman practice of guarding against the emergence of a hereditary aristocracy.[9] In most places, Kurdish tribes' land was organized into *tımar*s, the land grants given to support Ottoman cavalrymen, but in contrast to interior regions of the empire, the land remained in the possession of the family or tribe, and could not be confiscated or redistributed by the sultan.[10] The simultaneous existence of *tımar*s, which were a feature of regular Ottoman administration but uncommon in the periphery, along with preservation of a hereditary elite suggests that the Kurdish regions occupied a kind of intermediate space in Ottoman spatial thinking—neither fully "center" nor fully "periphery," a status they have retained in modern Turkey.

By the nineteenth century, geopolitical rivalry, the gradual extension of state power, and conflicts over resources between Kurds and Armenians led to attempts to more directly regulate Kurdish affairs. Efforts to extend central control were at once part of the larger process of modernization and centralization undertaken by Sultans Mahmud II (1808–39) and Abdülmecid I (1839–61), as well as a response to changing geopolitical conditions. The 1823 Treaty of Erzurum between the Ottomans and Qajars reduced the Kurdish emirates' importance as guardians of the frontier. Kurdish emirs in Bayazit, Kars, and Van who opposed Mahmud II's modernizing reforms remained neutral or backed St. Petersburg during the 1828–29 Russo-Ottoman War. Other Kurds expressed their support by attacking Armenian civilians, whom they perceived as sympathetic to the Russians.[11] Soon thereafter, agents of the rebellious Egyptian *vali* Muhammad Ali Paşa began making contact with the Kurdish emirs seeking a common front against the "infidel" modernizer Mahmud.[12]

In response, Mahmud ordered the *vali*s of Baghdad and Mosul to move against Muhammad Ali and his Kurdish supporters, setting the stage for the gradual elimination of the Kurdish emirates.[13] The abolition of the emirates prevented them from joining together or acting as the nucleus for a Kurdish nationalist movement.[14] The emirates were not, however, replaced by an effective system of administration. In 1847, Abdülmecid created a unified Kurdistan *eyalet* centered on Diyarbakır. In practice, though, Kurdish chieftains and religious networks remained the dominant political actors, as the elimination of the emirates paved the way for the "politicization of Islamic networks" that would be central to subsequent Kurdish mobilization.[15]

Meanwhile, the Ottoman Empire's integration into the globalizing economy of the late nineteenth century sparked economic growth that disproportionately benefited the better-educated, more cosmopolitan Armenian minority who formed the core of eastern Anatolia's emerging "petty merchant banking, and quasi-industrial classes."[16] In part to ameliorate the discontent of Kurdish tribal elites, Abdülhamid II's government encouraged them to appropriate new lands, some of which were also claimed by Armenians. Long-running disputes between Kurds and Armenians ensued, along with communal violence that reached a horrific denouement in the mass killing of Armenians (many at Kurdish hands) during World War I.[17]

The late nineteenth century saw both recurring tribal rebellions and the emergence of a Kurdish intelligentsia in Istanbul whose critique of Ottoman centralization informed a nascent Kurdish nationalist movement. Whether the revolts ultimately aimed at the establishment of a Kurdish state or a renegotiation of the political compact between Kurdish elites and Istanbul, they ultimately undermined efforts at imperial consolidation.[18] The largest broke out in 1880 under the Naqshbandi Sheykh Ubeydullah of Nehri, whose followers on both sides of the frontier sought to carve out a Kurdish polity free from both Ottoman and Qajar authority.[19] Later rulers were thus forced to find new mechanisms for securing the loyalty of Kurdish elites. Abdülhamid attempted to impose a uniform version of Islam based on the Hanafi *madhab* to encourage political and cultural consolidation.[20] This emphasis on Hanafi Sunnism sparked tensions with Kurds, even non-Hanafi Sunnis like Ubeydullah, who emphasized a common Kurdish identity inspired by Sufi spirituality.[21]

Abdülhamid also sought to win over Kurdish elites through extending patronage and protection, appealing to a common Muslim identity, and tolerating (or encouraging) abuses against their Christian neighbors[22] Abdülhamid presided over the establishment of the so-called Hamidiye Light Cavalry Regiments (*Hamidiye Hafif Süvari Alayları*), a force of largely Kurdish irregulars that provided employment and patronage, but also became a vehicle for state-sanctioned score-settling. The *Hamidiye* were implicated in both intertribal violence and repeated massacres of Armenian and other Christians in eastern Anatolia, including the mass slaughter of Armenians during World War I.[23] Despite the complex legacy of his reign, many Kurds would in later years look back fondly on the era of Abdülhamid, whom they called *Bave Kurdan* (Father of the Kurds), and the Ottoman Empire more generally, in contrast to the subsequent Young Turk era, and to the aspiring Turkish nation-state that emerged after the empire's collapse.[24] Kurds' more positive view of the Ottoman era would be an asset when the AKP began appealing to the Ottoman heritage to overcome Turkey's legacy of ethnic strife.

Kurdistan from Imperial Frontier to Republican Borderland

Imperial collapse transformed Ottoman Kurdistan from a vast frontier on the Ottoman Empire's southeastern periphery into components of the "interior" territory of Turkey and what were at the time the European mandates of Iraq and Syria. While Kurds did not receive a homeland, or even the autonomy promised them by the Treaty of Sèvres, they did not necessarily oppose the establishment of the Republic. Mustafa Kemal received significant Kurdish support during the War of Independence, in part from the lingering salience of religious identity and Kurdish concerns about the possible establishment of an Armenian state in eastern Anatolia.[25] Kemal also left the traditional tribal and administrative structures in place, reconciling tribal elites to the new order and inhibiting the emergence of a shared Kurdish political identity.[26]

Kurdish rebellions in Southeastern Anatolia were, however, endemic in the first decades of the Republic.[27] Religion remained a major driver of Kurdish grievance, especially following the abolition of the caliphate and banning of Sufi orders. As early as 1920, Kurds in Koçgiri revolted against efforts to include them in a new Turkish state. One of the most serious revolts broke out in late 1924 under the Naqshbandi Sheykh Said of Piran, who rejected Kemal's secularizing reforms and called for establishing an Islamically based state.[28] Sheykh Said's revolt precipitated Turkey's first experiment with one-party rule by Kemal's CHP, and

prompted a long-running campaign to control and transform the Kurdish regions.

Reflecting Ziya Gökalp's (possibly of Kurdish extraction himself) understanding of an Ottoman nation (*millet*) comprising multiple "tribes,"
the early Republic emphasized a common citizenship and culture as the
basis for integrating Kurds (and other non-Turks) into the new national
community.[29] Kurds were required to "call themselves Turks"—both by
assimilating to a dominant Turkish culture and by looking to the territorially bounded Turkish Republic, rather than the wider Kurdish milieu,
as the foundation of their identity. To ensure Kurdish populations' loyalty, the state demanded that, as Chief of the General Staff and former
Prime Minister Fevzi Çakmak wrote in 1931, "Kurdishness must be dissolved" into a wider Turkish identity.[30] Other figures associated with the
ruling CHP and the military went further, denying that Kurdish ethnicity
and language even existed. Kemalist writers and officials created myths
of common ancestry, and used terms like "mountain Turks" or "Turks of
Kurdish origin" to suggest that Kurds were merely a branch of the Turkish people.

In response to Kurdish revolts, the military carried out mass executions, destruction of villages, and expulsions of Kurdish civilians to
Turkish-dominated areas of western Anatolia.[31] Kemalist authorities re-
named territories throughout Southeastern Anatolia to emphasize their
inclusion within the Turkish nation and state. They created cultural institutions to impart Turkish language and high culture, and established
a regime of General Inspectorates with broad authority to suppress discontent. The use of the Kurdish language in public was banned; even in
private it was discouraged. Concerns about Kurdish loyalty perpetuated
patterns of discrimination in state employment, with officials from other
parts of the country usually sent to administer the southeast, where they
were discouraged from building relationships with locals lest their commitment to the Kemalist project be tainted. In the 1930s, administration
of the Kurdish regions was reorganized with an emphasis on central control and security. Discrimination against those espousing a Kurdish identity at odds with the "Jacobin" framing of Turkish nationalism remained
in place throughout the twentieth century, becoming particularly intense
in the wake of the military coups that punctuated Turkish politics in 1960,
1971, and 1980.

Even at the apogee of Kemalism, though, Ankara recognized the need
for a kind of "politics of difference" in Southeastern Anatolia. Hostility to

urban-based Kurdish nationalist groups and an embrace of divide-and-rule tactics left Republican Turkey dependent on Kurdish tribal elites to maintain order in the countryside, where centralized administration was harder to implement. Atatürk therefore made a "tacit alliance with the Kurdish aghas [tribal chiefs]," allowing them to continue managing disputes, acting as interlocutors with the state, and providing a bulwark against the spread of nationalist ideas. The aghas retained control of local education and preserved an essentially feudal social structure even after the onset of land reform.[32] During the 1950s and 1960s, the identification between Kurdish tribal elites and the state grew stronger thanks to a shared interest in containing left-wing activism and Soviet influence among Alevi Kurds and Kurdish migrants who had gone to cities looking for work.[33]

Perceiving the growth of left-wing Kurdish activism as a threat to Turkey's political order and territorial integrity, the junta that took power in 1980 adopted draconian restrictions such that "Kurds as Kurds ceased to exist in the official, public realm."[34] The junta passed a law prohibiting publication in languages other than Turkish, and enforced prohibitions on teaching or broadcasting in Kurdish as well. This discrimination was central to the outbreak of the PKK rebellion, which began in 1984 with a series of attacks on military outposts in the southeastern borderlands.[35] While Ankara sought to isolate the PKK from the wider Kurdish population, the difficulty of distinguishing loyalist from rebel Kurds resulted in the often indiscriminate use of force, which ended up reinforcing a shared identity among Kurds of different ideological persuasions.[36] One tool Ankara employed was recruitment of loyalist Kurds into so-called Village Guard (*Köy Korucuları*) units that, like the Ottoman-era *Hamidiye*, were charged with maintaining security on the ground in Southeastern Anatolia. Like the *Hamidiye*, too, they helped bring segments of the Kurdish population under state authority. They also reinforced the domination of the tribal elites commanding them and contributed to the generalized violence plaguing the region.[37]

If the Kemalist answer to the question of Kurds' place in the postimperial state centered on assimilation, conservative opposition parties (including the AKP) have long applied an Islamic lens to address the sources of conflict between Muslim Kurds and Muslim Turks. During the 1950s, the Democrat Party (*Demokrat Partisi*, DP) government under Prime Minister Adnan Menderes (1950–60) promoted a common religious framework based on the Naqshbandi *tariqa* to reconcile Sunni Turks and Kurds. Similarly, Özal, whose mother was Kurdish, emphasized his ties to the *Naqshbandiyya*, and Kurdish Naqshbandis from the traditional elite were among the main beneficiaries of his economic reforms.[38]

The AKP too framed its Kurdish Opening around the Ottoman practice of prioritizing religious over ethnic criteria, pointing to the historical ties uniting Turks and Kurds—both those living in Turkey and those in post-Ottoman Iraq and Syria.[39] The Kurdish Opening was part of an effort to address the sources of the conflict with the PKK, accelerate Turkey's path to European integration, and position Turkey as a regional power broker.[40] Of course, the Kurdish Opening had a more narrowly political objective as well, as Erdoğan calculated that he could win over enough support from conservative Sunni Kurds to help him secure a majority for his plan to amend the constitution and transform Turkey into a presidential republic. The Kurdish Opening coincided, though, with an upsurge in PKK attacks that that left the AKP vulnerable to criticism that it was soft on terrorism and separatism.

Though the constitutional referendum passed, and conservative Sunni Kurds continue to vote for the AKP in significant numbers, Kurdish support was also instrumental in the emergence of the liberal Peoples' Democratic Party (*Halkların Demokratik Partisi*, HDP), led by the Kurdish politician Selahattin Demirtaş, which called for a peaceful resolution to the conflict with the PKK, and whose success in the September 2015 general election helped cost the AKP its majority. The Kurdish Opening soon stalled, as the government stepped up security operations against the PKK; thousands were killed and over 350,000 civilians displaced in the ensuing fighting.[41] Ankara also used the state of emergency adopted after the failed July 2016 coup to crack down on the HDP, which had been acting as a go-between with the PKK. Hundreds of HDP members (including Demirtaş) were jailed on terrorism charges; Erdoğan blamed the HDP and Demirtaş personally for a clash where PKK supporters killed dozens of conservative Kurds during clashes in Diyarbakır over the siege of Kobani—a striking example of intra-Kurdish divisions over questions of identity and relations with the Turkish state.[42] In September 2020, prosecutors brought a case seeking to ban the HDP entirely.

This pivot back to a securitized approach to the Kurdish issue reflected the postcoup political environment, but also suggested the limits of the AKP's Ottoman-Islamic ideal as a solution to the Kurdish problem. As with the Kemalists who demanded Kurds "call themselves Turks," the AKP's emphasis on the Ottoman legacy and a shared Sunni identity excluded many Kurds who defined themselves along other lines. It left little space for Alevi, Yazidi, and other non-Sunni Kurds, and effectively sought to delegitimize secular, nationalist conceptions of Kurdish identity such as those promoted by the PKK and the HDP.[43] This struggle over the acceptable bounds of Kurdish identity was one element in the wider divides between urban and rural, secular and religious, driving political polarization in the AKP era.

The Kurds and Turkey's Postimperial Geopolitics

Exacerbating concerns about the loyalty of the Kurds to the Kemalist state was the post–World War I territorial settlement, which left Ottoman Kurdistan divided between Turkey, Iraq, and Syria. The growth of Kurdish nationalism and irredentism (sometimes with foreign backing) consequently posed a threat to the Republic's territorial integrity, even as nomads, smugglers, and guerillas continued to move back and forth across the remote, mountainous border region.[44] The importance of these cross-border connections is a result of enduring ties—tribal as well as political—among the Kurdish inhabitants of Turkey and its neighbors, and the failure of all three governments to make their Kurdish inhabitants full political stakeholders.

For that reason, Özal recognized that openness to expressions of a Kurdish identity at home could enhance Turkish influence with the Iraqi and Syrian Kurds too.[45] In addition to loosening restrictions on Kurdish culture, Özal cultivated the leading Iraqi Kurdish factions as allies against the PKK, allowing them to open offices in Ankara and giving their leaders Turkish diplomatic passports.[46] Yet the Iraqi and Syrian governments were equally capable of playing the Kurdish card in their regional competition with Turkey. While a shared hostility to Kurdish independence at times encouraged cooperation among Ankara, Baghdad, and Damascus, the wider frame of the Cold War and, more recently, the wars in Iraq (2003—17) and Syria (2011–present) provided incentives for all three governments (plus Iran, which faces its own Kurdish challenge) to instrumentalize the Kurdish question for their own ends.

The danger of a transboundary Kurdish uprising first became clear with the protests that erupted on all sides of the border following the return to Iraq of the nationalist leader Mullah Mustafa Barzani, who had escaped to the Soviet Union following Mohammad Reza Shah's suppression of the doomed Kurdish republic established in northern Iran at the end of World War II.[47] It was reinforced in the twenty-first century by the collapse of the Iraqi and Syrian states, which created new opportunities both for Kurdish militants to move back and forth across nominal state borders, and for Ankara to export its struggle against Kurdish separatism onto the territory of its neighbors.[48]

The permeability of Turkey's borders with Iraq and Syria was also an important asset for the PKK, which recruited among Kurdish refugees to Turkey and sought sanctuary for its fighters in the remote, poorly governed mountains on all sides of the border. Öcalan himself supervised preparations for the PKK's initial uprising from Damascus, while PKK fighters maintained camps in northern Iraq from which they slipped across the Turkish border.[49] The PKK's ranks in Turkey were, meanwhile, supplemented by Kurdish refugees escaping Saddam Hussein's *al-Anfal* campaign (which involved the use of air strikes and chemical weapons against Kurdish villages) and suppression of a U.S.-backed Kurdish revolt at the end of the 1991 Gulf War.[50]

Despite discriminating against their own Kurdish populations, both Baghdad and Damascus have also taken advantage of the frontier region's permeability and Kurdish discontent to put pressure on Ankara. Syrian president Hafez al-Assad (1971–2000) long used the PKK to press territorial and ideological disputes with Turkey. In addition to hosting Öcalan, Assad allowed PKK fighters to set up camps in Lebanon's Syrian-controlled Beqaa Valley and to recruit among the disaffected Syrian Kurds it was seeking to displace from its own border region.[51] Assad's Soviet ally, meanwhile, provided arms and training.[52]

Aligned with Turkey and against Syria and Iran, Saddam's Iraq initially cultivated the PKK as a counterweight to the separatist movements led by Barzani and his rival Jalal Talabani, rather than as a lever against Turkey. Saddam's calculation changed, however, when Turkey agreed to support the U.S.-led Gulf War in 1991. In response, the Iraqis began shipping arms and supplies to PKK fighters across the border.[53] After Saddam's forces put down the Kurdish uprising at the end of the war, the United States enforced a no-fly zone in northern Iraq, which allowed the Iraqi Kurds to consolidate an autonomous administration—the KRG—with many of the trappings of a state. Despite a tense relationship with the KRG leadership under Mustafa Barzani's son Masoud, the PKK managed to maintain a presence in northern Iraq from which to launch attacks into Turkey.

Such attacks prompted the Turkish military to conduct multiple cross-border operations into both Iraq and Syria. Tens of thousands of Turkish troops invaded northern Iraq in 1992, and again in March 1995, to push back PKK forces from the border.[54] Fearing the U.S.-led campaign to oust Saddam would touch off a new Kurdish uprising, Ankara also dispatched around 1,500 troops to northern Iraq in the first hours following the March 2003 U.S. invasion.[55] During the ensuing conflict, Turkey conducted several operations targeting PKK camps in the Qandil Mountains, and briefly occupied a swathe of northern Iraq in 2007–08, returning in force when Mosul fell to ISIS in the summer of 2014.

Turkish officials, however, recognized the limits of military intervention as a tool for containing Kurdish mobilization. After Iraq adopted a new constitution in 2005 that gave the KRG official status, Ankara decided to seek a modus vivendi with the KRG authorities. This rapprochement was based on Turkey's recognition that the KRG, which did not advocate separatism and was led by the tribal, conservative Barzanis, could provide a bulwark against the breakdown of governance, refugee flows, and strengthening of PKK-linked groups on the Iraqi side of the border.[56] Turkish support helped the KRG carve out a liminal existence on the margins of the Iraqi state. Erdoğan made his first visit to Erbil in March 2011 during the initial upheaval of the Arab Spring. Turkey soon opened a consulate in in the city and began allowing the KRG to export oil through Turkey over opposition from Baghdad (and Washington). Welcoming Masoud Barzani to Diyarbakır in late 2013, Erdoğan became the first Turkish leader to mention the word "Kurdistan" in public. Quoting the Diyarbakır-born Islamist Sezai Karakoç, Erdoğan noted that "just like Erbil, Diyarbakır is all of ours. We felt that Erbil is our city. You should feel that this city is your home."[57]

The relationship depended on maintaining what Davutoğlu called the KRG's "active support and solidarity" against Kurdish separatism.[58] After the collapse of the 2013–15 "solution process (çözüm süreci)," which saw demobilized PKK fighters take refuge in northern Iraq, Ankara looked to the KRG authorities to contain the renewed insurgency that resulted. Though the KRG had previously threatened that its *peshmerga* fighters would resist Turkish "hot pursuit" operations into Iraq, under the new agreement, *peshmerga* stood aside as Turkey carried out strikes against PKK camps or sent in ground forces to open a corridor to the PKK's redoubt in the Qandil Mountains.[59] The relationship deepened further as Ankara began supplying and training *peshmerga* forces, including the units it transported across Turkish territory to lift the siege of Kobani, an operation then-Prime Minister Davutoğlu praised as a "striking reflection of the trust" between Turkey and the KRG.[60]

That trust did not extend, however, to endorsing Barzani's decision to hold a September 2017 referendum on Kurdish independence from Iraq. Fearful lest the independence of Iraqi Kurdistan set a precedent for separatism inside Turkey, Ankara stood by as Iraqi government forces took control of much of the territory previously controlled by the KRG, including the city of Kirkuk. Nevertheless, Turkey sought to preserve the KRG as a distinct entity. It resisted Baghdad's calls to close the border or cut off trade, and reached a new deal with Erbil to conduct cross-border attacks on PKK targets once the KRG's bid for independence had been crushed, preferring the KRG's ambiguous sovereignty to the extension of Baghdad's authority up to the border.[61]

Turkey's approach to the Syrian Kurds was equally multifaceted, subordinated to larger considerations of border security and the evolution of relations with Damascus. In the mid-1990s, Turkish threats of cross-border intervention helped convince Syria to pull back its support for the PKK, leading to Öcalan's expulsion and eventual arrest, and a strategic rapprochement between Ankara and Damascus. When, however, Syrian-Turkish relations collapsed following Bashar al-Assad's bloody suppression of the Syrian Arab Spring uprisings, Damascus again looked to the Kurdish issue as a source of leverage against Turkey.

The strategic withdrawal of government forces from northern Syria in mid-2012 left much of the region along the Syrian-Turkish border under the control of Kurdish groups, among which the YPG's parent organization, the Democratic Union Party (*Partiya Yekîtiya Demokrat*, PYD), soon established its dominance. By mid-2016, the PYD/YPG was receiving U.S. military aid as the nucleus of the Syrian Democratic Forces, which were bearing the brunt of the fighting against ISIS. Thanks to U.S. assistance, the PYD/YPG found itself on the verge of connecting and consolidating the three north Syrian cantons of Afrin, Jazira, and Kobani into a unified administration covering the length of the Syrian-Turkish border.[62]

In contrast to the KRG, Ankara perceived this PYD-controlled statelet (known as Rojava)—with its expansive territorial ambitions and ties to the PKK—as a serious threat to its own security and territorial integrity. These concerns were exacerbated by the number of Turkish Kurds— including relatives of leading Kurdish politicians—who crossed the border to join the PYD at a time when the conflict with the PKK in Southeastern Anatolia was again growing following the end of the Kurdish Opening. Concerns about the emergence of a cross-border zone of PKK-PYD influence drove Ankara's decision to seal the border when ISIS laid siege to Kobani, despite the political and diplomatic backlash that ensued.[63]

Once the siege was broken, the Turkish army and aligned Sunni militias launched a series of cross-border operations to push back the YPG forces, dismantle the PYD administration in northern Syria, and resettle refugees who had fled to Turkey. Rather than devolve authority to local proxies as in Iraq, Ankara moved to extend elements of its internal administration into Syrian territory, pursuing political and cultural transformations to link the occupied regions more closely to Turkey. In the region between Afrin and Manbij occupied during 2016's Operation Euphrates Shield, Turkey established a "protostate," subordinated to the governor of neighboring Gaziantep province. Inhabitants reported an increasingly visible Turkish presence, including Turkish flags and schools adopting Turkish-language curricula.[64] In the pocket of Aleppo province occupied during Operation Olive Branch (2018), Ankara brought together Sunni rebel groups into a Turkish-backed interim government.[65]

Though Turkish officials deny any irredentist aspirations, this "Turkification" of northern Syria fed rumors that Ankara aimed to annex the occupied regions. Particularly in and around Afrin, pro-Turkish Sunni militias have been implicated in human rights abuses against (especially non-Sunni) Kurds, large numbers of whom have fled. Ankara has meanwhile encouraged Syrian refugees to settle in the region. Many of these settlers appear to be Arabs and other Sunnis from different parts of Syria.[66] Kurdish activists accuse Ankara of pursuing a deliberate strategy to dilute the Kurdish population of northern Syria and remove refugees who have become increasingly burdensome (and politically damaging) from Turkish territory.[67] Replacement of Yazidi and other Kurds with Sunni Arab refugees would not only implant a constituency supporting a long-term Turkish military presence, but isolate the Turkish Kurds inside the borders of the Republic and sever their physical link to Kurdish populations on the Syrian side of the border, thereby accelerating the transformation of Southeastern Anatolia from postimperial borderland to undifferentiated component of the Turkish state.

The Kurdish Borderland Between Empire and Nation

Turkey's approach to its Kurdish challenge remains balanced between the desire to consolidate and integrate Southeastern Anatolia more effectively into the Turkish Republic and an ambition to utilize the frontier region to extend Turkish influence into neighboring states—in other words, between nation-state and imperial approaches. Ankara pursued the nation-state approach throughout much of the twentieth century. The push to make Kurds call themselves Turks and wall off Southeastern Anatolia from the rest of historic Kurdistan weakened Turkish democracy and contributed to an endless cycle of insurgency and repression that Turkey's neighbors were only too happy to manipulate. The AKP's postimperial approach, conversely, aimed at reassessing the Kurds' place in the Turkish state, while taking advantage of the frontier's fluidity to pursue a defense-in-depth strategy by establishing buffer zones under different forms of ambiguous sovereignty on Iraqi and Syrian territory.

Like much else about the AKP's geopolitical vision, this approach worked as long as political conditions were favorable. Negotiations with Öcalan and the prospect of an end to the PKK insurgency provided an opportunity for reengaging with the Iraqi and Syrian Kurds on Ankara's terms. If the Kurds were not to have their own state, Davutoğlu's attempt to bring different parts of the Kurdish region together under Turkish protection—to see Diyarbakır and Erbil as part of the same patrimony—was perhaps the next-best alternative. Unfortunately, the collapse of the Kurdish Opening led to a resumption of conflict with the PKK and thousands of additional deaths. It also alienated many of the Iraqi and Syrian Kurds Ankara was hoping to cultivate.

Both the Kurdish Opening at home and the hybrid political arrangements in northern Iraq and northern Syria echoed imperial models, at least as understood by the AKP. The partnership with the KRG has become an effective and low-cost vehicle for ensuring security on the Iraqi border and exerting influence over Baghdad. The expansion of a Turkish military and administrative presence in northern Syria has contained the expansion of the YPG-PKK presence, but left Turkey isolated and dependent on the forbearance of Moscow, Damascus, and Tehran.[68]

Success, though, also depends on the willingness of multiple Kurdish populations to accept a framing of Kurdish identity emphasizing Sunnism and the interests of the Turkish state. The strength of secular Kurdish nationalists like the PKK and its offshoots, as well as the liberal HDP, suggests, however, that even if many Kurds see the Ottoman era in a positive light, they deny that what Ankara is offering them reflects their contemporary aspirations. Like the failure of the Kurdish Opening, the agony of Kobani showed that Ankara's imperial vision is not large enough to encompass Kurds whose political and territorial ambitions do not line up with its own vision for regional order.

CHAPTER SIX

The Geopolitics of the Post-Ottoman Space

R ESHAPING TIES WITH Turkey's post-Ottoman periphery is central to the AKP's foreign policy vision. Davutoğlu, Erdoğan, and other AKP figures portray Turkey as what Davutoğlu termed a "central country (*merkez ülke*)," whose organic connections with the Balkans, the Caucasus, and the Arab lands were severed at the founding of the Republic. As with most of the AKP's appeal to Ottoman legacies, this vision appeals to nostalgia for a glorious past while providing opportunities for the expansion of trade and influence. By restoring cross-border political, economic, and cultural ties, the AKP argues that Turkey can position itself at the center of a new regional order and, in the process, transform itself from a territorially confined state with its strategic ambitions largely subordinated to the West into an autonomous regional power with aspirations for global influence.[1]

In contrast to Russia's focus on military domination and institutional integration or China's emphasis on unequal economic relations, Turkey emphasizes a shared Ottoman heritage and the attraction of its own democratic Islamism as a model—though in recent years Turkish influence has come to rest partly on military power as well. While "neo-Ottomanism (*Yeni Osmanlıcılık*)" is a popular short-hand for this foreign policy vision, especially among critics, Ankara's ambitions are less about restoring political domination than about positioning itself as a hub for regional interactions—nor are they confined to the former Ottoman Empire.[2] Even as Turkey develops political, economic, and security ties with its neighbors, officials are careful to emphasize that Ankara follows "a policy based on equality, mutual goodwill, and developing cooperation," or what Davutoğlu famously described as ensuring "zero problems with neighbors" rather than imperial domination.[3]

In practice, however, Turkey's regional objectives often have imperial echoes. These include giving new impetus to longstanding irredentist claims, cross-border military interventions, creation of hierarchical, highly personalized relationships with neighboring leaders, and the mobilization of Sunni and Turkic-speaking minorities as a pro-Turkish constituency. Ambitions to transform other countries' domestic politics reached their apogee during the Arab Spring, which saw Turkey gamble that upheaval would bring sympathetic actors to power across the Arab world. Pursuing these aspirations left Turkey isolated when the Arab Spring cooled and pulled it into a disastrous war in Syria, but still shape its approach to neighboring states. Especially since Davutoğlu's departure from government in 2016, Turkey's approach to its neighborhood has taken on a more military cast, with Turkish forces and proxies active in Iraq, Syria, Libya, and the South Caucasus, and a Turkish military footprint in regions as diverse as Qatar and Somalia.

The Ottoman legacy matters to this vision both in terms of framing its geographic scope and as the source of the shared heritage that AKP officials claim provides a basis for Turkish leadership. As Erdoğan's close advisor and spokesman İbrahim Kalın suggested, the AKP's ascent signifies that Turkey had "returned to its past experiences, dreams, and aspiration in its greater hinterland."[4] This hinterland includes southeastern Europe, North Africa, Mesopotamia, the Arabian Peninsula, and the Caucasus, all of which broke away from Ottoman control during the nineteenth and early twentieth centuries (often with the assistance of rival empires), leaving behind a vast, but long unacknowledged, "post-Ottoman space" surrounding Anatolia on all sides—in addition to the "Turkic World," most of which never fell under Ottoman rule.

The Kemalist emphasis on the territory of the Republic as a national homeland (*vatan*) was a deliberate strategy for moving past this loss of Ottoman territory outside Anatolia. Yet from the very beginning, the process of separating Anatolia from the rest of the post-Ottoman space has been less clear-cut than Republican ideology sometimes claimed, and a kind of postimperial imagination has long existed toward parts of it. While irredentist undercurrents long tugged at these adjacent regions, the AKP both extended the geographic scope of that postimperial imagination beyond Turkey's immediate neighborhood and imbued it with a larger geopolitical and ideological significance. Although romantic nostalgia features prominently in public appeals, Erdoğan emphasizes that Turkish interest in the post-Ottoman periphery "is not a romantic neo-Ottomanism. It is a real policy based on a new vision of global order."[5]

That order, however, is one in which Turkey no longer has the luxury, according to the AKP, of hewing to the Western-centric vision that long dominated strategic thinking. Though Davutoğlu laid out this vision at a time when relations between Turkey and its NATO allies were comparatively good, Turkey's pursuit of regional influence has taken flight as relations with the West have frayed, and Turkey's own politics have become increasingly Islamist and illiberal. Many U.S. and European observers now worry that Ankara's regional ambitions represent a threat not only to the territorially satiated, Atlanticist foreign policy Turkey pursued during the Cold War, but to stability across the putative post-Ottoman space and beyond.

Discovering the "Post-Ottoman Space"

The idea of a "post-Ottoman space" is not just an ideological phenomenon, but also a product of changed post–Cold War strategic geography. Atatürk's emphasis on ensuring Turkey's territorial integrity by disentangling it from the periphery ensured that for most of the twentieth century, officials and analysts downplayed the very existence of a "post-Ottoman space."[6] Turkish nation-building involved drawing out contrasts with a non-Turkish other and forcing the millions of refugees from the periphery of the collapsing Ottoman Empire to subsume alternative identities, forgetting that their ancestors had been Albanians, Circassians, or Arabs rather than Turks. Other post-Ottoman states in the Balkans and the Arab Middle East underwent parallel nation-building processes that entailed rejecting their Ottoman past and downplaying lingering ties with Turkey. Ideological and geopolitical considerations encouraged that decoupling as well, since Turkey was on the opposite side of the Cold War divide from many other post-Ottoman states in the Balkans and Middle East.

Atatürk's decision to eschew irredentism notwithstanding, Turkey never fully separated from its near abroad. For most of the twentieth century, though, the most important map for Turkey's postimperial longings was not that of the Ottoman Empire at its height, but of the Republic at its inception. Turkey long evinced a degree of irredentism toward territories encompassed by the *Mısak-i Milli* but outside the borders established by the 1923 Treaty of Lausanne, including Cyprus, Alexandretta (Hatay), Mosul, Aleppo, Western Thrace, several Aegean islands claimed by Greece, and Batumi in Georgia's Ajaria region.[7] This irredentism manifested itself most starkly in Hatay, which Turkish forces seized from French Syria in 1938–39, and in Cyprus, where the breakdown of constitutional rule and an Athens-backed coup that aimed at fostering *enosis* (unification) with Greece led to a 1974 Turkish invasion and the establishment of the de facto Turkish Republic of Northern Cyprus. Erdoğan has more recently affirmed that Turkey retains special "rights" in the remaining regions covered by the *Mısak-i Milli* but left outside the Republic at Lausanne.[8]

Interest in the wider post-Ottoman space received new momentum from the end of the Cold War and the collapse of the USSR. With Russian power pushed back from its borders, Turkey acquired new opportunities to project influence throughout its neighborhood. Interest in a more assertive posture toward the Balkans, the Caucasus, and the Middle East thus predates the formation of the AKP. Invocations of the Ottoman Empire as a model for Turkey's foreign policy seem to have originated in the early 1990s with Özal's foreign policy adviser Cengiz Candar, who lauded Ottoman accomplishments and called for a "policy of 360 degrees that includes all of Turkey's many faces," and with Social Democratic Foreign Minister İsmail Cem, who argued that the Ottomans' tolerant multiculturalism presented a model for post–Cold War Turkey.[9] Though Ottoman nostalgia was primarily associated with Turkish Islamists, the interest of a Social Democrat like Cem in Ottoman models suggested that appreciation of the opportunities offered by Turkey's new strategic geography extended across the political spectrum.

Focus on the post-Ottoman space as an arena for Turkish influence gained mainstream currency, along with a more Islamic coloring, in large part thanks to Davutoğlu's academic work, especially his 2001 book *Strategic Depth* (*Stratejik Derinlik*). Davutoğlu emphasized Turkey's position as a "central country" at the intersection of the Balkans, the Middle East, and the Caucasus that, by reconnecting with its post-Ottoman periphery, could become the pivot for a regional system and mediate interactions among its neighbors.[10] Davutoğlu claimed that the emergence of Soviet domination over much of the former Ottoman periphery left Turkish foreign policy resting on "the National Pact borders and a nation-state defense strategy" instead of the Ottomans' traditional forward policy in the Balkans and the Black Sea.[11] Yet just because previous governments chose to turn their back on these regions did not mean that Turkey could isolate itself from them. Pointing to refugee flows streaming into Turkey from the conflicts in Bosnia, Kosovo, Nagorno-Karabakh, Chechnya, and Iraq, Davutoğlu argued that Turkey should "establish order in all these surrounding regions. . . . Because if there is no order, then we will pay the price together."[12]

According to Davutoğlu, establishing order around its periphery required Turkey to transform itself from a self-proclaimed nation-state into something more like a traditional empire. His description of Turkey as a "central state" implied that it maintained a natural hinterland, where it should seek out *Lebensraum* (Davutoğlu used the Turkish *hayat alanı* for this infamous German term, seemingly impervious to its Nazi connotations in the West).[13] Similarly, his notion of *tarihdaşlık*, and of Turkey's responsibility for its *tarihdaş milletler*, or nations sharing a common history, was likewise bound up with the belief in a natural sphere of influence extending beyond Turkey's borders. Taken together, this vision implied what a sympathetic analyst described as "making boundaries *de facto* meaningless while respecting national sovereignty."[14] Or as Erdoğan put it in 2016, "Our physical boundaries are different from the boundaries of our heart. . . . Naturally we show respect for our physical boundaries; but we cannot draw boundaries to our heart."[15] Since Davutoğlu's departure, this focus on a terrestrial post-Ottoman space has been supplemented by emphasis on the maritime dimension of Turkey's near abroad, a so-called Blue Homeland (*Mavi Vatan*), invoked to justify extensive claims in the Aegean and eastern Mediterranean.[16]

While the naval officers who developed the "Blue Homeland" idea are secular Kemalists, Erdoğan and Davutoğlu are Islamists, and Islam remains central to the AKP vision of Turkey's role at the center of a new regional order. Davutoğlu argued, according to Michael Reynolds, "that the conflicts and contrasts between Islamic and Western political thought originate mainly from their philosophical, methodological, and theoretical background" and, consequently, that the Western and Islamic worlds as distinct and incompatible.[17] The Turkey-centric order that the AKP aspires to construct is one in which Islam is a central organizing principle and the Islamic Middle East the main foreign policy priority. This emphasis on both Islam and the Middle East stems from many AKP members' dubious reading of the Ottoman past, especially a tendency to exaggerate the extent to which the Ottoman Empire was defined by its Islamic identity.

Yet in contrast to Saudi-style Salafism, Davutoğlu and Erdoğan's understanding of Ottoman Islam emphasizes its syncretic and tolerant nature.

Davutoğlu argued that the cosmopolitan Ottoman order had maintained a balance between the various cultural and religious communities—and that its breakdown led to the communal violence that long plagued the Balkans, the Caucasus, and the Middle East.[18] While politicians in many of these regions worry that Ankara's "neo-Ottoman" vision is a stalking horse for Islamization, Davutoğlu and Erdoğan perceive a Turkey-centric order based on Islamic principles as the foundation for stability and security, with Islamic practice (such as the Ottoman concept of *millets*) providing the framework for multiple communities to coexist under a Turkish-Islamic umbrella—though this assessment is not widely shared outside Turkey, where the appeal of such a Turkish-centric regional order based on Islamic principles remains limited.

The Balkans and Southeastern Europe

Unlike Mesopotamia or the Caucasus, the Balkan Peninsula was not a distant periphery of the Ottoman Empire but, along with western Anatolia, part of the Ottoman core. Thanks, however, to massive population movements and Atatürk's emphasis on the *Mısak-i Milli* borders, the fates of Anatolia and the Balkans grew apart. Nevertheless, like the Ottoman Empire, Turkey "is a Balkan country and has never, figuratively speaking, left the region."[19] Around 5 percent of Turkey's territory—Eastern Thrace and the European side of Istanbul—remains west of the Straits dividing Europe from Asia. At its height, though, the Ottoman Empire extended across southeastern Europe to the Danube. Though Ottoman forces were turned back from the gates of Vienna in 1529 and again in 1683, much of Hungary, Romania, Bulgaria, Albania, Greece, and the former Yugoslavia were for centuries under Ottoman authority.

South of a steppe frontier running from Hungary in the west to Crimea in the east—and excluding the tributaries Moldavia and Wallachia and the vassal principality of Transylvania—most of this region was integrated politically and culturally into the Ottoman interior.[20] Conquests were followed by the rapid installation of Ottoman administrative mechanisms such as *waqf*s (*vakıf*) and the Ottoman monetary system.[21] As in western and central Anatolia, Ottoman officials brought their holdings in the Balkans under direct rule and handed out *tımar*s, in contrast to peripheries where tax farming and other methods of indirect control predominated.[22] By the turn of the nineteenth century, though, indigenous elites controlled revenue collection and challenged central authority, providing a nucleus for movements seeking greater autonomy from Istanbul.

The disentanglement of Anatolia from the Balkans occurred amid the independence struggles waged by many Balkan Christian populations during the nineteenth and early twentieth centuries—usually with assistance from the European great powers. From the Habsburg advance into the Ottoman Balkans after the second siege of Vienna to the forced population exchange between Greece and Turkey at the end of the Turkish War of Independence, these struggles led to the mass expulsion and killing of Muslims from the Balkans, Crimea, and the Caucasus, with millions of refugees making their way to the ever-shrinking imperial rump.[23] Coupled with the Kemalist emphasis on assimilation, the exchanges of populations helped sunder the personal and cultural ties long binding Anatolia to the Balkans.[24]

Neither these population shifts nor the establishment of Turkey's post-Lausanne borders fully separated Turkey from its western periphery. To a greater degree than in the post-Ottoman Middle East or Caucasus, Ankara remained a factor in Balkan affairs throughout the Cold War era.[25] It participated in the two Balkan Pacts of 1934 and 1953, designed to insulate southeastern Europe from the ambitions of the major powers. It also inherited the Ottoman Empire's rivalry with Greece, which came to the fore in the 1950s and 1960s over Cyprus. Perhaps Turkey's most important link to the region remained its openness to refugees, primarily Muslims and Turks driven out by hostile governments, among them Turks from Romania and Bulgaria and Albanians from Yugoslavia. The largest flow came with the expulsion of around 300,000 Bulgarian Turks by the regime of Todor Zhivkov in 1989; another 20,000 or so Bosnian Muslims came with the outbreak of the Bosnian War in the early 1990s.[26]

As elsewhere around Turkey's periphery, the end of the Cold War opened up new opportunities—but also old fears. Just as the 1974 invasion of Cyprus rekindled European angst about Turkish imperialism, the rise of political Islam under Özal sparked U.S. and European concerns about radicalization and the creation of a Turkish-dominated "Islamic arc."[27] Such fears played a prominent role in the wars of the Yugoslav succession, where Serbian, Croatian, and Macedonian nationalists attacked the Muslims in their midst as "Turks" who had been implanted in the region by the Ottomans, and deliberately targeted elements of the Ottoman cultural heritage, such as cemeteries and mosques, for destruction.[28] Widely covered in the Turkish press, these events contributed to a new awareness of Turkey's connection to the Balkans.

The wars produced a renewed interest not only in historical ties, but also in Turkey's ability to affect events on the ground. Headed by the conservative True Path Party (*Doğru Yol Partisi*), Turkey's government was among the first to call for international military intervention to assist the Bosnian Muslims. Turkey cooperated with other Muslim-majority states (including Iran) to funnel weapons and assistance to Bosnian Muslim forces despite a UN Security Council arms embargo.[29] Even as it sought to rally international support for the Bosnian Muslims, though, Turkey was trying to position itself as a regional mediator. President Özal visited Sofia, Skopje, and Tirana in early 1993 "to put Europe on notice that Ankara has a strong interest in Macedonia and other Balkan countries that emerged from the Ottoman Empire after the Balkan wars of 1912 and 1913."[30] Turkey similarly supported the NATO campaign to stop the ethnic cleansing of Kosovar Albanians, and was at the forefront of calls to recognize Kosovo's independence from Serbia. Direct Turkish involvement in the wars in both Bosnia and Kosovo was limited, though, and was also coordinated with the EU and the United States, as Ankara sought to use its influence with the Balkan Muslims to demonstrate its value as a partner for the West at a time when EU accession remained a priority.[31]

The rise of the AKP did not initially portend a shift in this approach, but with Davutoğlu's 2009 appointment as foreign minister and the deterioration of ties with the West, Ankara launched a "dizzying diplomatic outreach" to the Balkans.[32] This Balkan pivot was in part about Davutoğlu acting on his longstanding vision of Turkey as an independent regional power, but it was also a response to the growing crisis in Turkey's relationship with the EU, which continued delaying Turkish accession. Apart from regional mediation, Turkish outreach included efforts to strengthen economic and cultural ties through *Diyanet*, the Yunus Emre Institute (Turkey's equivalent to the *Alliance Française*), and the Gülen movement, which established a network of schools throughout the region. TİKA contributed large sums to the reconstruction of mosques, cemeteries, and other Islamic sites destroyed by Serb forces during the Bosnian War.

Davutoğlu's efforts culminated in the 2010 Istanbul summit with the leaders of Bosnia and Serbia, which secured a commitment from Belgrade to respect Bosnia's territorial integrity. Along with a parallel initiative involving Serbia and Croatia, Ankara hoped its success would be read in Brussels as a demonstration of Turkey's ability to play a unique mediating role that would enhance its own attractiveness as a candidate for membership.[33] Davutoğlu suggested that because of "our [common] history we have a common past and a common wish for . . . peace and stability."[34] Yet Turkey's insistence on approaching its role through an Ottoman lens undermined its effectiveness as a mediator; when Erdoğan remarked at a 2013 rally in Kosovo that "Kosovo is Turkey and Turkey is Kosovo," Serbia ended the trilateral talks.[35]

Apart from regional mediation, Ankara's intervention in the Balkans emphasizes trade and appeals to the shared Ottoman heritage to boost Turkey's diplomatic and cultural presence. Unlike Russia, Turkey does not seek to undermine European unity or prevent states on its periphery from joining the EU and NATO. Turkish officials note that Ankara's higher profile in the Balkans is in line with EU norms, and in that sense compatible with the western Balkan states' own EU ambitions. As a former Turkish diplomat noted, "Turkey is not in the business of trying to dissuade the western Balkan countries from converging with the EU—on the contrary."[36] Yet, echoing concerns about Russian ambitions, many U.S. and European critics invoke the specter of neo-Ottomanism to suggest that Ankara aims to pull the region away from Europe into its own sphere of influence.[37]

Turkey's higher profile in the region does in fact have imperial echoes related to territory, ideology, and the shaping of domestic institutions. While Turkey remains largely committed to its post-1923 borders, its territorial disputes with EU members Greece and Cyprus have a whiff of irredentism. The presence of 30,000 Turkish soldiers in northern Cyprus ensures against efforts to reunite the island by force and serves as a bargaining chip with Nicosia and Brussels. Along with an expanded naval presence, a 2019 agreement with Libya established Turkey's claim to an exclusive economic zone in waters claimed by both Greece and Cyprus, bolstering its aspiration to become a regional energy hub and providing additional leverage.[38]

Despite efforts to play the role of balancer, moreover, Ankara places particular emphasis on cultivating Muslim "brethren" in Albania, Kosovo, North Macedonia, Serbia, and, especially, Bosnia. Ankara maintains direct ties to religious communities through *Diyanet*, which provides financial and material support, wrapped in "language that refers to the Ottoman past and of [sic] the shared Islamic heritage," attempting to inculcate a view of Islam congruent with Turkey's interests.[39] The most visible aspect of these activities is construction of Ottoman-style mosques, including the Namazgah Mosque in Tirana, which became the largest mosque in the Balkans when it opened in late 2019.[40] Erdoğan meanwhile depicts himself as the guardian of Muslim minorities in the Balkans. During a joint appearance in Serbia's Muslim Sanjak region in 2017, even Serbian president Aleksandar Vučić acknowledged that because Serbian Muslims looked to Turkey as a protector, "I am not going to be welcomed here like Erdoğan is."[41]

Turkey also exports aspects of its political model to the Balkans, a region with its own illiberal, populist currents. Turkish officials like to describe their country as an "elder brother" in the Balkans.[42] Relations are highly personalized, with Erdoğan eager to portray himself as a benevolent suzerain. Turkish support based on personal ties insulates Balkan leaders from demands from Brussels for further democratization (and to some degree from Russian influence), but in classic imperial form creates webs of obligation tying them to Ankara. Erdoğan's personalistic regime acts as a model that leaders like Albania's Edi Rama, Moldova's Igor Dodon, and even Vučić have followed as they move to establish state domination of the media and take control of patronage networks. Balkan leaders benefit from Turkish largesse in the form of trade and investment deals and, in exchange, defer to Turkish leadership in both substantive and symbolic terms, down to aping the AKP's de facto uniform of plaid sport coats during meetings.[43] The most glaring example may be Bosnian president Bakir Izetbegović's claim that his father, Bosnian independence leader Alija Izetbegović, entrusted Erdoğan with "safeguarding" Bosnia, implying a *Pax Ottomanica*–style protectorate.[44]

These relationships are also hierarchical in the sense that they give Turkey influence over its neighbors' internal affairs, sometimes in ways that suggest Ankara regards their sovereignty as conditional. Since the failed 2016 coup attempt, Ankara has placed significant pressure on its Balkan neighbors to close Gülen schools and extradite Gülenists, despite legal protections and condemnation from the EU. The 2018 seizure of six Gülenist suspects in Kosovo sparked a scandal that brought down the country's intelligence chief, police chief, and interior minister (President Hashim Thaçi, an Erdoğan ally, stonewalled the initial investigation).[45] With the Balkans emerging as an area of strategic competition between the EU/NATO and Russia, Turkey's ability to exploit connections with the region's leaders and populations, and to shape interactions between Balkan states, is a significant wildcard.

The Middle East

While the Ottoman Empire's political and economic core lay in the Balkans and western Anatolia, the AKP's own worldview is more Middle Eastern–centric. Because of the role they assign Islam as a constituent of identity, Erdoğan and Davutoğlu view "the Islamic Middle East as an organic whole with Turkey as its natural, rightful leader," and wax nostalgic for Baghdad and Jerusalem more than for Thessaloniki or Belgrade.[46] This turn to the Middle East has seen Ankara take on a higher profile as a security provider with forces stationed in several countries, to position itself as a mediator of the region's multiple conflicts, promote its own model of Islam, and boost trade ties.[47] From the beginning of the AKP era, Ankara sought to "creat[e] a new regional order and . . . [trigger] a process of Middle Eastern integration," which in turn depended on getting Arab states to reconnect to their own Ottoman-Islamic heritage, just as Turkey claimed to have done with the election of the AKP.[48]

The map of Turkey's interest in the Middle East owes much to the frontiers of the Ottoman Empire at its height, with Ankara seeking to shape outcomes not only in Iraq and Syria, but also in Libya, Israel/Palestine, and other states whose independence was the product of the breakdown of Ottoman rule. Most significantly, Turkey intervened in the conflicts in Iraq, Syria, and Libya in ways that portend a long-term extension of Turkish influence beyond its borders. While this intervention was prompted by the collapse of the Iraqi, Syrian, and Libyan states, it also reflects longstanding views of Iraq and Syria in particular as part of a Turkish sphere of influence based on their shared Ottoman-Islamic legacy—a view few Iraqis or Syrians share.

Compared to the Balkans and Anatolia, though, the Arab world was relatively peripheral to the Ottomans. After the 1639 Peace of Zuhab established an enduring frontier with Safavid Iran, local authority in the Aleppo, Mosul, and Baghdad *eyalet*s and in eastern Anatolia remained in the hands of influential families like the al-Azm of Damascus and the al-Jalili of Mosul, who maintained hereditary control of their lands in exchange for military and financial support. In the further reaches of the Arabian Peninsula and North Africa, Ottoman authority was often nominal. The Ottomans only introduced the *timar* system in Mosul, while revenue collection in Baghdad, Basra, and elsewhere derived mainly from tax farming.[49] In the 1830s, the Albanian-born *vali* of Egypt, Muhammad Ali Paşa, also occupied Syria and much of eastern Anatolia. Abdülhamid's emphasis on Islam and the caliphate aimed in part at securing Arab support as the Ottoman grip on the Christian Balkans slipped. Meanwhile, Arab activists challenged the Ottoman claim to the caliphate. Steps to integrate the Arab lands more firmly into the empire, including through recruitment and training of Arab officers, were nascent when World War I broke out in 1914.[50]

Late-Ottoman reform efforts colored by European-style colonialist assumptions made the situation worse. Though he encouraged Sunni-Shi'ite collaboration against European imperialism, Abdülhamid's promotion of the (Sunni) caliphate as a tool of legitimation alienated Iraq's large Shi'ite population. The CUP's campaign of centralization and Turkification, meanwhile, was resented by many Sunni Arabs who had supported Abdülhamid. These resentments encouraged figures like the onetime CUP member Aziz Ali al-Masri to approach the British, who saw such malcontents as the kernel of a vast Arab nationalist movement that could be used to challenge Ottoman rule throughout the Middle East.[51] Immortalized in the West by T. E. Lawrence, the Arab Revolt created a longstanding well of resentment between Turkish and Arab nationalists, and a view in Turkey that the Arab betrayal of their fellow Muslims was instrumental in the Ottoman defeat and the ensuing loss of Arab-majority Lebanon, Palestine, Syria, Iraq, and Jordan.[52]

The construction of the Republic entailed both an ideological and a geographic decoupling from the Arab world, whose future the *Mısak-i Milli* called for determining by referendum. If Atatürk's Republic viewed Europe as a source of enlightenment, it tended to look down on poor, tribal North Africa, Mesopotamia, and the Arabian Peninsula as backward peripheries best left behind in the push for modernization. Turkey largely stayed out of the region's twentieth-century conflicts, adopting a defensive posture focused on securing borders, containing the spread of Soviet influence, and impeding Kurdish nationalism. At U.S. insistence, Turkey participated in the 1955 Baghdad Pact and the CENTO alliance, but for much of the Cold War, Moscow's authority in Cairo, Baghdad, and Damascus posed an obstacle to Turkish influence in the region. So too did Turkish recognition of Israel and lukewarm support for the Arab states during the 1967 and 1973 Arab-Israeli wars. While some conservative governments (including Özal's and Erbakan's) sought a higher profile, engagement remained mostly opportunistic until the rise of the AKP in the early 2000s.

The major exception to this defensive approach centered on the northern reaches of Iraq and Syria that had been included in the *Mısak-ı*

Milli borders by virtue of being under Ottoman control at the time of the armistice, notably Aleppo, Alexandretta/Hatay, and Mosul. The Lausanne borders with Iraq and Syria were artificial, lacking geographic barriers and cutting off cities from their economic hinterlands. Especially in Syria, the border was also a source of insecurity, permeable to smugglers, drug traffickers, and Kurdish militants. Meanwhile, the centrality of the *Misak-ı Milli* in constructing the Republic's legitimacy meant these regions remained objects of longing; a 1926 agreement brokered by the League of Nations gave Turkey a percentage of Mosul's oil royalties, while many Turkish textbooks showed Mosul as belonging to Turkey. Along with the invasion of northern Cyprus, Republican Turkey's most direct violation of its neighbors' territorial integrity came with the annexation of Alexandretta, which Ankara had taken to calling Hatay (from "Hittite," to suggest its millennia-long attachment to the Hittites' homeland in Anatolia).[53]

Such longings outlasted the end of the Cold War and the rise of the AKP. At the start of the Iraq War in 2003, Turkish officials pointed to Ottoman-era property registers to suggest Ankara could claim northern Iraq's oil fields. When Baghdad then objected to the establishment of a small Turkish base in northern Iraq, Erdoğan noted that Turkey could not abandon the city because "we are present in Mosul's history."[54] Though it never recovered Aleppo, restoring Turkish influence and bolstering connectivity between Aleppo and its traditional hinterland—including Adana, Gaziantep, Urfa, and Hatay—was an important objective in the pre-2011 rapprochement between Ankara and Damascus. After that rapprochement soured, Erdoğan pointed to Turkey's historical ties to the city to justify intervention in the Syrian civil war.[55]

Even beyond these border regions, the AKP viewed the Middle East as central to its foreign policy aspirations. By virtue of sharing an Islamic-Ottoman pedigree with Turkey, Davutoğlu argued that the Arab states were the natural outlet for Turkey's efforts to break out of its strategic isolation. As in the Balkans, Davutoğlu also saw Turkey as a regional mediator for the Middle East; where his predecessors had shied away from regional disputes, Davutoğlu pursued ambitious initiatives seeking reconciliation between Israel and the Palestinians and aiming to resolve the Iran nuclear dispute. He also promoted trade, tourism, and cultural activities designed to bring Arabs and Turks together. These efforts culminated in a 2010 agreement on trade liberalization and visa-free travel with Jordan, Lebanon, and Syria, which Davutoğlu hailed as a step toward creating a single economic and security space "from Sinop to the equator, from the Bosporus to the Gulf of Aden."⁵⁶

AKP officials also used their platform to encourage democratization throughout the region. This grassroots appeal rested on an assumption that the status quo in the Middle East was unsustainable, since, just as Atatürk's Republic had severed Turks from their authentic identity, so too had secular dictatorships done in the Arab world. Though reluctant at first to embrace the idea of a "Turkish model," officials encouraged Arab Muslims to take inspiration from Turkey's own fusion of Islam and democracy. They were aided by Turkey's growing popularity in the region, the product of both the seeming democratic breakthrough of the early AKP era as well as the growing reach of Turkish soap operas and other aspects of popular culture. In particular, the AKP supported Islamist parties across the Arab world, especially those linked to the Muslim Brotherhood, which enjoyed a longstanding ideological affinity and personal ties with Turkish Islamists.⁵⁷ It also supported the Palestinian cause more actively; blistering criticism of Israel's 2008 war in Gaza and Turkey's involvement in the 2010 Mavi Marmara incident played well in the Arab world, but created a deep rift with Israel.⁵⁸

The contradiction between creating a regional system of intergovernmental cooperation and appealing over the heads of governments to a putatively Islamist national will became critical with the outbreak of the Arab Spring, which placed Arab governments and populations throughout the region on opposite sides of the barricades. AKP officials came to believe both that they had unique insights into the upheavals breaking out across the Arab world thanks to ties of history and religion, and that newly democratic governments would take their cues from Ankara.⁵⁹ As Kalın wrote a few months after the protests in Tunisia began, the "Turkish experience has gained greater salience in these countries" as they too attempted to "reconcile Islam, democracy, and economic development."⁶⁰

The Arab Spring's failure to bring lasting democratization (outside of Tunisia) was therefore a serious blow to Turkish ambitions for building a new regional order based on democratic Islamism. The Egyptian and Syrian counterrevolutions left Ankara with little influence in Cairo and Damascus. Spooked by the possibility of facing similar upheavals, Saudi Arabia, the UAE, Yemen, and other Arab states also turned against Ankara. The Arab Spring meanwhile pushed the Israeli-Palestinian issue into the shadows, depriving Ankara of whatever benefit its pro-Palestinian turn might otherwise have garnered. With the failure of the Turkish-backed opposition to push Assad from power in Damascus, Davutoğlu's ambition to position Turkey at the center of a new regional order lay in ashes, hastening the end of his tenure in office, and in the AKP.

While Erdoğan maintained the emphasis on civilizational bonds tying Turkey to its Arab neighbors, military power increasingly supplemented economic and cultural tools. In the process, Turkey developed a template (inspired in part by Russian models) for using military and proxy forces to project power. Syria, where Turkish forces had established a cross-border buffer zone as a bargaining chip and safe haven for anti-Assad rebels, became not only a proving ground for the AKP's geopolitical aspirations, but also a base for recruiting proxies deployed to Libya and, later, the South Caucasus.[61] These forces encompassed figures ranging from former Syrian officers to hardline Sunni militants whom Ankara allowed to cross through its territory to reach the front lines (including fighters from the Balkans and the Caucasus who had benefited from earlier efforts to facilitate movement across post-Ottoman borders).[62]

In the process, according to one of Davutoğlu's former students-turned-critics, "Turkey became merely one party among many in a sectarian war," sacrificing any hope of being accepted as an honest broker or hub for a new regional order.[63] Facing diminished returns in the face of extremist attacks at home and the intervention of Russian forces to prop up Assad, by mid-2017 Ankara pivoted to Libya, another post-Ottoman periphery whose political turmoil appeared to offer a new opportunity both to give Turkey's ambitions rein and to reinforce strained relationships with Western partners also backing Libya's UN-recognized interim government.[64] In both the transfer of forces between them and the overlapping geopolitical competition with rival Arab states and Russia, Turkey's intervention helped knit together the Syrian and Libyan conflicts, wittingly or not giving substance to its claims that these regions remained bound together by virtue of a shared past.

The Caucasus

While the Caucasus (North and South) was on the Ottoman Empire's outer periphery, the AKP includes them in its vision of a new Turkey-centric order (though its closest regional ally, Azerbaijan, was part of the Ottoman sphere only briefly); even in the 1990s, Ankara aspired to become the region's bridge to the West. Yet Turkish influence remained constrained by the prevalence of Russian power. The Turkish contribution to Azerbaijan's victory over Russian ally Armenia in the Second Nagorno-Karabakh War thus represented a sea-change in regional geopolitics, establishing Ankara as an important power broker and challenging Moscow's claim to an exclusive sphere of influence.

Long a fracture zone with the Iranian and Russian Empires, the Caucasus was a secondary concern for the Ottomans.[65] Though western Georgia and the western Armenian highlands came under Ottoman authority following the Peace of Amasya, Ottoman rule in most of the region was loose, exercised through vassals like the Kingdom of Imereti (western Georgia) or the tributary Crimean Khanate.[66] After the Russian conquest of Crimea in the 1780s, the Kabardians and other North Caucasus groups became pawns in the unfolding Russo-Ottoman struggle, which ended in 1829 with the Treaty of Adrianople, excluding Ottoman influence from the North Caucasus and securing Russian control of western Georgia.

As in the Balkans, Russia's advance displaced millions of indigenous, mostly Muslim inhabitants from Crimea, the Black Sea littoral, and the Caucasus, a majority of whom made their way to Ottoman shores, where they would help ensure the Caucasus remained on the political and diplomatic agenda.[67] With ethnic, religious, and social conflicts roiling the region after Russia's 1905 Revolution, Ottoman officials hosted Muslim guerrillas and Georgian revolutionaries, among them Nicolas, archimandrite of Georgia's largest monastery, who organized a Georgian Legion that fought under Ottoman command in World War I.[68] The defeat of Enver Paşa's forces at Sarıkamış in early 1915, however, left eastern Anatolia open to Russian invasion, and was instrumental in the CUP's decision to kill or expel the Ottoman Armenians whose homeland lay along the likely invasion route and who were perceived as aligned with the Christian Russians.

When the Russian Empire collapsed, Ottoman forces returned to the Caucasus. Ottoman troops participated in the capture of Baku and the establishment of the first Azerbaijan Democratic Republic in the summer of 1918. Ottoman forces also briefly controlled Ajaria's Black Sea port of Batumi, which was referenced in the *Misak-ı Milli* even after it had been claimed by the first Georgian republic and then included in the Soviet Union.[69] Under the 1921 Moscow and Kars treaties, Mustafa Kemal abandoned Turkey's claim in exchange for Soviet economic assistance and other territorial concessions, including regaining the Ottoman *vilayet*s of Kars, Ardahan, and much of Batumi (apart from the city itself).[70] Achieving a stable frontier in the Caucasus allowed Kemal to focus on ending the Allied occupation of western Anatolia, but left the Caucasus insulated from Turkish influence, particularly once Stalin began his campaign to construct "socialism in one country" in the late 1920s.

The end of the Cold War and Özal's effort to move beyond the "Jacobin" model of Turkish identity encouraged a renewed interest in the Caucasus on the part of Turkish officials and analysts. During the 1990s, Ankara promoted the "Turkish model" throughout the Caucasus and Central Asia, and positioned itself as the principal alternative to Russia for newly independent Azerbaijan and Georgia. Turkish officials participated in numerous state visits, focusing on establishing transit connections and seeking to contain the spread of both Islamism and Iranian influence.[71]

With the outbreak of conflict between Armenia and Azerbaijan over Nagorno-Karabakh, Turkey threw in its lot with the Azerbaijanis, closing its border with Armenia and imposing an embargo in response to Armenian troops' advance beyond the Soviet-era Nagorno-Karabakh Autonomous Oblast. Support for Azerbaijan prevented Ankara from taking on the role of an honest broker that it sought in its other peripheries. Instead, Turkey became an outlet to the West for Azerbaijan and Georgia, while using its influence to encourage political and economic reform.[72] Beginning with the Baku-Tbilisi-Ceyhan (BTC) oil pipeline, inaugurated in 2006, trilateral cooperation facilitated the development of new transit infrastructure that allowed Azerbaijan and Georgia to both reduce dependence on Russia and build new ties to Europe. Turkey meanwhile gained access to new sources of oil and gas that bolstered its ambitions to become a distribution hub. Economic ties also underpinned growing trilateral security cooperation, focused initially on protection of infrastructure, but expanding to include joint exercises and sales of Turkish military equipment that helped accelerate the decoupling of Azerbaijan's and Georgia's militaries from their Soviet heritage.[73]

Notwithstanding the emphasis on relations with Azerbaijan and Georgia, ambivalence about borders remains a source of friction. Batumi has, like Mosul or Aleppo, also been the subject of irredentist sentiments. Local officials suggest Turkey may account for as much as 90 percent of the foreign investment in Batumi and its environs.[74] Ankara also maintains a proprietary view of the city that some Georgians see as an infringement on their sovereignty. Turkish efforts to fund construction of an Ottoman-style mosque sparked a significant backlash, as did Erdoğan's calls for shutting down both bars and a Gülen school in the city. Nor are Turkish officials averse to claiming Batumi as part of a natural sphere of influence. Erdoğan's 2016 suggestion that Batumi was part of the natural hinterland of the neighboring Turkish town of Rize touched off a furor in Georgia.[75]

Meanwhile, Turkey's growing economic and security role across the Caucasus sparked both friction with Russia, which continues to maintain a military presence in Armenia, and Russo-Turkish efforts to manage regional security bilaterally. When Russian troops returned in force to the South Caucasus with the 2008 invasion of Georgia, Erdoğan and then-Foreign Minister Ali Babacan offered to mediate an end to the conflict, and, after its conclusion, proposed a Caucasus Cooperation and Stability Pact involving the three South Caucasus states, Russia, and Turkey.[76] The plan represented Turkey's attempt to apply its strategy for regional mediation and "zero problems" in the war-torn Caucasus.[77] While Moscow welcomed the idea of excluding outside powers, the pact failed to gain traction.

Erdoğan also pursued an "Armenian Opening" at home that coincided with similar efforts to reach out to Kurdish, Alevi, and other minorities. The Armenian Opening also entailed quiet diplomacy, backed by the United States, to unfreeze relations with Yerevan in the interest of expanding connectivity and bolstering Turkey's ability to shape the regional balance. Relations remained tense not only because of the Nagorno-Karabakh conflict, but also because of the legacy of the Ottoman collapse (Armenia's independence declaration mentioned the "killings of Armenians by Ottoman Turkey," and Yerevan balked at recognizing the border established between Moscow and Ankara in 1921).[78] Though Turkey and Armenia signed a protocol laying out a roadmap for opening the border and normalizing relations, opposition from Azerbaijan, which feared that Turkey would water down its commitment to securing the return of Nagorno-Karabakh in its eagerness for a deal, undermined the initiative and contributed to the breakdown of the broader Armenian Opening.[79]

The still-frozen relationship with Armenia remains an obstacle to Ankara's ambition to develop a more Turkey-centric regional order in the Caucasus. So too does the role of Russia, whose authority in both the North and South Caucasus has expanded significantly since the early 1990s. During the First Chechen War, Ankara maintained ties to Chechen and other North Caucasus separatist groups, which had strong backing from the descendants of Caucasian refugees in Turkey. Using its ties to the PKK as leverage, Moscow pushed Ankara to cut off support flowing to these groups. By the start of the Second Chechen War, Moscow had pulled back its support for the PKK, while Ankara clamped down on support going to separatists in Chechnya; activists also accused Ankara of allowing Russian security forces to assassinate Chechen exiles on Turkish soil. An attack on the BTC pipeline during the 2008 Georgia War that was initially claimed by the PKK, but later attributed to Russian security services, likewise provided a reminder of the power imbalance in the region.[80]

Despite the risks, Ankara's gravitational pull on Baku and Tbilisi represents a source of leverage that it has exploited as relations with Moscow have become increasingly complex. Russia's own interest in pulling Turkey away from its longstanding Western orientation has led it to tolerate a more visible Turkish presence even though the two countries' clashing objectives in both the Caucasus and the Middle East have sparked significant friction. Amid escalating tensions over Syria, Turkey extended its trilateral defense cooperation mechanism with Azerbaijan and Georgia in 2018, committing to helping Baku and Tbilisi to transform their militaries along NATO lines. In early 2020, Foreign Minister Mevlut Çavuşoğlu became one of the few allied officials to actively promote Georgia's NATO membership.[81] More significant still is Turkey's deepening strategic cooperation with Azerbaijan. Baku's victory in the Second Nagorno-Karabakh War depended on Turkish military supplies (notably drones), intelligence, and militia fighters recruited from Syria. The ceasefire ending the war established a joint Russo-Turkish monitoring center and a land corridor connecting Turkey to Azerbaijan, effectively formalizing Moscow's acceptance of a fundamentally new status quo between Baku and Yerevan, along with a recognition of Turkey as a legitimate regional player with interests that must be accommodated.

Is There a Post-Ottoman Space?

Given the economic and social disruptions Turkey has faced since the onset of the global economic crisis, the objective of positioning itself as the center of a regional order was likely beyond its capacity from the beginning.[82] These limitations are visible throughout the post-Ottoman region, but perhaps nowhere more so than in Syria, where Turkey is left holding onto small pockets of territory that it aims to use as leverage with not just Damascus, but also Tehran and Moscow. In the Balkans, both Russia and Europe offer competing visons of regional order that, while starkly opposed, have each garnered significant support. Pro-EU, but with a political model that more resembles Russia's, Turkey struggles to carve out a niche for itself, a middleweight among heavyweights. Throughout the putative post-Ottoman space, moreover, the AKP's uneasy balance between (illiberal) democracy and Islamism feeds distrust on many sides. Even after the Second Nagorno-Karabakh War, Azerbaijan continues its balancing act between Russia and Turkey, while Armenia's dependence on Moscow has only grown.

Underlying these ambitions is the longstanding belief among much of the Turkish right in the corporeal existence of a post-Ottoman space. Bonded to a geopolitical program by Davutoğlu and brought into the mainstream of Turkish foreign policy thinking by the AKP's rise, the idea of a post-Ottoman space waiting for Turkish leadership still exerts a hold within Turkey's political establishment. As with other aspects of the AKP's Ottoman imagination, nostalgia for an idealized past hangs over claims to regional leadership. The success of these claims thus depends, in part, on their acceptance by the states and peoples Turkey seeks to organize. Unfortunately for Turkey, efforts to appropriate the Ottoman legacy as a basis for regional order remain at odds with the founding narratives and historical memories of states in the Balkans, the Middle East, and the Caucasus, where in many cases the Ottoman period is still regarded as a time of foreign oppression.

The sheer diversity of the regions included in this imagined post-Ottoman space is also problematic; contemporary Georgia and Iraq, for instance, have little in common beyond the fact that they were once both Ottoman dominions. If the Ottoman Empire could manage its diverse peripheries through the politics of difference, Turkey's efforts at regional influence and integration entail a higher degree of coordination, one that Turkey—more so than wealthier and more powerful states like China and Russia—struggles to pull off. Unable to create a new *Pax Ottomanica* around its borders, Turkey has also had to take sides in conflicts between its neighbors (for example, siding with Azerbaijan against Armenia), in turn complicating efforts at regional mediation. The centrality of Islam to the AKP's regional vision contributes to this dilemma as well, since Turkey is often—fairly or not—seen as siding with Sunni populations against their Alawite, Christian, or Shi'ite neighbors.

In response to setbacks faced by its intervention in Syria and the exacerbation of social tensions set off by the presence of large numbers of refugees, Turkish observers close to the government point to a deemphasis of civilizational, Ottoman-inspired themes in discussions around Turkish foreign policy, and a greater focus on national interest. Still, as much as the AKP's Ottoman nostalgia drives these regional ambitions, twenty-first-century Eurasia's competitive, shifting geopolitical environment all but ensures that Turkey, no matter the color of its government, will remain more entangled with its periphery than was the case for most of the twentieth century. As the Syrian refugee crisis demonstrated, Davutoğlu was correct that instability around its periphery presents a threat to Turkey's own security. Surrounded on all sides by imperial shatter zones full of weak states, and with porous, hard-to-defend borders, Turkey retains a vital interest in containing threats outside its territory. Like its postimperial peers and rivals, Turkey maintains the military, political, and economic tools to establish buffer zones, spheres of influence, and other mechanisms of postimperial domination. And with ties to the West continuing to fray, the idea of repositioning Turkey as the hub of a regional order within the post-Ottoman space will retain its appeal.

IRAN

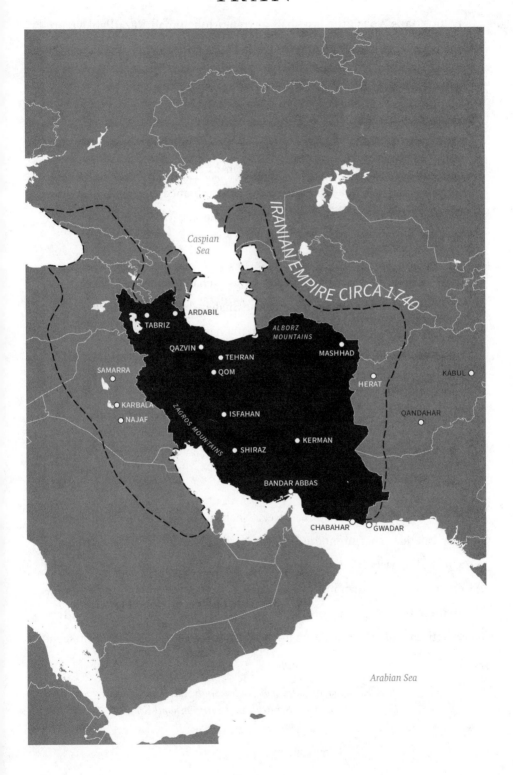

Caspian
Sea

IRANIAN EMPIRE CIRCA 1740

TABRIZ
ARDABIL
ALBORZ
MOUNTAINS
QAZVIN
TEHRAN
MASHHAD
SAMARRA
QOM
KABUL
HERAT
KARBALA
QANDAHAR
NAJAF
ZAGROS MOUNTAINS
ISFAHAN
KERMAN
SHIRAZ
BANDAR ABBAS
CHABAHAR
GWADAR

Arabian Sea

IN OCTOBER 1971, the last shah of Iran, Mohammad Reza Pahlavi, presided over an elaborate ceremony marking the 2,500th anniversary of the founding of Iran's empire by Cyrus the Great. Sparing no expense for this televised spectacle, Mohammad Reza Shah (1941–79) emphasized the connection between himself and Cyrus, and between the Achaemenid dynasty (549–336 B.C.E.) and his own Pahlavi dynasty, which, by the early 1970s, had established Iran as the dominant power in the Persian Gulf and a keystone of a U.S.-led alliance system. Speaking in front of the ruins of Cyrus's capital at Persepolis, Mohammad Reza Shah declared:

> O Cyrus! Great King, King of kings, Achaemenid King, King of the land of Iran [*Iranzamin*]. I, the Shahanshah of Iran, offer thee salutations from myself and from my nation. . . . At this moment, when the new Iran renews its bond with ancient pride, we all salute thee as the immortal hero of the history of Iran, the founder of the most ancient monarchy of the world, the great freedom giver, the precious child of mankind. . . .
>
> Cyrus! . . . Sleep in peace, for we are awake! And we always will be.[1]

A few years later, Mohammad Reza Shah went even further, adopting a new calendar that numbered the years since the foundation of the Achaemenid dynasty. This invocation of Cyrus and the Achaemenids, who had remained well known in the West thanks to the accounts preserved in the Hebrew Bible, was part of Mohammad Reza Shah's effort to portray Iran as both the inheritor of a long imperial tradition as well as a modern, secular state whose identity and history had more in common with Europe than the Middle East.

By the twentieth century, discussions of Iran's imperial legacy were associated with a critique of Islam, which nationalist thinkers portrayed as an Arab import that had ended the golden age represented by the Achaemenid and Sasanian (224–651 C.E.) dynasties such that, in the words of the twentieth-century historian Abdolhossein Zarrinkoub, "People long accustomed to listening to the murmuring of the Magi and the royal Sasanian anthems were now forced to listen to the grim chants of 'God is great' and the resounding calls of the muzzeins."[2] And since Cyrus had extended the frontiers of Persian rule far beyond the Iranian Plateau into the Balkans, Anatolia, Mesopotamia, and Central Asia, Mohammad Reza Shah's appeal to the Achaemenid legacy also suggested that he saw Iran as something greater than the medium-sized state left behind by the shrinkage of its frontiers in the nineteenth century in the face of Russian and British expansion.

Eight years after declaring himself heir to an empire founded two and a half millennia earlier, Mohammad Reza Shah was overthrown. What remained of Iran's traditional empire was replaced by a new kind of state, the Islamic Republic of Iran (*Jomhuri-ye Eslami-ye Iran*). Defined by a commitment to remake society, combat the influence of the United States (the "Great Satan"), spread Islamism, and assert its hegemony in the Middle East, the Islamic Republic frequently appears to be "more of a revolutionary movement than a country."[3]

From exile, the Islamic Republic's founder, Ayatollah Ruhollah Khomeini, was among the many observers—Iranian and foreign—who had mocked Mohammad Reza Shah's grandiloquent ceremony at Persepolis. Khomeini argued that "throughout a 2500 year history [Iran] has been under the rule of kings, kings who have brought it nothing but suffering and misery."[4] He condemned not only the waste of resources, but the very idea of commemorating Iran's imperial past. Khomeini and his supporters argued that the search for roots among Iran's ancient empires sought to divorce Iran from its Islamic, and particularly Shi'ite, identity, which it owed to the conquest and reunification carried out by Shah Ismail I (1501–24) and his successors in the Safavid dynasty (1501–1722).

Khomeini's rhetoric notwithstanding, the Islamic Republic did not break entirely from Iran's imperial past. After initially seeking to efface Iran's imperial legacy (one militant cleric threatened to bulldoze Cyrus's tomb), officials from the Islamic Republic began invoking imperial motifs and symbols during the bloody 1980–88 war with Saddam Hussein's Iraq. Imperial images have endured since the war to express pride in Iran's accomplishments as a civilization, supporting claims that Iran is entitled to a special status in the region and the world.

The Islamic Republic also inherited many structural legacies of Iran's old empires. As with Eurasia's other postimperial states, many of Iran's national and state borders are haphazard. Ancient Iran took its identity from the existence of a Persianate cultural realm stretching from the Euphrates to the Indus, defined by the use of Persian as a language of culture and administration and embodied in historical memory by the tales in Abolqasem Ferdowsi's tenth-century epic, the *Shahnahmeh*. With the coming of Islam, Iran became integrated with the wider Muslim world, but the "idea of Iran"—knowledge of its pre-Islamic history and a belief in Iran's imperial essence—endured, and with it the recognition of Iran as a distinct entity within the Muslim world.[5]

Iran's distinctive identity took on additional significance with the conversion to Shi'ism under the Safavids. Shi'ism helped set Iran off from its Sunni rivals, notably the Ottomans and Uzbeks, while establishing new connections with centers of Shi'ite learning outside Iran, including the shrine cities of Iraq, and Lebanon, which provided much of Safavid Iran's *ulema*. Since the Islamic Revolution, this Shi'ite dimension has become increasingly salient as a driver of Iranian foreign policy and imperial aspirations. While the Islamic Revolution initially appealed to Sunnis as well as Shi'as, the war with Iraq gave Iran's imperial ambitions a sectarian streak. Today, Tehran seeks to bring the Shi'ite populations of the Greater Middle East from Lebanon to Afghanistan under its influence, forging a Shi'ite counterweight to Sunni powers like Saudi Arabia, Egypt, and Turkey—even while continuing to support Sunni Islamists whose strategic objectives align with its own, such as the Gaza-based Hamas.

If Iran's traditional empires had been territorially fluid and ethnically diverse, the Islamic Republic also inherited a more recent tradition of Persian-centric nationalism, connected to Pahlavi efforts to replace Iran's imperial model of overlapping sovereignties—the "protected kingdoms of Iran (*Mamalek-e Mahruse-ye Iran*)"—with a Persian nation-state. This project of nation- and state-building required downplaying Iran's ethnic and linguistic heterogeneity, a process that sparked sometimes violent resistance. Areas with large minority populations, including Arab-majority Khuzestan, Azerbaijan, Baluchistan, Kurdistan, and the Turkmen region of Türkmen Sahra (Torkamansahra), all experienced uprisings at moments of political weakness at the center, notably when Allied forces occupied the country and deposed the German-leaning Reza Shah (1925–41) at the beginning of World War II, and again at the end of the war when Soviet occupation forces helped sustain short-lived Azeri and Kurdish statelets in northern Iran.

Resistance to assimilation later encouraged many non-Persians to support the 1979 revolution and fed a resurgence of unrest around Iran's frontiers in its aftermath. The Islamic Republic would nonetheless maintain much of the Pahlavis' Persian-centrism, even as the embrace of sectarianism further alienated non-Shi'ite Baluch, Kurds, Turkmen, and other minorities. Incapable of implementing a genuine "politics of difference" and lacking the resources to transform and integrate its periphery, the Islamic Republic administers its borderlands with securitized neglect.

The geographic imagination of the Islamic Republic has strong post-imperial echoes as well. Even though the larger Persianate world was rarely, if ever, under lasting Iranian control, the Safavids and their successors, including the Afsharid (1736–96), Zand (1751–94), and Qajar (1796–1925) dynasties, all regarded it as part of their legitimate patrimony. Only in the mid-nineteenth century, with the expansion of Russian and British power into the center of Eurasia, were Iranian claims decisively terminated. The erosion of Iranian influence in the Caucasus, Central Asia, and South Asia in the century and a half following the end of the Safavid dynasty shifted Iran's center of gravity from central Eurasia toward the Persian Gulf and the Levant, which remain the focal point for the Islamic Republic's foreign policy today. Many Iranian intellectuals nevertheless consider the territories on the Eurasian mainland comprising Iran's old empires part of Tehran's natural sphere of influence. Belief in the existence of a Greater Iran (*Iranshahr* or *Iranzamin*), which includes not only Mesopotamia but also the Caucasus and much of Central and South Asia, is often linked to nostalgia for the pre-Islamic age, and is used as a justification for Iran's claims to regional-power status.

Perhaps most important, the loss of Iran's imperial hinterlands feeds the Islamic Republic's narrative of victimization. In the nineteenth century, Iran lost much of its imperial periphery; in the twentieth century, the Iranian Plateau itself became the object of foreign imperialism, suffering intervention on multiple occasions and occupation during both world wars. Though the United States did not participate in the carve-up of Iranian territory, its collaboration with British ambitions to dominate Iran's energy industry—notably the British-inspired coup that ousted Prime Minister Mohammad Mosaddeq in 1953—and its support for the unpopular Mohammad Reza Shah thereafter—led many Iranians to associate the United States with the imperial powers that had earlier nursed territorial ambitions. The 1979 Islamic Revolution, with its combination of millenarianism, grievance, and appeals to thousands of years of Iranian greatness, is thus difficult to imagine absent the trauma accompanying Iran's loss of empire.

CHAPTER SEVEN

Iranian Identity and Iran's "Empire of the Mind"

S INCE THE ARAB CONQUEST and the coming of Islam, Iranian identity has been contested and plural. It comprises an indigenous culture based on the Persian language and Zoroastrianism, as well as an Islamic (and, since the sixteenth century, Shi'ite) identity tying it to the larger Islamic world—alongside territorial, linguistic, political, and other elements.[1] As in Turkey, the loss of a periphery inhabited by ethnic and religious minorities led nineteenth-century thinkers to begin reimagining Iran as a territorially delimited nation-state, a project that received renewed impetus with the replacement of the Qajar dynasty by the quasidynastic dictatorship of Reza Shah Pahlavi. The Pahlavis' attempt to transform Iran from a loose, culturally defined empire into something like a nation-state gave way in turn to the Islamic Republic, which emphasized the Islamic—and specifically Shi'ite—core of Iranian identity. Each of these shifts between different identity discourses accompanied radical upheavals.[2]

They also reconfigured the nature of Iran's relationship with its neighbors. Until the nineteenth century, the Persian language was used in chanceries from the Ottoman Empire in the west to Central Asia, Afghanistan, and India in the east. Scholarly and merchant networks tied Persian-speakers together everywhere from the shrine cities of Iraq to the Shi'ite courts of Bengal, with some of these regions becoming centers of Persianate culture in their own right.[3] Embodied most famously in

Ferdowsi's *Shahnahmeh*, this shared culture provided a reference point and set of symbols throughout territories comprising Iran in the pre-Islamic Sasanian era. The combination of different centers of Perso-Iranian culture and the continued influence of that culture far beyond the borders of modern-day Iran led Michael Axworthy to term Iran an "empire of the mind."[4] This "empire" was defined by a cultural idiom that encompassed a particular way of doing politics, a model of absolute kingship and dynastic inheritance with origins in the Sasanian era, along with a literate, urban bureaucratic class that maintained continuity during periods of upheaval.

Beginning around the turn of the nineteenth century, the shrinkage of Iranian frontiers, coupled with the decline of this larger Persianate world, prompted efforts to reimagine Iranians as a territorially bounded nation while emphasizing the "glorification of the country . . . centered on land."[5] As in Turkey, these efforts accelerated after the fall of the old empire and the establishment of a modernizing state. Much like Atatürk, Reza Shah sought to build a "territorially framed national identity," one which was "based on Persian identity and the idea of Aryanism."[6] The Pahlavi dynasty's promotion of a Persian-centric conception of Iranian identity at odds with the traditional notion of Iran as a pluralistic civilization bred resentment along Iran's non-Persian frontiers, leading many Azeris, Baluch, Kurds, and other minorities to support the revolution that overthrew the Pahlavis in 1979. Despite the aspiration to weld this Persian nation to the territory of contemporary Iran, moreover, the Pahlavis' glorification (and Persianization) of Iran's pre-Islamic empires implied belief in a privileged role for Iran in a Perso-Iranic world that included Kurds, Pashtuns, Tajiks, and others.

Without entirely abandoning this Persian-centric vision, the Islamic Republic replaced the Pahlavis' glorification of the nation with an emphasis on Shi'ism that was openly imperialistic—expansionary and heedless of both borders and nationality. For a time, its architects saw the revolution as not even Shi'ite so much as Islamic, calling on Muslims everywhere to take power from godless overlords in thrall to the non-Islamic West. While never abandoning this commitment to spreading the Islamic Revolution, Iran's clerical rulers had to make accommodations with the reality of Iranians' own ethno-cultural self-understanding, striking an uneasy balance between the Persian and the Islamic strands of Iranian identity.

They also had to navigate the Middle East's sectarian geopolitics, which the Islamic Revolution itself helped inflame. If the initial postrevolutionary period saw efforts to export the revolution throughout the Islamic world, by the first decade of the twenty-first century, Iranian foreign policy had an increasingly sectarian cast. While continuing to back Sunni movements with an anti-Israeli orientation like Hamas or Palestinian Islamic Jihad, Tehran threw its support behind Shi'ite groups during the wars in Iraq, Afghanistan, Yemen, and Syria, building up new Shi'ite proxies in the image and with the assistance of the Lebanese-based Hezbollah as part of its campaign of resistance against the "Domineering (or Arrogant) Powers" led by the United States.[7] That strategy relied upon organic connections among Shi'as on both sides of the historically fluid Iran-Iraq border, as well as on the prestige of Iranian religious authorities among foreign Shi'as in the wake of the Islamic Revolution.

It also entailed not only reconfiguration of the spatial limits of Iranian identity, but also the integration of Shi'as from different countries into a common political imaginary. Despite an enduring strain of pragmatism among Iran's foreign policy elite, the focus on Shi'ism as an organizing principle became linked with Tehran's ambitions for regional expansion, using patronage of Shi'ite communities in neighboring states as a tool for disrupting their politics and bringing them under Iranian influence. At the same time, the backlash within Iran against expensive interventions in Syria, Iraq, and elsewhere suggests that ordinary Iranians are not as willing to bear the costs of supporting foreign Shi'as as the ruling clerics would like. This backlash, like the ongoing confrontation between Iran and the United States, has not sufficed, however, to force Tehran to abandon its largely Shi'a-centric vision of regional order in the Middle East.

From "Empire of the Mind" to Persian Nation-State

To the extent historians have been able to reconstruct, "Iran" was initially a kind of ethnonym. The Achaemenid ruler Darius I (522–486 B.C.E.) described himself in the monumental inscription at his capital of Persepolis as "an Achaemenian, a Persian, son of a Persian, an Aryan [*ariya*], of Aryan stock."[8] Throughout the pre-Sasanian era, *ariya* appears to have described a group of people "aware of belonging to the one ethnic stock, speaking a common language, and having a religious tradition that centered on the cult of [the supreme Zoroastrian deity] Ahura Mazdā."[9] As Darius indicated, the Persians were one group of Aryans—specifically those from the Achaemenid homeland of Pars, or Persis—from which emerged the longstanding tradition of referring to Iran as "Persia" and all Iranians as "Persians."[10]

Applying a term from the sacred Zoroastrian text known as the *Avesta* for the mythical homeland of the *ariya*, the Sasanians designated the territory over which they ruled and worship of Ahura Mazda predominated as Iran (*Eran*).[11] Ardashir I Papagan (224–42), the first Sasanian ruler, is referred to on a relief carved to mark his investiture and on his coins as "Ardashir, King of Kings of Iran [*Ardashir shahan shah Eran*]," while Shapur I's (240–70) inscription of the subsequent generation replaces *Eran* with *Eranshahr* (Kingdom of Iran).[12] Since, moreover, the *ariyas*' homeland was held to be in Sistan, on the eastern periphery of the Iranian Plateau, the Sasanian adoption of the name for their kingdom suggested that Sasanian ambitions were not confined to Pars, but extended throughout regions where Zoroastrianism predominated.[13]

With the coming of Islam in the seventh century, usage of the terms *Iranshahr* and *Iran* declined. In part, the association of these terms with the old dynasty and with Zoroastrianism appears to have made them suspect in the early Islamic world.[14] While some Muslim authors, including Ferdowsi, continued referring to *Iranshahr* (and *Iranzamin*, which gradually replaced it), the terms *Fars*—that is, Pars, or Persia—and *al-Ajam*—originally an Arabic term for all non-Arabs—became increasingly common. Only under the Mongol Ilkhanate (1256–1335), which reunited much of the old Sasanian realm, did "Iran" again enter wide circulation as the name of the territory.[15] The later Safavids began referring to their empire as *Mamalek-e Mahruse-ye Iran* (protected kingdoms of Iran) in official correspondence and propaganda, thereby assigning a geographic basis to their rule and acknowledging the plurality and diversity of their realm.[16]

Only in the nineteenth century, with the shrinkage of Iran's borders and the emergence of Western-style nationalism, did Iranian intellectuals and, later, rulers begin speaking of Iranians as a nation and Iran—as opposed to the geographically fluid empires of the Safavids and Qajars—as a state.[17] The shrinkage of Qajar territory over the course of the nineteenth century precipitated efforts to mobilize Iran's Persian core behind European nationalist ideas to resist further onslaughts.[18] In line with prevailing European theories of race, late-Qajar intellectuals reconceptualized the heterogeneous and plural protected *kingdoms* of Iran as a unitary Persian nation-state, a project that would attain its apogee during the Pahlavi era. This process required overcoming the hostility of the *ulema* and many senior officials to emphasizing the will of the territorially restricted nation (*mellat*) over protection of the faith.

Late-Qajar reformers like the Armenian convert Malkum Khan took advantage of the ambiguity of Persian terminology, especially the concept of *mellat*—originally a religious community (like its Ottoman Turkish equivalent *millet*) that in the nineteenth century was repurposed along national lines—to maintain the support of the *ulema* for their campaign to reimagine Iran as a nation-state. While the Qajar court did not embrace the shift to nationalism, it did adopt some aspects of modern mass politics that were "crucial in laying the framework within which *the nation* could be imagined."[19] This shift toward mass politics and nationalization entailed an effort to Persianize (or "Farsify") Iran and its history, assigning an ethnic component to Iranian identity on top of competing discourses that emphasized religion, culture, or geography.[20] These steps provided a foundation for later efforts to think about Iran as a territorially contained nation-state rather than a fluid, heterogeneous empire.

Among the first to depict Iran as an ethnic nation, ironically, was the scholar and playwright Mirza Fath Ali Akhondzadeh (Akhundov)—a resident of the Russian Caucasus (and sometime Russian official) whose first language was Azeri.[21] Akhondzadeh portrayed Iranians locked in an enduring struggle with an Arab other whose introduction of Islam, he argued, was responsible for Iran's backwardness. Akhondzadeh pointed to the stories in the *Avesta* and the *Shahnahmeh* to assert that an Iranian nation—what Akhondzadeh termed the *mellat-e Iran*—had existed for thousands of years, in contrast not only to the "lizard-eating" Arab conquerors, but also to the Turkic Qajars, both of whom he blamed for Iran's nineteenth-century backwardness.[22]

A more explicit invocation of a racial basis for Iranian identity came from Akhondzadeh disciple Mirza Aqa Khan Kermani. Drawing on the work of European scholars such as Ernest Renan and Joseph Arthur de Gobineau, Kermani sought to differentiate the contributions of "Aryans" from their allegedly inferior "Semitic" neighbors, which, in the Iranian case, primarily meant Arabs.[23] The polarization between "Aryan" and "Semitic" provided a pseudoscientific basis for criticizing the Arab conquest and the subsequent conversion of Iran to Islam, and for locating in the pre-Islamic past a lost golden age.[24] Kermani argued that Iran's decline since the coming of Islam was the result of miscegenation with the Arab conquerors, and that "whenever I touch a branch of the ugly disposition of Iranians, I find its seed to be planted by Arabs."[25] With Akhondzadeh, Kermani was instrumental in what Kashani-Sabet calls the "glorification of the country . . . centered on land," describing the territory of Iran as a homeland (*vatan*) that embodied the history and culture of the Iranian nation.[26]

This focus on history, culture, and land became central to the Pahlavis' state-building project. Soon after taking power, Reza Shah embarked on a campaign to impose a uniform Persian identity—even though Reza Shah's own father was Mazandarani and his mother from a Georgian immigrant family. As in the new Turkish Republic, Reza Shah promoted a narrative of "common racial ancestry, linguistic affinity, shared mythology and certain stereotyped portrayals of minorities" that continues to inform nationalist thinking in the Islamic Republic.[27] It suggested that all Iranians belonged to a common "nation (*mellat*)," and was part of Reza Shah's ambition to replace the heterogeneous, ever-shrinking *Mamalek-e Mahruse-ye Iran* of the Qajars with a unified, territorially bounded "Sublime State of Iran (*Dowlat-e Aliyye-ye Iran*)." This "sublime state" was to be a nation-state of "Persian-speaking Shi'ite Iranian people" whose loyalties focused on their state, rather than tribal, religious, or ethnic solidarities.[28]

Reza Shah's Persianization campaign also helped mark off the Iranian state from its neighbors, many of which—including Turkey, Iraq, and Bahrain, following in the wake of nineteenth-century British India—were in the process of expunging Persian influence from their own languages. This simultaneous Persianization of Iran and decline of the wider Persianate world contributed to a territorialization of Iran at odds with many nineteenth-century nationalists' interest in using a shared Persianate culture to extend Iranian influence outward.[29] The emphasis on Iran's Persian identity continued under Mohammad Reza Shah, whose ascension coincided with the suppression of separatist revolts in both Azerbaijan and Kurdistan, and whose so-called White Revolution oversaw a dramatic expansion of education that spread Persian literacy and a reading of history emphasizing Iran's ancient heritage and national unity.[30]

The parallel campaigns of nation-building in Iran and its neighbors severed links tying them together and contributed to the forgetting of Iran's imperial past. Nevertheless, Persian remains an official language of Afghanistan (where it is known as Dari); under the name Tajik, it is also the main language of Tajikistan and an important minority language in Uzbekistan. Smaller numbers of (nondiaspora) Persian-speakers also reside in Kyrgyzstan, Pakistan, western China, and Azerbaijan. Related Iranic languages such as Ossetian, Kurdish, Pashto, and Baluchi are spoken across large swathes of the Caucasus, the Middle East, and South Asia, leading some Iranian nationalists to see speakers of these languages as at least proto-Iranians, and part of a Greater Iranian nation.

The Nation in the Islamic Republic

In the first years after the Islamic Revolution, the new regime sought to deemphasize the nationalist narrative promoted by the Pahlavis, focusing instead on the unity of the *umma*, or community of Muslim believers (Sunni as well as Shi'ite), both inside and outside Iran. The denigration of nationality as a category was a particular priority for Ayatollah Khomeini, who rarely even used the term "Iran." Rather, Khomeini viewed the idea of an Iranian nation as a Western construct aimed at keeping Muslims divided and as an obstacle to exporting the Islamic Revolution. Khomeini argued that in principle "Islam is against nationality" and that "our country includes all the Muslim world."[31] This was an explicitly imperial vision, even if its geographic parameters were not those of Iran's historic empires so much as the Muslim world as a whole.

The Islamic Republic nonetheless moved to invoke nationalist themes as a tool of popular mobilization during the 1980–88 Iran-Iraq War, when, to its chagrin, most Iraqi Shi'as remained loyal to Saddam Hussein. While export of the revolution remained a pillar of the Islamic Republic's foreign policy, officials quickly redefined the events of 1979 as an *Iranian* Islamic Revolution.[32] The influential Islamist thinker Morteza Motahhari, cofounder of the Combatant Clergy Association and a close associate of Khomeini, cited medieval Persian poetry to argue that Islam and Iranian nationhood were mutually compatible, while suggesting that Iranians embraced Shi'ism in part because of the ethnic discrimination they faced at the hands of the Sunni Arabs. Motahhari argued:

> As a principle, Islam, which is a universal creed, does not raise the issue of language. It never occurred to the Iranians even in their wildest flights of imagination that the reviving and speaking of the Persian language amounts to opposition to Islam—nor should they have imagined such a thing.[33]

Even Khomeini began paying tribute to the Iranian "fatherland" and "nation" to encourage resistance to the Iraqis, and noted that Persian was "the language of the revolution."[34] Revised textbooks assigned the Iranians a unique role within the Islamic world, celebrating "national" heroes like the Persian warrior Abu Muslim al-Khorasani—who led the rebellion against the Arab Umayyads—for their resistance to "foreign" domination. They also glorified Persian dynasties from outside the borders of contemporary Iran, such as the Samanids—who established a Persian-speaking dynasty in Transoxiana after the Arab conquest—for maintaining "Iranian" statehood while driving out the forces of the "tyrannical" Abbasid caliphate.[35] Such appropriation of Persian states from outside the Iranian Plateau hinted at the more expansive underpinnings of this approach to Iranian identity.

This synthesis of Islam and Persian-Iranian nationalism has become the dominant strand in the official identity propagated by the Islamic Republic, one that the state deploys instrumentally and in shifting combinations. Officials, up to and including Khomeini's successor as supreme leader, Ayatollah Ali Khamenei, contrast Iran, with its ancient culture and legacy of imperial achievements, with what they see as the less distinguished and less historically rooted Arab states, notably Saudi Arabia and the Gulf emirates, whose oil wealth has raised them to a level of prosperity and influence many Iranians regard as unwonted.[36] Khamenei celebrates the traditional Persian new year holiday of *Nowruz*, which he describes as a fusion of Iranian and Islamic traditions, and appeals to the "Iranian nation" in his calls to resist U.S. aggression.[37] These views have spread among the Shi'ite clergy as well, where Iran's "7000-year civilization, cultural discourse, and cultural impact" reinforce claims to exceptionalism.[38]

Invocations of the Persian "national" past also allow Iran to cultivate linkages to other states and peoples with a Persian component of their identity, notably Afghanistan and Tajikistan.[39] This trend was especially pronounced during the presidency of Mahmoud Ahmadinejad (2005–13), a populist-nationalist who sought to appropriate Iran's ancient past both to challenge the clerical establishment's supremacy and to justify an expansive foreign policy vision. Reflecting his own brand of nationalism tinged with Shi'ite millenarianism, Ahmadinejad attempted to fuse imperial and Islamic themes. He made a habit of celebrating *Nowruz* abroad, usually in Afghanistan or Tajikistan, emphasizing the unity of what remained of the Persianate world. During a 2010 ceremony marking the loan of the terracotta cylinder recording Cyrus's legal decrees from the British Museum, Ahmadinejad conferred an Iranian *keffiyeh* (a scarf associated with the Basij militia) on a Cyrus impersonator.[40] Ahmadinejad's top adviser, meanwhile, drew a link between Cyrus and the prophets to incorporate both into a narrative of Iranian exceptionalism.[41] Despite its overall hostility to civil society, Tehran also allows a series of nationalist, or "Iranist," civil society groups to operate. The most influential, known as the Cultural Society of Greater Iran (*Anjoman-e Farhangi-ye Iranzamin*, or Afraz), congratulated the "Iranian" people on their election of the Kurd (and thus speaker of an Iranic language) Jalal Talabani as president of Iraq in 2005.[42]

Islamic Republic and Islamic Empire

If appeals to a wider Persian identity allow Tehran to assert a claim on the loyalty of Persian-speakers outside the country, the centrality of Islam and, particularly, Shi'ism to the Islamic Republic's self-conception underpins an even more expansive and, at times, revolutionary approach to foreign policy, albeit one that is mostly directed at Mesopotamia, the Persian Gulf, and the Levant, rather than Iran's postimperial periphery in Eurasia. The ideology fueling Khomeini's seizure of power contributed to a strand of permanent revolution in Iranian foreign policy that entails not only confrontation with the United States and Israel (the "Lesser Satan"), but rejection of the existing international system as such. Like Napoleon and Trotsky, Khomeini couched his revolution in universal themes, declaring in a November 1979 sermon that "an Islamic movement, therefore, cannot limit itself to any particular country, not even to the Islamic countries; it is the continuation of the revolution by the prophets."[43]

The Islamic Republic is a hybrid of the wholly Islamic state envisioned by Khomeini and a republic with democratic trappings. While it has an elected president and parliament (Majles), the *rahbar*—literally "guide" or supreme leader—and leading members of the *ulema* hold the most important levers of power. The role of the supreme leader, and ultimately the *ulema* as a whole, is based on Khomeini's concept of the "Absolute Guardianship of the Jurist (*velayet-e mutlaqa-ye faqih*)," under which the authority of the cleric appointed supreme leader "is the most important divine laws [*sic*] and has priority over all other ordinances of the law . . . even praying, fasting and Hajj."[44] The supreme leader acts effectively as a "fourth branch of the government, which [is] stronger than the other three," and with its own set of parallel institutions, including the Islamic Revolutionary Guard Corps (IRGC).[45] Khomeini's notion of absolute *velayat-e faqih* positions the supreme leader above not just the political system but also, in theory, the remaining *ulema* both inside and outside Iran. The implementation of absolute *velayat-e faqih* in Iran thus serves as a prop for the Islamic Republic's ambitions to act as the center of a larger Shi'ite bloc.

From its origins in opposition to the domination of the Sunni caliphs, Shi'ism has long been entwined with notions of millenarian revolution, which figures like Safavid founder Ismail Safavi and Khomeini himself reinterpreted for their own ends.⁴⁶ This revolutionary potential has come to the fore during periods when alternative centers of power and legitimacy were weak, as during the last years of the Safavid, Qajar, and Pahlavi dynasties. The revolutionary dynamic stems too from the role of the Shi'ite *ulema* as an independent political force with no analogue in Eurasia's other great empires, where secular authorities were more effective at gaining ascendancy over their respective religious establishments. Unsurprisingly, the clergy's assumption of temporal power in the Islamic Republic gave voice to a maximalist, revolutionary approach to foreign policy that refers to divine law, rather than *raison d'état* or the well-being of Iranian citizens, as its principal reference point.⁴⁷

Iran's conversion to Shi'ism was itself the product of conquest by a revolutionary movement. After the fall of Tabriz in the autumn of 1501, Ismail Safavi, leader of the *Safawiyya* dervish order, mounted the pulpit of the congregational mosque, proclaiming himself head of a new dynasty and announcing that his realm would henceforth embrace Twelver Shi'ism. According to the chronicler Hasan Beg Rumlu, Ismail demanded that Sunni practice cease on pain of decapitation, adding that the Friday prayer should henceforth be read out in the name of the twelve Shi'ite Imams.⁴⁸ A later source claimed that when Ismail was told that two-thirds of the inhabitants of Tabriz were Sunnis, he drew his sword and stated that he would kill anyone who resisted conversion himself.⁴⁹

As Michael Mazzaoui notes, with the adoption of Shi'ism, "Iran became an identifiable entity" for the first time since the Arab conquest.⁵⁰ Conversion also reinforced Iran's isolation from its Sunni neighbors and, especially in the "exaggerated (Arabic *ghuluww*)" form espoused by Shah Ismail, provided a justification for imperial expansion.⁵¹ The early Safavids attempted to spread their ideology further afield through conquests in the Caucasus, eastern Anatolia, and Transoxiana. Catastrophic defeats to the Uzbeks at Ghijduvan in 1512 and the Ottomans at Chaldiran in 1514 thus limited the spread of both Safavid power and the revolutionary doctrines associated with the nomadic, mostly Turkic-speaking adherents of the *Safawiyya* known as Qizilbash (literally "red heads," from the red caps signifying their affiliation with the *Safawiyya*).⁵² These defeats also helped push Safavid Shi'ism away from its revolutionary *ghuluww* origins and encouraged Ismail's successors to focus more on consolidating Shi'ism at home.⁵³ Given the absence of native clerics trained in Shi'ite jurisprudence, Ismail's son Tahmasp I (1524–76) recruited *ulema* from Arab Shi'ite areas like Bahrain and southern Lebanon, helping bind Iran to the wider Shi'ite world.

The most notable Arab jurist in Iran during Tahmasp's reign was the Lebanese Ali al-Muhaqqiq al-Karaki al-Amili, who developed several key principles of jurisprudence that influenced the theorists of the twentieth-century Islamic Revolution—notably the idea that Shi'ite jurists (*mojta-heds*) should rule on a wide range of political and social matters through the practice of *ijtihad*, or critical reasoning.[54] Al-Karaki further empha-sized that while the shah's legitimacy rested on fulfilling his duty as a just ruler, ultimate religious authority resided with the clergy.[55] Al-Karaki's grandson-in-law, Mir Damad, went further, referring to the jurist rather than the shah as the "just ruler" and emphasizing the concept of *ijtihad mutlaq* (absolute, or infallible, interpretation not subject to question by other authorities).[56] This approach helped establish the clergy not only as an arbiter of political decision-making, but as the source of political authority in its own right. It also facilitated growing clerical influence at moments of weakness, which bred intolerance toward non-Shi'as and instability around Iran's mostly Sunni periphery. The growth of clerical authority, and with it persecution of non-Shi'as, was a major factor in the rebellion of the (Sunni) Abdali Pashtuns, who in 1722 occupied Isfahan and ended the Safavid dynasty, and in the upheaval of the late Qajar era.

With the Ottoman seizure of Baghdad and the holy cities of Najaf, Karbala, Kazemayn, and Samarra (known collectively as the *Atabat-e ali-yat*, or just *Atabat*, literally "sacred thresholds") in 1638, Iran lost control over the most important centers of Shi'ite learning. With the loss of the *Atabat*, the Safavids and their successors would look to build up indig-enous institutions like the seminaries at Qom and the shrine to the Eighth Imam, Ali al-Ridha (Ali Reza), in Mashhad to bolster their religious legiti-macy.[57] Beyond the reach of Safavid, Qajar, and Pahlavi rulers, meanwhile, clerics in the *Atabat* developed theological ideas out of favor in Iran. They also acted as tribunes, criticizing Iranian monarchs and providing refuge for dissident Iranian clerics, among them some of the key figures in the Iranian Constitutional Revolution (1905–11), as well as Khomeini and his followers in the 1960s and 1970s.[58]

While leading clerics in the *Atabat* had rejected Khomeini's doctrine of Absolute Guardianship and opposed the clergy's seizure of power, after 1979 the Iraqi Ba'athist regime persecuted them as a potential fifth col-umn. Saddam's fall therefore created new opportunities for Iran to mold the institutional bases of Shi'ite power in Iraq. Since 2003, Shi'ite parties have held the balance of power in Baghdad (Iraq's post-Saddam prime ministers have all been Shi'as), and Najaf has once again come to rival Qom as a center of Shi'ite piety and pilgrimage—thanks in part to the prestige of its leading cleric, the Iranian-born Ayatollah Ali Sistani.[59] For many non-Iranian Shi'as, Sistani and his followers in Najaf represent a more authentic scholarly tradition, one untainted by the controversies surrounding the Islamic Revolution—or the disputed circumstances surrounding Khamenei's elevation to the rank of ayatollah and the position of supreme leader following Khomeini's death.[60]

Tehran has consequently looked to southern Iraq's Shi'ite heartland as "something akin to Russia's concept of 'the near abroad,'" where it could secure itself from hostile forces and cement its status as a major regional power.[61] While Khamenei emphasized that Iraqis of all sects are "intimate brothers of Iran who enjoy [a] rooted, historical relationship with the Iranian people," in practice, the Shi'as who comprise a plurality of Iraq's population have been the focus of Iranian policy.[62] Tehran has sponsored a range of Shi'ite parties and movements in post-Saddam Iraq, including the Dawa Party, the Kata'ib Hezbollah Party-*cum*-militia, and especially, the Badr Organization (*Munazzama Badr*). Established in the 1980s by Iraqi Shi'ite exiles in Iran as the military wing of the Supreme Council of the Islamic Revolution in Iraq (SCIRI), the Badr Organization is closely integrated with the IRGC and commanded by Iranian officers. After Saddam's ouster, the Badr Organization transformed itself into a political party that gave Tehran a foothold in Iraq's electoral politics, while many of its members joined the Iraqi military and security forces.[63] Another important beneficiary of Iranian patronage was the militant cleric Muqtada al-Sadr, whose hardline stance and calls for the clergy to play a dominant role challenged Sistani's quietist approach, though Iran also maintained direct channels to Sistani, who favored enshrining Shi'ite political power through elections.

By balancing between the competing Shi'ite voices in Iraq, Iran established itself as a key power broker. Khamenei was able to appeal to Sistani to call for an end to the U.S. military's siege of Sadr and his allies in Najaf, which all three feared could damage the *ulema*'s prestige in the event of a bloody denouement.[64] Similarly, Sistani's June 2014 *fatwa* calling on Iraqi Shi'as to take up arms against ISIS provided what Khamenei termed a "divine inspiration" that allowed Iran to claim a leading role in organizing the anti-ISIS resistance inside Iraq.[65] Benefiting from the legitimacy conferred by Sistani's *fatwa*, Iranian troops under Quds Force commander Qassem Soleimani organized Shi'ite fighters into the Iraqi Popular Mobilization Forces (PMF), which were instrumental in beating back the ISIS threat to Baghdad. Many Iraqis recognized, though, that

Iran's influence over the PMF posed a threat to Iraq's sovereignty and the independence of the Iraqi clerical authorities.[66] Following the deaths of Soleimani and the PMF's top leader, Abu Mahdi al-Muhandis, in a January 2020 U.S. drone strike near Baghdad, Sistani gave his blessing to efforts to sever the PMF's tie to Iran by subordinating it to the Iraqi Ministry of Defense.[67]

Nor is Sistani alone in opposing Tehran's claim of a protectorate over Iraqi Shi'as. Notwithstanding the outpouring of grief over Soleimani's assassination, the roles of the PMF, the IRGC, and Iranian clergy have been sources of controversy and protests within Iraq. Perhaps the most sensitive issue centers on the succession to the elderly Sistani. Iran has made no secret of its desire to see Sistani replaced by a more pliable cleric, preferably one adhering to the doctrine of Absolute Guardianship, and who would thus defer in spiritual and temporal matters to the supreme leader.[68] Until his 2018 death, one of the most widely discussed candidates was the Iraq-born Ayatollah Mahmoud Hashemi Shahroudi, a one-time student of Khomeini who headed the Iranian judiciary and served on the Guardian Council. Shahroudi's state-backed efforts to build up a patronage network in Najaf sparked tensions with Iraqi Shi'as, who saw him as an agent of Iranian influence and a Khomeinist hardliner whose views were at odds with Najaf's quietist tradition.[69]

Appeals to Shi'ite solidarity are an important tool of Iranian foreign policy outside Iraq as well. Critics allege that Iran's goal is to establish a "Shi'ite Crescent" from Lebanon in the north to Yemen in the south, with Shi'a-dominated governments that look to Tehran for patronage and support.[70] While sometimes exaggerated, these claims reflect the fact that with the failure of attempts to spread the Islamic Revolution, Tehran has increasingly relied on regional Shi'as as a source of influence within neighboring states.[71] Outside Iraq, though, Iran's approach is less about coopting religious authority and more about promoting sectarian movements that look to Tehran for support and inspiration. By posing a threat to political order, such movements undermine the sovereignty of their host states and provide a platform for Iranian power projection. In places where such groups are active, borders and other aspects of sovereignty are compromised, as Iranian proxies move back and forth outside the effective jurisdiction of the states in which they operate.

The most powerful of Iran's Shi'ite proxies is Hezbollah, set up by the IRGC in the early 1980s in the wake of Israel's invasion of southern Lebanon. By the mid-2000s, Hezbollah had entrenched itself in the

Lebanese state and security institutions, effectively holding a veto over decision-making in Beirut. It also was instrumental in expelling Israeli forces and fought Israel to a draw in a 2006 conflict. Though in many ways autonomous of direct Iranian control, Hezbollah adheres to the doctrine of Absolute Guardianship, regards Ayatollah Khamenei as its overall leader, and remains closely connected with senior Iranian clerics, who use it to promote Khomeinist-style politicized Shi'ism in Lebanon. It also provides a military check on Israel and acts as a force multiplier by training and assisting similar Shi'ite forces throughout the region.[72] Whatever its own ambitions, Hezbollah "is not just a power unto itself, but is one of the most important instruments" in Iran's drive for regional supremacy, particularly valuable for giving this campaign an Arab face in light of concerns that an Iran-centric regional order would entail Persian domination.[73]

In that sense, Hezbollah is both a reflection of and a contributor to Iran's project of reshaping regional order by emphasizing sectarian over national or territorial loyalties. Since the U.S. invasion of Iraq, Iran has helped transform Hezbollah from an intra-Lebanese force into the nucleus of a wider struggle for influence throughout the Middle East, a Shi'ite "foreign legion" that supports Iran's ambition to create a regional Shi'ite bloc centered on Tehran.[74] The Islamic Republic used Hezbollah to train proxies in postinvasion Iraq, and in subsequent years Hezbollah fighters and Shi'ite militias trained by Hezbollah have participated in conflicts from Syria to Yemen (and have established toeholds for illicit business as far afield as South America).[75]

Hezbollah has been particularly visible in the Syrian conflict, which Tehran joined in large part to maintain the ability to ship weapons to Hezbollah through Syrian territory. Along with the Syrian army, Hezbollah fighters have borne much of the brunt of the fighting on behalf of Bashar al-Assad (though Iran's army has suffered upward of 2,000 casualties as well). Among its other consequences, the conflict helped Hezbollah reverse what had been a longstanding dependence on Damascus and, in the process, brought Assad's Syria further under Iranian tutelage. Hezbollah's success at infiltrating and controlling Lebanese politics, resisting Israeli military pressure, and turning the tide in Syria has made it an influential player throughout the Middle East, and led Iran to establish Hezbollah-style militias in Iraq, Syria, Bahrain, Yemen, Pakistan, and elsewhere.[76] Compared to the Arab Middle East, the Shi'ite dimension of Iranian foreign policy has been less pronounced in Iran's postimperial periphery in the Caucasus, Central Asia, and South Asia, where Shi'ite populations are more dispersed and comprise a smaller share of the population—and where Tehran has largely deferred to Russian leadership.

A Shi'ite Empire?

The Islamic Republic's emphasis on a Shi'ite identity as the basis for post-imperial expansion recalls the early Safavids, but is in other respects a departure from recent Iranian history—as well as from the pan-Islamic ideals in vogue in the early years of the Islamic Revolution. While Iran's own population is heavily Shi'a, the valorization of a sectarian over an ethnic or civic approach to Iranian identity is divisive, contributing to the almost perpetual volatility of Iran's non-Shi'ite borderlands. It is also a source of tension with even Shi'ite Iranians who reject a sectarian outlook or chafe at the restrictions on daily life associated with clerical rule.

In foreign policy terms, revolutionary Shi'ism has become a powerful lever for Iran to intervene in Iraq, Lebanon, and Bahrain with their large Shi'ite populations, as well as among disaffected Shi'ite minorities in Syria (whose Alawites are generally considered Shi'ite), Saudi Arabia, Yemen, Afghanistan, Pakistan, and elsewhere. As most of these states have a history of anti-Shi'ite oppression, Iranian appeals have resonated. For that reason, many non-Shi'as view Iranian-backed Shi'ite movements as a threat to the social order. One consequence has been growing sectarian conflict throughout the Middle East, or the sectarianization of existing conflicts. Almost inevitably, Sunni and Western rivals depict Shi'ite political movements—armed or not—as Iranian proxies. As with Yemen's Houthis, such accusations can become self-fulfilling when officials ignore legitimate grievances and see Iranian ayatollahs behind every public demonstration.[77]

This wager on Shi'ite grievance represents a deliberate strategy for enshrining Iran's standing as a regional power by destabilizing Sunni-ruled rivals and establishing pro-Iranian groups as kingmakers in local politics. It is a consciously imperial strategy in that it transcends borders and seeks to negate the importance of ethnic or civic conceptions of identity in the process of advancing Tehran's push for status: as far as Tehran is concerned, an Iraqi Shi'a should be Shi'ite first and Iraqi (or Arab) second—and, in being Shi'ite, should look to Iran as his or her primary source of political and religious inspiration. This approach rests on an understanding of Iranian identity defined by not just Shi'ism, but specifically Shi'ism as filtered through the Islamic Revolution and the thought of

Khomeini. The vision of the Islamic Republic as the nucleus of a transnational Shi'ite movement is most visible in Tehran's mobilization of Shi'as from one state as its proxies in another, not just with Hezbollah but also in the dispatch of fighters from Iraq's Badr Organization and recruitment of Afghan Shi'as for the so-called Fatemiyoun Division fighting for the Assad regime in Syria.[78]

As with Turkey's emphasis on Sunnism as the foundation for appealing to the populations of neighboring states, Iran's appeal to Shi'ism can stoke a backlash among those it is trying to recruit. Unlike Turkey, for which Ottoman-style Sunnism provides the framework for a (theoretically) inclusive regional order, Iran encourages disruption and stokes sectarian rivalries as a geopolitical tool, at times sparking a backlash among foreign Shi'as who reject the Islamic Republic's claim to speak on their behalf. Anti-Iranian protests have become a regular occurrence among Iraqi Shi'as (though less so elsewhere where Iranian influence has a more militant character). In one highly symbolic instance, Iraqi protestors burned down the Iranian consulate in the holy city of Najaf in late 2019.[79]

If Turkey's regional vision emphasizes integrating a collection of multiethnic, multiconfessional states united by a common Ottoman-Sunni heritage, Iran's vision is more about creating a unified community of Shi'as sharing the politicized faith of the Islamic Revolution and loyal above all to the Islamic Republic. In that sense it is closer to Russia's notion of a "Russian World," that is, citizens of other states who maintain a cultural or (in this case) religious connection to the postimperial center of gravity.

These regional ambitions and the disruptions they cause have positioned Iran at the center of the Middle East's complex geopolitical and sectarian rivalries, opposed by Sunni-majority states like Saudi Arabia (and, in a more complex manner, Turkey) as well as the United States. As Iran has found itself drawn deeper into sectarian conflicts in Syria and Yemen, it has also encountered a growing backlash from ordinary Iranians, who resent the scale of outlays on these foreign adventures as life in Iran grows more difficult.[80] In this backlash, which at times emphasizes symbols and language associated with the pre-1979 era, the Islamic Republic faces a population whose own sense of self is more nationalist than the ruling clerics would like, less religious (overall religiosity appears to have dropped significantly since 1979), and immune to the lure of imperial grandeur or Shi'ite millenarianism offered by the authorities.

CHAPTER EIGHT

Iran's Borderlands

The Non-Persian Periphery

AS WITH EURASIA's other postimperial states, Iran maintains an ambivalent relationship to the pluralism of empire, especially in borderlands with significant non-Persian populations. With the nineteenth-century shrinkage of Qajar Iran's territory, frontier regions turned into sites of disorder and strategic competition, with Turkmen incursions in the northeast, instability on the Afghan frontier in the southeast, and banditry among the Kurds and Arabs along the Qajar-Ottoman border all linked to the ambitions of rival powers. The intersection of local disorder with foreign intervention was both cause and consequence of the decline of Qajar authority. It became critical during both world wars, in which Iran was an unwilling participant, as the armies of foreign powers marched back and forth across Iranian territory, manipulating the aspirations of Iran's inhabitants as they went.

The continued volatility of Iran's borderlands is in part a legacy of this history of foreign powers using the discontent of ethnic and religious minorities to further their territorial ambitions at Iranian expense. The result, under the Pahlavis as under the Islamic Republic, has been a vicious circle of neglect, repression, and dissent. For the most part, though, peripheral unrest in Iran lacks a separatist dimension. From Azerbaijan in the northwest to Baluchistan in the southeast, Iranian ethnic and religious minorities agitate for greater rights and local autonomy, or around local issues (like the environmental degradation of Lake Urmia for Azeris), but rarely for independence. One important reason for the comparative absence of separatism is the durability of traditional understandings of Iran as a cultural and geographical expression, developed over the course of the twentieth century into a "settled territorial understanding" of the state.[1] Even as the majority holding power in the center has sought to make Iran at once more Persian and more Shi'ite, this cultural and territorial understanding helps non-Shi'as and non-Persians continue to perceive themselves as Iranians.

Unlike the role played by Ottoman Istanbul or pre-Petrine Moscow as nuclei for imperial expansion, Iran's geographic peripheries were sometimes politically central: the Safavids' first capital was in Azerbaijan (Tabriz), while Nader Shah Afshar's (1736–47) was in eastern Iran, or Khorasan (Mashhad), before the Qajars firmly established Tehran as the capital in 1792.[2] The ability of dynasties like the Azeri-Turkic Safavids and Qajars or the Turkmen Afsharids to hold together the diverse collection of peoples and territories comprising the "protected kingdoms of Iran" required maintaining a careful balance among different ethnic and religious communities. Around the periphery, acknowledgment of Iranian suzerainty was rarely guaranteed, especially among nomadic tribal populations like the Turkmen and the Baluch, where the central government "could only extend its authority . . . through the tribal khans and their subjects."[3] Diversity, as well as the problem of distance and the weakness of Iran's bureaucratic apparatus relative to its imperial rivals, all meant that Safavid and Qajar administration required a high degree of negotiation with local populations.

Borderlands in the Caucasus, Mesopotamia, and Khorasan were also sites of contestation with imperial rivals. By the Qajar era, Iran was the weakest of the Eurasian empires, and the nineteenth century saw it progressively cede its claims in these regions to the Russians and the British. Yet in contrast to the Ottoman Empire—whose shrinkage was accompanied by massive population movements that helped disentangle peripheries from the shrunken imperial core—Iran's losses entailed less ethnic and religious cleansing, leaving behind closely related populations on either side of the new borders. These cross-border connections remained a vulnerability well into the Pahlavi era, especially when foreign troops occupied Iranian territory during the two world wars.

This nexus of separatism and foreign intervention left Iranian governments, including that of the Islamic Republic, extremely sensitive about the vulnerability of Iran's non-Persian borderlands. While the Islamic Republic accepts in principle the diversity of Iran's population, it prioritizes unity and often fails to live up to its own commitments to respect cultural and religious pluralism. Khomeini set the tone, arguing that, while the differences between Persians, Kurds, Baluch, and others was real, "in Islam, race is fundamentally not an issue," and that the Islamic Republic's emphasis on religious solidarity was an antidote to both the Persian-centrism of the Pahlavis and the minority nationalism that threatened Iran's territorial integrity in the first years of the Islamic Republic.[4] This appeal to a supranational Iranian identity emphasized not only the role of Islam as a unifying factor (which is problematic for Iran's non-Muslim inhabitants), but also the long history of Iranian unity.[5]

In practice, though, the combination of religious prejudice and anxiety about territorial integrity has left the Islamic Republic with unstable borderlands on all sides. The mostly Sunni regions of Kurdistan, Türkmen Sahra, and Baluchistan suffer from underdevelopment and both cultural and religious discrimination. The problem is not just sectarian, though, as Shi'ite-majority Azerbaijan and Khuzestan are volatile too, in part because of concerns about their potential for loyalties divided with neighboring states. Tehran's inability to find a consensual basis for administering its borderlands remains a source of uncertainty, even if minorities' acceptance of the historical "idea of Iran" means that separatism is the exception rather than the rule.

From Protected Kingdoms to Sublime State

As in Eurasia's other great empires, Safavid and Qajar rule over the Iranian periphery remained largely indirect. In many places, the Safavids left in place native rulers who simultaneously served as viceroys, or *walis*, of the shah. The four *walis*—in Arabestan (modern Khuzestan), Georgia, Lorestan, and Kurdistan—were regarded as the seniormost "amirs of the frontier," hereditary rulers who acknowledged Safavid suzerainty but were effectively independent.[6] Peacetime Safavid rule in the eastern frontier zone appeared more direct, in that it was exerted through officials of the shah, including the crown prince, who until the reign of Abbas I (1588–1629) was normally governor of Khorasan. Yet this rule was often nominal because of the difficulties projecting power across the region's great distances and unforgiving geography. Dynastic authority over the tribal Baluch, Kurds, Lurs, Bakhtiyaris, Qashqa'is, Arabs, and Turkmen in particular was close to nonexistent.[7]

With limited administrative capacity and questionable legitimacy from the perspective of the Shi'ite *ulema*, the Qajars were "Shadows of the Almighty whose writ often did not extend beyond the capital; . . . sovereigns who sanctified the feet of their thrones but lacked the instruments of enforcing their decisions; [*shahanshahs*] who ruled not other kings, as they claimed, but through . . . tribal chiefs, local notables, and religious leaders."[8] They ruled the periphery of their empire by appointing the shah's relatives as provincial governors in the four provinces of Azerbaijan, Fars, Kerman-Sistan, and Khorasan (a fifth, centered on Tehran was formed in the late nineteenth century). These provincial governors established their own courts and maintained extensive autonomy from the center, but their authority was subject to the acquiescence of local tribes. To ensure a degree central of control, some senior officials in the provinces were appointed by the shah rather than the governor, including provincial viziers and chief financial officers (*mostawfi*s). Nonetheless, it was up to the provincial governors to collect and remit taxes to the center. The prevalence of tax farming created incentives for extracting the maximum possible amount of revenue from local populations and encouraged growing discontent with Qajar rule.[9]

Coupled with the gradual development of nationalist ideas among both Persians and non-Persians, the resulting abuses contributed to mounting unrest in the Qajar borderlands during the Constitutional Revolution and the First World War. Though the 1906 constitution rested on the assumption of imperial Iran as comprised of multiple, heterogeneous parts, "ethnic relations were subsumed under the general notion of the Iranian nation, whose identity was in part defined by the Persian language (and Twelver Shi'ism), and in part remained obscure."[10] This gradual shift to thinking of an Iran defined in ethno-cultural terms helped push non-Persians and non-Shi'ites to the margins—a process accelerated by foreign intervention.

During the First World War, first the Ottomans and then the Russians occupied Iranian Azerbaijan, while British forces occupied Khuzestan as part of their Mesopotamian campaign.[11] Reza Shah's consolidation of power included military expeditions to put down peripheral and tribal disturbances throughout the 1920s. Some of these revolts, like the uprising of the Gilan-based Jangalis or unrest among the Turkmen nomads in northern Khorasan, were motivated by frustration against the continued domination of the old elite, but had a strong regional or ethnic dimension.[12] Others were more explicitly separatist, or became so in the face of government intransigence.

As in post-Ottoman Turkey, which also experienced foreign occupation of its borderlands at the end of the war, the nationalist framework established by Reza Shah left little room for alternative framings of identity, particularly among groups with the potential to develop cross-border loyalties such as the Khuzestani Arabs, Azeris, Baluch, Kurds, and Turkmen. Reza Shah's Sublime State of Iran argued that "minorities were inseparably bound to Iran through shared linguistic, racial, and cultural roots."[13] It also suggested that ethnic and religious difference posed a threat to national unity. As a 1925 editorial in a pro-Pahlavi journal argued, "the Iranian state is in danger of crumbling as long as its citizens consider themselves not primarily as Iranians, but as Turks, Arabs, Kurds, Bakhtiyaris, and Turkmens. We must, therefore, eliminate minority languages, regional sentiments, and tribal allegiances, and transform the various inhabitants of present day Iran into one nation."[14]

To carry out this transformation, the Pahlavis conducted forced migrations and compulsory settlement of nomads to undermine regional power brokers and encourage cultural-linguistic melding.[15] Efforts to integrate the nomadic areas into a common economic space by opening the periphery to penetration by Persian/Azeri-dominated commercial agriculture both reinforced ethnic divides and hardened the division between consumers in the center and agricultural producers in periphery.[16] Some groups like the Qashqa'i and the Bakhtiyari, which lacked cross-border ties, adapted more or less willingly to the Pahlavi order (Mohammed Reza Shah even married a Bakhtiyari), while the Azeris, Baluch, Kurds, and others saw the emergence of modern nationalist movements in cooperation with their compatriots in neighboring states.

Iran's peripheral areas all experienced unrest during periods when the center was weak. The military's brutality in suppressing the revolts that broke out following the British-led ouster of Reza Shah in 1941, coupled with the renewed efforts at homogenization in the postwar era left behind grievances that would continue to fester. Unrest during the 1979 Revolution was especially sustained around Iran's periphery. And while the Islamic Republic was able to defeat these uprisings—often with significant loss of life—it has remained unable to reconcile much of its non-Persian and non-Shi'ite periphery to its rule, and has administered its borderlands with equal parts neglect and repression.

Just as with the Pahlavis, the Islamic Republic rejects the devolved, pluralistic approach of the old empires in favor of an exclusivist vision now premised on Shi'ism and the ideology of the Islamic Revolution. The constitution of the Islamic Republic, which came into effect in December

1979, acknowledges equal rights for all Iranians "regardless of the tribe or ethnic group to which they belong," along with the right of minority groups to use "regional and tribal languages" in addition to Persian. Laws recognize the corporate existence of the Arabs of Khuzestan, Baluch, Kurds, and Turkmen as "national minorities," and the Bakhtiyari and Qashqa'i as "tribes." Though ethnically inclusive, the constitution emphasizes the "Muslim nation (*mellat-e musalman*)" of Iran—excluding non-Muslims (though not, rhetorically at least, Sunnis) from the national community—while emphasizing that the "government of the Islamic Republic of Iran is required to base its overall politics on the merging and unity of the Muslim nations."[17] Christians, Jews, and Zoroastrians (though not Baha'is) are recognized as protected minorities and guaranteed one seat each in the Majles, though communal representatives often portray toleration as precarious.

Even Khamenei, whose father was Azeri and who speaks Persian with an Azeri accent, emphasizes the importance of Persian language and culture as a force for unity.[18] In practice, constitutional protections for minorities have never been implemented in full. Under the reformist government of Mohammed Khatami (1997–2005), Tehran made some efforts to create space for the expression of ethnic and national distinctiveness; Khatami's government announced in 1997 its commitment to "strengthening national unity and harmony while respecting local cultures," appointed minority officials to posts in their home provinces, and allowed the publication of newspapers in minority languages.[19] With the end of Khatami's term and the resulting conservative backlash, concern about the potential for separatism and foreign influence led Tehran to promulgate a new policy emphasizing that "the culture and civilization of Islam and Iran, the Persian language, and writing are key factors of solidarity."[20]

Azerbaijan

As Shi'as, Azeris—unlike Sunni Baluch or Kurds—do not face institutionalized ethnic discrimination in the Islamic Republic. Many Azeris hold prominent positions in business and in the Islamic Republic's administrative apparatus—notably Khamenei—though Azeri representation in the security organs, particularly the IRGC, is much lower.[21] Opportunities for upward mobility have been an important factor in reconciling many Azeris to the Islamic Republic and limiting support for separatism.[22] Yet individual Azeris' success remains contingent on acceptance of and participation in a supra-ethnic Iranian identity, and Azeris who articulate a distinct national identity or demand recognition of ethnic rights often face persecution.[23]

Tehran's sensitivity about Azerbaijan is partly a consequence of the region's history of vulnerability to invasion and the persistence of cross-border linkages with what is today the Republic of Azerbaijan. Iranian Azerbaijan was the center of the late medieval–early modern Iranian world, producing the dynasties of the Qara Qoyunlu (1375–1468), Aq Qoyunlu (1378–1501), and, ultimately, the Safavids. Yet the weak khanates that emerged on both banks of the Aras River after the collapse of Nader Shah's empire became objects of contention between the Qajars and the expanding Russian Empire. The treaties of Golestan (1813) and Torkamanchay (1828), which St. Petersburg imposed after inflicting crushing defeats on the Qajars, confirmed the extension of Russian power south of the Great Caucasus Mountains, establishing the Aras as the boundary between the Russian and Iranian realms and dividing the Turkic-speaking, largely Shi'ite inhabitants of the region between them.[24]

The loss of these territories bred resentment in Iran, but also created a platform for irredentism in the age of nationalism. Recognizing the region's strategic value on the frontier with the Russian and Ottoman Empires, Qajar founder Aqa Mohammad Shah (1796–97) began the practice of appointing his heir-apparent as governor of Azerbaijan. While "[Azeri] identification with the state seemed all but complete" by the time of the Constitutional Revolution, people continued to move across the border in both directions, helping maintain a common cultural and intellectual space covering Iranian Azerbaijan and the former khanates further north.[25]

These contacts provided a conduit for the cross-border flow of ideas, including the liberal and nationalist sentiments that northern Azerbaijanis acquired as part of the late Russian Empire's intellectual ferment, particularly in the industrializing oil city of Baku. Iranian Azeris also came under the influence of developments in the Ottoman Empire, where the rise of ethnic nationalism bred a greater emphasis on a Turkic identity and the Turkic Azeri language as a vehicle for cultural and literary production.[26] The spread of nationalist, liberal, and socialist ideas from the north contributed to mounting radicalization in Iranian Azerbaijan, which became an epicenter of opposition to the Qajar dynasty in the late nineteenth century and a hotbed of unrest during the overlapping Constitutional Revolution and the Russian Revolution of 1905.[27] Turbulence mounted further following the Russian-backed coup that restored Mohammad Ali

Shah (1907–09) to the throne. As Russian Cossacks terrorized the Constitutionalists, Azeri and Armenian socialists, Armenian nationalists, and
members of the Russian Social Democratic Workers Party all participated
in the resistance that finally compelled Mohammad Ali to flee into exile
in June 1909.[28]

While Russian forces withdrew at the start of the First World War,
Azerbaijan suffered successive invasions and occupations by Ottoman,
Russian (again), and British armies during the war. In May 1918, liberal
nationalists established an Azerbaijan Democratic Republic north of the
Aras, around the same time that reformists led by the Shi'ite cleric Mohammad Khiabani launched a revolt in Tabriz demanding greater self-rule
from the Qajars. Khiabani presided over the establishment of an autonomous administration in what he termed "Azadistan (Land of Freedom),"
designed as a model for democratized provincial governments across Iran.
Though Khiabani remained committed to keeping Azerbaijan within a
federal Iran and refused outside assistance, demands for regionaliza-
tion and autonomy isolated him from Iranian reformists committed to a
unitary state and contributed to the failure of his movement, which was
crushed by the Russian-led Cossack Brigade.[29]

The Communist Jafar Pishevari led another revolt for self-
determination in Iranian Azerbaijan at the end of the Second World War.
Aided by the Soviet occupation, Pishevari declared an autonomous Azerbaijan People's Government in November 1945. While Pishevari, unlike
Khiabani a generation earlier, sought independence in accord with the Soviet doctrine of national self-determination, his movement gained limited
traction. To many Iranian Azeris, Moscow's influence (including establishing Soviet-trained militias and security services), the presence of Soviet
military forces, and the existence of the Soviet Azerbaijan SSR just across
the Aras made the revolt appear part of a Soviet campaign to seize Iranian Azerbaijan. After the withdrawal of Soviet forces in November 1946,
support for Iranian Azerbaijan's independence collapsed and Mohammad
Reza Shah's military put down the revolt within a month.

Azerbaijan was also the site of large-scale violence during the 1979
Revolution. Backed by the Azeri Ayatollah Kazem Shariatmadari, Azeri
activists set up a Muslim People's Republican Party (MPRP) in Tabriz that
opposed efforts to establish a centralized state under clerical domination.
Widely considered to outrank Khomeini as a scholar, Ayatollah Shariatmadari criticized the doctrine of Absolute Guardianship, arguing that "the
role of the clergy is a spiritual one. . . . I don't think we should involve
ourselves in government."[30] Shariatmadari was instrumental in mobiliz-

ing opposition to the Islamist constitution that Khomeini pushed through in the summer of 1979. As Touraj Atabaki notes, though, opposition to the principle of Absolute Guardianship cut across ethnic lines in Azerbaijan, and references to Azeri nationalists like Khiabani and Pishevari were absent during the uprising.[31] For all its intensity, the 1979 uprising emphasized demands for local rights within a less centralized Iran rather than national self-determination. The scale of the violence was significant, though, and after local troops sided with the insurgents, Khomeini was forced to call in units from outside Azerbaijan to put down the revolt.

Azerbaijan's position within the Islamic Republic changed fundamentally with the collapse of the Soviet Union and the independence of the Baku-based Republic of Azerbaijan. The Republic of Azerbaijan inherited the Soviet Union's secularism and, especially with the development of Caspian oil and gas resources, was more economically developed than Iranian Azerbaijan. Its secular culture became a pole of attraction for many Iranian Azeris in a way that Soviet culture never was, especially given relatively free movement across the border. Many Iranian Azeris unhappy with life in the Islamic Republic saw in the north and its music, films, and television a more attractive example of modern, secular, increasingly globalized Azeri culture. One example of the shift was increasing use of the ethnonyms "Azeri" (or less commonly, "Azerbaijani") rather than "Turk" among Iranian Azeris. The 1990s also saw efforts not only to expand the use of the Azeri language, but to bring the version used by Iranian state broadcasters closer to the version spoken in the Republic of Azerbaijan.

Meanwhile, some leaders of independent Azerbaijan (notably its second president, Abulfaz Elchibey) and nationalist activists portrayed it as the homeland for all ethnic Azeris. Elchibey (1992–93) spoke of a "southern Azerbaijan question" and predicted that the two segments of Azerbaijan could be unified within five years.[32] In response, Tehran threw its weight behind Armenia in the conflict over Nagorno-Karabakh, while Azerbaijan developed a strategic partnership with Israel that faced Tehran with the prospect of a second front should a conflict break out in the Middle East. Iran's support for Armenia helped mobilize more Iranian Azeris on behalf of Baku and contributed to, rather than inhibited, the consolidation of a shared cross-border identity, as Azeri deputies to the Iranian Majles called for sending assistance and Iranian Azeri civilians organized humanitarian aid to the Republic of Azerbaijan.[33]

Despite Tehran's emphasis on Shi'ism as the foundation of Iranian identity, inherited Persian-centrism and concerns about Azeri loyalty also contribute to discrimination. Iranian Azeris cite the partition of historic

Azerbaijan into the provinces of Ardabil, East Azerbaijan, West Azerbaijan, and Zanjan as an example of Tehran's dilution of Azeri influence and pursuit of self-determination. In 2006, a proregime newspaper published a cartoon comparing Azeris to cockroaches, touching off large-scale protests. The government's response, declaring the cartoon "an offense to the Iranian people as a whole," only emphasized its unwillingness to accept the reality of Azeri grievances or the existence of a distinct Azeri identity.[34]

Khuzestan (Arabestan)

At the head of the Persian Gulf, the Iranian Plateau gives way to the sparsely populated deserts and marshes of the Arabian Peninsula, a region historically known in Iran as Arabestan, and today the state of Khuzestan. The region's tribes—Arabs along the coast and Bakhtiyaris further inland—long enjoyed substantial autonomy at the intersection of the Iranian and Ottoman/Arab spheres of influence. With the Bakhtiyaris in the highlands and the Arab Banu Tarf and Banu K'ab tribal confederacies dominating the coastal plain, there was, according to Abbas Amanat, "limited space for Tehran's presence" in the region's few large towns, and relations with the tribes were typically distant and indirect.[35]

Interest in expanding that presence grew with the discovery of oil and the arrival of the British. In exchange for protection and a share of the revenue, the Banu K'ab leader Sheykh Khazal of Mohammareh signed an agreement in 1909 allowing the Anglo-Persian Oil Company to build a refinery on the island of Abadan. In exchange, the British helped the Banu K'ab consolidate regional power at the expense of their tribal rivals and Tehran. The implications for Iranian sovereignty were considerable, as similar agreements led to the formation of independent states in Kuwait, Qatar, and what became the United Arab Emirates. During the unrest that shook Iran at the end of the First World War, Sheykh Khazal launched a separatist revolt that dragged on until 1924 before Reza Khan's forces were able to subdue it—but only after reassuring London that Tehran would not challenge the arrangements with the Banu K'ab and Bakhtiyari that ensured access to the oil.[36] The Pahlavis then prioritized anchoring Khuzestan more firmly to the Iranian nation and state not only because of its oil, but also because of its legacy as the heartland of the Achaemenid empire, whose legendary capital of Susa was there. For Mohammad Reza Shah, "restoring Khuzestan [to its pre-Islamic glory] was pivotal to selling Persian nationalism for all of Iran," which, in turn, meant seeking to efface the region's non-Persian character.[37]

Like the Arab tribes in Iraq's neighboring Basra province, members of the Banu Tarf and Banu K'ab are mostly Shi'as who continued adhering to the Akhbari school of Shi'ism even after most Shi'as in Iran and the *Atabat* adopted the rival Usuli school during the Safavid era.[38] In contrast to the more numerous Usulis, Akhbaris do not acknowledge a clerical hierarchy and reject the ability of living clerics to exercise independent legal analysis (*ijtihad*). The Arabs of Khuzestan therefore strongly opposed efforts to vest supreme power in the Shi'ite *ulema* through the doctrine of Absolute Guardianship, by which Khomeini took the Usuli concept of emulation (*taqlid*) to its logical conclusion.[39]

The combination of ethnic distinction and theological opposition made the Khuzestani Arabs' loyalties suspect in the eyes of the clerical regime. Saddam Hussein further stoked these fears by appealing to pan-Arab sentiments in a bid to encourage a revolt in Khuzestan during the opening phase of the Iran-Iraq War—even as Tehran called on Iraqi Shi'as to overthrow Saddam's secular, Sunni-dominated Ba'athist regime. Saddam apparently harbored plans to annex Khuzestan, thereby cutting off Iran from the headwaters of the Gulf, and use it as a base for a new provisional government aiming to liberate Iran from the Islamic Republic.[40]

Though these efforts proved fruitless, Khuzestan was on the front lines of the war and suffered enormous damage. While many locals point to their sacrifices in the war with Iraq to advance a claim to membership in the national community, Tehran continues to approach Khuzestan through a highly securitized lens. Even the insistence on the name Khuzestan, rather than Arabestan, is connected to concerns about the potential for pan-Arab mobilization. More than three decades after the end of the war, much of Khuzestan remains in ruins and has experienced bouts of unrest from residents protesting perceived discrimination. While cracking down on protests, Tehran often blames Saudi Arabia and other Arab rivals for provoking the unrest and spreading pan-Arab ideas in the interest of destabilizing Iran.[41]

Compounding the difficulty for Tehran is the more open border with post-Saddam Iraq, which has allowed for the reestablishment of tribal and family ties between Khuzestan and Iraq's neighboring Basra province. Activists, rebels from the left-wing Mojahedin-e Khalq (MEK), and Sunni jihadist groups have all taken advantage of the porous frontier to conduct

hit-and-run attacks on targets in Khuzestan. And while pan-Arab sentiments found little resonance during the Iran-Iraq War, the combination
of tribal, ethnic, and doctrinal ties uniting Arabs on either side of the border remains a source of enduring concern for the Islamic Republic and
provides a justification for Tehran's interest in dominating Iraq.[42]

Kurdistan

So too does the challenge posed by Iran's Kurdish borderland. This region's status is complicated both by cross-border ties with Kurdish populations in Syria, Turkey, and, especially, Iraq, as well as by the complex
position Kurds hold in the Iranian national mosaic. A classic imperial borderland, Greater Kurdistan remains a buffer zone and arena for strategic
competition between its neighbors.

After the Battle of Chaldiran, the bulk of the Kurdish emirates in the
borderlands of eastern Anatolia and upper Mesopotamia came under Ottoman influence. Safavid efforts to limit the effectiveness of Ottoman propaganda by disrupting tribal hierarchies and encouraging conversion to
Shi'ism had limited success. The Safavids were eventually forced to make
accommodations with the emirs of Ardalan, who remained (along with,
later, the ruler of Mukriyan) a nominally independent vassal and Safavid
"emir of the frontier."[43] Qajar attempts in the 1840s to tighten control
over the Kurdish tribes while the Ottomans were distracted by Muhammad Ali Paşa's revolt and conflicts between Kurds and Assyrian Christians contributed to a series of tribal rebellions. The fallout from Sheykh
Ubeydullah's revolt a generation later led the late Qajars to impose more
direct administration, appointing governors from the ruling family and
attempting a policy of divide-and-rule toward Kurdish tribes.[44]

Like Azerbaijan (with which it partly overlaps), Iranian Kurdistan was
at various times subjected to Ottoman, Russian, and British invasion and
occupation during the First World War, resulting in "the total collapse
of authority and administration and the disruption of agrarian production and trade."[45] Amid the demise of both Ottoman and Qajar power
after World War I, a series of Kurdish uprisings broke out, including a
Social Democratic revolt in Sanandaj and the Ottoman-backed insurrection of the chieftain Ismail Aqa Shakak, or Simko, whose forces controlled
much of western Azerbaijan from 1918 to 1922.[46] Simko's aspirations were
mostly limited to tribal and religious grievances (among other exploits,
Simko was implicated in the massacre of Assyrian Catholicos Shimun XIX

and his retinue), despite the appearance of some nationalist propaganda among his forces.[47]

The Pahlavis' focus on administrative consolidation and Persianization encouraged the parallel nationalization of Kurdish resistance, and with it, deepening ties with Kurds in neighboring states. Reza Shah imposed restrictions on the Kurdish language, confiscated land, and displaced tribal chiefs. Pahlavi state-building paralleled Atatürk's efforts in Turkey, which likewise regarded Kurdish mobilization as a threat to territorial integrity, and Ankara cooperated with Tehran to secure the border and dilute tribal power. However, in contrast to Turkey, where Kurdish identity as such was perceived as a threat to state-building, the Pahlavis' attitude was more ambiguous. As Denise Natali notes, "Unlike Atatürk, Reza Shah's objective was to destroy the political and military organization of the Kurdish tribes, not their ethnic identity."[48]

As speakers of a spectrum of Iranic languages who claim a long-standing presence on the Iranian Plateau (many Kurds identify as the descendants of the Medes, whose empire dominated Iran before the Achaemenids), some Iranian Kurds embraced the Pahlavi-era nation-building project as their own. The Pahlavi state's official view was that "the Kurds are a branch of the Iranian race and are therefore part of Iran . . . therefore, no Kurdish problem exists."[49] Yet in practice, the Pahlavis adopted policies that favored Persian-speakers (and Shi'as), including the Persianization of education and appointment of Persian officials to Kurdish regions. As in Turkey, this pursuit of assimilation prompted the mobilization and development of Kurdish nationalism in response.[50]

Kurdish aspirations were further enhanced by the Soviet occupation of northern Iran during World War II. In January 1946, with Soviet troops still in the country, the Sunni jurist Qazi Muhammad proclaimed an independent Kurdish Republic based in Mahabad (the former capital of the Mukriyan emirate and the base of the Kurdish Democratic Party of Iran, KDPI). Despite Qazi Muhammad's religious background and Moscow's preference for keeping Kurdistan within Pishevari's autonomous Azerbaijan, Soviet occupation forces provided military protection and assistance to the new republic. As with Pishevari, the role of the Soviet occupation enhanced Tehran's suspicions about the Mahabad republic's objectives, which appeared to have both social revolutionary and nationalist elements.

Amid internecine rivalries, including tension between the mostly urban nationalists and the tribal elite that provided the most effective local military forces, Mohammad Reza Shah's troops captured Mahabad and

ended the Kurdish Republic soon after the withdrawal of Soviet forces
in the summer of 1946. The suppression of the Mahabad republic—the
only independent Kurdish state of the modern era—was exceptionally
brutal. Qazi Muhammad was publicly hanged, and many Kurds who did
not flee into exile would remain unreconciled to the Pahlavi state. Despite
being driven underground, the KDPI launched another revolt in 1967.
It was suppressed in part thanks to the willingness of Mustafa Barzani,
Qazi Muhammad's Iraq-based former military commander, to collaborate
with Tehran—in the process acting very much in the spirit of a Safavid
frontier emir.

Along with Azerbaijan, Iranian Kurdistan saw some of the heaviest
fighting during the conflict that led to the establishment of the Islamic
Republic. Participants in the 1979 uprising demanded Kurdish self-rule,
in part in response to anti-Sunni discrimination and the revolutionary
government's rejection of regional autonomy. KDPI-aligned forces seized
several cities, including Mahabad, which they defended from Revolutionary Guard attacks for over a year.

The danger posed by unrest among the mostly Sunni Kurds grew
with Saddam's September 1980 invasion. During the Iran-Iraq War, both
sides organized Kurdish detachments to stir unrest across the border. The
KDPI went out of its way to disclaim separatist ambitions, emphasizing
its all-Iranian character and commitment to regional autonomy rather
than independence. Yet elements within the KDPI collaborated with and
sought assistance from Iraq and from Kurdish activists outside Iran. Before subduing the rebellion, the Islamic Republic bombed villages, conducted mass executions, stationed large numbers of security forces in the
Kurdish regions, and expelled many Kurdish civilians.

The years since the final suppression of the KDPI uprising in 1983
have seen sporadic battles between Kurdish fighters and the Iranian
military. Like Iran's other ethnic peripheries, the Kurdish regions suffer from underdevelopment and a pervasive sense of disenfranchisement,
exacerbated by the continued emphasis on centralization and Persianization.[51] Unrest has grown since the establishment of the Party for a Free
Life in Kurdistan (*Partiya Jiyana Azad a Kurdistanê*, PJAK), an Iranian
offshoot of the Turkey-based PKK, which carried out its first attacks in
2003–04. The PJAK's activity suggests that Iranian Kurds' commitment
to the idea of Iran as a homeland is less solid than even a generation ago,
and that the idea of a trans-boundary Kurdish identity driving the PKK
rebellion in Turkey is taking root in Iran as well. Though the PKK once

operated openly in Iran, the emergence of the PJAK and, even more, the growth of trilateral Iranian-Russian-Turkish cooperation in Syria have inclined Tehran to become more supportive of Turkey's anti-PKK campaign—though Ankara still accuses Tehran of turning a blind eye to PKK operations in areas it controls in Iraq.

Türkmen Sahra

Today divided between the Iranian states of Golestan, Khorasan-e Shomali (North Khorasan), and Mazandaran, the Türkmen Sahra ("Turkmen Steppe") region suffers from the same pattern of underdevelopment and ethnoreligious discrimination as Iran's other Sunni peripheries. Well into the nineteenth century, the nomadic Turkmen of northern Khorasan were effectively independent of outside authority, though the Qajars and the Central Asian khanates of Khiva and Bukhara attempted to control them. Qajar interest centered largely on disrupting the Turkmens' role in the slave trade, which carried off tens of thousands of Iranians and travelers to the slave markets in Khiva and Bukhara—itself an indication of the limited scope of Iranian influence.[53]

Opposition to the slave trade, however, also drew Russia into regional geopolitics as a rival to the khanates and their Turkmen confederates, but also to the Qajars. An 1861 expedition launched by Naser al-Din Shah (1848–96) to aid the Sarïq Turkmen against their Tekke rivals met with disaster at Merv (in modern Turkmenistan), opening the way to Russia's conquest of Central Asia over the next two decades.[54] The Russian-Iranian Treaty of Ahal, signed in the wake of Russia's crushing victory over the Tekke at Gök Tepe in 1881, left just the southern periphery of the Turkmen steppe south of the Atrek River under Qajar authority.

As with Iran's other eastern borders, the bifurcation of the Turkmen steppe was the product of interimperial confrontation that took no account of demographic realities or migration patterns. The limited ability of both states (Iran in particular) to project power into the region left the frontier porous and loosely governed. With the establishment of Soviet power in the north, the enduring linkages between tribes on either side of the border came to be seen by Tehran as a strategic vulnerability, and the Turkmen region was a site of resistance to the consolidation of the centralized power of both the Pahlavis and the Islamic Republic.

In May 1924, Iranian Turkmen under Osman Ahund proclaimed independence. Hinting at the emergence of an ethnonationalist, as opposed to a tribal, identity among the Turkmen, Ahund's forces received assistance and training from the nascent Turkish Republic, and aligned themselves with the still-flickering campaign for Turkic unity proclaimed by the late Enver Paşa.[55] Meanwhile, the Soviet government established a Turkmen SSR in October 1924, part of "a shift from a genealogical to a territorial conception of Turkmen identity" that divided Soviet from Iranian Turkmen.[56]

Once his troops defeated Osman Ahund in 1925, the newly enthroned Reza Shah attempted to dilute the Turkmen presence in northern Khorasan through compulsory resettlement of Kurds, Azeris, and other tribal populations, and through a policy of forced Persianization. Tehran stationed troops in the region, while members of the Pahlavi family and other Persian elites appropriated Turkmen pastureland for landed estates. Coupled with the deployment of Iranian troops, this effort at frontier integration was in keeping with Reza Shah's wider policy of nation- and state-building.[57]

Iranian Turkmen, like many other non-Persians around the periphery, played an active role in the 1979 Revolution. While raising issues related to autonomy and linguistic rights, Turkmen demands focused largely on economic issues, especially land redistribution. As Sunnis, though, many Turkmen objected to the establishment of the Islamic Republic and voted against its constitution in a referendum. While violence in Türkmen Sahra was on a smaller scale than in Azerbaijan or Kurdistan, it was not until 1983 that Tehran fully pacified the region, following large-scale protests over compulsory veiling of women (a practice not traditionally followed by the nomadic Turkmen).

As in other borderlands, Tehran's (re)drawing of state borders has helped dilute Turkmen populations, who comprise around one-third of the inhabitants of Golestan and much less in the other states. Turkmen object to restrictions on teaching in their native language (which the state allows in principle, but does not fund), as well as ethnic discrimination, forced in-migration of non-Turkmen, brutality by the security forces, and the killing of community leaders and activists. While the region likely holds significant natural gas reserves, Tehran has inhibited their development, wary of enhancing local bargaining power against the center.[58] Discrimination often has a sectarian element, with activists complaining about the shuttering of Sunni mosques and forced conversions to Shi'ism.[59]

Given the paucity of sources from either side of the border, it is difficult to get a sense of the degree of connections between Iranian Turkmen and their ethnic kin in Turkmenistan. As one of the most isolated and closed societies in the world, and with increasingly serious economic problems of its own, Turkmenistan does not exert the same magnetic pull on Iranian Turkmen as Azerbaijan does on Iranian Azeris. Ashgabat also took steps shortly after independence to assuage Iranian concerns about cross-border linkages, prioritizing border security and economic cooperation over efforts to cultivate ties with Iranian Turkmen.[60] While Türkmen Sahra remains loosely integrated into the Islamic Republic, the lack of cross-border ties guards against even tacit irredentism.

Baluchistan

Similar problems plague Iran's Baluch, around 1.5 million of whom live in the border province of Sistan and Baluchistan (*Sistan-o Baluchestan*), which is among the poorest and least developed in Iran, with the lowest per capita income and the highest level of infant mortality.[61] For much of the Qajar era, Baluchistan was an unstable frontier on the margins between Iran, the Sultanate of Oman, and a British-led regional coalition that included Afghanistan and the Baluch-dominated Khanate of Kalat (part of modern Pakistan's Balochistan province), whose administrative machinery was largely operated by Persian-speaking Tajiks. In the late 1830s, the Qajars occupied Bampur as a base for projecting power in the region, and played off local Baluch tribes and leaders with the lure of the right to supervise tax collection.[62] Instability along this frontier and an interest in building a telegraph along the Makran coast led the British to pursue border demarcation, which in turn encouraged the Qajars to emphasize Iran's historical and cultural claim to the entire region. In 1870, a British-led boundary commission partitioned Baluchistan at the Helmand River, with Kalat joining the British Raj and the remote western regions of Baluchistan, including the coastal area around Chabahar, remaining under Qajar suzerainty.[63]

In practice, Iranian authority was loose. From Bampur, the Qajar governor collected taxes and appointed local officials, but the Baluch tribes often fought to avoid payment. The largest Baluch rebellion broke out amid the uncertainty following Naser al-Din Shah's death, when tribes across the region united around a demand for lower taxation. The fighting only ended in 1900 when Mozaffar al-Din Shah (1896–1907) agreed to appoint the Baluch leader Hosayn Khan governor in exchange for acknowledging that western Baluchistan constituted part of the legitimate Qajar domains.[64]

This agreement marked a potentially important step toward the closure of the Baluchistan frontier, though Baluchistan's subsequent volatility during the First World War and the establishment of the Pahlavi state suggested that neither the Qajars nor their successors were powerful enough to bring that process to its conclusion. Although a combination of military force and tribal divisions allowed Reza Shah's forces to quell a revolt that broke out in 1924 over tardy subsidy payments, ensuring stable administration proved more difficult. The Pahlavis' initial approach emphasized expanding bureaucratic administration, neutralizing the tribal khans (*sardar*s), and preventing the emergence of transboundary ethnic consciousness. The failure of these efforts, however, led Tehran to turn to indirect rule, coopting Baluch chieftains to maintain order.

Because of their role in sustaining Pahlavi rule, the tribal chieftains were marginalized after the founding of the Islamic Republic, which has also struggled to enforce its writ along its remote eastern frontier.[65] Instead, Sunni religious leaders have become the most influential tribunes for Baluch grievances, which are usually articulated in sectarian, rather than national terms, focusing on issues like gaining permission to construct Sunni mosques.[66] Following the 1979 Revolution, the Baluch-majority Muslim Unity Party (led primarily by Sunni clerics) emerged as a voice opposing the establishment of Shi'ism as a state religion and the compulsory use of the Persian language. It presided over an uprising that took the Islamic Republic two years to quell. Tehran subsequently viewed the Sunni Baluch as a potential fifth column that rivals like Saudi Arabia and Pakistan could manipulate.

Along with smugglers, Baluch insurgent groups like Jaish al-Adl and Jundullah (which also cooperates with the Pakistani Taliban and other hardline Sunni groups in Pakistan) have proliferated in the lawless wastes of Sistan and Baluchistan.[67] While they primarily target Iranian officials and security personnel, both groups have also attacked Shi'ite religious sites and non-Baluch civilians. This low-level insurgency has reinforced Tehran's proclivity for repression in the region. Human rights groups estimate that at least 20 percent of those executed by the Islamic Republic since 2006 are Baluch, who comprise less than 2 percent of the country's population.[68] At the same time, Iranian ambitions to develop Baluchistan's port of Chabahar as a node for global trade aim to promote the region's economic development. As with China's approach in Xinjiang, Iran hopes that economic development will reconcile peripheral minorities to integration with an increasingly nationalizing state.

Nor does Tehran's sometimes heavy-handed approach prevent it from maintaining a kind of postimperial regard for the Baluch living in Pakistan. Criticism of Pakistan's oppression of its Baluch minority is a rhetorical staple for many Iranian journalists and politicians. Unlike Azerbaijanis and Iranian Azeris, interactions between the Baluch of Pakistan and Iran never faced a hard border or a Communist state intent on carrying out a social revolution on one side. Given both states' failure to integrate their Baluch minorities, these cross-border linkages are a source of insecurity for both Tehran and Islamabad, with Baluch guerillas, smugglers, and jihadists working across the rugged border region and targeting both states. Jaish al-Adl has at times absconded with Iranian hostages across the border into Pakistani Balochistan, which Iranian observers believe is only possible due to the support of Pakistani intelligence.[69] More frequently, Tehran claims that Islamabad has failed to do enough to clamp down on groups like Jundullah and Jaish al-Adl on its territory, and has threatened to launch raids into Pakistani Baluchistan to root out militants.[70] Neither country wants to see the emergence of a powerful Baluch movement straddling the border, but sectarian agendas on the part of both governments and the Baluch themselves have created a series of cross-cutting interests. The Islamic Republic thus continues to prioritize concern about Sunni militancy on its frontier over efforts to use the Pakistani Baluch to exert leverage on Islamabad.

The Islamic Republic's Postimperial Mosaic

Compared to China, Russia, or Turkey, a striking element of Iran's approach to its borderlands is the prioritization of security over power projection. Since the end of the Iran-Iraq War, Tehran has downplayed efforts to position itself as a pole of attraction for (non-Shi'ite) Arabs, Azeris, Baluch, Kurds, or Turkmen in neighboring states. Tehran's obsession with limiting its own minorities' cross-border ties can go to extreme lengths: Tehran discourages Iranian Azeris from crossing the Aras to celebrate *Nowruz* in the Republic of Azerbaijan, and when Baku hosted the Eurovision song contest in 2012, Tehran recalled its ambassador.

This largely defensive orientation is less a reflection of Iranian weakness or a rejection of the tools of empire—as extensive support for Shi'ite proxies in much of the Middle East indicates—than a consequence of the Islamic Republic's tenuous legitimacy in its non-Persian borderlands that the encouragement of cross-border ties could further erode. Tehran's

commitment to Shi'ite supremacy at home leaves it few tools for addressing the grievances of the non-Shi'as along its periphery. Where Russia
actively accepts ethnoreligious diversity, Turkey (which is more religiously
homogeneous) allows all its inhabitants the option of "calling themselves
Turks," and even China embraces a vision of community defined by commitment to a loosely defined civilization, Iran's vision of a "(Shi'ite) Muslim
nation" offers the roughly one-tenth of the population that is non-Shi'a
few positive inducements. The Islamic Republic's continued adherence to
the Persian-centrism of the Pahlavi era, however downplayed, is equally
exclusive of Shi'ite Arabs and at least those Azeris who choose to define
themselves in national terms. Not only do poor conditions on the Iranian
side limit Iran's ability to use cross-border connections as a geopolitical
tool, they continue to represent a vulnerability that rivals can exploit, as
Saddam tried to do in the 1980s.

Absent a positive vision for coexistence, Tehran largely neglects its
borderlands except as a problem of security. All of Iran's borderlands have
seen ethnic unrest, especially at moments of more general upheaval such
as the Green Movement of 2009. Iranian thinkers from across the political
spectrum recognize the continued failure to integrate the ethnic periphery; a number have called for a new approach. Calls for giving peripheral
regions more autonomy frequently invoke models from the imperial era,
whether Achaemenid-style satrapies or the devolved *Mamalek-e Mahruse-
ye* of the Qajars.[71] Given the Islamic Republic's sclerosis and vulnerability,
such reforms are unlikely to take hold anytime soon. Ethnic unrest is thus
one subset of the larger governance challenge facing the Islamic Republic,
and cannot be solved in the absence of a larger effort to secure popular
legitimacy among Shi'as and Sunnis, Persians and non-Persians.

CHAPTER NINE

Greater Iran (*Iranzamin*) and Iran's Imperial Imagination

W HILE THE CENTER of recent Iranian history lies on the western half of the Iranian Plateau, historical and cultural links to other areas once subject to Iranian imperial control have endured. These links contribute to an understanding that has persisted down to the present of a Greater Iran where imperial longings are more abstract and Iranian influence more diffuse. At its most extensive, this Greater Iran encompasses Mesopotamia and Bahrain, whose large Shi'ite populations provide an obvious target for Iranian outreach; but also the southern Caucasus and eastern Anatolia, pieces of Central Asia, and South Asia east to the Indus River.[1] These latter regions have fallen into and out of Iranian control several times, but have for a millennium or more been regarded as part of Iran's cultural and political patrimony. Only in the nineteenth century, with the shrinkage of Qajar Iran's territory in the face of Russian and British pressure, was Iranian influence attenuated, such that, according to Firoozeh Kashani-Sabet, "the Iranian space could no longer be termed imperial, even if Iran's imperial imaginings lingered."[2]

Drawn from ancient sources, the most commonly used terms for this Greater Iran (lit. *Iran-e Bozorg*) are *Iranshahr* or, especially, *Iranzamin*. They imply a contrast between the territorially restricted entity that emerged in the nineteenth century and an idealized vision of the

Sasanian Empire that includes, in addition to modern Iran, the bulk of the Eurasian landmass between the Euphrates and the Indus. Despite the shrinkage of borders, post-Qajar Iran has remained entangled both culturally and politically with much of this onetime imperial periphery. Bound together by a shared, if distant, history and a Persianate high culture whose extent has shrunk dramatically in the age of nation-states, this *Iranzamin* is perceived by many Iranians as Iran's "legitimate" sphere of interest.[3]

Though both the Pahlavis and the Islamic Republic have been—with a few notable exceptions—cautious in their aspirations to reconnect with Iran's historical periphery, this Greater Iran has remained the object of an implicit desire. For the Pahlavis, the idea of *Iranzamin* mattered primarily as a cultural phenomenon, linked as it was to the emphasis on reconnecting with an imagined Persian past. The primary vector of the Islamic Republic's foreign policy has remained the Middle East and the Persian Gulf, where sectarian considerations trump appeals to a shared imperial legacy. Yet amid its shift toward acceptance of Iran's "national" history, recognition of connections to this wider postimperial space in Eurasia grew. Persian nationalists, including those opposed to the Islamic Republic, invoke the memory of the Sasanian *Iranzamin* as an argument for Iranian exceptionalism and a claim to regional leadership. Tehran today points to this Greater Iran of the past as a monument to and argument for Iran's status as a major power. More so than the Pahlavi state, it also looks to the historical *Iranzamin* as an outlet for foreign policy.

Unlike its postimperial rivals, though, Iran's engagement with the South Caucasus and Central/South Asia rarely has irredentist implications (the only territory outside its current borders to which Iran lays claim are some small islands in the Persian Gulf). Whether because Tehran was too weak or because, with the loss of these territories, its strategic geography became more Middle Eastern than Eurasian, Iran's approach to its onetime periphery in Eurasia has been opportunistic, focusing more on creating buffer zones and enhancing connectivity to the outside world rather than exporting the Islamic Revolution or reshaping regional order. Tehran has nonetheless made clear its ambition of becoming an important player in the Caucasus and Central/South Asia in order to secure itself from external threats, assert its standing relative to its neighbors, and, more recently, take advantage of the region's potential to expand connectivity to the east, west, and north.[4]

Aiding this ambition are geopolitical shifts underway in Iran's wider neighborhood. The Soviet invasion of Afghanistan encouraged Tehran to intervene more directly to shape Afghan politics and society to check Soviet influence on its borders. The USSR's collapse then opened up new opportunities to restore old connections with the Caucasus and Central Asia. The most significant impetus for Iran to attempt applying its hitherto ephemeral interest in building something like a new *Iranzamin* came in the twenty-first century, though, with the U.S.-led invasions of first Afghanistan and then Iraq. The removal of hostile Sunni-dominated regimes and Washington's inability to impose stability in their wake provided Tehran with an opportunity to bolster strategic, economic, and cultural ties across its onetime imperial hinterland. The Islamic Republic poured significant resources into establishing influence in both countries, supporting pro-Iranian militants and politicians, investing in media and cultural institutions, and taking advantage of refugee flows to create proxy forces. In the process, Iran set out to ensure its own security by preventing the consolidation of hostile actors (including those connected to the United States) along its borders.

The difference between Iraq and Afghanistan is nonetheless instructive: given its vulnerability to developments in the former, Iran's ambitions toward Iraq were more extensive, centered on using the large Shi'ite population to "shap[e] Iraq's domestic politics and strategic orientation."[5] In Afghanistan, conversely, Iran sought to influence but not dominate the political space, focusing mainly on containing cross-border security threats on Afghan territory. Indeed, Iranian involvement throughout the Greater Khorasan region (encompassing much of eastern Iran as well as western Afghanistan and southern Central Asia) and the Caucasus has limited objectives, in part because of the visible presence of rival powers like Russia and Turkey, not to mention the United States. Rather than seek to change borders or forge a new regional order, Iranian ambitions in Eurasia are therefore mostly about ensuring security around its periphery and breaking out of the isolation imposed in the wake of the Islamic Revolution.

Greater Iran, *Iranshahr, Iranzamin*

Historically, the Iranian imperial ecumene extended far beyond the borders of the modern Islamic Republic. In Iranian nationalist thought, the usual name for this imperial space, stretching from the Euphrates to the

Indus, is *Iranzamin*, a Sasanian-era term whose popularity stems from its use in the *Shahnahmeh*. Originally, *Iranzamin* referred to the lands under the sway of the Sasanian monarch and inhabited by people who identified themselves as *Ariya*. This region was defined less by its political boundaries or the ethnic composition of its inhabitants than by a shared Persian high culture and the presence of Persian-speaking officials in chanceries from Bursa to Mumbai.[6] Within this *Iranzamin* was the political entity known as *Iranshahr*, the Kingdom of Iran. Over time, though, the distinction was lost and both *Iranshahr* and *Iranzamin* came to refer in one way or another to a legendary Greater Iran whose existence was sanctified in historical memory largely thanks to the *Shahnahmeh*.[7]

The territories outside the present borders of the Islamic Republic with the most extensive historical, cultural, and political ties to Iran—the modern *Iranzamin*—are in eastern Iraq, Bahrain, the South Caucasus, and the historical region of Greater Khorasan, which encompasses—along with Iran's own eastern provinces—western Afghanistan, western Pakistan, and parts of Turkmenistan, Uzbekistan, and Tajikistan.[8] Though the entirety of this territory was rarely under the control of a single dynasty after the fall of the Sasanians, the notion of a Greater Iran as the legitimate patrimony of dynasties ruling on the Iranian Plateau endured, as did the Iranian "empire of the mind," the organically entangled Persianate cultural space. Continued invocation of *Iranzamin* suggested the durability of an ideological claim to these territories rooted in historical and cultural ties.

While its exact parameters have always been shifting and fluid, the notion of a Greater Iranian space distinct from Iran proper has ancient roots. The *Avesta*, parts of which date back as far as the eighth century B.C.E., lists the regions created by the supreme deity Ahura Mazda, called *Airyana Vaejah*, which contain the peak at the center of the world from which Zoroaster handed down his teachings, and which lie in the eastern reaches of the Iranian Plateau.[9]

From their capital at Ctesiphon in Iraq, the Sasanians later extended the frontiers of Iranian rule into the Caucasus, the Arabian Peninsula, and in the direction of India. In addition to the provinces described as *Eran*, which stretched from Azerbaijan to Herat and the Makran coast, the rock inscription of Shapur I lists separately areas under Sasanian control in India, Oman, the South Caucasus, and "Balasagan up to the Caucasus at the Gate of the Alans."[10] These territories comprised a region that Sasanian writers referred to as *Aneran*, or *Aneranshahr*—the "Kingdom of the non-Aryans."[11] In Sasanian usage, the concept of *Aneran* appears to apply to territories under Sasanian rule but outside the traditional core regions, suggesting both a distinction between inner and outer domains, as well as a geographic limit to Sasanian claims.[12]

The *Shahnahmeh*, which dates to the tenth century, provides a rough, somewhat contradictory geographic outline of what Ferdowsi alternately terms *Iranzamin*, *Shahr-i Iran* (Kingdom of Iran), and the world.[13] Ferdowsi's discussion of the pre-Sasanian period refers to the Oxus (Amu Darya) and Helmand Rivers as Iran's eastern frontiers, while his narrative about the Sasanian era centers on Mesopotamia.[14] Acknowledging that the extent of actual sovereignty might vary, the fourteenth-century historian and geographer Hamdallah Mostawfi Qazvini outlined the legitimate frontiers of *Iranzamin* as encompassing

> the province of Sind, then by Kabul, Saghaniyan, Transoxiana, and Khwarizm to the frontier of Saqsin and Bulghar. The western frontier lies on the province of Niqsar (Neo-Caesarea) and Sis, and thence to Syria. The northern frontier lies on the land of the Ossetes and the Russians, the Magyars and Circassians, the Bartas and along the Khazar desert . . . with the country of the Alans and the Franks. The dividing line between these last and the lands of Iran is formed by Alexander's Cut (the Hellespont) and the Sea of the Khazars (the Caspian). . . . The southern frontier lies on the desert of Najd, across which the road passes to Mecca, and on the right hand of this desert the line goes up to the frontiers of Syria, while on the left hand it comes down to the Persian Gulf . . . from whence the frontier reaches India.[15]

The extent of the territory subject to the *Shahanshah* (a Sasanian title revived a few centuries into the Islamic era) nonetheless varied over time. Even when dynasties were strong, the Iranian periphery was littered with semi-independent states that paid tribute to the *Shahanshah* and provided troops for his military, but were otherwise self-governing. During periods of disunity or state breakdown in the Iranian heartland, regional dynasties also emerged, particularly in Khorasan, which challenged the claims of rulers located further west to the title of *Shahanshah*. Under dynasties like the Samanids (834–999) and Ghaznavids (977–1186), the political and cultural centers of the Persian world shifted east, with cities like

Bukhara and Herat coming to rival the splendor of Baghdad and other traditional Islamic capitals. In part for this reason, efforts at nation- and state-building in Afghanistan and Tajikistan have likewise sought to appropriate aspects of the Iranian imperial heritage, including by claiming figures such as Zoroaster, Ferdowsi, and the poet Rudaki—all natives of Greater Khorasan—as their own.

Mohammad Reza Pahlavi promoted the idea of *Iranzamin* as a cultural realm where the influence of Iran's ancient empires remained visible.[16] In the Islamic Republic too, the idea of *Iranzamin* embodies a source of longing linked to an idealized vision of Iran's (pre-Islamic) past. In that sense, belief in an Iranian imperial restoration is separate from, and often hostile to, the founding mythology of the Islamic Republic, with its appeals to the community of believers and emphasis on areas like the Levant that never fell into the Achaemenid, Sasanian, or Safavid imperial orbit.

Yet since the Islamic Republic has appropriated much of the language of Iranian nationalism and maintains a fundamentally imperial vision of Iranian foreign policy, ideas of *Iranzamin* remain very much part of Tehran's vocabulary and worldview. Though mostly associated with Persian nationalism (and thus inclined to identify *Iranzamin* with the anachronistic idea of a Persian nation-state), discussion of *Iranzamin* appears in the Islamic Republic's textbooks and remains part of official rhetoric. Even Ayatollah Khamenei points to the loss of Iran's "legitimate territory" outside the borders of the Islamic Republic as a factor in the Qajars' and Pahlavis' downfall, since "one of the matters that Iranians . . . regard as the most important basis of their historical judgments is the question of their country's territorial integrity," even if this territory now lies within other states.[17]

The Caucasus

Though less visible in the region than its postimperial rivals Russia and Turkey, Iran too is an important player in the Caucasus—especially the South Caucasus, which was long an integral part of the Iranian imperial space. Iranian influence in the Caucasus was more prominent in the 1990s, a period of great fluidity in the wake of the Soviet collapse. With the improvement of Iranian-Russian relations over the past two decades, Tehran has aligned itself with Russian objectives in the region, contributing to the formation of a north-south axis including Russia, Armenia, and Iran underpinned by trade and transportation linkages.[18] At the same time,

Tehran has its own postimperial dilemmas to manage, notably its relationship with Azerbaijan, which has long been dominated by concerns about Baku's influence on the population of Iranian Azerbaijan.

Iranian influence on the southern slopes of the Caucasus and the Armenian highlands, which stretch into eastern Anatolia, dates back to the ancient period, when a single Bronze Age culture united northwestern Iran, Armenia, and southern Georgia. Into the medieval era, the Armenian and Georgian kingdoms served as buffer states between the empires of the Seleucids (312–63 B.C.E.), Arsacids (247 B.C.E.–224 C.E.), and Sasanians to the east and the Romans and Byzantines to the west. To the southeast, nomadic migrations of the medieval period resulted in the presence of Oghuz Turkic speakers on both sides of the Aras River dividing Iranian Azerbaijan in the south from the region known as Arran and Shirvan, roughly the modern Republic of Azerbaijan, to the north.[19] While Armenia and Georgia managed to maintain a distinct identity, reinforced from the fifth century by their adoption of Christianity, they remained within the Iranian imperial space until the expansion of Russian power south of the Caucasus in the nineteenth century. The Safavid conquest of Tabriz in 1501 was followed by expansion northward along the Caspian littoral to Shirvan, Baku, Nakhichevan, Qarabagh (Karabakh), and Yerevan. The 1555 Peace of Amasya bifurcated the Caucasus between a Safavid east and an Ottoman west, an arrangement made more or less permanent in 1639 under the Peace of Zuhab.[20] The Iranian zone encompassed the eastern Georgian kingdoms of Kartli and Kakheti, and eastern Armenia centered on Yerevan.

As in many other imperial peripheries, Safavid rule in Georgia was generally indirect, relying on native kings who were also *wali*s of the shah. At times, however, the Safavids sought to subject Kartli and Kakheti to more direct control and to impose Islam by force. In 1540–41, Tahmasp I sent forces against Kartli, whose ruler had, according to the chronicler Eskandar Beg Monshi, "repeatedly forgotten his position [as a Safavid vassal] and had ravaged the Muslim lands on his borders." In response, the Qizilbash "subdued all the infidels living in those regions, and all those who were blessed by good fortune and divinely guided to make the twin professions of the Muslim faith were spared; the rest packed their bags and took their abode in hell."[21] Georgia suffered devastating invasions at the hands of Shah Abbas, Nader Shah, and Aqa Mohammad Khan Qajar as well. As early as the 1630s, these invasions persuaded Georgian leaders to look for protection from their fellow-Orthodox Russians, who in the following century would begin pushing both Iranian and Ottoman influence out of the region.[22]

Despite its location on the periphery of the Safavid empire, the Caucasus played an integral role in Safavid administration from the reign of Abbas I. To balance the influence of both the nomadic, mostly Turkic Qizilbash and the urban Persian-speakers (Tajiks) who dominated the bureaucracy, the Safavids promoted a third faction comprised of elite, mostly Georgian and Circassian slaves (*ghilman*, sing. *ghulam*). These slaves became a crucial element in the power structure of Isfahan, a link between the center and the periphery, and warriors whose lack of dynastic ambitions encouraged the Safavids to deploy them to other frontier zones, such as Khorasan. The slave system thus became a tool binding the Caucasus, central Iran, and the eastern periphery into a single imperial space. By the end of Abbas's reign, more than two-thirds of Iran's then-thirty-seven provinces had *ghulam* governors.[23] The most successful Caucasian *ghulam* was Allahverdi Khan, a Georgian who became governor of Fars province, *qollar-aqasi* (commander of the *ghulam* corps), *sipahsalar* (commander in chief of all the military forces), and one of the richest men in Iran—but whose descendants were massacred by Shah Safi I (1629–42) for backing the wrong side in a dynastic struggle inside Georgia.[24]

Safavid forces also made brief forays north of the Caucasus in the 1510s, when Shah Ismail's Qizilbash brutally subdued the Lezgin and Tabasaran tribes in Dagestan.[25] In concert with the Ottomans, the inhabitants of Shirvan and the ruler of the Lak-Kumyk confederation (known as the shamkhal) then aided the rebellion of Tahmasp's brother Alqas Mirza in 1547.[26] The subsequent, gradual expansion of Safavid power north of the Caucasus became a source of concern not only for the Ottomans, but also for the Russians, who established their first fort on the Terek River in the 1560s. Russian emissaries warned the Safavids off from attacking the Kabardians and Kumyks and aided (along with the Ottomans) the Sunni tribes who rebelled against Safavid rule after the death of Tahmasp.[27]

While Safavid influence in the North Caucasus outside Dagestan was ephemeral, it was the wider breakdown of Safavid authority in the early eighteenth century that encouraged the Ottomans and Russians to press forward into the South Caucasus. After the fall of Isfahan to the Pashtuns in 1722, Peter I of Russia forced the Iranians to cede Derbent and Baku, along with the southern Caspian littoral, while the Ottomans secured Georgia, Armenia, Shirvan, Azerbaijan, Hamadan, and parts of western

Iran.[28] Nader Shah's (successful) demand for the return of these territories, on the basis that they comprised part of the Safavid realm, suggested the growing hold of the idea of an Iran with "legitimate" borders extending beyond the Iranian Plateau.[29]

Meanwhile, the tenuousness of Iran's hold on the Caucasus sparked repeated conflicts and paved the way for Russian conquest. Russia launched a punitive expedition against Iran in early 1796, following Catherine II's failure to defend Kartli-Kakheti from Aqa Mohammad's forces. The invasion effectively halted Qajar ambitions in the Caucasus and served as a prelude to Russia's formal annexation of eastern Georgia in 1801.[30] Under Catherine's successors, the Treaties of Golestan and Torkamanchay confirmed the extension of Russian power south of the Great Caucasus Mountains leaving the territory of modern Armenia, Azerbaijan, Georgia, Dagestan, and a slice of eastern Chechnya firmly within the Russian Empire.[31]

While Georgia posed the biggest challenge to Safavid and Qajar authority in the Caucasus, since the late nineteenth century Azerbaijan—both the region of northwest Iran historically known as Azerbaijan and the former khanates north of the Aras River now comprising the Republic of Azerbaijan—has been the most complex of Iran's Caucasian peripheries. For much of the twentieth century, the closure of the Soviet-Iranian border limited contacts between Soviet (Northern) and Iranian (Southern) Azerbaijan. Azerbaijani nationalism—the idea that Shi'ite Oghuz Turkic-speakers on both sides of the border comprise a single nation and should have their own state—became much stronger in Soviet Azerbaijan, which had the advantage of a standardized language and state sponsorship of cultural production.[32]

For Tehran, Azerbaijan's independence was thus a two-edged sword: while removing the Russian/Soviet threat on its borders, independent Azerbaijan represents a potentially subversive force on the Azeri population of the Islamic Republic, a population that has remained restive since the 1979 Revolution. While Tehran at first hoped to pull the Republic of Azerbaijan into its own sphere of influence, Iranian leaders soon came to worry about the attraction independent Azerbaijan was exerting on its own Azeri population. These concerns led Tehran to support Armenia in the conflict over Nagorno-Karabakh in the early 1990s, and more broadly to align itself with Moscow and Yerevan in the Caucasus.

If Tehran accuses Baku of promoting irredentism among Azeris in northern Iran, Baku accuses Tehran of supporting Shi'ite militants and

ethnic separatists within the Republic of Azerbaijan. Iran criticizes the
Azerbaijani government's militant secularism, including its banning of
the *hijab* and closure of mosques; Azerbaijan in turn criticizes Iran for
interfering in its internal affairs, including through the backing of militant Shi'ite organizations such as the banned Islamic Party of Azerbaijan
(whose leader called for the ouster of Azerbaijan's secular government)
and a militant group known as Muslim Unity.[33] Baku also charges that
Iran has assisted Shi'ite extremists from Azerbaijan get to Syria to fight
with militias supporting Bashar al-Assad.[34] Underlying these concerns is
fear that Tehran is seeking not only to subvert the secular nature of the
Azerbaijani state, but also to manipulate cross-border linkages to undermine Azerbaijani independence in the name of renewed imperial aspirations; in one notable instance, the editor of a hardline Iranian newspaper
and adviser to Ayatollah Khamenei called for Baku to hold a referendum
on joining the Islamic Republic.[35]

Only in recent years have Tehran and Baku begun making cautious
efforts at overcoming the legacy of mistrust that the Soviet collapse and
the emergence of the "southern Azerbaijan question"—the idea first put
forward by Elchibey about Iranian Azerbaijan becoming part of the independent republic in the north—precipitated. The basis for this cautious
rapprochement is an attempt to recast the region's economic and political geography by restoring some of the connections between northern
and southern Azerbaijan that existed before the Treaties of Golestan and
Torkamanchay.

With the Islamic Republic attempting to break out of its international isolation following the signing of the Joint Comprehensive
Plan of Action (JCPOA) in 2015, Azerbaijan became an important conduit to the outside world. By tying northern and southern Azerbaijan together through a web of trade and transit links, Tehran aimed to side-
step the questions of ethnicity and irredentism by shifting the focus to
mutually beneficial economic cooperation that, at the same time, would
strengthen Baku's economic dependence on Tehran—even as Tehran
deepens its strategic alignment with Azerbaijan's other former hegemon,
Russia. Iran's leaders viewed the completion of a rail line connecting Iranian Azerbaijan to the Republic of Azerbaijan, part of the International
North-South Transit Corridor between India and Russia, as part of a
larger process of restoring Iran to its rightful place as a "point of equilibrium in the region," and allowing it to adopt a more balanced position
between Baku and Yerevan. Azerbaijan's warming ties with Turkey and
victory in the Second Nagorno-Karabakh War, however, soon disrupted

this regional equilibrium, prompting concern about renewed threats along Iran's northern border, while reviving calls for irredentism in both Baku and Tehran.[36]

Asserting itself as a point of equilibrium has also led Iran to focus on deepening its engagement with Georgia, as well parts of the Russian North Caucasus once connected with the Iranian Empire (notably Dagestan, parts of which were under nominal Iranian rule for the bulk of the millennium preceding the Treaty of Golestan). Reestablishing Iranian influence after a century-plus of Russian domination and closed borders is the main priority, though Tehran is also interested in maintaining a regional balance and limiting the spread of outside, notably U.S., influence. Iran was therefore wary of Georgia's 2003 Rose Revolution, which Tehran believed was part of a U.S.-led campaign of regime change in which it too was a target. Following the 2008 war between Russia and Georgia, though, Tbilisi pursued a rapprochement with Tehran, which it viewed as a potential hedge against Russian domination, even as Tehran sought to guard against U.S. influence in Tbilisi.[37] Iranian engagement with the North Caucasus is more limited, but has accelerated in recent years as Moscow has become less concerned about alienating the United States and has sought to bolster ties with Iran at the regional level. Apart from economic opportunities, Iran sees investment in Chechnya, Dagestan, and Ingushetia as a low-cost means of checking the growth of Saudi influence among the region's Muslims.[38]

Central/South Asia (Greater Khorasan)

The historical region of Greater Khorasan—now divided between Iran, Central Asia, and Afghanistan—remains entangled with Iran because of porous borders and overlapping populations, as well as the strategic competition over Afghanistan and Central Asia that has dragged on, in some form, since Soviet troops first invaded Afghanistan just months after the start of the Islamic Revolution. Iran's own objectives, especially in Central Asia, are limited and largely defensive. Since the 1980s, Tehran has endeavored to prevent the consolidation of a hostile regime in Afghanistan—whether controlled by the USSR, Sunni extremists, or the United States—and to ensure Afghanistan's instability does not spill across the porous Afghan-Iranian border.[39] Iran is therefore largely a status quo power across Greater Khorasan, even as it cultivates allies and seeks to reshape politics within neighboring states.

The Sasanians first articulated the idea of Khorasan ("where the sun rises") to define the easternmost expanse of their realm. Recognition of Khorasan as a distinct entity endured after the demise of the Sasanian empire, and it remained part of the Iranian imperial space even when ruled by outsiders up until its partition at the hands of the Russians and British in the nineteenth century.[40] The extent of actual Iranian control often fluctuated.[41] As Rudi Matthee notes, Safavid-era Khorasan was larger than France, but sparsely inhabited, with Kandahar (in modern Afghanistan) the only sizable town.[42] Imperial authority in the vast deserts and mountain fastness of Khorasan amounted to little more than securing the frontiers and preventing rebellions that could threaten the power of the dynasty; standard state activities such as collecting taxes and recruiting soldiers were often impossible.[43]

Even though actual Iranian control over towns like Balkh, Merv, and Herat would come and go, the Safavids regarded the entire region as an integral part of their realm, in contrast to the Caucasus, which had relatively few Persian-speakers and where Iranian cultural influence was more tenuous.[44] The early Safavid poet Helali described Khorasan as "the heartland of the world," while the royal chronicler Eskandar Beg Monshi termed Herat "the greatest of the cities of Iran."[45] Despite being pushed out of eastern Khorasan in the nineteenth century, Iran's rulers continued to angling for its return, encouraged by Afghanistan's perpetual weakness and the persistence of economic and cultural linkages with both Afghanistan and the Persianate regions of Russian/Soviet Central Asia.

While Aqa Mohammad Shah Qajar and his successor Fath Ali Shah (1797–1834) brought western Khorasan, centered on Mashhad, back under Iranian control after decades of upheaval, Herat, Kandahar, and Kabul would remain under loose Iranian suzerainty following the death of Ahmad Shah Durrani in 1773 and the decline of the first Afghan empire.[46] The position of Herat in particular was contested, with local rulers nominally owing tribute to the Qajars but often resisting attempts to assert more direct control, intriguing with Afghan rulers further east, and occasionally leading troops against Iran directly. Instability at the center also contributed to renewed incursions into eastern Iran by Turkmen, Afghan, and Baluch nomads. Most aimed at capturing slaves and other booty, but, as the Afghans' 1722 conquest of Isfahan demonstrated, could, if unchecked, pose a threat to the core of the empire.

Instability also opened up the Iranian periphery to the ambitions of its imperial rivals. As British general Sir Frederic Goldsmid observed, with the loss of the Caucasus to Russia, Iran was now "confined in its move-ments to one particular quarter, the Afghan and Baluch frontiers" to the east.[47] In 1837, Mohammad Shah (1834–48) set out to subdue Herat, plan-ning a subsequent campaign against the Turkmen tribes and the Uzbeks in Merv, Khiva, and Bukhara. The assault awakened British fears that Iranian control of Herat would threaten the route from Central Asia to India and encourage Russia to exert greater influence over Iran (the presence of a Russian envoy with the Qajar army reinforced these fears).

In response, the British sought to build up Afghanistan as a buffer state, with territory tacked on from eastern Khorasan. The 1857 Treaty of Paris, imposed by the British following another abortive effort to retake Herat, forced the Qajars to "relinquish all claims to sovereignty over the territory and city of Herat and the countries of Afghanistan."[48] The treaty also raised the issue of border demarcation and granted the British the right to participate in the commissions that would be formed to delin-eate the boundaries between Iran and the new Afghan state, which "al-lowed the finalization of the partitioning of Khorasan and paved the way for the creation of Afghanistan."[49] It established, moreover, a precedent for British-dominated boundary commissions to fix Iran's eastern borders, which confined Iran well to the west of what most Iranians considered to be their traditional territories.

These commissions, in which Goldsmid played a central role, lopped off much of eastern Khorasan, Sistan, and Baluchistan to the benefit of British India and British-backed Afghanistan, leaving the border west of the Helmand River that Qajar delegates had claimed as the legitimate boundary. While the commissions were whittling away Iranian claims in Khorasan and Baluchistan, Russian armies were taking over the Central Asian khanates of Khiva, Bukhara, and Khoqand, followed by tracts of northern Khorasan (the south of modern Turkmenistan and Uzbeki-stan) in the 1880s.[50] By the first decade of the twentieth century, Iran's much-shrunken eastern frontiers were largely set, bequeathing Iran a series of postimperial ties that have shaped relations with Afghanistan, Central Asia, and Pakistan down to the present—and contributing to the sense of grievance and loss that remains a consistent theme in Iranian foreign policy.

Notwithstanding Naser al-Din Shah's recognition of Afghanistan's independence and territorial integrity in 1857, Iran maintained signifi-cant cross-border influence, especially in western Afghanistan and Herat, which have ever since allowed it to exert significant influence over Afghan politics. Mohammad Reza Shah's Iran never entirely reconciled itself to the loss of western Afghanistan, and pursued a range of cultural and economic projects with a sometimes irredentist subtext. The Islamic Republic has abandoned overtly irredentist ambitions, but continues putting down roots in places like Herat, Balkh, and other western regions that were once part of Iran's empires, in part to ensure security along its vulnerable eastern border. The Islamic Republic pursues analogous ambitions toward Tajikistan, whose 1991 independence and subsequent civil war opened up new opportunities. In both Afghanistan and Tajikistan, Tehran channels trade and investment, supporting Shi'ite communities in Afghanistan and promoting the Persian language as a lingua franca throughout the region.

When Afghanistan's king Muhammad Zahir Shah was overthrown in 1973, Tehran expelled around a million Afghan laborers and flirted with the idea of fomenting a promonarchy uprising in western Afghanistan.[51] After the Communist People's Democratic Party of Afghanistan (PDPA) seized power in a coup, Iran offered support for the large anti-Communist uprising that broke out in Herat in the spring of 1979 and called on Afghan Shi'as to oppose the PDPA government. Despite the hardships it faced at home following the 1979 Revolution and the invasion of the country by Iraq, the Islamic Republic sent Revolutionary Guard troops into Afghanistan to fight against Soviet forces and spread the ideology of the Islamic Revolution.

Iran also admitted as many as 2 million Afghan refugees into the country, whom it has used as a source of leverage ever since.[52] After providing military training, Tehran employed some of these refugees in its own war with Iraq; others returned to Afghanistan to serve as proxies in the chaotic period following the Soviet withdrawal. Iran also brokered the creation of an alliance of Shi'ite *mujahedeen*, which became the nucleus for the Hezb-e Wadhat (Party of Unity) to protect its interests in the Afghan civil war. Tehran later encouraged these groups to participate in the coalition opposing the Soviet-backed government of Muhammad Najibullah, ensuring that Tehran's allies would remain at the center of Afghan politics.[53]

Iran also sought to leverage ethnic and cultural ties to Afghanistan to make inroads among non-Shi'ite segments of the population. During the Afghan civil war, Iran was instrumental in consolidating Afghanistan's Dari-speaking minorities against the mostly Pashtun groups backed by Saudi Arabia and Pakistan. It forged an agreement with the Sunni Jamiat-e Islami, led by the Tajik commanders Burhanuddin Rabbani and Ahmed

Shah Masoud, which it encouraged to collaborate with Hezb-e Wadhat and other Shi'ite proxies. When Masoud's forces overthrew Najibullah in April 1992, Iran supported the creation of a new, Tajik-dominated government headed by Rabbani—though it would back competing warlords as well when Rabbani and Masoud proved ineffective.[54]

Once the militantly Sunni and Pashtun-dominated Taliban ousted Rabbani in 1996, Iran worked with India, Russia, the United States, and Tajikistan to forge the so-called Northern Alliance between militias representing the Tajiks, Uzbeks, Hazaras, and anti-Taliban Pashtuns such as future president Hamid Karzai. Iran's proxies and allies in Afghanistan included Herat's main power broker, the Tajik warlord Ismail Khan; Afghanistan's leading Shi'ite cleric and founder of the Islamic Movement of Afghanistan (originally organized in Qom), the Qizilbash Ayatollah Asif Mohseni; and Karzai's former foreign minister and rival for the presidency, the Tajik Abdullah, who became Afghanistan's chief executive in 2014.[55] As in the Levant, support for Shi'ites and Persian-speakers has not prevented Tehran from engaging the Sunni Taliban, despite the sectarian divide and a history of hostility predating the U.S.-led invasion.

Based on shared opposition to the U.S. presence and an interest in maintaining a foothold following the 2021 withdrawal of U.S. forces, Iranian engagement with the Taliban suggests the limited importance of sectarian considerations in Iran's eastern periphery.[56] In addition to guarding against a permanent U.S. presence, Tehran seeks to prevent Afghanistan's problems from spilling over the remote, poorly mapped border. Both drug smuggling and illegal migration are major concerns, and much of Iran's engagement focuses on containing these problems on the Afghan side, including through development initiatives. Iranian-backed projects include infrastructure (roads, bridges, power plants, telecommunications), as well as "softer" projects such as education, agriculture, and mosque construction. Many of these projects connect western Afghanistan to Iran, including road and railway connections to Herat and the "Eastern Corridor" connecting Iran's Chabahar port to Afghanistan's ring road.[57] By promoting investment and trade, Tehran hopes to create economic interdependence and develop new opportunities for both economic connectivity and political leverage.

Until the Taliban's 2021 takeover, these initiatives were also a tool for Iran to limit the presence of rival powers, notably the United States, and expand the number of pro-Iranian actors in the country. A number of Iranian development projects are operated by companies connected to the

Islamic Revolutionary Guard Corps. The Imam Khomeini Relief Committee, which works across Afghanistan, is particularly active in Herat, where it disburses funds to groups that support Iranian interests. Tehran also promotes transit trade through Chabahar, where it gives Afghans preferential access as it seeks deeper regional integration and an alternative to U.S.-backed plans that skirt Iran. Tehran also sponsors seminaries across western Afghanistan and has reportedly used its consulate in Herat to recruit fighters for its militias in Syria. Such steps suggest an interest in building up Iranian influence, while recognizing that Afghanistan will remain a locus of strategic competition with other powers whose capabilities overmatch Iran's, but who may not have the same staying power as a country with such extensive historical and cultural links.

Protection of Hazaras, Tajiks, and other Shi'as and Persian-speakers remains "a core strategic objective" for Iran in Afghanistan, and a source of leverage that Tehran employs with Tajikistan as well.[58] Apart from his custom of celebrating *Nowruz* in Afghanistan and Tajikistan, former President Ahmadinejad proposed creating a joint Iranian-Afghan-Tajik television station. While Dushanbe and Kabul rejected this proposal, Iran's Revolutionary Guard supports the Afghan network *Tammadon* (Civilization), founded by Ayatollah Mohseni and staffed by Shi'ite Hazaras. Iranian publishers translate and export significant quantities of books and magazines to Afghanistan and Tajikistan, whose own publishing industries are miniscule, while Tehran targets much of its development assistance to Afghanistan's Shi'as and Tajiks including funding for schools and a university (Kabul's Khatam Al-Nabieen University, established by Ayatollah Mohseni).[59]

Tehran similarly maintains strong educational and cultural ties to Tajikistan, which Khamenei termed "an inseparable part of the Iranian culture."[60] In the 1990s, Iran was deeply involved in Tajikistan's civil war, nominally supporting the secular post-Communist government of Emomali Rakhmon(ov), but also providing refuge and material support for members of the Islamist opposition. Together with Russia, Iran helped broker the 1997 ceasefire ending the conflict. Today, Tehran sponsors a range of Tajik-language media outlets that it uses to promote its interests in Tajikistan, including the Revolutionary Guard–controlled Radio Tajiki ("the Voice of Khorasan"). Tajikistan and other areas of Greater Khorasan also receive a significant amount of assistance from the Imam Khomeini Relief Committee, and Tajikistan remains an important destination for Iranian outward investment.[61]

Iranzamin and Eurasian Regional Order

In both the Caucasus and Greater Khorasan, Iran recognizes that it lacks the capacity to dominate its periphery and must modulate its ambitions in line with the region's complex strategic balance. Nor have these regions been a first-order foreign policy priority for the Islamic Republic. Consequently, the idea of *Iranzamin* as an Iranian-centric regional order has never gained wide traction, either in Tehran or in the region itself.

An influential subset of Persian nationalists still believes the Sasanian map represents Iran's natural sphere of influence. While the Islamic Republic shares some of their underlying assumptions and regards Iran as the inheritor of a grand imperial legacy that entitles it to a special world-historical role, its emphasis on the sectarian aspect of Iranian identity, not to mention Iran's straitened circumstances relative to its major rivals, have left Iranian engagement with its postimperial periphery in Eurasia comparatively modest, certainly in comparison with its role in the Persian Gulf and the Levant. While Tehran has its clients in Afghanistan and Pakistan (less in the secular post-Soviet republics, where Russia remains the most powerful external actor), its focus has been more on promoting concrete geopolitical interests rather than undermining existing regimes or exporting the Islamic Revolution. Its efforts to reconnect with the Caucasus and Central/South Asia are thus more modest than those pursued by Beijing, Moscow, or even Ankara.

This conscious downplaying of sectarian elements so visible in Iranian policy in the Arab world helps explain why Moscow and Beijing, at least, believe they can work pragmatically with Iran, especially given their increasingly difficult relations with the United States. In the Caucasus in particular, Iran has been willing to align its objectives with those of Russia, while in Central and South Asia, it has done nothing to challenge the larger projects of reshaping regional order undertaken by Russia and China (indeed, Iran was admitted to Sino-Russian–dominated Shanghai Cooperation Organization in 2021).

Whether this pragmatic approach to Eurasia will endure, of course, will depend to a significant extent on Iran's internal development, not to mention the success or failure of its revolutionary aspirations in the Middle East. The idea of *Iranzamin* nonetheless represents a deeply rooted vision of Iran's "legitimate" sphere of influence that long predates—and will likely outlive—the Islamic Republic. The very durability of this idea, which transcends the Islamic Republic's deep ideological divides, is perhaps the clearest indication of how Iran, despite over two centuries of repeated geopolitical setbacks, remains indelibly shaped by its millennia-long imperial legacy.

CHINA

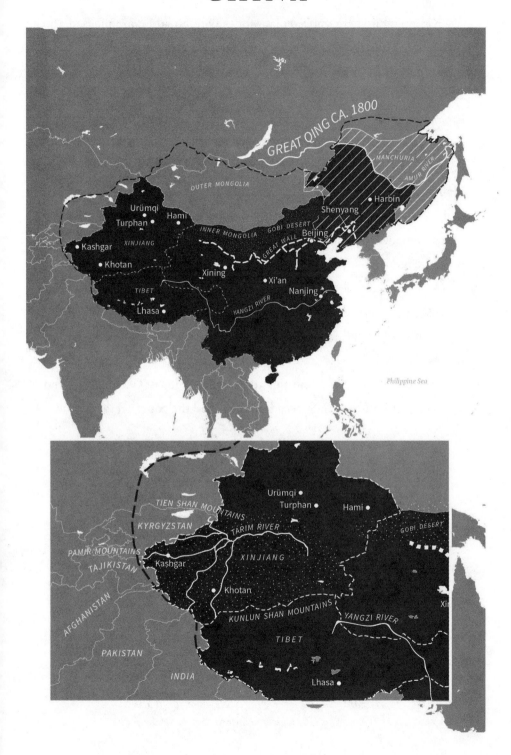

Xi Jinping first announced plans for the Silk Road Economic Belt, the overland leg of China's ambitious Belt and Road Initiative (BRI), in September 2013 in Kazakhstan's capital of Astana. Evoking the ancient Silk Road, which carried Chinese goods all across Eurasia, Xi pointed to the exploits of the Han dynasty (202 B.C.E.–220 C.E.) envoy Zhang Qian who, the Chinese leader suggested, "was sent to Central Asia twice to open the door to friendly contacts between China and Central Asian countries."[1] Since Xi's Astana speech, Zhang Qian has become a prominent symbol of China's Eurasian ambitions. Museum exhibitions, television shows, and other elements of popular culture depict Zhang's exploits, even as Xi and other leaders invoke him to promote the BRI.

As a metaphor for Beijing's aspirations in twenty-first-century Eurasia, Zhang's journeys to the "Western Regions (*Xiyu*)" encapsulate the ambiguities of Chinese intentions. While Xi and other leaders emphasize his contribution to peace, cooperation, and mutual benefit, Zhang Qian was an agent of empire.[2] Returning to the Han capital of Chang'an around 150 B.C.E. after more than a decade, Zhang told the court

> [places] such as Dayuan as well as Daxia and Anxi were all large states with many rare goods . . . however their forces were weak, and they prized Han goods and wealth. . . . to their north there were . . . the Yuezhi and Kangju, whose forces were strong; it would be possible to present them with gifts and hold out advantages with which to bring them to court. If they were really won over and made into subjects . . . it would be possible to extend [Han] territory for ten thousand *li*.[3]

Discussions of China's rise frequently emphasize the parallels between Beijing's current geopolitical ambitions and an idealized vision of the role imperial China played prior to the "century of humiliation (*bainian guo-chi*)" that followed the arrival of European navies in the mid-nineteenth century. They rest on a narrative of unbroken continuity from the earliest dynastic states to emerge on north China's "Central Plain (*zhongyuan*)" during the Neolithic era to the present. Whether emphasizing the myth of descent from a common ancestor like the legendary Yellow Emperor (*Huangdi*) or the existence of a unified Confucian culture, the PRC government and most Chinese view themselves as heirs to a long imperial tradition.[4] In part, however, because China itself was the victim of European and Japanese imperialism during the "century of humiliation," officials downplay the imperial elements of China's own past, to the point of eschewing the term "empire (*diguo*)" to describe the dynastic states that ruled what is now China prior to the fall of the Qing dynasty in 1911. The rebranding of Zhang Qian as a cultural ambassador is in keeping with Beijing's efforts to portray Chinese aspirations as uniquely benevolent and promote the idea of "win-win" cooperation as the basis for relations with smaller states in China's neighborhood.

The structure of the Chinese state nevertheless reflects legacies of imperial expansion. Both the Republic of China (ROC), which ruled on the mainland until 1949 and still holds sway on Taiwan, and the post-1949 People's Republic of China (PRC) struggled to reconcile claims to the territorial legacy of the Qing (1644–1911) with aspirations to transform this vast realm into something like a nation-state. Both acknowledge the existence of a composite nation, termed *zhonghua minzu* (roughly, "people of the central civilization") made up of multiple populations but nevertheless "speaking" Mandarin Chinese. While the ROC's ruling Nationalist Party, or *Guomindang*, was openly assimilationist during its mainland rule, the Chinese Communist Party (CCP) that came to power in 1949 acknowledges non-Han aspirations for cultural and political rights. It provides legal recognition to fifty-six *minzu* (a term variously rendered in English as "race," "nation," "nationality," "people," or "ethnic group"), including the Han, within the multiethnic *zhonghua minzu*.[5] Yet Han identity and culture remain the normative standard against which others are measured (like whiteness in the United States).[6] The PRC is thus a kind of hybrid state, a "'national empire' defined by—but not divisible into—its fifty-six national components."[7]

The challenge of diversity is especially acute along China's Inner Asian periphery, which encompasses Northeastern China, previously referred to as Manchuria (historic Manchuria comprised the provinces of Heilongjiang, Jilin, and Liaoning, along with part of Russia's Far East); and the autonomous regions of Inner Mongolia, Tibet, and Xinjiang—called East Turkestan by its Turkic-speaking inhabitants. These areas were intermittently controlled by Sinitic states based on the Central Plain, but most comprehensively integrated with "China proper" during periods of rule by Inner Asian dynasties like the Mongol Yuan (1279–1368) and the Manchu Qing. The Qing nevertheless maintained a distinction between the polity known as the Great Qing (*Da Qing*), whose borders shifted with each wave of dynastic expansion and were defined solely by the extent of the emperor's authority (*jiangyu*), and a smaller, largely fixed "China (*Zhongguo*)" within it. Bureaucratic order based on Confucian norms reigned in the interior, while, at least until the late nineteenth century, the Qing maintained various forms of indirect rule around its northern and western periphery.

By the last decades of Qing rule, new ideas about national identity and the threat to Qing sovereignty posed by European and, later, Japanese, imperialism sparked efforts to extend the system of provincial administration prevailing in the eighteen provinces of "China proper" to Inner Asia, and to make all of *Da Qing* into *Zhongguo*. These efforts sparked anti-Qing revolts in Tibet and Outer Mongolia, both of which remained effectively beyond the authority of the post-1911 ROC (while the PRC recognized Mongolian independence, its forces reconquered Tibet in the 1950s). Russian/Soviet support was instrumental in sustaining Mongolia's statehood, and Moscow sought to extend its authority from Central Asia (West Turkestan) to Chinese-ruled East Turkestan, exacerbating concerns about Beijing's ability to hold this territory together. Today, both Tibet and Xinjiang remain only partly integrated into the political and social fabric of the PRC. In recent years, this legacy of foreign intervention and separatism has led Beijing to intensify efforts to secure its hold in both Tibet and Xinjiang, adopting a strategy mirroring the approaches of Eurasia's other postimperial states, albeit magnified by China's comparative wealth and access to modern technology.

China's Inner Asian periphery borders territories in neighboring Russia, Mongolia, Kazakhstan, Kyrgyzstan, and Tajikistan lost during the final decades of Qing rule, and toward which the PRC maintains a still-ambivalent relationship. Though much of this territory was remote and sparsely inhabited, its loss—at a time when the British and French were also slicing off Qing possessions along the maritime periphery—fed into the narrative of China's "century of humiliation."[8] Beijing has resolved its border disputes with Russia and its Central Asian neighbors, but observers in these states worry about the possibility of future Chinese irredentism. Already, Chinese investment in infrastructure, farming, and resource extraction contribute to growing Chinese influence.

These worries have grown more acute since the announcement of the BRI, by which the CCP aspires to reshape the economic, political, and potentially, military balance across central Eurasia. Over the longer term, the BRI could help consolidate a regional order that is more Sino-centric, with recipient states compelled to adopt much of China's own security paradigm; for instance, the region's governments support Beijing's campaign against East Turkestan independence, even though their own citizens largely sympathize with the region's Muslim, Turkic inhabitants.

The BRI is thus both a development project and—at least to some of its proponents—part of a wider effort to rewrite the rules of global cooperation, with partnerships based on deference replacing the system of rules and alliances built up by the United States after 1945. Supporters of these efforts often couch them in language and ideas drawn from traditional Confucian culture, which the CCP has reembraced as a source of legitimacy in the years since the 1989 Tiananmen Square uprising.

Even if the CCP's invocation of Confucian ideals is instrumental, it is based on ideas deeply rooted in Chinese history. Among the concepts invoked to support Beijing's aspirations to reshape regional order is "Great Unity (*datong*)," first discussed in the *Book of Rites* (*Liji*), one of the five "Confucian" classics that would become the basis for China's imperial ideology from the Han to the Qing. The idea of Great Unity, with its emphasis on a single ruler for "all under the sky [*tianxia*] as one Family, and . . . all the Middle states [*zhongguo*] as one man," would later exert a profound influence on late Qing intellectuals seeking to maintain the territorial integrity of the Qing realm in the guise of a Chinese nation-state.[9]

Today, such ideas are invoked as an alternative to a Western model of geopolitics based on the rivalry between nation-states. They imply that Chinese preeminence throughout the historical *tianxia*—essentially the then-known world radiating out from northern China—was benign, and that Beijing's contemporary aspiration to create what Xi calls a "Community of Common Destiny (or Shared Interests, *Mingyun gongtongti*)" is similarly based on a desire for "win-win" outcomes. With their roots in ancient political thought and backed by the political and financial weight of the CCP, they represent an ambitious model of imperial geopolitics that holds the potential to reshape the balance of power all across Eurasia.

CHAPTER TEN

Civilization and Imperial Identity in China

FROM THE EASTERN ZHOU era (776–225 B.C.E.), the most important marker dividing the Sinitic realm (anachronistically, "China") from the rest of the world was Confucian culture, later admixed with elements of Daoism, Buddhism, and Islam.[1] This cultural complex was associated with states that rose and fell in the watersheds of the Yellow and Yangzi Rivers, a region Chinese authors referred to as "civilization (*huaxia*)" or the "central states (*zhongguo*)," and which sat at the center of the known world, or "All Under Heaven (*tianxia*)."[2] This Confucian culture provided both a foundation for political legitimacy within the "central states," as well as a rationale for imperial expansion, justified by the belief in Confucianism as the source of universal civilization.

The major dilemma facing imperial rulers lay in reconciling the aspiration for Confucian-inflected unity with the reality of ruling over peoples from outside the Confucian cultural realm, especially nomads from the Inner Asian steppe. The Qing, China's last imperial dynasty, was unsurpassed in its ability to establish stable administration over territories from Central Asia to the Pacific, in part by adopting different strategies for ruling in the Confucian realm and mostly nomadic Inner Asia. By the mid-nineteenth century, political crises and territorial losses, beginning with the British seizure of Hong Kong in 1841, left the Qing confronting the same dilemma as its Ottoman and Qajar contemporaries, namely, how to mobilize the empire's diverse inhabitants to resist colonial encroachment imperiling not just the dynasty, but China's "territorial, cultural, and, in the opinion of some, even racial survival."[3]

Overcoming this peril required ending the Qing's "politics of difference," by uniting the Manchus constituting the Qing elite with Han, Tibetans, the Turkic Muslims who later adopted the autonym Uyghur, and
others into a single community. In the process, a new generation of thinkers
reimagined the diverse, politically variegated Qing lands as a historically
unified nation-state, inhabited by a people sharing a common cultural and
even biological essence. With this new framing, the Manchu-dominated
Qing was—like the similarly "foreign" Qajars—unable to transform itself
into the nucleus of a movement for "national" salvation. It would be liberal
constitutionalists from the class of Confucian literati, men like Kang Youwei and his disciple Liang Qichao, who were instrumental in calling for
what Liang termed a "national imperialism" to ensure the survival of the
state in a Darwinian world of empires.[4] The implications of that shift were
profound, for Kang, Liang, and their allies were proposing nothing less
than transforming China from the center of universal civilization (*tianxia*)
to a state and a nation hemmed in by the borders of the late Qing empire.[5]

To give substance to this transformation, Liang articulated the idea
of an all-Chinese nation, which he termed *zhonghua minzu*. Combining
a character signifying China as the central state or middle kingdom—
zhongguo—with one signifying civilization—*huaxia*—this neologism
suggested that the Chinese nation is comprised of all those who live in
China and participate in its civilization, regardless of their ethnic origin
or native language.[6] Like most Confucian scholars, though, Liang and
Kang believed in the universality and superiority of Confucian culture.
While expressed in a nationalist vocabulary, their notion of *zhonghua
minzu* was thus shaped by traditional ideas about the civilizing potential
of Confucian civilization. They emphasized Confucian thought, classical
script, and other cultural elements traditionally associated with the Han
population—itself comprising a vast range of linguistic and lineage groups
united by little more than a common literary language and membership in
the Confucian cultural ecumene.

This emphasis on Chinese-Confucian culture as the basis for unification became the foundation for nation-building in the ROC and, with
some modifications, the PRC. Both states remained committed to the idea
from the Confucian tradition of Chinese culture as the pinnacle of civilization, which the state was responsible for spreading to less enlightened
peoples. Especially during the *Guomindang* dictatorship (1928–49), the
ROC emphasized assimilation. The PRC acknowledged the existence of
non-Han populations and enshrined protections for now fifty-five offi-

cially recognized minority *minzu*, whose members are encouraged to assimilate to a Han-centric mainstream while their own cultures remain stereotyped and commodified.[7] That Han-centrism has received new emphasis in the Xi era as a deliberate strategy for combating "splittism" along China's frontiers and mobilizing the population behind the Communist Party's ambition to position China as a major global power.

For much of its existence, the PRC's Han-centrism was expressed in Marxist terms, with the Han portrayed as having achieved the highest level of technical development. In the wake of the 1989 Tiananmen Square protests and the demise of the USSR, though, Beijing turned to traditional Confucian themes and topics. While selective, this embrace of Confucian symbolism allowed for a more aggressive assimilation of non-Han, similar to the campaigns against the Kurds in Kemalist Turkey or non-Persians in Pahlavi Iran. The most prominent victims in recent years have been the Uyghurs, who face a comprehensive assault on their language, culture, and religious practices as part of the CCP's campaign against East Turkestan separatism that also echoes strategies adopted by powerful past dynasties like the Han and Tang (618–907 C.E.) to pacify northern "barbarians" by inducing them to follow Chinese cultural ways.

While nation-building in the PRC aimed at securing the loyalty of China's multiethnic population within the postimperial state's borders, Chinese identity also has its imperial elements. A Confucian-inflected belief in Chinese exceptionalism always existed beneath the PRC's Marxist veneer and, with China's reemergence as a global power, underpins efforts to forge something like a new *tianxia* based on deference to and imitation of Chinese models. On a more basic level, the emphasis on culture and civilization as the defining elements of Chinese identity means both the pre-1949 ROC and the PRC have perceived the tens of millions of "Chinese" people living outside China's borders as being at least partly connected to this all-Chinese nation. The PRC in particular has cultivated ties with these "overseas Chinese (*huaqiao huaren*)" as a target for outreach and a resource in the campaign to establish Chinese influence globally.

From *Huaxia* to *Zhonghua Minzu*

The Confucian tradition encompasses different approaches to managing relations with "barbarians (usually *yidi*)" who exist outside the Confucian cultural space. Within this tradition, the dominant criterion distinguishing civilization from its absence was proper performance of *li*, or ritual. *Li* entailed a complex system of behaviors, acting as a form of "social regula-tor" facilitating the achievement of Confucian objectives such as perfec-tion of the self and social harmony.[8] *Li* also acted as a sort of "customary law," and anyone who acted in accordance with it was regarded as *huaxia*, or "civilized," which in turn was equivalent to what, anachronistically, could be considered "Chinese."[9] New populations could become *huaxia*—that is, "Chinese"—by accepting the dictates of this system and engag-ing in correct performance of *li*. As an ideal, *huaxia* remained capacious enough to include "different polities occupied by diverse peoples who had inherently different languages, beliefs, and practices."[10]

Nevertheless, scholars and statesmen were divided on the question of how, and to what degree, nomadic and other populations from outside the Confucian heartland could be transformed by exposure to Confucian civilization. Pan Yihong identifies two contending discursive frameworks that underlay traditional thinking about identity and empire, both rooted in the Confucian canon.[11] One, based on separation, held that "barbar-ians" were by their very nature alien, savage, and incapable of accepting the virtues of civilization. According to proponents of this view, a wise ruler should "have the various states of Xia (Chinese speakers) within and [keep] the Yi-Di . . . out."[12] With respect to Inner Asia, this approach was associated mainly with dynasties like the Southern Song (1127–1279) and the Ming (1368–1644)—whose extension and reconstruction of the Great Wall was probably its most visible manifestation—that did not control the steppe.

The other framework emphasized the transformative power of Chinese-Confucian culture. While its proponents held that China's cul-ture was more advanced than that of neighboring peoples, they also be-lieved that culture held universal appeal, and that exposure to it would in time cultivate and civilize the "barbarians."[13] This more universalist vision of Chinese culture facilitated imperial expansion and the assimilation of new populations, on the premise that "the king should leave nothing and nobody outside his realm," and the belief that the extension of Chinese cultural and political influence would ensure permanent peace.[14]

Dynasties like the Han that originated in the Confucian realm south of the Great Wall but also controlled the steppe beyond it were the most ardent advocates of "civilizing" the "barbarians," while so-called conquest dynasties originating outside the Confucian realm, like the Yuan and the Qing, tended to use Confucian norms as a basis for ruling within the Con-fucian cultural space, but ruled nomadic populations on the basis of their own traditions. Such differentiation was particularly salient under the Qing, a conquest dynasty that originated among the Tungusic-speaking forest-dwellers known from the seventeenth century as Manchus. Central to the Qing's ability to bridge the gap between its inner and outer realms were its heterogeneity and the adoption of multiple personas on the part of the Qing emperor, who was simultaneously "the Bodhisattva Manjusri when he went to worship the Buddha . . . the Ruler of Rulers when he went to the Potala Palace in Lhasa . . . the Aisingioro [the Manchu royal clan] chief when he was in Manchuria,"—and the Son of Heaven (*Tianzi*) in Beijing.[15]

The social and institutional basis of Qing rule was a Manchu elite, whose defining feature was membership in the army *cum* "social formation and . . . political structure" known as the Eight Banners (Mandarin *ba qi* /Manchu *jakun gusa*). Devoted to preserving what the Qianlong Emperor (1733–96) termed the "Old Manchu Way (*Manjusai fe doro*)," the Eight Banners served as a reservoir of military and civilian officials that allowed a small conquest elite to maintain its sovereignty over a largely peasant population that vastly outnumbered them.[16] While the Banners initially comprised Mongol and *Hanjun* ("Han-martial") units in addition to Manchus, in time membership in the Banners, rather than linguistic or cultural markers, became the defining characteristic of Manchu identity, as *Hanjun* were assimilated or expelled.[17] Being a member of the Qing ruling elite meant being a member of the Banners, which, by the late eighteenth century, increasingly meant being considered Manchu.

As the institutional core of the ruling class, the Banners—and hence, the Manchus—thus became the target of nationalist ire over their inability to fend off foreign aggression from the Opium Wars (1839–60) to the post–Boxer Rebellion occupation (1900–1901). The result was both racialized violence, as vast numbers of Manchus were slaughtered during periods of upheaval like the 1850–64 Taiping Rebellion, and calls for the Qing to root its legitimacy in "the people (*min*)" rather than the narrow Manchu elite.[18] As Liang Qichao lamented in 1901:

> In the present-day international struggles in which the whole citizenry participate (and compete) for their very lives and properties, people are united as if they have one mind. The international competitions of the past, which were the concerns of the rulers and their ministers, would subside after a period. But the current international struggle will last forever because it is constantly a

matter of concern for the life and property of the people. How dangerous this is![19]

Seeking to mobilize the largely non-Manchu public behind the cause of holding the Qing empire together, liberal reformers like Liang and his mentor Kang Youwei promoted the idea of an all-Chinese nation uniting Han, Manchus, Mongols, Tibetans, Turkestani Muslims (Uyghurs), and others. They sought to bridge the gap between rulers and subjects and maintain the full extent of Qing territory by denying that Mongols, Tibetans, Muslims, and other Qing subjects had a basis for claiming independence. According to Liang, "Viewed from the righteousness of making the empire public, then all the people of the nation have the duty to love and worry about the nation, and so divisions between Manchu and Han . . . are not permissible."[20] Yet Liang's vision remained colored by Confucian assumptions about the role of culture—language, script, and tradition— as the basis of the "Chinese" nation. Liang's acceptance of Manchus as part of the nation rested, moreover, on his belief that they, like the elites of most other conquest dynasties, had long since assimilated to Confucianism's superior culture.[21] And while Kang had called for "preserv[ing] China (the nation) through the Qing (the state)," the fact that the dynasty was non-Han meant that, in contrast to the Ottoman Empire (or Meiji Japan, which Kang viewed as a model), the nationalist movement could only triumph by replacing the dynasty.[22]

Revolutionary nationalists like Zou Rong and Zhang Binglin (Zhang Taiyan), meanwhile, were more explicit about the need to replace the Qing with a state based on the sovereignty of the Han majority and, in Zou's formulation, to "destroy the five million furry Manchus."[23] Zhang adopted familiar terminology of ancestral lineage to suggest that the people he called Han, or "Han people (variously *hanzu, hanren, hanzhong, hanren-zhong*)" were all part of a common lineage traceable back to the legendary Yellow Emperor. With this framing, Zhang sought not only to highlight the alien nature of the Qing, but, as Kai-wing Chow suggests, to more generally liberate China's history from the dynastic cycle by making the Han people—rather than the various Han and non-Han ruling houses— the subjects of a new *national* history. In that way, the history of the Sinitic and Inner Asian worlds was nationalized, such that affronts to the Qing dynasty like the burning of the Old Summer Palace were reinterpreted as affronts to the nation. While the concept of "Han" or "*Hanzu*" had under the Qing been essentially an "institutionalized distinction" between

Banner and non-Banner populations, by the early twentieth century, it had taken on an ethnonational coloring, subsuming in the process the multiplicity of other identities within "China proper," where Fujianese, Cantonese, and other "dialects" of Chinese could have acted as crucibles for their own claims to nationhood.[24]

Kang, Liang, and their post-Qing heirs rejected the idea of a state based on Han ethnonationalism because it would struggle to hold on to territories like Tibet and Xinjiang. Their conception of an all-Chinese nation, which Liang termed *zhonghua minzu*, was nevertheless colored by a belief in the necessity of spreading Chinese-Confucian culture to prevent separatism. As Kang Youwei argued:

> If Mongols, [Uyghurs], and Tibetans are all ordered to establish schools and are taught by using the Classics, script, language, and customs, they will unify and become the same as the Central Plain (Zhongtu).[25]

In choosing the name *zhonghua*, Liang rejected his earlier preference for *zhongguo*, which emphasized the state (*guo*), rather than the cultural ideals bound up with *hua*. Influenced by Zhang Binglin, Liang also increasingly described *hua* in racial terms—identifying the Hua people as the original descendants of the Yellow Emperor who later assimilated other neighboring populations to form the *Hanzu*. The term *zhonghua* would eventually comprise part of the name of both the Republic of China (*Zhonghua Minguo*) and the People's Republic of China (*Zhonghua Renmin Gongheguo*)—suggesting a Chinese nation comprised of all those who live in China and participate in its civilization, regardless of ethnic origin or native language.[26] The term *minzu*, meanwhile, was Liang's translation of the German *Nation*. In picking it, Liang once again rejected an alternative formulation (*guomin*) that emphasized the state and its territory. Unlike a *guomin* that would be confined to the state's borders, a culturally defined *minzu* could exist across borders—leaving future rulers an enduring ambiguity about the Chinese state's relationship to both non-Han minorities at home and various peoples outside China with links to its history and culture.[27]

Building the Nation in the State: *Zhonghua Minzu*

Liang's vision of an all-Chinese *zhonghua minzu* would underpin nation-building efforts throughout the post-Qing era. In both the ROC and the

PRC, though, nation-building remained colored by assumptions drawn from the Confucian tradition about the civilizing and transformative power of "Chinese" culture. While the language, especially in the PRC, was modern and "scientific," the underlying assumptions were similar to those guiding older dynasties like the Han and the Tang, which also struggled to integrate the Inner Asian periphery into a common political space. Always implicit, the Confucian basis for these assumptions has become more categorical in the twenty-first-century PRC, as the Communist Party has embraced Confucian imagery and ideas to emphasize China's role as a great power and nucleus of its own regional order.

It rests on the formula enshrined in the PRC constitution that China is a "unitary, multi-national State," which implies that "claims of secession based on nationality [*minzu*] are illegitimate . . . and, second that claims to exclusive domination over the country [*guojia*] and its policy by any one nationality are likewise illegitimate."[28] Despite this ethnically neutral framing, the numeric domination of the Han (who comprise around 92 percent of the PRC's population) and the centrality of Confucian culture in shaping Chinese identity have meant that in both the ROC and the PRC, *zhonghua minzu* has typically "spoken" (or, more accurately, "written") Mandarin Chinese—while Tibetan, Uyghur, Manchu, Dai (Thai), or other minority languages and identities have limited scope.

As in Eurasia's other postimperial states, the tension between diversity and assimilation—between the territorial legacy of empire and the ideology of nationalism—has been a source of contention and instability. In his January 1912 inaugural address as president of the ROC, Sun Yat-sen called for "unifying the Han territories, Manchuria, Mongolia, the Muslim lands, and Tibet . . . [by] uniting the Han, Manchu, Mongol, Hui [Muslim], and Tibetan ethnicities [*zu*] as one people [*yiren*]."[29] This vision of a "five-lineage republic (*wuzu gonghe*)" originated among Manchu exiles seeking a basis for Manchu acceptance in a post-Qing state, and was symbolized by the adoption of a five-striped flag for the new Republic.[30] Sun's "Three Principles of the People" called on the Han "to sacrifice [their] separate nationality, history, and identity" to merge with China's other four historic peoples.[31]

The civic nation Sun sought to construct nonetheless reflected Han language and culture. Sun demanded minorities' rapid assimilation into a Han-centric identity—and was in his private capacity critical of the five-striped flag. Yuan Shikai (1912–16), Sun's successor as head of the ROC, was more committed to the five-lineage republic, but his time in power saw continued fragmentation around the periphery that undermined support for the idea within the ruling elite.

Chiang Kai-shek, who seized power in 1928, argued conversely that all Chinese "belong to the same nation, as well as to the same racial stock. . . . That there are five peoples designated in China is not due to differences in race or blood, but to religion and geographical environment," thereby implying that minority groups were merely branches of the Han.[32] Chiang meanwhile pointed to the Qing's cultivation of Manchu distinctiveness through the Banner system and practice of the "politics of difference" as the source of its failure.[33] Chiang's portrayal of non-Han as biologically indistinguishable from the Han borrowed elements of both Liang's emphasis on cultural unity and Zhang's focus on ideas of race to provide a "modern" argument for the classical concept of unity.

This lack of regard for non-Han identity was, however, a liability for Chiang's *Guomindang* during the Civil War, one Mao Zedong's Communists would exploit. Mao criticized the *Guomindang* for its "wrong Han-chauvinistic ideology and policy," and repression of secessionist movements in the borderlands, even promising non-Han peoples the right to maintain their own armed forces.[34] The CCP's acknowledgment of diversity was in part a response to the experience of the guerrilla campaign it conducted in the 1930s from areas inhabited by non-Han, as well as to the influence of Marxist and Soviet thinking about the "national question."[35]

The constitution of the first Chinese Soviet republic, proclaimed in Jiangxi in November 1931, established equal citizenship for "Chinese, Manchurians, Mongolians, [Muslims], Tibetans, Mao, Li as well as all Koreans, Formosians, Annamites [Vietnamese], etc. living in China," and guaranteed that "all Mongolians, Tibetans, Miao, Yao, Koreans and others living on the territory of China, shall enjoy the full right to self-determination, i.e., they may either join the Chinese Soviet state or secede from it and form their own state," or voluntarily rejoin China in a federal arrangement.[36]

While eager to secure the support of non-Han in the fight against the *Guomindang*, the CCP was, however, never prepared to go as far as its Soviet comrades in assigning political content to ethnic distinctions. Mao, in particular, was affected by the loss of Korea and Taiwan, the partition of Manchuria, and other indignities inflicted on the late Qing, and therefore remained committed to preventing China's further fragmentation or subjugation by foreign powers.[37] In 1938, Mao replaced his support for self-determination with the formula of minorities' "equal rights . . . under the principle of their own volition to unite and establish a unified government."[38] In contrast to the *Guomindang*'s demands for rapid, overt fusion, CCP leaders argued that ethnic assimilation (*minzu ronghe*) should be a lengthy process, but sought to induce it through efforts to shape and channel nationalist sentiments.[39] Their view of national identity was colored by assumptions drawn from both Confucius and Marx—with different minorities portrayed as having achieved different levels of class consciousness, and the Han as the source of universal enlightenment and civilization (the Party itself has also remained both centralized and dominated by Han Chinese throughout its existence, with only a few non-Han cadres holding senior positions).[40]

While assimilation had been an explicit aim of the *Guomindang*, the PRC's construction as a "unitary multinational state" ensured some acceptance of diversity. The 1954 PRC constitution provided for the creation of national autonomous areas, but affirmed that they "are inalienable parts of the People's Republic of China."[41] Under this system, recognized *minzu* received limited autonomy in territorial units ranging from large "autonomous regions" (*zizhi qu*) like Tibet and Xinjiang down to counties (*xian*). "Autonomy" encompassed certain cultural rights, notably the use of indigenous languages, within the framework of the unitary multinational state. Unlike the Stalinist Soviet Union, the PRC did not regard specific regions as the homeland of particular ethnic groups, instead adhering to the longstanding belief that all the lands of "China" have been under Chinese control since the Han era.

Like other empires, the early PRC also undertook an ambitious campaign to map and categorize its inhabitants. These efforts drew on the tradition, dating to the Ming, of categorizing and shaping communal solidarities along the southwestern frontier.[42] The first PRC census, conducted in 1953–54, produced more than 400 *minzu* labels. A subsequent "ethnic classification (*minzu shibie*)" project compressed the number substantially. The ethnic classification project assigned large numbers of people, especially in sensitive border areas, to the category of "Han," while consolidating other *minzu* categories through linguistic standardization. Among newly consolidated *minzu* were the Zhuang (officially the second largest in the PRC), whose recognition aimed in part to "obfuscate" the political demands of Uyghurs, Tibetans, and other large communities.[43]

By the 1980s, the number of officially recognized groups had been set at fifty-six, with the fifty-five non-Han groups the bearers of the autonomy provisions laid out in the constitution.[44] At least twenty of the fifty-five recognized non-Han *minzu* live on both sides of the PRC's borders—including Koreans, Mongolians, Uyghurs, Kazakhs, and others—creating opportunities for cross-border influence even though one of the main aims of the classification project was to bind the non-Han populations to the state.[45] Containing these nations within the PRC has become increasingly difficult as Mongols, Hmong, Dai, and others have established online communities with coethnics in neighboring states.[46]

That development is particularly ironic, since the portrayal of China as a "unitary multinational state" was designed to emphasize that institutions and identities existing outside the framework of the state, such as the Qing-era Manchurian and Mongolian Banner system, are illegitimate in the postimperial era.[47] Beijing implies that Turkic Uyghurs are part of the core of a Sinocentric solar system along with the Han, rather than part of a wider community of Turkic-speaking Muslims in Central Asia and beyond, and that Tibetans' identity should be defined by the inclusion of Tibet within the PRC, rather than by loyalty to the India-based Dalai Lama. Under Xi, Beijing justifies this strategy not only on the basis of historical claims, but also as a bulwark against the spread of dangerous ideas (like pan-Islamism) into the borderlands.[48] Beijing thus allows non-Han to maintain aspects of their culture, to an extent determined by the state, but strictly controls their interactions with foreign compatriots, for instance by restricting the ability of Uyghurs to participate in the *hajj* or other rituals that reinforce their identification with a transnational Islamic *umma* rather than the Chinese *zhonghua minzu*.[49]

The overriding emphasis on unity also means that the CCP approaches its ethnic minorities largely through the prism of assimilation. Official rhetoric continues to emphasize the rights of non-Han *minzu*, but much of the academic and policy discussion adheres to a teleological assumption, drawn from both Confucianism and Marxism, about the inevitable disappearance of ethnic distinction (including minority languages) in the process of economic development. The CCP argues that the Han have reached a more developed stage of production than Mongols, Tibetans, or other groups, who are portrayed as "less evolved branches of people who need the moral and legal guidance of the 'Han' . . . to ascend on the scales of civilization."[50] In the post-Mao era, minorities seen as less developed have benefited from affirmative action, including exemption from the one-child policy in place from 1979 to 2015, and preferential access to education.[51] At the same time, this Marxist-inflected portrayal of China as the source of civilization allows the CCP to justify Han political domination in materialist terms, with non-Han expected to undergo transformation through "modernization (*xiandai hua*)," a contemporary analogue to the Confucian emphasis on bringing civilization to the "barbarians."[52]

During the 1950s and 1960s, Beijing relied on the process of "socialist transformation" to accelerate ethnic assimilation, arguing that non-Han populations remained stuck at the feudal or prefeudal level of development, and therefore required tutelage from the more developed Han to advance to modernity. Large numbers of Han youth were "sent down (*xia fang*)" to the provinces during the Cultural Revolution (1966–76). This campaign had both a class element—insofar as the "bourgeois" youth were forced to perform manual labor—but also a cultural one, as the "sent down" youth were to bring Han-style modernity to the minority regions, the product of what June Dreyer calls a perceived "Han man's burden."[53] Moreover, while the Cultural Revolution's widespread destruction targeted both Han and non-Han cultural relics, in minority regions, the destruction of temples, graveyards, texts, and other artifacts paved the way for increased homogenization into a Han-centric cultural mode. Han-centrism became more explicit after the launch of Deng Xiaoping's (1978–89) reforms, and by the mid-1980s, the CCP was in the process of rehabilitating Confucian culture, which Mao's Red Guards had sought to eradicate less than a generation earlier.[54]

This embrace of Confucian culture became more fulsome amid the ideological vacuum that opened up following the suppression of the 1989 Tiananmen Square protests and the demise of the USSR, with the CCP invoking Confucian ideals to justify both authoritarian politics and pursuit of global power out of a recognition that if the Party was "no longer communist, it must be even more Chinese."[55] In principle, the CCP's post-Tiananmen nationalism was ethnically inclusive and state-focused— the Party preferred the term "patriotism (*aiguo zhuyi*, lit. "loving the state")" to "nationalism (*minzu zhuyi*)." It fused loyalty to country with loyalty to the Party and the socialist system, making support for the political status quo equivalent to being patriotic, while highlighting aspects of Confucian culture that prioritized obedience and social harmony.[56] A more explicitly assimilationist "second-generation" ethnic policy then emerged in the aftermath of large-scale unrest in Tibet and Xinjiang in 2008–09, the result of official frustration that the combination of autonomy and investment had failed to secure Tibetans' and Uyghurs' loyalty to the state.

Part of that shift involved reembracing the language of *zhonghua minzu* as a foundation for assimilating Tibetans, Uyghurs, and other minorities to guard against separatism. For most of its history, the CCP termed its conception of the Chinese nation *zhongguo renmin* rather than the *zhonghua minzu* of the late-Qing reformers and the ROC. Prioritization of the state (*guo*) as the arbiter of Chinese identity supported territorial unity and aligned with the Party's emphasis on writing disfavored classes (such as landlords) out of the national community. As in the pre-1949 ROC, the CCP's revival of *zhonghua minzu* as the name for the nation highlighted the (Han-centric) cultural dimension to Chinese identity. Xi frequently speaks of the Chinese *zhonghua minzu*, and in 2017, the CCP adopted a resolution to add a provision on forging a *zhonghua minzu* "collective consciousness" to the Party constitution.[57] Still, as Mark Elliott, notes, hardly anyone in China describes him- or herself as a member of the *zhonghua minzu*, rather than one of the fifty-six *minzu* comprising it.[58]

Limited resonance of the *zhonghua minzu* idea among the Han majority underpins demands for more explicit nationalization measures, which the CCP increasingly sees as a path to unity. While adhering to the fifty-six-*minzu* framework, and encouraging "all ethnic groups [to] work together for common development and prosperity," the CCP increasingly emphasizes common descent from figures associated with Han culture like the Yellow Emperor and the Flame Emperor (*Yandi*), suggesting a lineage-based bond uniting the various peoples living on the territory of the PRC regardless of *minzu* classification.[59] The placement of Confucius statues in, for instance, Xinjiang's capital of Ürümqi, became a way for the Chinese state to claim ownership of these borderlands for a Han-centric Chinese nation defined by its embrace of Confucian values.

The PRC's historical narrative also increasingly attempts to Sinicize non-Han conquest dynasties like the Yuan and Qing, describing them as presiding over "ethnic fusion" that contributed to the "national unification" of China, rather than foreigners who conquered and dominated the Han majority.[60] A growing number of commentators, meanwhile, advocate a completely assimilationist approach that would do away with the entire edifice of minority preferences in favor of strengthening minorities' identification with the *zhonghua minzu*, and hence with the Chinese state. Beijing's ongoing campaign to transform Xinjiang reflects this emphasis on coercing non-Han populations into abandoning their ethnic, cultural, and religious distinctiveness in the name of becoming "civilized"—as defined by the CCP itself.

Zhonghua minzu Beyond *Zhongguo?*
The Overseas Chinese Imperial Nation

Although the idea of *zhonghua minzu* was specifically linked to the territory of the Chinese state (the *Zhonghua* of the ROC and PRC), its theorists and implementers never wholly separated it from populations outside China's borders. One of the most significant ambiguities centers on
the place of "overseas Chinese," particularly those living across Southeast
Asia and in North America, in the Chinese nation. With China's return
to global power status, its complex relationship to these populations is
emerging as an important source of influence, with Beijing appealing to
these groups on the basis of a common ethnocultural identity, suggesting
that, whatever their origins or current citizenship, they too are part of a
Chinese nation defined by an amorphous historical and cultural logic that
transcends borders.

In some ways, belief in a Chinese "imperial nation" is more modest
than in Eurasia's other postimperial states; Beijing's claims fall short of the
"Russian World" project, much less Turkish- or Iranian-style arming of
coreligionists. While Beijing does assert a claim to the loyalty of Taiwan,
Hong Kong, and Macao residents, it does so on a political basis—since
the CCP regards these places as legitimate components of the Chinese
state (even if their salience for Beijing is comparatively recent). Efforts
to bring the overseas Chinese (and, in a different way, inhabitants of a
"new *tianxia*") under Beijing's influence nevertheless suggest that the territorialization of Chinese identity adopted at the end of the Qing remains
compromised by the wider diffusion of the culture on which that identity
is based.

Communities of Chinese émigrés and their descendants have lived
across maritime Southeast Asia since the 1840s, when the post–Opium
War Treaty of Nanjing forced the Qing to lift restrictions on emigration.
More recently, large numbers of Chinese citizens have traveled overseas
to study, with many remaining abroad after graduation. Today number-
ing around 30 million in Southeast Asia and roughly 42 million in total,
these overseas Chinese give the *zhonghua minzu* something of an imperial cast, even though the category of overseas Chinese includes a wide
variety of communities whose relationship to China as a political entity is
complex. Many families who settled in Southeast Asia in the Qing era did
not experience the process of nationalization at work in the ROC/PRC,
and today identify more with their native province or lineage than with

a "Chinese" nation.[61] Others are anti-Communists, whether adherents of
the ROC who fled after 1949 or dissidents with no desire to return to the
PRC. Many more are apolitical and, like immigrants everywhere, mostly
interested in making a new life for their families.

Despite such ambiguities, Beijing looks to the overseas Chinese community as an important vehicle for Chinese economic and cultural outreach. As the PRC seeks to position itself as a global power, it has taken
advantage of the overlapping discourses of Chinese identity to mobilize
overseas Chinese in Southeast Asia, Australia, New Zealand, North America, Latin America, and elsewhere as a political resource. That process requires identifying the overseas communities as being in some ineffable
way "Chinese," insofar as they participate in the same cultural complex
that defines *zhonghua minzu*.

Such appeals to the loyalty of overseas Chinese rest on the ambiguous framing of Chinese identity that emerged at the end of the Qing.
Despite their emphasis on the territory of the Qing empire, even liberal
nationalists like Liang regarded the overseas communities as part of the
Chinese nation. Indeed, support from overseas Chinese was instrumental
in the foundation of the Chinese nationalist movement. Sun Yat-sen established his Revive China Society (*Xingzhonghui*), dedicated to ousting
the "Tatar" Qing, among émigrés in Hawaii, and overseas communities
provided much of the funding for the anti-Qing movement.[62] Sun, Liang,
Kang Youwei, and other anti-Qing dissidents also took refuge in overseas
Chinese communities during periods of reaction or disorder back home.
The revolutionaries Zou Rong and Zhang Binglin, meanwhile, popularized the use of *huaqiao* among émigré communities—emphasizing that, as
fellow *hua*, they shared a responsibility to the cause of overthrowing the
Qing, while their status as *qiao*, or sojourners, implied an enduring tie to
their homeland.[63]

Developments within the late Qing contributed to the ambiguous
relationship between China and the overseas Chinese as well. Drawing
on the European concept of nationality by blood, or *jus sanguinis*, the
nationality law adopted in 1909 at the end of the Qing era invoked the
"principle of blood lineage (*xuetong zhuyi*)" as the basis for inclusion in
the *zhongguo ren* ("people of the Chinese state"). Under this statute, anyone whose father was *zhongguo ren* (in practice, meaning any native of the
Qing lands) was also considered *zhongguo ren*—or Chinese—regardless of
birthplace. Adopted primarily to ensure Qing jurisdiction over individuals
living under European colonial rule in Southeast Asia, *xuetong zhuyi* was

"considered an effective tool for maintaining the unconditional obedience of Chinese overseas," and allowed the state to claim the allegiance of any "Chinese" person anywhere in the world.[64]

With some modifications, the Qing-era nationality law remained on the books throughout the ROC era on the mainland; in practice, the PRC also abided by *xuetong zhuyi* until it adopted its own nationality law in 1980 allowing some overseas Chinese to claim the nationality of their birth state. The ROC set up an Overseas Chinese Affairs Commission whose main goal was fundraising for the *Guomindang*, but also encouraged identification with the ROC as the motherland of all Chinese.[65] The PRC initially was more cautious, in part because of its early–Cold War interest in building ties with governments across Southeast Asia, many of which suspected that the application of *xuetong zhuyi* meant that the loyalties of their overseas Chinese communities were suspect. Only in the late 1970s, as China was coming out of the upheaval caused by the Cultural Revolution, did Beijing begin actively cultivating these communities, including by establishing its own Overseas Chinese Affairs Office (OCAO) under the State Council, along with other state and Party organs devoted to relations with overseas Chinese. Initially focused on PRC citizens abroad (*huaqiao*), the OCAO has since the 1990s also targeted its appeals to non-citizen "ethnic Chinese (*huaren*)," suggesting the two groups—now officially referred to as *huaqiao huaren*—comprise a common "overseas Chinese" community.

These efforts took on a wider scope as China's economy boomed and the number of Chinese students overseas expanded. Since the 1990s, Beijing has come to view the overseas Chinese as a potential source of investment and technical knowledge to tap.[66] The end of the Cold War sparked discussion about creating various forms of a "Greater China," including free-trade areas and even EU-style supranational entities uniting PRC citizens and ethnic Chinese abroad.[67] In the context of escalating economic competition with the West, the CCP has taken steps to encourage overseas Chinese to invest or settle in China. Officials emphasize that the concept of a "Chinese Dream," first articulated by Xi in 2013, includes overseas Chinese, and that Beijing will "promote the organic linkage of the Chinese Dream with the dreams of overseas Chinese."[68] Xi's 2017 acknowledgment that Beijing would "maintain extensive contacts with overseas Chinese nationals . . . so that they can join our endeavors to revitalize the Chinese nation" became the basis for a decision to grant foreign citizens of Chinese heritage (on the basis of *xuetong zhuyi*) five-year multiple-entry visas to encourage their resettlement.[69]

The most significant development of recent decades though has been Beijing's recognition of the overseas Chinese as not only economic assets, but also a source of political leverage on questions related to Taiwan, Hong Kong, Xinjiang, and other issues where its line is contested. Working through local community groups, the OCAO positions itself as an intermediary for the interests of overseas Chinese with host governments, while seeking to mobilize them on behalf of PRC foreign policy goals. In 2018, the OCAO was brought under the authority of the Communist Party's United Front Work Department, Beijing's main organ for establishing influence over groups and individuals outside the Party, in order to bring its activities in line with the CCP's overall strategy for recruiting foreign sympathizers.[70] One particular target is "ethnic Chinese" entrepreneurs as far afield as Central America, who are encouraged not only to invest in China, but also to promote Beijing-friendly figures to their boards and local chambers of commerce.[71]

The CCP encourages these overseas Chinese organizations to hold events critical of Taiwan during periods of cross-Straits tension, and to mobilize against Tibet or East Turkestan "splittism." Campaigns for overseas Chinese investment focus on Tibet and Xinjiang, with overseas Chinese encouraged to "contribute more to safeguarding China's territorial integrity, realizing its reunification, as well as passing on Chinese cultural values" by investing in projects that will boost development and integration with the PRC.[72] The biannual World Congress of Overseas Chinese Associations, the largest gathering of overseas Chinese community organizations, has in recent years made national unity—both securing Tibet and Xinjiang and promoting "reunification" with Taiwan—a central theme.[73] From the Party's perspective, a Chinese person in New York or Kuala Lumpur should take as much personal interest in the unity of the Chinese state as a PRC citizen in Beijing.

As part of this campaign to mobilize overseas Chinese on behalf of the PRC's territorial integrity, Beijing has also widened its focus to include outreach to overseas Tibetans, Uyghurs, and other minority communities, termed "overseas Chinese ethnic minorities (*shaoshu minzu huaqiao huaren*)," as pillars of the transnational, multiethnic Chinese nation. Application of the term *shaoshu minzu* (ethnic minority) to foreign Tibetans and Uyghurs reflects Beijing's understanding that such individuals remain "Chinese" no matter where they live, and that their loyalties should therefore line up with other "Chinese," rather than with external actors like the Dalai Lama or the World Uyghur Congress led by Rebiya Kadeer. Beijing thus regards foreign Uyghurs or Tibetans who reject this framework and criticize its actions in Xinjiang or Tibet as disloyal—regardless of whether or not they are PRC citizens.[74]

Another target is students; security services in several states have noted the extent of CCP influence among overseas Chinese student associations. As Chinese student organizations abroad include citizens of both the PRC and other states, Beijing's efforts to rally them behind its geopolitical objectives imply an assertion that being "Chinese" is equivalent to being loyal to the PRC. Beijing directs and assists these associations to mobilize around high-profile events, for instance bussing in demonstrators for rallies to welcome visiting CCP officials, or staging protests against supporters of the Dalai Lama.[75] In some cases, student associations receive talking points on sensitive subjects like Hong Kong or Xinjiang directly from PRC officials connected to the United Front Work Department.[76] Many overseas student associations have seen serious quarrels between pro- and anti-Beijing factions.

Beijing's interest in cultivating such populations suggests the emergence of a more imperial conception of Chinese identity, somewhat analogous to Russia's appeals to "compatriots" and Turkey's cultivation of Muslim minorities in Europe. For overseas Chinese communities themselves, Beijing's interest is a dual-edged sword. On the one hand, the increased attention and funding are a boon; on the other, increased scrutiny from host countries and fears of overseas Chinese as a fifth column are for some a source of anxiety that may, ironically, end up reinforcing their identification with the PRC in the long run.

CHAPTER ELEVEN

China's Inner Asian Borderlands

SINCE 2014, A VAST SOCIAL and political experiment has been underway in China's far-western region of Xinjiang. Following a spate of terrorist attacks perpetrated by Uyghurs, the Muslim, Turkic-speaking community comprising around half of Xinjiang's population, Xi Jinping ordered "an all-out struggle against terrorism, infiltration, and separatism."[1] Encompassing massive surveillance and detention of enormous numbers of Uyghurs—as well as Kazakhs and other Muslims—in "reeducation" camps, this crackdown, according to documents leaked from the highest levels of the CCP, aims at forcibly secularizing and assimilating Xinjiang's inhabitants while transforming them into loyal citizens of the PRC. It also involves severing Xinjiang—the Chinese political entity in the historical region of East Turkestan—from its past through the eradication of mosques, graveyards, historical neighborhoods, and other physical symbols of Xinjiang's otherness.

On the surface, China seems to have been more successful than Eurasia's other postimperial states in forging a common national identity anchored to a specific territory with borders widely regarded as legitimate.[2] That transition, however, rests on a view of the imperial past that subsumes the multiplicity of relationships that existed between Sinitic dynasties based on the Central Plain and the mostly nomadic societies of Inner Asia under the claim that a unified "China" has always existed more or less within its current borders. This portrayal of China as a historically united state—rather than an overlapping collection of sovereignties with shifting

borders—conflates pre-1911 polities, known by a dynastic name (for example, *Da Qing*), with the aspiring nation-states of the ROC and PRC
that came after. Beijing thus views both the Qing conquests and the consolidation of CCP rule over the borderlands after 1949 through the lens
of national reunification rather than as a colonial or imperial enterprise.

In fact, these borderlands were not only imperial frontiers, but, more
than with Eurasia's other postimperial states, often nuclei of competing
political entities. Their inclusion in China in something like its current
borders emerged during periods when the Central Plain came under Inner Asian rule, particularly the Mongol Yuan and Manchu Qing dynasties.
Both the ROC and the PRC have sought to legitimate their rule over both
China's Sinitic core and the sparsely populated Inner Asian periphery—
Inner Mongolia, Tibet, Xinjiang, and the three northeastern provinces of
Heilongjiang, Jilin, and Liaoning that constitute the region historically
referred to as Manchuria—by depicting these empires as episodes in Chinese history and the entirety of their territory as part of a historically
unified China.

Comprising more than half the PRC's territory, Inner Asia is ethnically and culturally distinctive. Until the modern era, these regions
remained under indigenous rulers whose loyalty to China-based states
was conditional and shifting. At times, they paid tribute to the Son of
Heaven in exchange for titles, seals of investiture, and economic benefits. At others, they contested Chinese influence across their shared frontier, or, as with the Mongols of the Yuan and the Manchus of the Qing,
conquered the Sinitic heartland itself.[3] Chinese dynastic control in this
frontier was, in Liu Xiaoyuan's memorable description, "as fluctuating as
a seasonal lake."[4]

Even when these disparate regions were united into a single imperial
formation, they were ruled through a variety of indirect arrangements different from those prevailing at the center, and were regarded as distinct
from "China proper." As the nineteenth-century statecraft scholar Wei
Yuan noted, "The seventeen provinces [of China proper] and the three
eastern provinces [of Manchuria] are *Zhongguo*. To the west of *Zhongguo*
are the Muslim areas, to the south the Tibetans, to the east Korea, and to
the north Russia."[5] Traditional Chinese bureaucratic order reigned in the
interior, while, at least until the late nineteenth century, the Qing maintained various forms of indirect rule throughout the periphery, managing relations with its Inner Asian dependencies through a special bureau
known as the *Lifan Yuan*—roughly, Court of Colonial Affairs, though the

Manchu name (*Tulergi golo be dasara jurgan*) means something closer to "Ministry Ruling the Outer Provinces"—whose top officials were always Manchus or Mongols.[6]

The indirect nature of Qing rule left Inner Asia open to the ambitions of the rival British, Japanese, and Russian Empires. As in the Qajar and Ottoman Empires, the intersection of imperial rivalry and local separatism exacerbated concerns about the loyalty of borderland populations. Efforts to impose administrative uniformity were interrupted by the Xinhai Revolution, but were again taken up by the *Guomindang*. Yet because the ROC was constantly fighting for its life, the Inner Asian borderlands attained a substantial degree of self-rule in the first half of the twentieth century, even as they remained objects of contestation between China and its rivals. This history of de facto sovereignty made the PRC's attempts to establish control particularly difficult. After 1949, Beijing adopted a hybrid approach combining a watered-down version of the Soviet Union's territorialization of identity with an ethnocentric pursuit of integration echoing Kemalist Turkey.

Reflecting the different relationships existing in the Qing era, integration has been uneven. Qing Manchuria is now effectively part of China's interior, and Inner Mongolia is losing much of its identity as a borderland. Thanks to their remoteness and recent history of self-rule, Tibet and Xinjiang remain very much postimperial borderlands, with strong movements demanding autonomy or even independence. In the past decade, Beijing has moved aggressively to integrate both Tibet and Xinjiang through economic connectivity with the interior, infrastructure investment, education, and migration. Its approach has also become increasingly securitized. Yet the very scale of Beijing's ongoing crackdown in Xinjiang, which many foreign observers have come to characterize as a form of genocide, testifies to how far China remains from being the consolidated nation-state the CCP likes to portray.

From the Qing to China

Only in the late nineteenth century, in the face of mounting pressure around its periphery, did the Qing move to integrate its Inner Asian borderlands into the core of the empire. By gradually eroding the political and institutional barriers between core and periphery, this process allowed a later generation of thinkers to regard the entirety of the Qing domains as "Chinese."[7] As in Eurasia's other empires, though, attempts to tighten administrative control in the name of national unification sparked a backlash, and contributed to the difficulties faced by Chinese regimes ever since in establishing durable control over these borderlands. The anti-Manchu violence of the Xinhai Revolution, moreover, alienated not just Manchuria but the bulk of the non-Han periphery, since "in building a China for the Chinese . . . [the revolutionaries] had made no place for Tibetans, Mongolians" and other Inner Asians, who in turn sought to break away when central authority collapsed.[8]

The period after 1911 saw debate between supporters of a state centered on the Han-majority provinces of "China proper (*Benbu Zhongguo*)," and those favoring a "Greater China (*Da Zhongguo*)" encompassing the entirety of the Qing territories, even as the ROC struggled to specify where, precisely, these territories lay.[9] For both strategic and ideological reasons, the "Greater China" principle won out; even the virulent Han nationalist Zhang Binglin concluded that without the Inner Asian periphery, China's Han population would remain vulnerable to foreign attack.[10] Adoption of the "Greater China" principle left subsequent governments confronting the challenge of reconciling concentrated minority groups with vastly different lifestyles to inclusion in a state organized around Han Chinese identity and culture.

Though the ROC set up special provinces, and later, autonomous regions, in Inner Mongolia and parts of Tibet, in practice, political weakness prevented it from exercising real sovereignty over much of Inner Asia, which remained contested among China, Japan, and the Soviet Union until the end of World War II. Both Tibet and Xinjiang enjoyed periods outside Chinese control lasting until after the foundation of the PRC in 1949. The CCP, which gained substantial support in the borderlands during the Civil War, attempted to coopt movements seeking greater autonomy, adopting a form of mixed rule designed to reconcile minorities' demands for self-determination with the imperative of maintaining unity. Beijing recognized autonomous regions in Inner Mongolia (1947), Xinjiang (1955), Guangxi and Ningxia (1958), and Tibet (1965), plus numerous lower-level autonomies throughout the country with "the power to enact regulations . . . in the light of the political, economic and cultural characteristics of the nationality or nationalities in the areas concerned," subject to the approval of higher CCP organs.[11]

Yet Chinese law emphasizes that ethnic autonomy must prioritize the interests of the state and its continued unity.[12] The PRC's embrace of local autonomy was based on the Soviet experience of nationality policy, but

China never created anything like the Soviet "affirmative action empire," with territories designated as "homelands" for specific minorities or efforts to promote what Moscow termed "indigenization (*korenizatsiya*)" of local institutions. And while autonomous regions in theory enjoy rights denied to ordinary provinces, in practice, implementation of these privileges is uneven, in part because the CCP itself remains centralized and Han-dominated, its administration of the borderlands overseen by the State Ethnic Affairs Commission—a modern analogue to the Qing's *Lifan Yuan*.[13]

The balance between autonomy and centralization has also shifted over time, with the pendulum moving in the direction of centralization since the crushing of the Tiananmen Square protests in 1989. Investment designed both to improve living standards (and thereby reduce socio-economic grievances) and to promote economic integration with the rest of the country has played an important role. So too has an influx of Han settlers, especially to the cities of Xinjiang and Tibet. These better-educated Han not only administer Beijing's development programs, they are gradually transforming the cultural and physical landscape along "Chinese" lines. Given the sheer scale of China's Han population and the educational disparities with Tibetans and Uyghurs, the effects of this settlement campaign exceed those of similar efforts in Kemalist Turkey or Pahlavi Iran, even if the process remains far from complete.

The Northeast (Manchuria)

Homeland of the forest-dwelling Manchu (previously known as Jurchen) tribes who established the Qing, "Manchuria" no longer formally exists. Denuded of population and resources by the Qing's quixotic commitment to preserving it as a reservation for the "Old Manchu Way," nineteenth-century Manchuria came under increasing pressure from the Russian and Japanese Empires, which loosened the ties binding it to the rest of China. Russia annexed "Outer Manchuria" (now much of the Russian Far East) from 1858 to 1860, while the remaining "Inner Manchuria" (that is, Heilongjiang, Jilin, and Liaoning, plus parts of the Inner Mongolian Autonomous Region) remained an object of contention until the end of World War II. Today a struggling rustbelt whose Manchu population has mostly assimilated, Chinese Manchuria—now usually referred to as "the Northeast (*Dongbei*)"—has lost much of its character as a borderland in a process that many in Beijing see as a template for the PRC's other Inner Asian peripheries.

Paradoxically, Manchuria's loss of identity grew out of failed Qing efforts to maintain it as an "ethnic preserve" for the Manchus. Heavily garrisoned by Banner troops, Qing Manchuria was isolated from the Chinese "mainland" by the so-called Willow Palisade, which Han Chinese required passports to enter. Banner garrisons in Mukden/Shenyang, Jilin, and Heilongjiang provided administration in place of the normal civilian bureaucracy.[14] To maintain the region's Manchu character, Qianlong promoted traditional Manchu culture and practices (notably archery and horsemanship), and banned Han settlement, decreeing that all officials serving in Manchuria were to be Manchus.[15]

These restrictions failed due to a combination of corruption, inefficiency, and concern about the expansion of Russian power. Han farmers and merchants bought land illegally from Manchu owners, who were prevented from productive employment by government insistence they maintain the Old Manchu Way. Migration restrictions did, however, keep Qing Manchuria's population small and limited its economic development, in turn making it vulnerable to penetration by rival empires.[16] After Russia cleaved off much of northern, "Outer" Manchuria in the mid-nineteenth century, the Qing moved to bring "Inner Manchuria" under regular provincial rule. Imperial Japanese troops nevertheless conquered much of it in the 1890s, and long maintained control of the so-called Kwantung (Guandong) Leased Territory and the railroad connecting Dalian (Port Arthur) with Harbin, from which Japan launched its devastating invasion of China at the start of World War II.

In 1932, the occupying Japanese established the dependent state of Manchukuo, and in 1934, placed it under the nominal control of Puyi, the former Xuantong Emperor of Qing (1908–12). While Manchukuo was a Japanese satellite and a source of raw materials for Tokyo's Greater East Asian Coprosperity Sphere, the installation of the last Qing emperor as its nominal sovereign and the adoption of the name "Manchukuo (*Manzhouguo*, lit. State of the Manchus)" suggested an attempt to fuse the Qing legacy and Manchu nationalism on behalf of the Japanese war effort.[17] The ROC effectively recognized Manchukuo's independence in May 1933 in the hope of staving off war with Japan, and likely would have acquiesced in its permanent loss had the Japanese army not subsequently marched into Inner Mongolia and "China proper."[18]

Despite this ambivalent attitude toward Manchukuo, postwar Chinese governments vilified Manchus for "treason" and denied them the autonomy granted to other minorities in the early PRC—hence the absence of "Manchuria" as a distinct administrative or political entity. The first Manchu autonomous areas were only created in the 1980s, and then just at the level of counties rather than prefectures or regions. This "deterritorialization" of Manchuria underpins the PRC's claim that the three northeastern provinces are a "natural part" of the PRC's territory—and that the Qing era was thus part of *Chinese* history, rather than a foreign conquest.[19]

Only in recent years have significant numbers of individuals begun acknowledging a Manchu identity openly, in part to take advantage of the minority preferences adopted in the wake of Deng Xiaoping's 1979 reforms. Manchus are now the PRC's third largest *minzu*, comprising around 10.4 million people (around half in Liaoning province), although, culminating a decline that began in the eighteenth century, the number of native Manchu-speakers may be in the single digits.[20] Observers in China's other Inner Asian borderlands fear that this combination of assimilation and deterritorialization points to a larger strategy of eroding the boundaries between core and periphery that Beijing would like to apply elsewhere.

Inner Mongolia

If Manchuria has been effectively deterritorialized, Inner Mongolia retains aspects of distinctiveness, not least its status as an autonomous region, but is undergoing a similar process of assimilation. Aiding this process is the region's majority-Han population, as well as the linguistic and cultural assimilation of most Inner Mongols, encouraged since Qing times to guard against the emergence of Mongol confederations that could challenge Chinese authority or give birth to a new Mongol empire. With the independence of the Republic of Mongolia (Qing Outer Mongolia) in 1912, concerns about pan-Mongol consciousness took on new life, especially once the new republic became a Soviet client state. Both the ROC and the PRC have thus followed their Qing predecessors in seeking to bind the Inner Mongols more tightly, in part by portraying China itself as the legitimate embodiment of Mongolian identity and statehood.

Like China's other borderlands, Mongolia was united with the Sinitic realm when Inner Asian dynasties such as the Yuan or the Qing took power south of the Great Wall. Nurhaci, the founder of what became the Qing, appealed to the Inner Mongols for support in his campaign to displace the Ming, arguing that while Manchus and Mongols spoke different languages, "our clothing and way of life is the same."[21] The Mongols recognized Nurhaci as a khan, allowing him and his successors to claim authority in the Mongol steppe as heirs to the political charisma of Ching-gis Khan. Forty-nine Inner Mongolian princes then attended the 1636 *qurultai* where Nurhaci's son Hong Taiji proclaimed the establishment of the Qing dynasty.[22]

The Qing divided the Mongolian steppes into the directly controlled "Internal" or "Court" Mongolia (*Neishu Menggu*) and the peripheral regions of Inner Mongolia (*Nei Menggu*) and Outer Mongolia (*Wai Menggu*).[23] Inner Mongolian tribes such as the Khorchins and Kharachins retained their hereditary nobility, though, in contrast to Outer Mongolia, the Qing sought to weaken tribal solidarity by limiting mobility and mandating court confirmation of local rulers (*jasak*s), who acted under the supervision of the *Lifan Yuan* and Qing military governors.[24] The Qing also opened Inner Mongolia to settlement by farmers, with the result that the population was more agricultural and more Han than in Outer Mongolia. The different approaches to Inner and Outer Mongolia not only impeded the emergence of a pan-Mongol identity in the age of nationalism, they also kept Inner Mongolia bound to the wider state even when Qing authority began crumbling.

Though anti-Han resentment was fierce, the outnumbered Inner Mongols' push for self-determination after the fall of the Qing made little headway. In the 1920s, though, many nurtured hopes of either achieving independence or joining a Greater Mongolia. Facing growing exploitation from warlords associated with the ROC, Inner Mongols carved out an autonomous administration in the early 1930s.[25] It was taken over in 1947 by indigenous Mongol Communists, who ensured that autonomy would be maintained under the PRC in the newly established Inner Mongolian Autonomous Region (IMAR). While Tibetans and East Turkestanis viewed the revolution through the lens of imperial conquest, Inner Mongols' sense of ownership was an important factor in reconciling them to inclusion in the PRC and in explaining Inner Mongolia's comparative tranquility ever since.[26]

Like other frontier regions, Inner Mongolia was subjected to severe repression during the Cultural Revolution, which saw a sharp decline in the use of the Mongolian language, the near eradication of the Inner Mongolian Tibetan Buddhist religious establishment, and a renewed push for assimilation. Han migration continued as well (according to the 2010 census, ethnic Mongols comprised only 17.1 percent of the IMAR's population).[27] The large Han presence means that Mandarin is the primary language not only of education, but also of commerce and the mass media.

Knowledge of the Mongolian language and participation in traditional pastoral society are declining, especially among younger generations.[28] Intermarriage between Mongols and Han is common, in contrast to the situation in Tibet or Xinjiang.[29]

The PRC's approach to Inner Mongolia is also colored by the existence of an independent Mongolian state to the north, which for much of the Cold War was a Soviet client (relations between Beijing and Ulaanbaatar were only normalized in 1986, following the withdrawal of Soviet troops). The PRC inherited the *Guomindang*'s efforts to reorient Inner Mongols away from a pan-Mongolian consciousness and toward membership in the multiethnic *zhonghua minzu*.[30] While Ulaanbaatar adopted the Cyrillic alphabet, with a written language based on the Khalka dialect, Beijing left the traditional script in place (after a brief experiment with Latin script). The "Khalka-centric" project of nation-building in the Republic of Mongolia excluded Inner Mongols, not to mention Oirats, Buryats, and other Mongol-speakers from the national community.[31] The result was to strengthen the Inner Mongols' identification with the Chinese state, and the perception of them as "Chinese" when traveling in Mongolia.[32] This cultural divide has limited the appeal of pan-Mongol ideas, much less irredentism originating from the Republic of Mongolia.[33]

To further cement Inner Mongolia's identification with the PRC, Beijing also promotes Chinggis Khan and other Mongol heroes as actors in *Chinese* national history, and portrays the Yuan as a legitimate Chinese dynasty rather than a foreign conqueror. Reinforcing this claim are the location of Chinggis's mausoleum in Inner Mongolia's Ordos Prefecture and preservation of the traditional Mongolian script in Inner Mongolia—both of which allow the PRC to depict itself as the custodian of the Mongols' traditions.

Moreover, although Mongols comprise less than one-fifth of the IMAR's population, its roughly 4.2 million Mongols outnumber the 2.85 million or so in the Republic of Mongolia. They also enjoy a much higher standard of living (per capita GDP in the IMAR is roughly $10,000, compared with $4,000 in Mongolia), limiting the attraction of the Republic of Mongolia as a pan-Mongol homeland.[34] Nevertheless, improved relations between Beijing and Ulaanbaatar, plus the PRC's outward-looking approach to development, have boosted trade and personal ties with Mongolia, leading some Inner Mongols to look across the border for inspiration and raising concerns in Beijing about potential separatism—and in Ulaanbaatar about creeping Chinese domination.

Compared to Tibet and Xinjiang, Inner Mongolia has experienced only sporadic mobilization against Chinese rule, though protests against environmental degradation, Han migration, and, in 2020, Beijing's plans to downgrade Mongolian as a language of instruction have occurred. Exacerbating the challenges to collective action are the numeric domination of the Han as well as divisions between Mongol factions and tribes in the IMAR (the post of regional chairman is normally rotated between residents of eastern and western Inner Mongolia). And, as Enze Han notes, Inner Mongolia lacks both the religious institutions that in Tibet and Xinjiang have become a rallying point for mobilization, as well as a charismatic leader abroad such as the Dalai Lama capable of putting Inner Mongolia on the global agenda.[35] Despite lingering tensions, Inner Mongolia's assimilation to the Chinese nation and state appears underway as the IMAR gradually loses the character of a postimperial borderland—perhaps following Manchuria and providing a more recent model for what the PRC hopes to achieve in Tibet and Xinjiang.

Tibet

Thanks to the charisma and visibility of the Dalai Lama, Tibet has received the most international attention of any Chinese borderland. From exile in India, the Dalai Lama—the fourteenth holder of that title signifying leadership in the Gelug (Yellow Hat) sect of Tibetan Buddhism, remains a powerful symbol of Tibet's distinct culture and history. The Dalai Lama is not only a spiritual leader, but was also the de facto ruler of Tibet until the PRC's 1959 invasion, and his lineage is bound up with Tibet's history as a self-governing polity under the leadership of Buddhist monks.

And while the fourteenth Dalai Lama has reconciled himself to Tibet's inclusion in the Chinese state, other Tibetan nationalists and their supporters in the West have not. Emphasizing the discontinuity between the Qing empire and modern China, they argue that Tibet voluntarily accepted Qing suzerainty, but reverted to independence when the Qing collapsed—and thus that subsequent Chinese claims to Tibet are illegitimate. In line with its aspiration to embody the political and territorial legacy of previous empires, the PRC however maintains that Tibet is "an integral part of China, and the Tibetan ethnic group has been a communal member of the Chinese nation sharing a common destiny" for thousands of years, but only the coming of CCP rule allowed Tibet to pursue "the socialist road to development and progress."[36]

Isolated by the high mountains leading up to the Tibetan Plateau and sparsely populated, Tibet was only sporadically subjected to Sinitic authority before the early eighteenth century, when the struggle for mastery in Inner Asia between the Qing and the federation of western Mongols known as Zunghars led to a permanent Qing presence. Conflicts between Dalai Lamas and China-based regimes seeking to coopt the Buddhist hierarchy's religious-political authority have characterized relations between Beijing and Lhasa ever since. According to Timothy Brook, "Each rupture has resulted from the irreducible conflict between the Beijing-centered state, striving to assert exclusive territorial control of a grandiose national geo-body, and the aspirations of local authorities in Lhasa, striving for autonomy from external patrons."[37] Like Xinjiang, Tibet has also been the object of foreign attention, with the British, the Russians, and, later, the Indians contesting Chinese claims, thereby reinforcing Beijing's concerns about the durability of its rule.

From the seventh to the ninth centuries, Tibet was an empire in its own right that challenged claims of Chinese centrality to the East Asian political order. According to a treaty from the late Tang era, "As for the whole of China, Tang is the sovereign, and as far as the whole region of the western frontiers, Great Tibet is the ruler" (the very notion of treaties was an accommodation to Tibet's demand for equal status).[38] For a time, the Tang even paid tribute to the Tibetan ruler, known as the *btsang po*. Only under the Yuan did Tibet and China come under common rule. Yet even the Mongols did not describe Tibet as part of the Yuan state, much less "China."[39] Rather, Tibet's clerical authorities paid tribute to the Yuan emperor, who in turn formally invested the head of the Sakya Buddhist order as Tibet's ruler. Qubilai Khan (1260–94) eventually developed a separate administrative structure for Tibet known as the *Xuanzheng Yuan* (roughly, Tibetan and Buddhist Bureau) headed by a cleric and outside the regular administrative apparatus.[40]

The Qing similarly ruled Tibet through its indigenous Buddhist clergy, relying especially on the Gelug sect and its leader, the Dalai Lama, to rival the more Mongol-oriented Sakya. In 1652, the Shunzhi Emperor (1644–61) invited the fifth Dalai Lama to visit Beijing, conferring on him a seal designed to signify that the Qing was now the ultimate source of authority in Tibet.[41] The growing Qing presence eventually led the "Great Fifth" to seek assistance from the Khoshot Mongols to reunify the Tibetan lands and pursue parity with the Qing.[42]

This balancing act between Manchus and Mongols came to an end in the mid-eighteenth century as a consequence of the titanic struggle for Inner Asian supremacy between the Qing and the Zunghars, in which Tibet and its Buddhist hierarchy became pawns. After Qing troops had rescued the child seventh Dalai Lama from Zunghar custody and restored him to the Tibetan throne, the Kangxi Emperor (1661–1722) sent him a public letter calling him "a true reincarnation, and everyone must show him true respect. . . . The Dalai Lama is requested to advise [the Mongols] to remain obedient to the Emperor."[43] Kangxi, however, also installed a nobleman who had served loyally during the conflict as the head of a new council of ministers, and left behind both a Qing garrison and Manchu commissioners known as *amban*s.[44] The Dalai Lama remained the visible embodiment of Buddhist sovereignty and Tibetan identity, but his authority ultimately rested on Qing military power.[45]

This arrangement endured until 1903–04, when British troops under Col. Francis Younghusband fought their way to Lhasa.[46] Younghusband forced the thirteenth Dalai Lama's representatives to sign an agreement barring the influence of foreign powers (including the Qing) and establishing a preferential trade regime with British India. A belated Qing attempt to tighten administrative control and promote Han colonization sparked a backlash and the assassination of a deputy *amban*. Qing troops then toppled the Tibetan government and forced the thirteenth Dalai Lama to flee. The undisciplined soldiers sparked widespread ethnic violence and reduced much of Lhasa to rubble. This upheaval shattered the foundations of Tibet's accommodation to Chinese suzerainty, laying a foundation for much of the Sino-Tibetan enmity of the subsequent century.[47]

Tibet then remained effectively independent for over four decades following the Qing collapse. The role of British, Soviet, U.S., and Indian support in sustaining it fed into fears of encirclement that long colored Beijing's attitude toward Lhasa. In 1914, British, Chinese, and Tibetan representatives negotiated a convention at Simla codifying the divide between Chinese-controlled "Inner Tibet" (now mostly in Sichuan and Qinghai provinces) and an autonomous "Outer Tibet." The convention specified that "Tibet is under the suzerainty of China, and recognizing also the autonomy of Outer Tibet, [the parties] engage to respect the territorial integrity of the country, and to abstain from interference in the administration of Outer Tibet."[48] With its recognition of Tibet's right to conduct diplomatic negotiations and promises of autonomy, the Simla Convention remains central to Tibetan claims to sovereignty. Beijing, which quickly withdrew its signature, counts the Simla Convention among the "unequal treaties" forced on it by foreign imperialists before

1949, though—in contrast to other such agreements—it does not regard the convention's terms, among them the Tibetan negotiators' cession of territory in what is today the Indian state of Arunachal Pradesh to the British, as binding. Throughout the Republican era, this nominally independent Tibet endured both British and Soviet intrigues (with Moscow seeking to extend its Mongolian protectorate to Tibet), with clear implications for Chinese security.[49]

Following the Chinese Civil War, the CCP recognized that Tibet's remoteness, history of de facto independence, and the almost complete absence of a Han population required a gradual approach to integration. Mao consequently sought to make the fourteenth Dalai Lama an ally in Tibet's "modernization." When Lhasa refused to accept incorporation, however, Mao ordered Red Army troops into Tibet to impose a settlement.[50] The resulting Seventeen Point Agreement, signed in May 1951, mirrored the indirect arrangement under which the Qing ruled Tibet before the Younghusband Expedition. Beijing promised to eschew force, and to respect Tibet's "current political systems" and "the Dalai Lama's inherent power and position," while Lhasa acknowledged that Tibet was part of the PRC. Beijing, as Liu Xiaoyuan notes, was not committing to maintaining what it saw as Tibet's "theocratic dictatorship" so much as to allowing the Tibetans themselves to implement the reforms it deemed necessary to bring Tibet into the modern world, and into the Chinese state.[51]

The Seventeen Point Agreement, though, applied only to "political Tibet," not to the territories earlier incorporated into Sichuan and Qinghai. Beijing's promotion of land reform in these regions in the mid-1950s sparked an uprising that spread to "political Tibet" as well, leading to the arrival of Chinese troops and the flight of the fourteenth Dalai Lama to India in March 1959. Even if the Communist Party had always anticipated that autonomy under the Dalai Lama would be temporary, the violence of the 1950s accelerated the shift from what Sulmaan Wasif Khan terms "empire-lite" into a "harder, heavier imperial formation" that sought to impose the same kind of homogenization to which the rest of the PRC was subjected.[52]

Beijing abolished Tibet's Buddhist government, replacing it in 1965 with the Tibetan Autonomous Region (TAR). It also closed the majority of Tibet's monasteries, which had sat at the apex of a feudal economy, breaking up the monastic estates and giving land to peasants in the expectation that they would place class loyalties above those of religion or nationality (attacks on the Buddhist establishment reached their apogee during the Cultural Revolution). Institutions modeled on those in in the interior, from schools to post offices, were also introduced, often staffed by Han Chinese.[53] Beijing sought to delineate and close down movement across its Himalayan frontiers to both limit contacts with the Dalai Lama's government-in-exile and extend state power throughout the TAR. The closure of the border was also a response to concerns that India was using the unrest in Tibet to pursue its territorial ambitions at Chinese expense.[54]

While the atheist CCP imposed significant damage on Tibet's Buddhist institutions during the 1950s revolt and again during the Cultural Revolution, Buddhism's endurance as an element of Tibetan identity has also led the PRC to manipulate the Buddhist hierarchy along lines pioneered by the Qing. Beginning in the 1950s, Beijing promoted the more malleable Panchen Lama as an alternative to the Dalai Lama.[55] When the tenth Panchen Lama died in 1989, Beijing attempted to prevent the exiled Dalai Lama from picking his successor—kidnapping the boy proclaimed as the new incarnation and replacing him with its own candidate, who was then selected through a system of lots first established by Qianlong in the 1790s.[56] Beijing similarly asserts its prerogative to name the fourteenth Dalai Lama's eventual successor.

Unlike Manchuria and Inner Mongolia with their large Han populations, more than 90 percent of the TAR's inhabitants are ethnic Tibetans, since almost all Han who lived in Tibet during the Qing era fled during the upheavals of the early twentieth century.[57] As in other borderlands, though, top cadres have always been Han Chinese, and Beijing's emphasis on economic development has since the 1980s led to an influx of Han laborers and businesspeople, as the overall share of Han increased from less than 3 percent in 1964 to 8.2 percent in 2010. Lhasa and other large towns now have a non-Tibetan majority, though rural areas remain heavily Tibetan in population and language use.[58]

This influx of better-educated Han and the infrastructure that many of them have come to build, including a highway and railway connecting Lhasa with Chengdu, have begun integrating Tibet economically and politically with the rest of China. As in Xinjiang, moreover, the influx of Han professionals has sparked a debate between Tibetans seeking to preserve the ethnic character of the TAR and officials who argue that development will provide a higher standard of living and reconcile the Tibetan population to Chinese rule. The better-educated Han population acts as a pro-Beijing "constituency," whose appeals for official assistance in periods of unrest contribute to the expansion of the state's presence. They thus play a role out of proportion to their numbers in promoting Tibet's political and cultural integration with the rest of the PRC.[59]

Xinjiang

China's most complex borderland lies in the Xinjiang Uyghur Autonomous Region (XUAR), combining the steppe region of Zungharia in the north and the dry Tarim and Turfan Basins—collectively known to their Turkic inhabitants as Altishahr (the "six cities") in the south and east. Beijing established the XUAR in 1955 in an effort to give the region's inhabitants a stake in the PRC's state-building project and to guard against Soviet-backed movements for independence.[60] Beijing argues that Xinjiang "has been an important part of China [since the first century B.C.E.], and played a significant role in the construction and development of a unitary multiethnic country," as "home to several of China's ethnic peoples."[61] Many of the region's Muslim inhabitants, including Uyghurs, Kazakhs, Kyrgyz, Hui (Dungans), and others, point to the ancient kingdoms and city-states of the Tarim Basin, to more recent periods of self-rule, as well as to the independence of the Turkic Central Asian states from the USSR, to support their own political aspirations.[62]

The steppes, oases, and deserts of modern Xinjiang have been linked to the Sinitic world since the ancient era thanks to their location along the main route of the Silk Road. The Han and Tang dynasties developed distinct institutions for projecting power into the loosely governed "Western Regions (*Xiyu*)," such as the Tang's Protectorate of the Pacified West (*Anxi duhufu*), which provided a security umbrella and dispute-resolution mechanism for the region's approximately 850 "loose-rein commands and prefectures (*jimi fuzhou*)."[63] Chinese influence declined dramatically, however, after the end of the Tang. Preserved in the artifacts of Dunhuang, Khotan, and other Silk Road sites, the legacies of Chinese rule would be little remembered until the modern era, and despite the CCP's claim that Xinjiang has always been part of "China," it was only under the Qing that East Turkestan became firmly attached to the geobody of what became the Chinese state.

The culmination of the Qing conquest came with the brutal annihilation of the Zunghars, who had controlled the steppes of northern Xinjiang, the Ili River valley, and the Altai Mountains until the 1750s.[64] Following Qianlong's command to "show no mercy at all to these rebels," a combination of Qing forces and smallpox decimated the Zunghar population in the conflict's final stages, leaving behind a depopulated steppe open to settlement by Dungans/Hui and the settled Turkic farmers known as Taranchis, whose contemporary descendants mostly consider themselves Uyghurs.[65] The final piece of Qing expansion in Inner Asia was the conquest of the oasis cities of the Tarim Basin that had been tributaries of the Zunghars through a complex process of manipulating rivalries between competing Sufi orders and the local aristocracy, commonly referred to as *begs*.[66]

Until the creation of Xinjiang province in 1884, Qing rule in these lands remained diverse, reflecting the distinct political and economic arrangements that prevailed in Zungharia, the Tarim Basin oases, and the eastern cities of Hami (Qumul) and Turpan (Turfan). A governor general in Huiyan (Yining) exercised overall control, while security was in the hands of military garrisons in Zungharia. Chinese-style administration was gradually introduced in Ürümqi and other areas with larger Han populations. The linchpins of Qing power in oasis cities like Yarkand, Khotan, and Kashgar were members of the local elite, or *begs*, who agreed to accept appointment in the Qing administrative order and exercised power under the supervision of the *Lifan Yuan* and imperial representatives in Ürümqi.[67] In the east, the Qing maintained tributary relations with the hereditary rulers of Hami/Qumul and Turpan, who had supported the campaign against the Zunghars.[68]

As in Tibet, these arrangements broke down in the late nineteenth century in the face of growing interimperial competition. Russia's penetration into Central Asia was particularly threatening because the longstanding connections between eastern and western Turkestan gave St. Petersburg the ability to influence developments across the Qing frontier. Further complicating the situation was the rebellion of Yaqub Beg, a commander in the force dispatched by the neighboring Khanate of Khoqand to support a Dungan uprising in Qing Shanxi and Gansu. En route, Yaqub deposed his nominal superior and took command of the army, which he then used to set up a Kashgar-based Islamic emirate that dominated East Turkestan for over a decade (1865–77). Yaqub Beg's revolt and Russia's conquest of Khoqand led the Qing to reorganize Zungharia and Altishahr into a Chinese-style province named Xinjiang (New Frontier).

Though Xinjiang had the trappings of a regular province, the combination of distance and the influence of local power brokers kept central authority weak, allowing governors to act with little oversight and facilitating abuses of power.[69] Tenuous control from the center also complicated efforts to keep Xinjiang within the Chinese orbit when Qing authority collapsed. After 1911, Xinjiang endured "Chinese warlord satrapies paying lip-service to weak central Chinese governments, hopeful Turkic republics and satellites of the Soviet Union" until its eventual incorporation into the PRC.[70] This period of upheaval saw the outflow of large numbers of Han and other settlers who had arrived as part of the Qing's efforts at imperial consolidation.

The breakdown of Chinese authority also provided a pretext for Soviet intervention. Always adaptable, Moscow backed a range of proxies with divergent ideas about East Turkestan's identity and relationship to China. The USSR aided the rise of Sheng Shicai, the warlord whose largely Han forces dominated Xinjiang for most of the 1930s and defeated a nascent East Turkestan Republic (ETR) in 1934. Yet when Sheng pivoted back to the *Guomindang* after the German invasion of the USSR, Moscow began arming Uyghur and Kazakh separatists along the border with Soviet Kazakhstan instead.[71]

Moscow's backing was also instrumental to the success of the Second East Turkestan Republic, proclaimed in November 1944 by Turkic separatists in the three Ili Valley districts of northern Xinjiang. With a program calling for friendly relations with Moscow and a ban on Han migration, the Second ETR promoted an East Turkestani identity uniting speakers of various Turkic languages against Han domination. Fighting between ETR and Chinese Nationalist forces was exceptionally bloody, with widespread massacres of civilians, motivated in part by the ETR's desire to eliminate the Han presence.[72]

The CCP did not, however, challenge the Second ETR's claim to independence—both out of deference to Soviet leadership and because the conflict with the ETR forced the Nationalists to fight on two fronts during China's civil war. Soviet support for the ETR was, however, conditional, and at the end of World War II, Moscow brokered an agreement leaving the three Ili districts in separatist hands in exchange for their joining a coalition with the *Guomindang*. After the ETR's top leaders were killed in a suspicious plane crash in August 1949, Moscow convinced the remaining leadership to accept incorporation into the new PRC.

Despite the legacy of Soviet influence, the Second ETR remains the most successful and enduring effort to create an independent East Turkestani state, and therefore a source of great sensitivity in the PRC. The CCP's own acquiescence in what amounted to an attempt at creating a Soviet protectorate is not a page of history that the modern CCP is eager to revisit. Historical scholarship, much less public discussion of the Ili Revolt, is thus carefully regulated. Beijing's fears about East Turkestan separatism and Uyghur activism are also colored by the specter of foreign support, now exacerbated by the expansion of cross-border ties between Xinjiang and the independent Central Asian states.

Since 1949, Xinjiang has experienced the same pressures for consolidation and integration as the rest of the PRC's Inner Asian periphery. While a concession to the Uyghur population, the creation of the XUAR did not confer on them a specific claim to the territory. Indeed, Beijing emphasizes that the XUAR "has been a multiethnic region . . . since ancient times," but never a Uyghur homeland.[73] Following a post-1949 influx of Han (and Hui), Xinjiang's demographic profile today is similar to that of the mid-nineteenth century; according to the 2010 census, Xinjiang's population was 46.4 percent Uyghur, down from more than 80 percent in 1941, with most Han concentrated in Ürümqi and other cities.[74] The shift is largely the result of state policy encouraging Han settlement, which was most pronounced during the Great Leap Forward (1958–62) and Cultural Revolution. While the PRC no longer explicitly promotes Han colonization, emphasis on economic development still encourages poor Han and Hui to move to Xinjiang in search of work. One of the main drivers of Han settlement is the so-called Xinjiang Production and Construction Corps (*Xinjiang shengchan jianshe bingtuan*), which is modeled on agricultural settlements used since Han times to support occupation forces along the frontiers.[75]

Unlike other autonomous regions, the XUAR comprises numerous smaller autonomous districts, counties, prefectures, and towns for its non-Uyghur *minzu*. Although non-Uyghurs were a small fraction of the population in the 1950s, these "subautonomies" make up more than half the territory of the XUAR. Representatives of non-Uyghur populations like Kazakhs and Kyrgyz are thereby embedded in the political apparatus of the XUAR out of proportion to their overall share of the population. As beneficiaries of the system who would stand to lose from a more representative distribution of benefits, non-Uyghur *minzu* were long allies of the state. Beijing nevertheless worries about their Islamic identity and loyalties that are potentially divided with neighboring Central Asian states.

The PRC's dragnet in Xinjiang has thus swept up large numbers of Kazakhs, Kyrgyz, and other non-Uyghur Muslims, potentially eroding Beijing's longstanding divide-and-rule strategy and consolidating more widespread opposition.[76] In any case, the position of regional Party secretary and leading positions at the regional, prefectural, and county levels have always been held by Han cadres.[77] Han domination is especially pronounced within the Communist Party and the security organs, whose influence outstrips that of formal state institutions where Uyghurs and other Muslims have greater representation.

Beginning with the announcement of the Great Western Development (*Xibu da kaifa*) program in 1999, Beijing has sought to address regional disparities in income, investment, and living standards by combining state-directed investment with efforts to improve the investment climate and migration of skilled (mainly Han) workers to underdeveloped regions in western and northern China. The bulk of the ensuing investment focused on transportation, energy, communications, and irrigation infrastructure.[78] Though China's economy overall has slowed, growth in Xinjiang has averaged 8.5 percent per year since 2009, further widening the income gap between Uyghurs and (mostly better-educated) Han, and driving further Han migration.[79] Even Xi acknowledges, though, that "economic development does not automatically bring lasting order and security."[80] Without abandoning the commitment to development, Beijing's post-2014 crackdown suggests a new conviction that only surveillance, "reeducation," and the wholesale erasure of Uyghur culture will accelerate Xinjiang's transformation from postimperial borderland to undifferentiated component of the Chinese state.

China's Accelerating Postimperial Transformation

Xinjiang is the starkest example of how the PRC faces the same dilemma as its peers in balancing the imperial and national strands of its identity. While claiming the full territorial inheritance of the Qing (apart from Mongolia), the PRC is, if anything, moving further from the segmented, differentiated model that allowed a figure like Qianlong to encompass China proper and Inner Asia within the bounds of *Da Qing*, and toward a unified, Han-dominated administrative model. If Beijing succeeds in consolidating its grip on Xinjiang (and Tibet), as it has already done to a greater or lesser degree in Manchuria and Inner Mongolia, it will have moved further down the path from empire to national state. As in other states that experienced this transition, the human cost is liable to be high.

While revelations of the CCP's campaign against the Uyghurs in Xinjiang shocked many foreign observers, they are in keeping with the steps Eurasia's other postimperial states have taken to consolidate their control over volatile borderlands. From Kemalist Turkey's campaigns in Kurdistan to Stalin's deportations of Chechens, to multiple excesses committed by the Islamic Republic of Iran after 1979—not to mention the CCP's own actions in Cultural Revolution–era Tibet—concern about losing control of borderlands tends to spark violent repression. The Xinjiang case is distinguished mainly by the role of information technology for surveillance and greater global visibility.

The Xinjiang crackdown may also have more lasting effects, since Beijing faces limited obstacles. Despite an escalating confrontation with the United States, China's international environment in Inner Asia is comparatively benign. Russia—its only potential regional rival—is a de facto ally, while regional governments (including in Central Asia, with its close historical and cultural links to Xinjiang) are cowed by Chinese economic and military power. Freed from longstanding concerns that imperial rivals could stoke instability in service of their territorial aspirations, China has a generally free hand in Xinjiang (and other borderlands). It also has technological capabilities, from facial recognition software to mobile tracking apps, of which Stalin or Atatürk could only dream, plus a large Han population whose resettlement is itself an important tool for integration. The main factor determining the success or failure of this effort therefore is less Xinjiang itself and more the durability of CCP rule in China as a whole.

CHAPTER TWELVE

Sinocentrism and the Geopolitics of *Tianxia*

URING THE 2017 BELT and Road Forum in Beijing, Xi called on participants in the BRI to work together to build a "Community of Common Destiny," a term that has taken on increasing visibility as a framework for Chinese foreign policy in Eurasia and beyond.[1] Beijing portrays the Community of Common Destiny as "a borderless order with China at its center; a benign hierarchical order guided by morality and administered for the benefit of all . . . informed by a sense of the superiority of the Chinese civilization."[2] First articulated by Xi's predecessor, Hu Jintao (2002–12), the Community of Common Destiny concept has in the Xi era come to echo ideas from the Confucian canon depicting China as the source of universal civilization whose influence radiates outward across "All Under Heaven (*tianxia*)." This vision provides intellectual underpinning for Beijing's pursuit of great power status and aspiration to transform the international system to reflect Chinese interests.

The prominence of *tianxia* and related concepts in contemporary Chinese foreign policy debates is not motivated by a concern for historical accuracy so much as by a desire on the part of the CCP to give the Chinese people "the sense that China is back in its natural place in the world."[3] At their most ambitious, historical analogies suggest an aspiration to create something like an entirely new system of international relations, a "New *Tianxia*" in place of the Westphalian model of sovereignty that European imperialists introduced to Asia in the nineteenth century.

Scholars and officials invoke them to support Beijing's claim that its aspirations are qualitatively different from those of the European colonial
powers and the United States, and that neighboring states should not fear
a more powerful China.[4]

The reemergence of *tianxia* as a framework for twenty-first-century
Chinese foreign relations has particular implications for the relationship
between the PRC and states around China's periphery in regions once
subject to Qing rule. On the Eurasian landmass, these include the Republic of Mongolia (Qing Outer Mongolia) and vast swathes of Central
Asia and the Russian Far East—along with Hong Kong, Korea, Macao,
Taiwan, and other onetime Qing dependencies on the Pacific Rim. Compared to these domains along China's maritime periphery, late Qing territorial losses in Eurasia were large in spatial terms, but of limited strategic
significance. Despite their commitment to maintaining the geobody of
the late Qing, both the ROC and the PRC were therefore comparatively
willing to move beyond the loss of territories in Manchuria, Central Asia,
and—eventually—Mongolia (in contrast to the PRC's attitude to Tibet
and Xinjiang).

Beijing's relatively accommodating approach to the former Qing territories now encompassed in Mongolia, Russia, Kazakhstan, Kyrgyzstan,
and Tajikistan is at odds not only with its commitment to maintaining
control of Tibet and Xinjiang, but also with its vigorous pursuit of claims
to Hong Kong and Taiwan, or with its "Nine Dash Line" maritime claims
in the South China Sea. Unlike Eurasia's other postimperial states, China
does not have military forces deployed across its borders against the wishes
of neighboring governments, and does not maintain irredentist claims toward them (excepting a disputed border region with Bhutan, India, and
Nepal that Beijing claims it never ceded in the first place).[5] The idea of a
wider "post-Qing space" in Eurasia would seem somewhat puzzling not
just in Beijing, but in neighboring states as well.

Yet China's consolidation as a territorially bounded state did not
completely efface either the political/cultural bonds tying former Qing
dependencies in Eurasia to China, or the influence of *tianxia* as an order-
ing concept for Chinese foreign policy. Both took on new prominence
as the CCP embraced Confucian culture as a source of legitimacy in the
wake of the 1989 Tiananmen Square protests and the end of the Cold
War. They have received new momentum in the twenty-first century
with China's emergence as a major global power; especially since the
2013 launch of the Belt and Road Initiative, Chinese "neighborhood di-

plomacy" on the Eurasian landmass bears hallmarks of traditional thinking about China as the center of a regional system and source of political legitimacy. The BRI itself thus represents not only a strategy for economic development, but part of a framework for regional cooperation based on Chinese leadership and the export of Chinese norms and ideas. As the liberal critic Liu Qing notes, Beijing's pursuit of regional influence rests on an inherent ambiguity about the boundary separating China as a state from the wider *tianxia*, giving rise to an assumption "that China can develop a superior, more universal civilization based on its own unique cultural tradition."[6]

The role of hard and soft infrastructure within the BRI, meanwhile, is eroding the salience of Eurasia's post-Qing borders, recreating something like the ambiguous territorial arrangements characteristic of the traditional *tianxia* paradigm. In exchange for investment and trade opportunities, states within China's erstwhile sphere of influence are expected to align themselves with Chinese positions on issues like the status of the South China Sea or opposition to the "three evils (*sange shili*)" of extremism, terrorism, and separatism. The penetration of their economies, moreover, creates conditions for expanding China's security role in ways that local officials worry will erode their sovereignty and, over time, potentially give rise to irredentism. Even if such concerns prove excessive, China's aspiration to construct a new regional order based on investment and the export of its own political and security paradigms is in some ways the most ambitious project for reshaping regional order of all Eurasia's post-imperial states.

Tianxia and Twenty-first-Century Sinocentrism

As early as the Zhou era, the understanding of territory subject to dynastic control referred to as *zhongguo* or *huaxia* contrasted with a more ideological description of the space known as *tianxia*, within which dynastic states' geopolitical ambitions operated, and which described the imagined legitimate boundaries of Zhou influence.[7] As Zhou authority grew, *huaxia*—the "civilized" world that recognized Zhou suzerainty—became increasingly coterminous with *tianxia*—the culturally linked realm that marked the outer frontier of Zhou aspirations.[8] While *tianxia* was coterminous with what was at the time the known world, it was also a cosmological concept that provided a framework for imperial expansion. With its reference to "Heaven (*tian*)," it implied a connection between the physical and the ethereal. It suggested a kind of cosmically sanctioned unity, "a political order in which the world [as opposed to individual states] is primary."[9] As described in the Zhou-era *Book of Odes:*

> Everywhere under vast Heaven
> There is no land that is not the king's.
> To the borders of those lands
> There are none who are not the king's servants.[10]

After the unification of much of the Sinitic realm by the First Emperor of Qin (*Qin Shihuangdi*) in 221 B.C.E., *tianxia* took on universalist pretensions; the Son of Heaven was not the ruler of a territorially bounded state so much as a universal sovereign to whom all others were expected to pay deference. Within this system, territorial control at the edges of the known world was not, for the most part, a priority. As described by Qin Yaqing, "If you stand on top of the hill in the Imperial Garden behind the Forbidden City, you see a square-shaped complex of buildings surrounded by a larger square surrounded by an even larger square. . . . This is the Chinese understanding of the world, which is infinite in space and time with the Chinese emperor's palace at the center."[11] In this idealized conception, the Son of Heaven administered *tianxia* on the basis of Confucian principles, while surrounding rulers "visited the imperial court, performed *ketou* [kowtow], or obeisance, and presented gifts of local produce. In return, their legitimacy as rulers was affirmed."[12]

Of course, this vision of tributary relations centered on the Son of Heaven was, at best, an ideal to which Chinese rulers aspired, especially outside the Confucian cultural space.[13] Access to material wealth was always important for securing participation in this system, what the Han dynasty statesman Jia Yi termed the "five baits (*wu er*)" for attracting the nomadic Xiongnu: "elaborate clothes and carriages to corrupt their eyes; fine food to corrupt their mouths; music to corrupt their ears; lofty buildings, granaries, and slaves to corrupt their stomachs; [and] gifts and favors for [those] who surrendered."[14]

Because this order rested on Confucian authority over the whole of *tianxia*, it treated "foreign" relations as an extension of internal administration. As Liu Xiaoyuan notes, before the settlements imposed at the end of the Opium Wars, the Qing "did not have neighboring states as we understand [the term] today."[15] Liu recounts a case from the 1720s when the Yongzheng Emperor (1722–35) agreed to resolve a territorial dispute with the kingdom of Annam (northern Vietnam) by ceding territory. Yongzheng justified the concession by noting: "[the disputed territory] is my interior land if assigned to Yunnan [province], and my outer territory if to An Nam. There really is no difference. I will bestow this piece of land to the king and let him guard it for me."[16]

Even after the end of the Qing, *tianxia* continued to provide an intellectual framework for thinking about China's place in the world. Kang Youwei invoked *tianxia* in his discussion of a unified world that "transcends the state, ethnicity, class, gender, and other relations of hierarchy," while Mao Zedong claimed that the annihilation of social class under communism represented the true path to "the great unity of *tianxia*."[17] Some Chinese scholars likewise see these ideas underpinning the policy of Peaceful Coexistence proclaimed by Premier Zhou Enlai and Indian prime minister Jawaharlal Nehru in 1954, and later adopted as the basis for relations within what became the Nonaligned Movement.[18] A more explicit turn to the geopolitics of *tianxia* emerged, however, in the wake of Deng Xiaoping's "Reform and Opening Up (*gaige kaifang*)," which both downplayed Marxism-Leninism and ushered in a period of rampant materialism that repelled many Chinese elites. The subsequent embrace of Confucian ideas and symbols helped legitimate ideas about global order drawn from traditional Chinese sources among influential scholars and, increasingly, in the rhetoric and actions of PRC officials.[19]

Proponents of this "New *Tianxia*" contrast the allegedly peaceful Confucian world order of the past with the violence that has been a central feature of Westphalian geopolitics. As Zhao Tingyang, whose 2005 book *The Tianxia System* (*Tianxia tixi*) did much to popularize the idea of a specifically Chinese model of international relations, argues, the Westphalian order, a product of the Western intellectual tradition, has created a "failed world" of conflict and disorder because of the primacy it assigns to the separate perspectives of states and individuals.[20] In Zhao's idealized "*Tianxia* System," political legitimacy derives from the ethical conduct of relations, which are equivalent across the different types of relationships comprising the family, the state, and *tianxia*, and which owes something to belief in the acculturating potential inherent in Confucianism, with its ability to "civilize" the "barbarians."[21]

Making this system work, though, requires that other states subsume their own aspirations and accept Chinese leadership. Focusing on the Han-era thinker Xunzi's notion of "true kingship," the nationalist scholar Yan Xuetong suggests that "voluntary submission, rather than force," is the basis for stable relations.[22] Yan calls for China to advance new international norms drawn from its Confucian tradition such as benevolence, righteousness, and etiquette that can "transcend liberalism" and position China for a different kind of global leadership role.[23] While noting that hierarchy as an organizing principle may be unpopular, Yan argues that a hierarchical international system is fair because states' power objectively differs. He approvingly cites Xunzi's observation that "when power and positions are equally distributed . . . there is certain to be contention."[24]

The importance of Zhao's *Tianxia* System and Yan's normative hierarchy derives less from their logical force or their grounding in the realities of China's imperial history than from their influence among the policymaking elite of the People's Republic.[25] Regardless of whether concepts like Sinocentrism and *tianxia* are explicitly acknowledged, they comprise part of the intellectual architecture, or "habits of mind," of Chinese leaders.[26]

Xi has come closer than his predecessors to "framing his vision for a new world order . . . as a 21st century version of the tianxia model," specifically in his portrayal of the Community of Common Destiny.[27] According to Xi, this community is simultaneously about making the world amenable to China's governance model and promoting China's emergence as a global power by "facilitat[ing] a favorable external environment for realizing the Chinese Dream of national rejuvenation."[28] This vision encapsulates old ideas, not only about China's great power aspirations, but about its centrality to global order and the universality of the Chinese experience. As described by Foreign Minister Wang Yi, "China must combine domestic development with opening up, linking its own growth to world economic growth and increasingly integrating its interests with the common interests of mankind."[29]

China's initiatives for reforming global governance center on establishing Chinese influence within existing international institutions such as the United Nations, creating parallel institutions outside the Western-centric framework established at the end of World War II, and establishing increasingly hierarchical relationships with smaller states. Within the UN, Beijing seeks to leverage increased financial contributions to embed its own officials, who in turn adopt positions favorable to Chinese interests—for instance, attaching BRI programs to the UN's Millennium Development Goals.[30] Beijing also promotes alternative regional institutions, including the SCO and the Asian Infrastructure Investment Bank (AIIB), one of the main funding sources for the BRI. These institutions, which lack the emphasis on promoting liberalism and democracy central to U.S.-backed international bodies, are among the most prominent manifestations of what scholars have termed "illiberal internationalism."[31] They represent an alternative vision of international cooperation and, at a minimum, help erode the normative hegemony of their liberal rivals.

Beginning with the creation of the Shanghai Five (precursor to the SCO) in 1999, China has also exported its security paradigm—combating the "three evils" of terrorism, extremism, and separatism, as exemplified by its aggressive crackdown on Uyghur activism—as a basis for both multilateral and bilateral cooperation.[32] Following the 2009 Ürümqi uprising, Beijing worked through the SCO's Tashkent-based Regional Anti-Terrorism Center (RATS) to persuade Kazakhstan and Kyrgyzstan to extradite activists associated with Uyghur diaspora organizations that it blamed for the violence. In this way, the SCO "expands the fight against 'East Turkistan' [i.e., the movement for an independent state in Xinjiang] from China to the SCO itself."[33] Beijing also uses bilateral investment and development assistance to incentivize states to support Chinese goals, including nonrecognition of Taiwan, but also adoption of Chinese technology standards and acceptance of PRC narratives around the situation in borderlands like Hong Kong, Tibet, and Xinjiang.

In contrast with the alliance relations the United States maintains in both Europe and Asia, Xi has called for "partnerships based on dialogue, non-confrontation and non-alliance."[34] Such partnerships rest on the idea of mutual obligation, rather than on specific rules, such as commitments to democracy. Without the institutional and legal basis of the United States' treaty alliances, these partnerships are by their nature hierarchical, with smaller states initially joining to secure economic benefits, and in time coming (in theory) to share China's political and security perspective. The best-known example is Beijing's use of financial leverage to compel adherence to its claim of an exclusive economic zone in the South China Sea. Over the course of Xi's presidency, though, China has signed new partnership agreements with dozens of states, both in its own neighborhood and further afield, suggesting what Wang Yi describes as "foster[ing] a new type of international relations and firming up" the Community of Common Destiny, above all for countries in China's immediate neighborhood.[35]

Does China Have a Eurasian Near Abroad?
Central Asia, Mongolia, and the Russian Far East

China's apparent success in making the transition from empire to nation-state is in part a consequence of having what appear to be stable, legitimate borders, which largely coincide with the extent of the Qing at the time of the Xinhai Revolution. Since 1949, moreover, Beijing has made significant progress in demarcating boundaries with most of its terrestrial neighbors (apart from its dispute with Bhutan, India, and Nepal).[36] While maritime claims in the East and South China Seas—not to mention the status of Hong Kong and Taiwan—are sources of tension, China's ability to secure itself within clearly defined land borders sets it apart from Eurasia's other postimperial states.

Yet both enduring linkages and the increasingly popular vision of a Sinocentric *tianxia* call into question portrayals of the PRC as a territorially bounded state—not only at sea, but on land as well. The most obvious example is the unsettled frontier with India, stemming from Chinese rejection of the 1914 Simla Convention with its cession of northern Arunachal Pradesh, as well as from an undemarcated frontier in the Himalayas, where construction of a road connecting Tibet to Xinjiang through the remote Aksai Chin region helped spark a 1962 border war and sporadic violence ever since—including a major clash in June 2020.[37] Bhutan and Nepal similarly accuse China of encroaching on their territory in remote stretches of the Himalayas.

The PRC has, conversely, reached border demarcation agreements with most of its other terrestrial neighbors, including Mongolia, Russia, Kazakhstan, Kyrgyzstan, and Tajikistan. A degree of ambiguity nevertheless exists about Beijing's ultimate intentions, especially toward territories acquired by Russia during the "century of humiliation." For much of the post-Qing era, Chinese governments were reluctant to regard the cession of territories on the Eurasian mainland as final, in line with efforts to adopt the full territorial inheritance of the Qing. The Republic of Mongolia and the territories that came under Russian control from 1858 to 1944—including "Outer Manchuria" (now part of the Russian Far East), the northern Ili region (in modern Kazakhstan, Kyrgyzstan, and Tajikistan), and Tannu-Uriankhai (roughly, Russia's Republic of Tuva)—were sparsely populated and seemingly of limited strategic value. The circumstances of their loss, however, imbued them with a "symbolic importance beyond [their] obvious strategic significance" that today contributes to anxiety in neighboring states about the PRC's willingness to continue abiding by these settlements.[38]

Efforts to demarcate a Qing-Muscovite boundary date back to the seventeenth century, when Cossack settlers in Siberia first encroached upon Qing frontiers. Under the 1689 Treaty of Nerchinsk, Moscow agreed to demolish its fort on the northwestern reaches of the Amur River and abandon its territorial claims in the Amur Basin; in exchange, the Qing acknowledged Muscovite control of the region between Lake Baikal and the Argun River and authorized trade at the border. Most important from the Qing perspective, Moscow agreed to maintain neutrality in the conflict with the Zunghars. The Treaty of Nerchinsk was the Qing's first agreement with a European power, one that signified the gradual emergence of ideas about China as a territorially bounded state. The Nerchinsk settlement and the follow-on Treaty of Kyakhta (1727), which extended Russian claims south to the Kerülen River, secured the Qing's northern frontier against Russian penetration and would govern relations into the mid-nineteenth century.[39]

By the 1850s, though, the Opium Wars and Taiping Rebellion encouraged renewed probing, as Russia took advantage of the Qing's distraction to claim vast territories stretching from the Pacific coast to what is now southeastern Kazakhstan. Under the Treaties of Aigun (1858) and Beijing (1860), Russia acquired more than 800,000 square kilometers of land north of the Amur and east of the Ussuri Rivers.[40] These acquisitions then allowed St. Petersburg to project economic and political influence further into Qing Manchuria, which became the object of a sustained Russo-Japanese rivalry lasting until the end of World War II. In October 1864, with the Qing occupied by Yaqub Beg's revolt, Russia also imposed the Treaty of Tarbaghatai, acquiring additional territories in the mountains of what is today southern Kazakhstan and Kyrgyzstan. Following subsequent adjustments, by 1881 Russia had gained more than 900,000 square kilometers of formerly Qing Central Asia.[41]

Russia was also instrumental in the loss of Qing Outer Mongolia, which declared its independence in the wake of the Xinhai Revolution. As in Tibet, belated Qing attempts to tighten control by abolishing the prohibition on Han settlement and intermarriage led the dominant Khalka Mongols to fear dilution of their identity and authority.[42] In December 1911, the Khalka nobility convinced the eighth Jebtsundamba Khutukhtu, Outer Mongolia's "living Buddha," to proclaim himself the Bogd Khan (Holy Khan) of an independent Mongol khanate. This new khanate aspired to encompass not just the Khalkas, but in principle Inner Mongols, Barguts, Oirats, and Uriankhai as well. The Bogd Khan's argument for independence was that the Khalkas' submission to Kangxi in 1691 bound them to the Qing dynasty, but not to the newly established ROC, explicitly rejecting the ROC's claim of continuity with the Qing.[43]

Mongolia was able to maintain its independence during and after the post-Qing upheavals thanks in large part to Russian military intervention.[44] The Bogd Khan initially kept Chinese forces at bay thanks to a White Russian detachment under Baron Roman von Ungern-Sternberg. In June 1921, the Bolshevik Red Army invaded, scattering Ungern-Sternberg's forces and establishing a Communist-led Mongolian People's Republic.[45] The presence of Soviet troops then helped secure Mongolia's independence against the various armies and warlords contending for power in China.[46] Soviet patronage was likewise instrumental in the establishment of a Communist regime in Turkic-speaking Tannu-Uriankhai, a Qing tributary annexed to the USSR in 1944 as Tannu-Tuva (today, Russia's Republic of Tuva)—the last piece of the old Qing empire to come under Russian rule.

More than elsewhere along the Eurasian periphery, Beijing's attitude toward the Republic of Mongolia remains colored both by concerns about cross-border ties and by the legacy of the Chinese Civil War. Moscow secured international recognition of Mongolia's independence following a plebiscite in 1945. While the ROC acquiesced to the loss, in part from fear that Stalin would encourage claims to Inner Mongolia as well, the *Guomindang* later withdrew its recognition, and would long emphasize Russia's role as the primary villain in the "century of humiliation."[47] As the internationally recognized government of China, the *Guomindang*-led ROC blocked Mongolia's admission to the United Nations until 1960, and only after the *Guomindang* lost power in elections in the early 2000s did Taiwan recognize Mongolian independence. Meanwhile, whatever irredentist sentiments existed within the PRC were muted by the legacy of wartime deference to Moscow, as the CCP could not criticize the loss of Mongolia without raising uncomfortable questions about its own wartime position. Instead, the CCP preferred to blame its Nationalist rivals for failing to prevent the Bogd Khan's declaration of independence and acquiescing to Mongolia's independence at the end of World War II, holding them up as examples of the fragmentation that could overtake other borderlands should CCP control waver.

Elsewhere, the early PRC maintained a classically imperial view of frontiers as transition zones, delaying efforts to demarcate borders and using territorial concessions to secure political influence with neighbors. During the 1950s, Beijing acceded to territorial demands from Burma, Nepal, North Korea, and Mongolia. As Zhou Enlai promised, "We pledge to observe our borders: should a transgression take place, we will immediately acknowledge our mistake and retreat within our own borders."[48] These concessions were made with a view to securing neighbors' support during the Sino-Soviet split and the larger territorial dispute with India.[49] Crises along the frontier, including the flight of the Dalai Lama to India in 1959 and the 1962 Ili crisis, when Moscow encouraged Chinese Kazakhs to flee across the border at the height of the Cultural Revolution, encouraged the PRC to adopt a more territorially bounded form of state-building, which in turn required an attenuation of the cultural, economic, political, and social ties binding Chinese-ruled Inner Asia to neighboring states.

Despite its strategy of territorial accommodation, moreover, the PRC became embroiled in militarized border disputes with both the USSR and India from the late 1950s.[50] Amid the Sino-Soviet split, Mao deliberately sabotaged border talks by demanding Moscow acknowledge the unequal nature of the nineteenth-century Qing-Russian treaties as part of his campaign against Soviet "revisionism." The dispute eventually sparked a clash over Zhenbao (Damansky) Island in March 1969 that left dozens dead on both sides; smaller skirmishes broke out that summer in northern Xinjiang along the border established by the Treaty of Tarbaghatai as well. By establishing deterrence, these border skirmishes marked an end to "the era begun in the mid-nineteenth century during which Russia could exert military superiority to expand its borders over Chinese resistance."[51] The price, however, was a further erosion of the links between the PRC and the former Qing territories controlled by the Soviet Union and whose restoration—in contrast to Hong Kong or Taiwan—Beijing has avoided demanding.[52]

Efforts by Deng Xiaoping and Mikhail Gorbachev to demarcate the border helped drive the gradual rapprochement between Beijing and Moscow that began in the mid-1980s, and has continued down to the present (with the last stretch of the Sino-Russian border demarcated in 2005). Despite the broader alignment between Xi's China and Vladimir Putin's Russia, though, the legacy of the nineteenth-century treaties remains a source of sublimated anxiety in Russia. Beijing still considers the Aigun, Beijing, and Tarbaghatai agreements "unequal treaties," and some textbooks show the regions ceded to Russia as "temporarily" lost. Putin has (unsuccessfully) requested the description of "unequal treaties" with

Russia be removed from Chinese textbooks. Some Russian officials and commentators also fear that the demarcation agreement represents only a temporary truce, and that the changing power balance between Moscow and Beijing will eventually lead China to make revisionist claims, a fear exacerbated by (exaggerated) reports in the Russian media about Chinese migration.[53]

Concerns about Chinese irredentism are more pronounced in Central Asia, where the power disparity is greater, and where China has already used its leverage to compel territorial and other concessions. Despite the progress Deng and Gorbachev made toward demarcating the border, Beijing had to negotiate new arrangements with independent Kazakhstan, Kyrgyzstan, and Tajikistan once the Soviet Union fell. A 1996 agreement led to demilitarization of the common border and the formation of the Shanghai Five (China, Kazakhstan, Kyrgyzstan, Russia, and Tajikistan), but also reopened disputes seemingly resolved in the months leading up to the Soviet collapse. In subsequent years, Beijing sought to address territorial issues with Kazakhstan and Kyrgyzstan (negotiations with Tajikistan were shelved because of that country's civil war), employing both carrots and sticks to convince the two countries to cede large swathes of land.

These negotiations and the concessions that ensued were unpopular within Central Asia; the backlash nearly brought down Kyrgyzstan's government in the mid-1990s, and Tajikistan faced similar anger when its government finally approved a demarcation agreement in 2011.[54] Apart from the lack of transparency with which the agreements were prepared, opposition in Kazakhstan and Tajikistan centered on both the territorial concessions and announcements that Chinese farmers would receive leases on farmland inside the Central Asian states.[55] Altogether, these negotiations resulted in China gaining around 16,000 square kilometers from its three Central Asian neighbors.

Beyond border rectification, Beijing also envisioned economic integration between China's western regions and neighboring states as part of its development strategy for Xinjiang. As early as 1998, the Prosperous Borders Wealthy Minorities (*Xingbian fumin xingdong*) program mentioned the link between "wealthy people, happy borders . . . and harmonious and friendly neighbors."[56] The Great Western Development program adopted the following year gave form to this vision with investment in transportation, energy, communications, and irrigation infrastructure situated along existing or planned transit routes into the center of Eurasia. Following the upheaval in Xinjiang in the summer of 2009, Beijing proposed opening up

Xinjiang's borders and transforming the region into a logistics corridor as a step in China's gradual opening to central Eurasia.[57] The resulting "dual opening" aimed to integrate borderlands like Xinjiang more firmly into the PRC while developing them as bridges to neighboring states through cross-border supply chains and cooperation zones like the Khorgos special economic zone on the Sino-Kazakh border.[58] China's role in building and operating much of this infrastructure, as well as the imbalanced trading relationships that it underpins, however, feed perceptions in Central Asia that the project aims at transforming the region into a Chinese sphere of influence.[59] Wang Jisi, one of the first thinkers to champion investing in Eurasian connectivity, suggested such infrastructure would give China "a good opportunity to participate in the multilateral coordination of major powers and enhance its international status."[60]

For many Central Asians, Chinese investment and infrastructure also raise the specter of irredentism. One concern is that infrastructure investment will encourage a Chinese security presence that could be used to enforce territorial claims. The role of infrastructure—notably roads—in opening up Tibet and Xinjiang to Chinese military penetration reinforces these fears, which are also emerging in Nepal and Bhutan as Beijing more actively presses claims along remote, undemarcated frontiers.[61] Another worry is that the reorientation of the region's economy toward China will leave Central Asia vulnerable to economic coercion, as already appears to be happening with the Central Asian governments' silence about Beijing's internment of not only Uyghurs, but also Kazakhs and Kyrgyz (some of them not even Chinese citizens) in Xinjiang.[62] Even if Beijing has no interest in territorial revisionism as such, its neighbors' growing dependence on China as an economic driver and security provider is gradually whittling away borders, moving back toward a classically imperial model, where formal sovereignty matters less than effective authority. The resulting model of interaction bears traces—sometimes deliberately emphasized—of the Sinocentric system that allegedly dominated eastern Eurasia before the age of European imperialism.

Imperial Ambitions Along the Belt and Road

Much of this infrastructure linking western China to its neighbors has since 2013 been subsumed within the BRI, now the principal vehicle by which Beijing aims to export its own economic, political, and security paradigm. Many Chinese officials see the BRI as a tool for building a new regional order within which Chinese norms and standards predominate, Chinese firms reap most of the economic benefit, and Beijing uses financial leverage to compel concessions in the political and security realms.[63] Notwithstanding its focus on development and infrastructure and the rhetoric of "win-win" cooperation, not to mention smaller states' own calculations, the BRI's ambitions, as Jonathan Hillman notes, "are imperial, even if they may not succeed."[64]

On maps, the BRI is portrayed as a web of six east-west transport corridors connecting China with all corners of the Eurasian landmass (hence the reference to the Silk Road), even if precise details and routes are lacking from official statements.[65] It contrasts with competing visions for Eurasian connectivity not only in its sheer scale—including the amount of money Beijing has made available—but also in the scope of China's aspiration to use infrastructure and trade to rewrite the rules of regional cooperation. While Chinese officials emphasize that the BRI represents a contribution to global development, many foreign, especially Western, observers see it as a form of "strategic cunning" underpinning what Nadège Rolland calls "a grand strategy that advances China's goal of establishing itself as the preponderant power in Eurasia and a global power second to none."[66]

Xi's 2013 speech in Kazakhstan referenced not only transportation, but also coordination of policy, trade, monetary, and people-to-people ties.[67] According to a 2015 white paper, the BRI "aims to promote the connectivity of Asian, European and African continents and their adjacent seas, establish and strengthen partnerships . . . set up all-dimensional, multitiered and composite connectivity networks, and realize diversified, independent, balanced and sustainable development."[68] By enhancing connectivity across all these dimensions, Beijing aspires to establish itself as the region's primary trade partner and source of development financing, promote its own technology standards, and create opportunities for Chinese companies to access global markets. To implement these projects, China seeks connections with politicians and other elites throughout Eurasia to secure market access, political influence, and the gradual expansion of its own security footprint.[69]

The core of the BRI is Chinese investment in new connectivity infrastructure such as roads, ports, railways, and power grids that collectively will integrate the Eurasian landmass and its maritime periphery into a more unified economic space. Reflecting the CCP's Marxist-inflected belief that "development holds the master key to solving all problems," the BRI also aims at creating economic opportunities in places where Beijing believes poverty drives radicalization, not just in Xinjiang, but across the border as well, since "China needs a peaceful neighboring environment in order to concentrate on development."[70] At the same time, the BRI is an element of China's "neighborhood diplomacy," by which it seeks to align neighboring states' incentives with pursuit of the Chinese Dream and the creation of the Community of Common Destiny.[71] And while Beijing argues that the BRI is an open network that is "harmonious and inclusive," it also emphasizes that the initiative signifies China's commitment "to shouldering more responsibilities and obligations within its capabilities, and making greater contributions to the peace and development of mankind."[72]

Those contributions include construction of infrastructure projects and economic relationships that advance Sinocentric regional integration. Railway construction provides a boon for Chinese construction companies and allows Chinese firms to ship their products to new markets (even though transit has little direct impact on the economies of states along the route and trains often return to China empty).[73] Apart from roads and railways, one of Beijing's main priorities has been energy and pipelines. Accessing its neighbors' oil and gas resources is a tactic for escaping from what Hu Jintao termed the "Malacca dilemma," that is, the vulnerability of seaborne imports to interdiction (especially by the U.S. Navy) at chokepoints like the Malacca Strait, thereby enhancing the PRC's energy security at a time of mounting great power competition.

Pipelines, though, also deepen supplier states' dependence on the Chinese market, while allowing China to play suppliers off one another. This dependence is especially pronounced for Central Asia; even before completion of the planned fourth branch of the China–Central Asia gas pipeline, around three-quarters of the region's gas exports (including 90 percent of Turkmenistan's) went to China.[74] Debt-financed construction also allows Beijing to acquire equity in energy and other projects as collateral, which then provides political and economic leverage—even if Chinese banks appear no more predatory in their lending than Western institutions.[75] Dependence also allows Beijing to export its own security narrative. The Central Asian governments' rhetorical and practical support for the Chinese crackdown in Xinjiang—despite the risk of a domestic backlash—is a striking testament of Beijing's ability to leverage infrastructure and investment for geopolitical ends.

Before the economic slowdown associated with the Covid-19 pandemic, China had earmarked over $1 trillion for investment in BRI projects through Chinese banks, the AIIB, and a dedicated Silk Road

Fund.[76] Most of the projects financed by these institutions are also being implemented by Chinese companies, with workers and materials imported from China. The lack of opportunities for local firms and workers has been a source of tension, especially in Central Asia, which has seen occasional protests and even riots targeting Chinese laborers.[77] Given the scale of these investments, Beijing has also been taking on a higher-profile security role through participation in regional dialogues (including a quadrilateral security mechanism with Afghanistan, Pakistan, and Tajikistan), weapons sales and training, construction of border posts and other facilities, and the quiet deployment of security forces in neighboring states.[78]

In line with the thinking behind the Community of Common Destiny, the BRI is also a vehicle for promoting new forms of regional cooperation reflecting China's own interests. The emphasis on policy coordination outlined in Xi's 2013 Astana speech points to the importance of aligning BRI participants' approaches to everything from regulation to security. Given the power disparities between participating states, this alignment primarily entails the export of Chinese norms and standards, or what then-Vice Foreign Minister Liu Zhenmin termed "promoting Asia's common development on the basis of China's own development."[79] Beijing, for instance, encourages the use of the *renminbi* in transactions and the adoption of Chinese telecommunications standards in other BRI participant states.[80]

Chinese investment and assistance lack much of the conditionality imposed by Western-backed development institutions like the International Monetary Fund, which demand transparency and accountability in exchange for lending. While Beijing downplays the existence of conditionality, in practice recipients are expected to support Chinese political priorities, including Chinese maritime claims, the "three evils" framework, and China's crackdown in Xinjiang. The lack of transparency, meanwhile, allows corruption to flourish, strengthening ties among corrupt elites and undercutting Western-backed governance norms that, in Beijing's view, are themselves elements of the West's political hegemony. Likewise, the role of "people-to-people" connectivity as a pillar of the BRI allows Beijing to reinforce support for its worldview through publications in local media (coordinated by a Belt and Road Media Cooperation Alliance under the State Council), academic and analytic exchanges, business alliances, and other networks in keeping with the United Front Work strategy at the heart of Beijing's international outreach.[81]

From Belt and Road to *Tianxia*?

Even when couched in the explicit or implicit language of *tianxia*, Chinese infrastructure and investment appear to offer a more attractive inducement for cooperation than the closed institutions promoted by Russia, or the distant and sometimes unreliable cooperation offered by the United States and EU. Many states and officials point to Eurasia's deficit of infrastructure as an impediment to development and prosperity. Whatever their concerns about China's geopolitical ambitions, they largely welcome Chinese investment. And as most of the Eurasian states targeted for inclusion in the BRI have nondemocratic and nontransparent political systems, a lack of democratic accountability makes Chinese investment an attractive alternative to development assistance or commercial loans from the West. Even the expansion of China's security footprint is welcomed in neighboring capitals as a hedge against the spread of instability (and, in Central Asia, against Russia). With no explicit territorial ambitions and no legacy of domination, China is also a welcome partner in the South Caucasus, the Balkans, and other postimperial "shatter zones" far from its own borders—including by leaders who see it as a hedge against the postimperial domination of Moscow, Ankara, or even Brussels.[82]

China's aspiration to reshape regional order is more far-reaching than that of Eurasia's other postimperial states: it is not limited to a "post-Qing space," and it is backed by significantly greater financial and other resources than are available to Iran, Russia, or Turkey. China is also more ambitious in seeking not just economic and political influence, but also a shift in the normative basis of interstate relations. At a minimum, the idea of a Community of Common Destiny and the concrete steps taken to give it form represent an increasingly geopolitical understanding of China's relationship with its neighborhood, one based on the CCP's own reading of Chinese history.

These ambitions are in keeping with a narrative of China's returning to its rightful position at the center of the political cosmos after recovering from the "century of humiliation." Invocation of the historical Silk Road and of figures like Zhang Qian are part of an effort to depict China's rise in light of the role played by the PRC's dynastic predecessors and its critique of the Western-dominated international order that has prevailed in East Asia since the mid-nineteenth century. The narrative of continuity with China's imperial past helps legitimate Beijing's aspiration to play a larger role domestically and in the wider region. Both the "hard" infrastructure comprising the BRI and the "soft" norms of cooperation underpinning it reinforce the idea of China's position at the center of a new regional order stretching from Southeast Asia to Europe (and, with the 2018 announcement of the so-called Polar Silk Road, to the Arctic as well).[83] These ambitions have developed in conjunction with China's emergence as a global power in the years since Deng's Reform and Opening Up. Underpinning them are a still-growing economy that will likely surpass that of the United States before 2030, an increasingly powerful military, and a more active diplomatic posture in Eurasia and beyond.

Of course, Beijing faces real constraints, and historical analogies only go so far. Whatever the reality of the historical *tianxia*, participants in the BRI today are well aware of the potential pitfalls and seek to guard their sovereignty from Chinese encroachment. As both a development initiative and a framework for transforming regional order, the BRI has delivered less than its acolytes in Beijing have promised; much Chinese investment has been unproductive or simply wasted, and China itself has grown more cautious as the CCP worries about the sustainability of its economic model and prospects for growth in the wake of the Covid-19 pandemic.[84]

Xi Jinping has, nevertheless, staked his legacy on both the philosophical underpinnings and the political/economic benefits of the BRI, to the point of including it in the PRC constitution in 2017. Emphasis on the BRI as a vehicle for reshaping regional and global order will likely endure in some form at least throughout Xi's (now indefinite) time in office. Whether the BRI in fact lays the foundation for something like a new *tianxia* may be the most consequential question for Eurasia's future security and prosperity, both within and beyond the old Qing frontiers.

Conclusion

A World Safe for Empire?

A
S LARGE, DIVERSE STATES with long histories at the center of distinct regional orders, China, Iran, Russia, and Turkey are different in both internal construction and external ambition from the smaller states surrounding them. What these four states share is less a commitment to a particular political system or ideology than a sense of themselves as something more than "normal" states. They appeal to peoples living outside their borders, securitize relations with borderland populations, intervene in neighbors' affairs, and seek to reshape regional (and, in the cases of Russia and China, global) order not because they are "ideological grievance states," or because they have megalomaniacal rulers, but because they were constructed out of the rubble of empires and remain shaped on some fundamental level by their respective imperial pasts.

The onset of Eurasia's new imperial age has been unexpected for many observers in the West not only because of the pervasive post–Cold War belief in the "end of history," but also because the upheavals and rivalries of the decades leading up to 1989 disguised the imperial legacies that continued to shape the Soviet Union, Turkey, Iran, and China. Hard borders replaced the fluid frontiers of an earlier era, closing off opportunities for trade and exchange. The Sino-Soviet rivalry turned what had been a relatively open frontier into a heavily militarized border. The consolidation of Soviet rule in the Caucasus and Central Asia isolated these regions from longstanding connections to Turkey, Iran, and China; the reassertion of Beijing's control over Xinjiang and Tibet had a similar effect. Iran's strategic focus shifted to the Middle East while Turkey increasingly pivoted to Europe, especially after joining NATO.

Since the end of the Cold War, though, the imperial legacies that still linger in the political and social fabric of these states have grown more salient and more visible. Russia, Turkey, Iran, and China have remained on the margins of a post–Cold War order that emphasizes democracy, self-determination, equal sovereignty, and territorial integrity. In place of the West's invocation of "universal" values, leaders like Erdoğan and Putin have instead looked to the imperial past for inspiration and legitimation. Meanwhile, the collapse of the USSR; China's attempt to expand development from its eastern coast to its western borderlands; wars in Afghanistan, Iraq, and Syria; and, more recently, Eurasia's reintegration with global markets through new transit, infrastructure, and trade linkages have created opportunities for China, Iran, Russia, and Turkey to project power and influence into their Eurasian hinterlands in patterns structurally, institutionally, and ideologically shaped by the imperial legacies they each inherited. The persistence of these imperial legacies suggests that the challenge these four states pose to a global order based on sovereign equality and territorial integrity is also likely to persist, regardless of political shifts or changes in leadership.

Across much of Eurasia, China, Iran, Russia, and Turkey are rivals. The interstices between them in the Balkans, the Caucasus, Mesopotamia, and Greater Central Asia (including Afghanistan) will likely remain zones of contestation. Competition between Russia and Turkey in Syria, Libya, the Balkans, the Caucasus, and even Ukraine is a source of strain that Putin and Erdoğan spend significant time and diplomatic capital managing. The long-predicted rivalry between Russia and China over Central Asia appears subdued for the moment, but the growth of not only China's economic footprint but, potentially, its security presence could create friction in the future. Turkey and Iran continue jousting over Syria and across the Middle East more broadly, championing not only different religious sects, but different political models and strategic orientations. Growing Chinese investment in distant locales like the Balkans poses important, and underexplored, questions for Beijing's relations with its postimperial peers as well.[1]

Power disparities are also a source of tension. China's growing economic and military might poses a quandary for Iran, Russia, and Turkey—much as it does for the United States or smaller states in East Asia. While

Beijing makes an effort to respect the amour propre of the other three, such deference only goes so far—whether manifested by forcing Erdoğan to tie himself in rhetorical knots over Xinjiang, imposing a lopsided deal to bail out Iran's floundering oil industry, or expelling Russian state companies from energy projects in the South China Sea.[2] The power disparity between Russia and Turkey shapes their interactions in peripheries like Syria and Libya as well, not to mention the controversy over Turkey's purchase of a Russian S-400 air defense system.[3] Iran's isolation and economic distress, meanwhile, have left it vulnerable to exploitation by both Russia and China.[4]

Notwithstanding the competition between these four powers within Eurasia, they maintain at the global level a shared interest in challenging the political, institutional, and normative leadership of the West. Rather than accept the legitimacy of what successive U.S. administrations have referred to as a "rules-based" international order, China, Iran, Russia, and Turkey all claim what amounts to the right to ignore the rules and constraints facing their smaller neighbors. Each prizes its own sovereignty—including the right to choose its own political system and to decide which foreign nongovernmental organizations to allow on its territory. Yet all four also embrace the idea that, de facto, some states are more sovereign than others. Perhaps only Putin would go so far as to say that one of Russia's neighbors "is not even a state," but it is a sentiment widely shared among political elites in China, Iran, and Turkey as well.[5] Thus, while Eurasia's postimperial states may be divided over the future of Syria, all adhere to the proposition that Syria's future will be decided by its powerful neighbors—rather than by abstract principles or the will of the Syrian people. To the extent these four states share a common goal, then, it can perhaps be characterized as making the world safe for empire—which in turn means eroding the dominance of U.S.-backed norms and institutions that reject the legitimacy of empire and imperial geopolitics.

Since the end of the Cold War, the United States has been the principal underwriter of an international system based on the ideas of sovereign equality and territorial integrity—in principle, if not always in its own practice. It has also not only promoted democracy abroad, but sought to encode it in the operating system of international institutions in a way that suggested alternate political models were illegitimate.[6] The endurance of imperial legacies in China, Iran, Russia, and Turkey has consequently left them on the sidelines, or excluded entirely, from institutions emphasizing democracy, equal sovereignty, and territorial integrity. Meanwhile, efforts to change their behavior, usually through sanctions, are perceived in Moscow, Tehran, and, increasingly, Beijing and Ankara as well, as aiming at regime change—and therefore an indication that the United States and its allies regard them in some fundamental way as illegitimate. Relative to U.S.-backed norms and institutions, these four states have, therefore, come to comprise something like an "axis of the excluded."[7]

Increasingly, and in shifting geometries, they have instead begun laying out alternative visions of both regional and global order. These alternatives are embodied in multilateral initiatives like the SCO, the Eurasian Economic Union, the BRI, and, more loosely, the Astana peace process for Syria—as well as in informal and unequal bilateral relationships with smaller states and their elites. The relationships and institutions China, Iran, Russia, and Turkey are creating are less about ideology (both democratic and authoritarian states are welcome to participate in the BRI, for instance) than about using informal ties, fluid frontiers, ethnic-religious connections, and other tools to build hierarchical, differentiated relationships with their neighbors—that is, the "'rimless hub-and-spoke systems" characteristic of empires. All seek to establish themselves as pivots for political order in their respective regions, where relations with smaller states are determined less by impartial rules and more by the logic of hierarchy, layered sovereignty, and informal relationships.

Meanwhile, Ankara, Beijing, Moscow, and Tehran manage internecine disputes among themselves with little reference to or regard for U.S.-led international institutions. The lengths to which Putin and Erdoğan have gone to smooth over the fallout from clashes between their militaries and proxies may be the most striking example: even Russian airstrikes that killed dozens of Turkish soldiers near Idlib in April 2020 did not spark a conflict or a fundamental rupture between the two states—though Turkey remains a member of a military alliance Russia regards as hostile. Moscow recognizes that a more "imperial" Turkey, which prioritizes strategic autonomy and expanding its influence in Eurasia over reinforcing a U.S.-led security architecture in Europe, is worth the occasional clash in Syria, Libya, or the South Caucasus. Turkey, meanwhile, sees in Putin's Russia both a model for conducting postimperial geopolitics and a buttress for its own ambitions. Likewise, the strategic rapprochement between Moscow and Beijing—despite a growing power imbalance and possibly incompatible visions for reshaping Eurasia—is a product of the two countries' shared interest in eroding liberalism's normative hegemony and legitimating their respective ambitions to establish spheres of influence around their borders. In a world made safe for empire, such managed competition over "shatter zones" will likely be a permanent feature of Eurasian geopolitics.

Of course, the endurance of Eurasia's imperial moment over the longer term depends on many factors, including the stability of the regimes in Moscow, Ankara, Tehran, and Beijing. To a significant degree, however, the persistence of empire is built into the very nature of these states. Their location on the Eurasian landmass, history as centers of regional order, vast and unguardable borders, heterogeneous populations, and patchwork political structures all suggest that even regime change may not be sufficient to dramatically alter their ambitions for regional leadership and intervention in their neighbors' affairs. A more democratic Russia would still worry about the spillover of refugees, violence, and extremism from its neighbors. A more democratic Iran would still seek to shape the theological and political orientation of the *Atabat* and take an interest in the fate of Shi'as across the Middle East. A more democratic Turkey would still oppose the establishment of an autonomous Kurdish region under the PYD in Syria.

Indeed, the imperfect history of democratic rule in these states suggests that freely elected leaders can be, and often are, just as "imperial" as authoritarian regimes. Of the four states, Turkey has the most extensive experience with democracy, which has endured in some fashion—despite sporadic military coups—since the 1950s. It was Adnan Menderes, Turkey's first freely elected prime minister, who pointed to accomplishments of the Ottoman period, created space for Islam in mainstream politics, and called for reengaging with Turkey's post-Ottoman periphery. Erdoğan, who openly identifies with Menderes, operates from a more ambitious version of this playbook seven decades later.[8] His unprecedented electoral success suggests that imperial nostalgia is not merely an elite phenomenon, but a potent resource political entrepreneurs can tap.

Like Erdoğan, Putin did not create imperial nostalgia so much as mobilize it, using the annexation of Crimea—over Western protests and in the face of Western sanctions—to make a symbolic statement that Russia was returning to its imperial roots in the wake of the "chaotic 1990s," NATO expansion, the U.S.-led bombing of Serbia, "colored revolutions" in Georgia and Ukraine, and other indignities. Even if Putin's post-Crimea popularity boost proved fleeting, moreover, its very existence provides a template, and a temptation, that not just Putin but his successors too may be tempted to emulate.[9] Aleksey Navalny's support for the annexation of

Crimea suggests that identification with Russia's imperial legacy remains entrenched within the democratic opposition to Putin as well.

In China, meanwhile, the embrace of Confucian symbolism and imperial nostalgia helped the CCP fill the intellectual and ideological vacuum opened up by the Tiananmen Square crisis. Today, the CCP promotes an expansive vision of China's role in the region and the world, in part to compensate for public discontent over slowing growth, corruption, environmental degradation, and other challenges. Beijing's ambitions are directed more at maritime East Asia (including the South and East China Seas, Hong Kong, and Taiwan) than at the Eurasian mainland, but the underlying belief in China as the center of a historically and culturally defined regional order has implications extending far beyond China's coastlines. The narrative of a powerful and united China returning to its proper place in the world provides an opportunity to mobilize the country's billion-plus inhabitants behind a party that long ago abandoned any pretext of being Communist and now faces mounting challenges to its legitimacy. It is this fear of the CCP channeling accumulating social pressures outward— a variant of what the German historian Hans-Ulrich Wehler identified in pre-1914 Germany as "manipulated social imperialism"—that drives many comparisons of the contemporary U.S.-China competition with the Anglo-German rivalry that sparked World War I.[10]

Though Iran's embrace of imperial nostalgia is more tentative, it is equally real. As in post-1989 China, the inability of the Islamic Republic to secure mass support for its ideological claims induced it to reemphasize imperial motifs as the price of survival during the Iran-Iraq War—despite not merely the opposition of leading clerics, but also the ways in which Mohammad Reza Shah's clumsy imperial nostalgia helped discredit the very idea of continuity with the Achaemenid and Sasanian eras. The tension between the Islamic and the imperial strands of Iranian identity remains acute today, even as the Islamic Republic pursues a different kind of imperial vocation through its cultivation of Shi'ite allies and proxies throughout the Greater Middle East. Meanwhile, the Islamic Republic's democratic opponents look to the imperial past as an alternative source of legitimacy, even reembracing aspects of the Pahlavi era (and sometimes, the Pahlavi family) as avatars of a more authentic Iranian identity.[11]

Of course, changes to the fundamental shape and extent of these states could reverse the drift toward postimperial geopolitics. Turkey without its Kurdish periphery would be much more of a nation-state, as would China without Tibet and Xinjiang (even if Han identity itself remains more variegated than official discourse would suggest), or Russia without the North Caucasus. Iran without its non-Persian periphery would be more of a nation-state as well, though the overall absence of separatism among Iran's embattled minorities suggests the durability of a supraethnic, suprareligious "idea of Iran" even today. In any case, though, officials in Beijing, Tehran, Moscow, and Ankara have all made state preservation a top priority, and there is little to suggest they will not be successful at least for the foreseeable future. The scale of Russia's effort to hold onto Chechnya, or of China's pitiless campaign in Xinjiang, is evidence of that commitment to holding onto the vestiges of empire—and of the linkage between the difficulty of maintaining the unity of postimperial states and authoritarian politics.

The challenge these four states pose to the U.S.-led post–Cold War order centers on their support for an alternative conception of international politics, one based not on laws or the Westphalian principles of equal sovereignty and territorial integrity, but on power derived from longstanding historical, cultural, religious, and other ties. The tension between postimperial states' claim to special status and the United States' insistence that all states—apart from the United States itself—subject themselves to rules and institutions codified by the victors in World War II and given universal scope at the end of the Cold War has become perhaps *the* principal fault line in the emerging era of great power competition. This competition pits the United States against Russia and China, not just over primacy in the strategically important regions of Europe and East Asia, but also over the shape of global order and international institutions.

Within this competition, Tehran's sympathies clearly lie with Beijing and Moscow. Ankara's attitude is more complex, but the internal transformation of Turkey under AKP rule and deepening ties with Russia are a source of mounting angst across the trans-Atlantic West too. That transformation itself is evidence of the imperial legacies that always lurked beneath the surface in Atatürk's republic, and in Eurasia's other postimperial states as well. Neither "grievance states," civilizational states, nor merely great powers, China, Iran, Russia, and Turkey are something much older and more enduring. They are heirs to long imperial traditions whose specter, a century after the end of formal empire, haunts Eurasia once more.

Notes

Abbreviations

AHR: American Historical Review
CAS: Central Asian Survey
CHC: Cambridge History of China
CHI: Cambridge History of Iran
CHR: Cambridge History of Russia
CHT: Cambridge History of Turkey
CSIS: Center for Strategic and International Studies
EAS: Europe-Asia Studies
EI2: Encyclopedia Islamica, New (2nd) Edition
EIr: Encyclopedia Iranica
HJAS: Harvard Journal of Asiatic Studies
HUS: Harvard Ukrainian Studies
IJMES: International Journal of Middle Eastern Studies
IS: Iranian Studies
JAOS: Journal of the American Oriental Society
JfGO: Jahrbücher für Geschichte Osteuropas
MES: Middle Eastern Studies
PONARS: Program on New Approaches to Research and Security in Eurasia
SEER: Slavonic and East European Review
TPQ: Turkish Policy Quarterly
WdI: Welt des Islams
WZKM: Wiener Zeitschrift für die Kunde des Morgenlandes

Introduction

1. Fiona Hill and Clifford G. Gaddy, *Mr. Putin: Operative in the Kremlin* (Washington, DC: Brookings, 2013) 63–77. Soner Cagaptay, *Erdogan's Empire: Turkey and the Politics of the Middle East* (London: I. B. Tauris, 2020) xvi–xviii, 5–7.

2. Steven Lee Myers, *The New Tsar: The Rise and Reign of Vladimir Putin* (Oxford: Oxford University Press, 2014). Soner Cagaptay, *The New Sultan: Erdogan and the Crisis of Modern Turkey* (London: I. B. Tauris, 2017).

3. Charles Tilly, *Coercion, Capital, and European States, AD 990–1992* (London: Blackwell, 1992) 2–3.

4. Geoffrey Hosking, "The Freudian Frontier," *Times Literary Supplement*, 10 Mar 1995: 27. Also see Mark R. Beissinger, "The Persisting Ambiguity of Empire," *Post-Soviet Affairs*, 1995, 11(2): 149–84.

5. Christopher Ashley Ford, "Ideological 'Grievance States' and Nonproliferation: China, Russia, and Iran," U.S. Department of State, 11 Nov 2019, https://www.state.gov/ideological-grievance-states-and-nonproliferation -china-russia-and-iran/.

6. The term "a world safe for empire" was used—with a somewhat different meaning—in Erez Manela, *The Wilsonian Moment: Self-Determination and the International Origins of Anticolonial Nationalism* (Oxford: Oxford University Press, 2007) 197–214.

7. For instance, Michael McFaul, *From Cold War to Hot Peace: An American Ambassador in Putin's Russia* (New York: Houghton Mifflin, 2018). Timothy Snyder, *The Road to Unfreedom: Russia, Europe, America* (New York: Tim Duggan, 2019). Newt Gingrich, *Trump vs. China: Facing America's Biggest Threat* (New York: Center Street, 2019). Bill Gertz, *Deceiving the Sky: Inside Communist China's Drive for Global Supremacy* (New York: Encounter, 2019). Michael Pillsbury, *The Hundred-Year Marathon: China's Secret Strategy to Replace America as the Global Superpower* (New York: Henry Holt, 2014). Ilan Berman, *Iran's Deadly Ambition: The Islamic Republic's Quest for Global Power* (New York: Encounter, 2019). Özgür Tüfekçi, *The Foreign Policy of Modern Turkey: Power and the Ideology of Eurasianism* (London: I. B. Tauris, 2017). Michael Rubin, "Shifting Sides? The Problems of Neo-Ottomanism," *National Review*, 10 Aug 2004, http://www.michaelrubin.org/918/shifting-sides.

8. Hal Brands, "Democracy vs. Authoritarianism: How Ideology Shapes Great Power Competition," *Survival*, Oct–Nov 2018, 60(5): 66.

9. Charles Kupchan, *No One's World: The West, the Rising Rest, and the Coming Global Turn* (Oxford: Oxford University Press, 2012). Andrei P. Tsygankov, *Russia and America: The Asymmetric Rivalry* (Cambridge: Polity, 2019). Andrew Radin and Clint Reach, "Russian Views of the International Order," RAND Corporation, 2017, https://www.rand.org/content/dam/rand/pubs/ research_reports/RR1800/RR1826/RAND_RR1826.pdf. Elias Götz and Camille-Renaud Merlen, "Russia and the Question of World Order," *European Politics and Society*, 2019, 20(2): 133–53. Yong Deng, *China's Struggle for Status: The Realignment of International Relations* (Cambridge: Cambridge University Press, 2006). Alistair Iain Johnson, "Is China a Status Quo Power?," *International Security*, 2003, 27(4): 5–56. Shaun Breslin, "China and the Global Order: Signalling Threat or Friendship?," *International Affairs*, May 2013, 89(3): 615–34. Martin Jacques, *When China Rules the World: The End of the Western World and the Birth of a New Global Order*, 2nd ed. (New

York: Penguin, 2012). Philip Robins, "Turkey's 'Double Gravity' Predicament: The Foreign Policy of a Newly Activist Power," *International Affairs*, 2013, 89(2): 381–97.

10.   Christopher P. Coker, *The Rise of the Civilizational State* (Cambridge: Polity, 2019). Amitav Acharya, "The Myth of the 'Civilization State': Rising Powers and the Cultural Challenge to World Order," *Ethics & International Affairs*, 2020, 34(2): 139–56.

11.   Samuel Huntington, *The Clash of Civilizations and the Remaking of World Order* (New York: Simon & Schuster, 2011) 21–28.

12.   Dominic Lieven, "The Russian Empire and the Soviet Union as Imperial Polities," *Journal of Contemporary History*, Oct 1995, 30(4): 607.

13.   Theoretical works and comparative histories of empire are numerous. See especially Michael W. Doyle, *Empires* (Ithaca: Cornell University Press, 1986). Peter Fibiger Bang and C. A. Bayly, *Tributary Empires in Global History* (London: Palgrave, 2011). Jane Burbank and Frederick Cooper, *Empires in World History: Power and the Politics of Difference* (Princeton, NJ: Princeton University Press, 2011). Anthony Pagden, *The Burdens of Empire: 1539 to the Present* (Cambridge: Cambridge University Press, 2015). Alexei Miller and Alfred J. Rieber, eds., *Imperial Rule* (Budapest: CEU, 2004). Stephen Dale, *The Muslim Empires of the Ottomans, Safavids, and Mughals* (Cambridge: Cambridge University Press, 2009). Krishan Kumar, *Visions of Empire: How Five Imperial Regimes Shaped the World* (Princeton, NJ: Princeton University Press, 2017). Dominic Lieven, *Empire: The Russian Empire and its Rivals* (New Haven: Yale University Press, 2002). Karen Barkey, *Empire of Difference: The Ottomans in Comparative Perspective* (Cambridge: Cambridge University Press, 2008). Odd Arne Westad, *Restless Empire: China and the World since 1750* (New York: Basic Books, 2015). Ilhan Niaz, *Old World Empires: Cultures of Power and Governance in Eurasia* (London: Routledge, 2014). Alfred J. Rieber, *The Struggle for the Eurasian Borderlands: From the Rise of the Early Modern Empires to the End of the First World War* (Cambridge: Cambridge University Press, 2014).

14.   On the Delian League, see Alexandros Koutsoukis, "Building and Empire or Not: Athenian Imperialism and the United States in the Twenty-first Century," *Global Discourse*, 2013, 3(1): 12–30. On the European Union, see Jan Zielonka, *Europe as Empire: The Nature of the Enlarged European Union* (Oxford: Oxford University Press, 2006).

15.   John Gallagher and Ronald E. Robinson, "The Imperialism of Free Trade," *Economic History Review*, 2nd series, 1953, 6(1): 1–25.

16.   David Armitage, *The Ideological Origins of the British Empire* (Cambridge: Cambridge University Press, 2000) 1–24.

17.   Daniel Immerwahr, *How to Hide an Empire* (New York: Farrar, Straus, and Giroux, 2019).

18.   Lieven, *Empire*, xi.

19.   Daniel H. Nexon and Thomas Wright, "What's at Stake in the American Empire Debate," *American Political Science Review*, May 2007, 101(2): 253–71. Joseph M. Colomer, "Bringing the Empire Back In," *Revista*, 2008, 2(1):

48–58. Charles S. Maier, *Among Empires: American Ascendancy and Its Prede-cessors* (Cambridge, MA: Harvard University Press, 2007) 24–77. Alexander Cooley, *Logics of Hierarchy: The Organization of States, Empires, and Military Occupation* (Ithaca: Cornell University Press, 2005) 20–63.

20. Barkey, *Empire of Difference*, x, 1.

21. Nexon and Wright, "What's at Stake," 253. Charles Tilly, "How Empires End," in Karen Barkey and Mark von Hagen, eds., *After Empire: Multiethnic Societies and Nation-Building* (Boulder, CO: Westview, 1997) 1–11.

22. Kumar, *Visions of Empire*, 15.

23. Burbank and Cooper, *Empires in World History*.

24. Rieber, *Struggle for the Eurasian Borderlands*, 59–64.

25. Ronald Grigor Suny, "Ambiguous Categories: States, Empires, and Na-tions," *Post-Soviet Affairs*, 1995, 11(2): 185.

26. Ayşe Zarakol, *After Defeat: How the East Learned to Live with the West* (Cam-bridge: Cambridge University Press, 2010) 9–12.

27. On Eurasia, see Christopher I. Beckwith, *Empires of the Silk Road: A History of Central Eurasia from the Bronze Age to the Present* (Princeton, NJ: Princeton University Press, 2009). Peter Frankopan, *The Silk Roads: A New History of the World* (New York: Vintage, 2017). Niaz, *Old World Empires*. Rieber, *Struggle for the Eurasian Borderlands*. Bruno Maçães, *The Dawn of Eurasia: On the Trail of the New World Order* (New Haven, CT: Yale University Press, 2018). Kent E. Calder, *The New Continentalism: Energy and Twenty-first Century Eurasian Geopolitics* (New Haven, CT: Yale University Press, 2012). Robert Kaplan, *The Return of Marco Polo's World: War, Strategy, and American Interests in the Twenty-First Century* (New York: Random House, 2018).

28. Beckwith, *Empires of the Silk Road*, xx. See also Alexei Miller and Alfred J. Rieber, "Introduction," in Miller and Rieber, eds., *Imperial Rule*, 1–8. Rieber, *Struggle for the Eurasian Borderlands*, 1–4. Burbank and Cooper, *Empires in World History*, 93–116.

29. Frankopan, *Silk Roads*, xiv–xix. Beckwith, *Empires of the Silk Road*, 12–28. Ste-phen Kotkin, "Mongol Commonwealth? Exchange and Governance Across the Post-Mongol Space," *Kritika*, Summer 2007, 8(3): 487–531.

30. J. A. Hobson, *Imperialism: A Study* (London, 1902). Vladimir Lenin, "Imperi-alism: The Highest Stage of Capitalism," in Lenin, *Selected Works* (Moscow: Progress, 1970 [1916]).

31. Rieber, *Struggle for the Eurasian Borderlands*, 8–10. Jin Noda, *Kazakh Khan-ates Between the Russian and Qing Empires: Central Eurasian International Re-lations During the Eighteenth and Nineteenth Centuries* (Leiden: Brill, 2016) 293–303.

32. Benedict Anderson, *Imagined Communities: Reflections on the Origins and Spread of Nationalism* (London: Verso, 2006) 88.

33. Stefan Berger and Alexei Miller, "Introduction: Building Nations in and with Empires—A Reassessment," in Berger and Miller, eds., *Nationalizing Empires* (Budapest: CEU, 2015) 1–30. Stefano Taglia, "Ottomanism Then

and Now: Historical and Contemporary Meanings: An Introduction," *WdI*, Nov 2016, 56(3–4): 279–89.

34. Most of the vast literature on imperial legacies overlooks Eurasia. Exceptions include Lieven, *Empire*, 343–412. Berger and Miller, eds., *Nationalizing Empires*. Pagden, *Burdens of Empire*, 243–62. Joseph W. Esherick, Hasan Kayalı, and Eric van Young, eds., *Empire to Nation: Historical Perspectives on the Making of the Modern World* (Lanham, MD: Rowman & Littlefield, 2006). Barkey and von Hagen, eds., *After Empire*. Krishan Kumar, "Nation-states as Empires, Empires as Nation-states: Two Principles, One Practice?," *Theory and Society*, Mar 2010, 39(2): 119–43. Kumar, *Visions of Empire*, 465–76. L. Carl Brown, ed., *Imperial Legacy: The Ottoman Imprint on the Balkans* (Ithaca: Cornell University Press, 1996). Niaz, *Old World Empires*, 471–522. C. A. Bayly, *Remaking the Modern World, 1900–2015: Global Connections and Comparisons* (London: Wiley-Blackwell, 2018) 270–86. Also see the 2005 special issue of *Ab Imperio* devoted to imperial legacies.

35. Miguel Angel Centeno and Elaine Enriquez, "Legacies of Empire?," *Theory and Society*, 2010, 39(3): 343–60.

36. Krishan Kumar, "Nations and Nationalism: Civic, Ethnic, and Imperial," in *The Making of English National Identity* (Cambridge: Cambridge University Press, 2003) 18–38.

37. L. Carl Brown, Mark von Hagen, and Karen Barkey, "In Search of Imperial Legacy: Historians' Recollections and Historiographic Milestones," *Ab Imperio*, 2005, 4: 23–38.

38. Gerard Toal, *Near Abroad: Putin, the West, and the Contest Over Ukraine and the Caucasus* (Oxford: Oxford University Press, 2017) 3.

39. Lieven, *Empire*, 22.

Russia

1. Vladimir Putin, "Obrashcheniye prezidenta Rossiyskoy Federatsii," The Kremlin, 18 Mar 2014, http://kremlin.ru/events/president/news/20603.

2. Vladimir Putin, "Poslaniye Federal'nomu Sobraniyu Rossiyskoy Federatsii," The Kremlin, 29 Apr 2005, http://kremlin.ru/events/president/transcripts/22931.

3. Jeffrey Mankoff, "Will Belarus Be the Next Ukraine?," *Foreign Affairs*, 5 Feb 2020, https://www.foreignaffairs.com/articles/belarus/2020-02-05/will-belarus-be-next-ukraine.

4. Putin, "Obrashcheniye prezidenta."

5. David G. Rowley, "Imperial Versus National Discourse: The Case of Russia," *Nations and Nationalism*, 2000, 6(1): 23–42. Oxana Shevel, "Russian Nation-Building from Yel'tsin to Medvedev: Ethnic, Civic, or Purposefully Ambiguous?," *EAS*, Mar 2011, 63(2): 180–81, 189. Valerie Kivelson and Ronald Grigor Suny, *Russia's Empires* (Oxford: Oxford University Press, 2017) 6–8, 18–32.

6. "Vserossiyskaya perepis' naseleniya 2010: 1—Natsional'nyy sostav naseleniya," http://www.gks.ru/free_doc/new_site/perepis2010/croc/Documents/Vol4/pub-04-01.pdf.

7. Julie Wilhelmsen, "Inside Russia's Imperial Relations: The Social Constitution of Putin-Kadyrov Patronage," *Slavic Review*, 2018, 77(4): 919–36.

Chapter One. Russian Identity Between Empire and Nation

1. Geoffrey Hosking, *Russia: People and Empire 1552–1917* (Cambridge, MA: Harvard University Press, 1997) xxiii. James Cracraft, "Empire Versus Nation: Russian Political Theory Under Peter I," *HUS*, Dec 1986, 10(3–4): 524–41.

2. Theodore R. Weeks, "Managing Empire: Tsarist Nationalities Policy," *CHR* I-2: 27.

3. Jeffrey Mankoff, *Russian Foreign Policy: The Return of Great Power Politics*, 2nd ed. (Lanham, MD: Rowman & Littlefield, 2011) 219–62.

4. Janet Martin, "Russian Expansion in the Far North: X to Mid-XVI Century," in Michael Rywkin, ed., *Russian Colonial Expansion to 1917* (London: Mansell, 1988) 8–22. John W. Slocum, "Who, and When, Were the *Inorodtsy?* The Evolution of the Category of Aliens in Imperial Russia," *Russian Review*, Apr 1998, 57(2): 173–90.

5. Ronald Grigor Suny, "The Empire Strikes Out: Imperial Russia, 'National' Identity, and Theories of Empire," in Ronald Grigor Suny and Terry Martin, eds., *A State of Nations: Empire and Nation-Making in the Age of Lenin and Stalin* (Oxford: Oxford University Press, 2001) 37.

6. Cracraft, "Empire Versus Nation," 527. Andreas Kappeler, *The Russian Empire: A Multiethnic History*, trans. Alfred Clayton (London: Longman, 2001) 131–34.

7. Suny, "The Empire Strikes Out," 37–43 (quote, p. 40).

8. Quoted in Ernest A. Zitsner, "Boris Ivanovich Korybut-Kurakhin," in Stephen M. Norris and Willard Sunderland, eds., *Russia's People of Empire: Life Stories from Eurasia, 1500 to the Present* (Bloomington: Indiana University Press, 2012) 66n7.

9. Paul Bushkovitch, "What Is Russia? Russian National Identity and the State, 1500–1917," in Andreas Kappeler et al., eds., *Culture, Nation, and Identity: The Ukrainian-Russian Encounter (1600–1945)* (Edmonton: Canadian Institute of Ukrainian Studies, 2003) 144–62.

10. Suny, "The Empire Strikes Out," 47–48. Alexei Miller, "'Official Nationality'? A Reassessment of Count Sergei Uvarov's Triad in the Context of Nationalism [sic] Politics," in Miller, ed., *The Romanov Empire and Nationalism: Essays in the Methodology of Historical Research* (Budapest: CEU, 2008) 139, 146. Cynthia H. Whittaker, "The Ideology of Sergei Uvarov: An Interpretive Essay," *Russian Review*, Apr 1978, 37(2): 158–76.

11. Bushkovitch, "What Is Russia?," 153–54.

12. Laura Engelstein, *Slavophile Empire: Imperial Russia's Illiberal Path* (Ithaca: Cornell University Press, 2009) 10. Susanna Rabow-Edding, *Slavophile Thought and the Politics of Cultural Nationalism* (Albany: SUNY Press, 2006) 1–14, 117–34.

13. Andreas Renner, "Defining a Russian Nation: Mikhail Katkov and the 'Invention' of National Politics," *SEER*, Oct 2003, 81(4): 659, 669–72. G. P. Izmest'yeva, "Istoricheskiye portrety: Mikhail Nikiforovich Katkov," *Voprosy istorii*, 2004, (4): 71–92.

14. Suny, "The Empire Strikes Out," 53–54. Edward C. Thaden, Introduction, in Thaden, ed., *Russification in the Baltic Provinces and Finland, 1855–1914* (Princeton, NJ: Princeton University Press, 1981) 7–9. Alexei Miller, "Russification or Russifications?," in Miller, ed., *The Romanov Empire and Nationalism*, 51–53.

15. A. A. Ivanov, "'Rossiya dlya russkikh': pro et contra. Pravye i natsionalisty kontsa XIX-nachala XX vv. o lozunge 'russkogo Vozrozhdeniya,'" *Tribuna russkoy mysli*, 2007, (7): 92–102.

16. Theodore R. Weeks, *Nation and State in Late Imperial Russia: Nationalism and Russification on the Western Frontier, 1863–1914* (DeKalb, IL: Northern Illinois University Press, 1996) 172–92. Faith Hillis, *Children of Rus': Right-Bank Ukraine and the Invention of a Russian Nation* (Ithaca: Cornell University Press, 2017) 225–43, 249–54. Hans Kohn, "Was There a Russian Fascism? The Union of Russian People," *Journal of Modern History*, Dec 1964, 36(4): 398–415. Suny, "The Empire Strikes Out," 43–44. Alexei Miller and Alfred J. Rieber, "Introduction: Imperial Rule," in Miller and Rieber, eds., *Imperial Rule* (Budapest: CEU, 2004) 1–26.

17. Sergey Kryzhanovskiy, *Vospominaniya* (Berlin: Petropolis, 1938) 117.

18. Weeks, *Nation and State*, 172–92. Hillis, *Children of Rus'*, 225–43.

19. Eric Lohr, *Nationalizing the Russian Empire: The Campaign Against Enemy Aliens in World War I* (Cambridge, MA: Harvard University Press, 2003) 6–8, 17–22, 31–120.

20. Ibid., 121–65. Peter Gattrell, *A Whole Empire Walking: Refugees in Russia During World War I* (Bloomington: Indiana University Press, 2005).

21. Suny, "The Empire Strikes Out," 43–44. Miller and Rieber, "Introduction: Imperial Rule."

22. Ilya Prizel, *National Identity and Foreign Policy: Nationalism and Leadership in Poland, Russia, and Ukraine* (Cambridge: Cambridge University Press, 1998) 185–86. Lenin's letter is available in *Lenin's Final Fight: Speeches and Writings, 1922–23* (New Delhi: Pathfinder, 2010) n.p.

23. Prizel, *National Identity*, 182–84.

24. Timothy Snyder, "Ivan Ilyin, Putin's Philosopher of Russian Fascism," *New York Review of Books*, 16 Mar 2018, https://www.nybooks.com/daily/2018/03/16/ivan-ilyin-putins-philosopher-of-russian-fascism/.

25. J. V. Stalin, "Toast to the Russian People at a Reception in Honour of Red Army Commanders Given by the Soviet Government in the Kremlin on

Thursday, May 24, 1945," https://www.marxists.org/reference/archive/
stalin/works/1945/05/24.htm.

26. Dmitry Gorenburg, "Soviet Nationalities Policy and Assimilation," in Blair
Ruble et al., eds., *Rebounding Identities: The Politics of Identity in Russia and
Ukraine* (Cambridge: Cambridge University Press, 2006) 273–303.

27. Marlène Laruelle, "The Yuzhinskii Circle: Rediscovering European Far
Right Metaphysics in the Soviet Underground," in Laruelle, ed., *Entangled
Far Rights: A Russian-European Intellectual Romance in the Twentieth Century*
(Pittsburgh: University of Pittsburgh Press, 2018) 203–18.

28. Pål Kolstø, "The Ethnification of Russian Nationalism," in Pål Kolstø and
Helge Blakkisrud, eds., *The New Russian Nationalism: Imperialism, Ethnicity
and Authoritarianism 2000–2015* (Edinburgh: Edinburgh University Press,
2016) 28–30.

29. Prizel, *National Identity*, 189–91.

30. Tomasz Kamusella, "The Change of the Name of the Russian Language in
Russian from Rossiiskii to Russkii: Did Politics Have Anything to Do with
It?," *Acta Slavica Iaponica*, 2012, (32): 73–96.

31. "Konstitutsiya Rossiyskoy Federatsii," 12 Dec 1993, http://www.constitution
.ru/1000300/10003000-3.htm.

32. Vladimir Putin, "Zasedaniye mezhdunarodnogo diskussionogo kluba <Val-
dai>," The Kremlin, 18 Oct 2018, http://kremlin.ru/events/president/news/
58848.

33. Vladimir Putin, "Vladimir Putin. Rossiya: natsiona'lnyy vopros," *Nezavisimaya gazeta*, 23 Jan 2012, https://www.ng.ru/politics/2012-01-23/1_national
.html.

34. "Peskov prokommentiroval popravku k Konstitutsii o narode," RIA-Novosti,
4 Mar 2020, https://ria.ru/20200304/1568137099.html.

35. "V Rossii vyrosli ksenofobskiye nastroyeniya," Levada-Tsentr, 27 Aug 2018,
https://www.levada.ru/2018/08/27/v-rossii-vyrosli-ksenofobnye-nastroeniya/.

36. Putin, "Vladimir Putin. Rossiya: natsiona'lnyy vopros."

37. Snyder, "Ivan Ilyin." Marlène Laruelle, "Is Russia Really 'Fascist'?,"
PONARS, Sep 2018, http://www.ponarseurasia.org/memo/russia-really
-fascist-reply-timothy-snyder.

38. Quoted in Helge Blakkisrud, "Blurring the Boundary Between Civic
and Ethnic: The Kremlin's New Approach to National Identity Under Putin's Third Term," in Kolstø and Blakkisrud, eds., *The New Russian
Nationalism*, 254.

39. Vladimir Putin, "Stat'ya Vladimira Putina 'Ob istoricheskom yedinstve
russkikh i ukraintsev,'" The Kremlin, 12 Jul 2021, http://kremlin.ru/events/
president/news/66181.

40. Robert Paul Magocsi, *Galicia: A Historical Survey and Bibliographic Guide*
(Toronto: University of Toronto Press, 1983) 52–53. *The Hypatian Codex II*
(Paderborn: Wilhelm Fink, 1973) 58. Serhii Plokhii, *The Origins of the Slavic
Nations: Premodern Identities in Russia, Ukraine, and Belarus* (Cambridge:
Cambridge University Press, 2010) 49–121.

41. Timothy Snyder, *The Reconstruction of Nations: Poland, Ukraine, Lithuania, Belarus 1569–1999* (New Haven, CT: Yale University Press, 2003) 15–30. Nancy Shields Kollman, *The Russian Empire, 1450–1801* (Oxford: Oxford University Press, 2017) 72–79.

42. Zenon E. Kohut, "Origins of the Unity Paradigm: Ukraine and the Construction of Russian National History (1620–1860)," *Eighteenth Century Studies*, Fall 2001, 35(1): 70–76 (quote, p. 71). Vera Tolz, *Russia: Inventing the Nation* (London: Bloomsbury Academic, 2001) 209–34.

43. Kohut, "Origins."

44. Zenon E. Kohut, "Servant of the Tsar, Defender of the Ukrainian Church Autonomy, and Promoter of the Kyivan Caves Monastery: The Political World of Inokentii Gizel' (1650s–1670s)," *HUS*, 2011–14, 32/33, Part 1: 437–54.

45. Innokentyy Gizel', *Mechta o russkom yedinstve: Kievskiy sinopsis (1674)*, O. Ya. Sapozhnikov and I. Yu. Sapozhnikova, eds. (Moscow: Yevropa, 2010) 103.

46. Kohut, "Origins," 73.

47. John P. LeDonne, "The Territorial Reform of the Russian Empire, 1775–1796, Part 2: The Borderlands," *Cahiers du monde russe et soviétique*, 1983, 24(4): 414.

48. Terry Martin, "The Empire's New Frontiers: New Russia's Path from Frontier to 'Okraina' 1774–1920," *Russian History*, 1992, 19(1: 181–201.

49. Darius Staliūnas, "Affirmative Action in the Western Borderlands of the Late Russian Empire?," *Slavic Review*, Winter 2018, 77(4): 988–89. Theodore R. Weeks, "Territorializing Ethnicity in the Russian Empire? The Case of the Augustav/Suvalki Province," *Ab Imperio*, 2011, (3): 147–50.

50. Darius Staliūnas, "Between Russification and Divide and Rule: Russian Nationality Policy in the Western Borderlands in Mid-19th Century," *JfGO*, 2007, 55(3): 367–68.

51. Anna Veronika Wendland, *Die Russophilen in Galizien: Ukrainische Konservative zwischen Österreich und Rußland 1848–1915* (Vienna: Österreichische Akademie der Wissenschaften, 2001).

52. Stephen Velychenko, "The Bureaucracy, Police, and Army in Twentieth Century Ukraine: A Comparative Quantitative Study," *HUS*, Dec 1999, 23(3: 63–103.

53. P. I. Kovalevsky, quoted in Alexei Miller, *Ukrainian Question: Russian Empire and Nationalism in the 19th Century* (Budapest: CEU, 2003) 207.

54. "La mort de M. Sazonof," *Journal de Genève*, 29 Dec 1927. Hoover Institution, Sergei D. Sazonov Papers, Box 4 Folder 1.

55. Shane O'Rourke, "From Region to Nation: The Don Cossacks 1870–1920," in Jane Burbank et al., eds., *Russian Empire: Space, Power, People, 1700–1930* (Bloomington: Indiana University Press, 2007), 218–38.

56. Terry Martin, *The Affirmative Action Empire: Nations and Nationalism in the Soviet Union, 1923–1939* (Ithaca: Cornell University Press, 2001) 75–124.

57. Yaroslav Bilinsky, "Mykola Skrypnyk and Petro Shelest: An Essay on the Persistence and Limits of Ukrainian National Communism," in Jeremy

Azrael, ed., *Soviet Nationality Policies and Practices* (Westport, CT: Praeger, 1978) 105–43.

58. Serhy Yekelchyk, "Stalinist Patriotism as Imperial Discourse: Reconciling the Ukrainian and Russian 'Heroic Pasts,' 1939–1945," *Kritika*, Winter 2002, 3(1): 51–80.

59. Paul Robert Magocsi, *A History of Ukraine: The Land and Its People*, 2nd ed. (Toronto: University of Toronto Press, 2010) 639–41, 670–74.

60. Brezhnev's 1947 passport, available at https://commons.wikimedia.org/wiki/File:Brezhnev_LI_Pasport_1947.jpg?uselang=en.

61. Gorenburg, "Soviet Nationalities Policy."

62. Aleksandr Solzhenitsyn, "Kak nam obustroit' Rossiyu? Posil'nye soobrazheniya," http://www.solzhenitsyn.ru/proizvedeniya/publizistika/stati_i_rechi/v_izgnanii/kak_nam_obustroit_rossiyu.pdf.

63. Igor A. Zevelev, "Russia in the Post-Soviet Space: Dual Citizenship as a Foreign Policy Instrument," *Russia in Global Affairs*, Jun 2021: 10–37, https://eng.globalaffairs.ru/wp-content/uploads/2021/06/010-037.pdf.

64. Grigory Ioffe, "Understanding Belarus: Belarusian Identity," *EAS*, Dec 2003, 55(8): 1241–72.

65. "O Soyuznom gosudarstve," Informatsionno-analiticheskiy portal Soyuznogo gosudarstva, https://soyuz.by/o-soyuznom-gosudarstve.

66. Dmitry Butrin, "Druzhba nalogov," *Kommersant*, 16 Sep 2019, https://www.kommersant.ru/doc/4094365.

67. David Remnick, "Putin's Pique," *New Yorker*, 10 Mar 2014, https://www.newyorker.com/magazine/2014/03/17/putins-pique.

68. Vladimir Putin, "Zasedaniye mezhdunarodnogo diskussionogo kluba <Valdai>," The Kremlin, 24 Oct 2014, http://www.kremlin.ru/events/president/news/46860.

69. "Ukrainskiy general obvinil Rossiyu v namerenii doyti do Dnepra," *Gazeta.ru*, 13 Aug 2018, https://www.gazeta.ru/army/news/2018/08/13/11902561.shtml.

70. Velimir Razuvayev, "Ul'trapravye poshli nalevo," *Nezavisimaya gazeta*, 15 Jul 2016, http://www.ng.ru/politics/2016-07-15/3_pravye.html.

71. John O'Laughlin et al., "A New Survey of the Ukraine-Russia Conflict Finds Deeply Divided Views in the Contested Donbas Region," *Washington Post*, 12 Feb 2021, https://www.washingtonpost.com/politics/2021/02/12/new-survey-ukraine-russia-conflict-finds-deeply-divided-views-contested-donbas-region/.

72. Mark Bassin, "Russia Between Europe and Asia: The Ideological Construction of Geographic Space," *Slavic Review*, Spring 1991, 50(1): 9–12.

73. Lev Gumilev, "Lev Gumilev: Istoriko-Filosofskiye sochineniya knyazya N.S. Trubetskogo," 1990, Tsentr L'va Gumileva, https://www.gumilev-center.ru/lev-gumiljov-istoriko-filosofskie-sochineniya-knyazya-n-s-trubeckogo/.

74. Aleksandr Dugin, *Osnovy geopolitiki*, Part 4 (Moscow: Arktogeya, 2000), chapter 2, n.p.

75. Vladimir Putin, "Obrashcheniye prezidenta Rossiyskoy Federatsii," The Kremlin, 18 Mar 2014, http://kremlin.ru/events/president/news/20603.

76. "O vnesenii izmeneniy v federal'nyy zakon 'O gosudarstvennoy politike Rossiyskoy Federatsii v otnoshenii sootechestvennikov za rubezhom,'" *Rossiyskaya gazeta*, 27 Jul 2010, https://rg.ru/2010/07/27/sootech-dok.html. "O gosudarstvennoy politike Rossiyskoy Federatsii v otnoshenii sootechestven-nikov zarubezhom," The Kremlin, 24 May 1999, http://www.kremlin.ru/acts/bank/13875.

77. "Kontseptsiya vneshney politiki Rossiyskoy Federatsii," Ministry of Foreign Affairs, 30 Nov 2016, https://www.mid.ru/ru/foreign_policy/official_documents/-/asset_publisher/CptICkB6BZ29/content/id/2542248.

78. Igor Zevelev, "The Russian World Boundaries," *Russia in Global Affairs*, 7 Jun 2014, https://eng.globalaffairs.ru/number/The-Russian-World-Boundaries-16707.

79. Sergey Lavrov, "Voynu my ne nachnem, eto ya vam obeshchayu," *Kommersant*, 26 Sep 2019, https://www.kommersant.ru/doc/4103946.

80. Marlène Laruelle, "The 'Russian World': Russia's Soft Power and Geopolitical Imagination," CGI, May 2015, http://globalinterests.org/wp-content/uploads/2015/05/FINAL-CGI_Russian-World_Marlene-Laruelle.pdf.

81. M. D. Suslov, "'Holy Rus': The Geopolitical Imagination in the Contemporary Russian Orthodox Church," *Russian Politics and Law*, May–Jun 2014, 52(3): 18–21.

82. "Sobraniye 'Russkogo mira,'" Moscow State University, 22 Nov 2007, https://www.msu.ru/news/sobranie_russkogo_mira.html.

83. "Ideologiya," Fond Russkiy Mir, https://russkiymir.ru/fund/.

84. Orysia Lutsevych, "Agents of the Russian World: Proxy Groups in the Contested Neighbourhood," Chatham House, Apr 2016, https://www.chathamhouse.org/sites/default/files/publications/research/2016-04-14-agents-russian-world-lutsevych.pdf.

85. Suslov, "Holy Rus'," 67–86.

86. Putin, "Zasedaniye mezhdunarodnogo diskussionogo kluba <Valdai>."

87. Anton Troianovski, "Branding Putin," *Washington Post*, 12 Jul 2018, https://www.washingtonpost.com/graphics/2018/world/putin-brand/.

Chapter Two. Russia's Borderlands and the Territorialization of Identity

1. "Vserossiyskaya perepis' naseleniya 2010: 1—Natsional'nyy sostav naseleniya," http://www.gks.ru/free_doc/new_site/perepis2010/croc/Documents/Vol4/pub-04-01.pdf.

2. Michael Khodarkovsky, "Four Degrees of Separation: Constructing Non-Christian Identities in Muscovy," in A. M. Kleimola and G. D. Lenhoff, eds., *Culture and Identity in Muscovy, 1359–1584* (Moscow: ITZ-Garant, 1997) 248–66.

3. Vladislav Inozemtsev, "Russia, The Last Colonial Empire," *American Interest*, 29 Jun 2017, https://www.the-american-interest.com/2017/06/29/russia-last-colonial-empire/.

4. Willard Sunderland, "The 'Colonization Question': Visions of Colonization in Late Imperial Russia," *JfGO*, 2000, 48(2): 225.

5. Sergey Mikhailovich Solov'yev, *Istoriya Rossii s drevneyshchykh vremen*, Vol. 4, http://www.lib.ru/HISTORY/SOLOVIEV/solvo4.txt. Willard Sunderland, *Taming the Wild Field: Colonization and Empire on the Russian Steppe* (Ithaca: Cornell University Press, 2006) 3–4. Nicholas B. Breyfogle, Abby Schrader, and Willard Sunderland, "Russian Colonizations: An Introduction," in Breyfogle et al., eds., *Peopling the Russian Periphery: Borderland Colonization in Eurasian History* (London: Routledge, 2008) 1–18.

6. Alan Bodger, "Nationalities in History: Soviet Historiography and the Pugačëvščina," *JfGO*, 1991, 39(4): 561–81.

7. Sunderland, "The 'Colonization Question,'" 213–15.

8. David Moon, "Peasant Migration and the Settlement of Russia's Frontiers, 1550–1897," *Historical Journal*, 1997, 40(4): 866–67. S. I. Bruk and V. M. Kabuzan, "Migratsiya naseleniya v Rossii v XVIII–nachale XX veka (chislennost,' struktura, geografiya)," *Istoriya SSSR*, 1984, 4(52).

9. Moon, "Peasant Migration," 864–65.

10. Yuri Slezkine, "The USSR as a Communal Apartment, or How a Socialist State Promoted Ethnic Particularism," *Slavic Review*, Summer 1994, 53(2): 423.

11. Alfred J. Rieber, "Stalin, Man of the Borderlands," *AHR*, Dec 2001, 106(5): 1651–91. J.V. Stalin, "Marxism and the National Question," 1913, https://www.marxists.org/reference/archive/stalin/works/1913/03.htm.

12. Quoted in Terry Martin, *The Affirmative Action Empire: Nations and Nationalism in the Soviet Union, 1923–1939* (Ithaca: Cornell University Press, 2001) 5.

13. Ibid., 33.

14. Elise Giuliano, "Who Determines the Self in the Politics of Self-Determination? Identity and Preference Formation in Tatarstan's Nationalist Mobilization," *Comparative Politics*, Apr 2000, 32(3): 304–5.

15. Mark Kramer, "Why Did Russia Give Away Crimea Sixty Years Ago?," Woodrow Wilson Center/Cold War International History Project, 19 Mar 2014, https://www.wilsoncenter.org/publication/why-did-russia-give-away-crimea-sixty-years-ago.

16. Dmitry Gorenburg, "Soviet Nationalities Policy and Assimilation," in Dominique Arel and Blair A. Ruble, eds., *Rebounding Identities: The Politics of Identity in Russia and Ukraine* (Washington, DC: Woodrow Wilson Center, 2006) 273–303.

17. Valery Tishkov, *Ethnicity, Nationalism and Conflict in and After the Soviet Union: The Mind Aflame* (London: SAGE, 1997) 54–60.

18. Giuliano, "Who Determines the Self?," 305–10. Henry E. Hale, *Patronal Politics: Eurasian Regime Dynamics in Comparative Perspective* (Cambridge: Cambridge University Press, 2014) 123–77.

19.   Tishkov, *Ethnicity, Nationalism, and Conflict*, 54–62.

20.   Ibid., 62.

21.   V. A. Karatashkin and A. Kh. Abashidze, "Autonomy in the Russian Federation: Theory and Practice," *International Journal on Minority and Group Rights*, 2004, (10): 203–5.

22.   Stergos Kaloudis, "The Institutional Design of Russian Federalism: A Comparative Study of Three Republics; Tatarstan, Dagestan, and Chechnya," *Demokratizatsiya*, Winter 2017, 15(1): 143–46.

23.   Lena Smirnova, "Tatarstan, the Last Region to Lose Its Special Status Under Putin," *Moscow Times*, 25 Jul 2017, https://www.themoscowtimes.com/2017/07/25/tatarstan-special-status-expires-a58483.

24.   "KS RF raskritikoval resheniya konstitutsionnykh sudov Bashkirii, Tatarstana i Yakutii," *NEWSru.com*, 9 Jun 2009, https://www.newsru.com/russia/09jun2009/ks.html.

25.   "Vserossiyskaya perepis'."

26.   "Natsional'nyy Proyekt <Obrazovaniye>," 24 Dec 2018, https://strategy24.ru/rf/education/projects/natsional-nyy-proyekt-obrazovaniye.

27.   "Starye schety Kiriyenko. Tatarskiye natsionalisty otkryto vystupayut protiv politiki Kremlya," *Rambler*, 24 Oct 2017, https://news.rambler.ru/other/38234193-starye-schety-kirienko-tatarskie-natsionalisty-otkryto-vystupayut-protiv-politiki-kremlya/?updated.

28.   Kamil Galeev, "Fear and Loathing in Russia's Catalonia: Moscow's Fight Against Federalism," *War on the Rocks*, 31 Jan 2018, https://warontherocks.com/2018/01/moscows-fight-against-federalism-fear-and-loathing-in-russias-catalonia/.

29.   "V Yakutii prodolzhayutsya napadeniya na migrantov," *Regnum*, 28 Mar 2019, https://regnum.ru/news/2600214.html.

30.   Michael Khodarkovsky, "The Indigenous Elites and the Construction of Ethnic Identities in the North Caucasus," *Russian History*, 2008, 35(1–2): 130.

31.   Walter Richmond, "Circassia: A Small Nation Lost to the Great Game," in Alexander Laban Hinton et al., eds., *Hidden Genocides: Power, Knowledge, Memory* (Trenton: Rutgers University Press, 2013) 110–12. Charles King, "Imagining Circassia: David Urquhart and the Making of North Caucasus Nationalism," *Russian Review*, Apr 2007, 66(2): 238–55.

32.   Julietta Meskhidze, "Imam Shaykh Mansur: A Few Stanzas to a Familiar Portrait," *CAS*, 2001, 21(3): 301–24.

33.   "Shamil's Testament," trans. Dibir M. Mahomedov, *CAS*, 2002, 21(3): 243. Michael Reynolds, "Myths and Mysticism: A Longitudinal Perspective on Islam and Conflict in the North Caucasus," *MES*, Jan 2005, 41(1): 41.

34.   Alexandre Benningsen, "Un mouvement populaire au Caucase du XVIIIe siècle: La 'Guerre Sainte' du Sheikh Mansur (1785–1794), page mal connue et controversée des relations Russo-Turques," *Cahiers du monde russe et soviétique*, Apr–Jun 1964, 5(2): 159–205.

35. Moshe Gammer, "The Beginnings of the Naqshbandiyya in Dāghestān and the Russian Conquest of the Caucasus," *WdI*, 1994, 34(2): 204–17. Gammer, *Muslim Resistance to the Tsar* (London: Routledge, 2003) 39–46.

36. Marie Bennigsen Broxup, "The Last *Ghazawat:* The 1920–1921 Uprising," in Broxup, ed., *The North Caucasus Barrier: The Russian Advance Towards the Muslim World* (New York: St. Martin's, 1992) 112–45 (quote, p. 114).

37. Abdurahman Avtorkhanov, "The Chechens and the Ingush During the Soviet Period and Its Antecedents," in Broxup, ed., *North Caucasus Barrier*, 146–94.

38. Amjad Jaimoukha, *The Chechens: A Handbook* (London: RoutledgeCurzon, 2005) 58–71.

39. Irma Kreiten, "A Colonial Experiment in Cleansing: The Russian Conquest of Western Caucasus, 1856–65," *Journal of Genocide Research*, 2009, 11(2): 227–31.

40. Anatol Lieven, *Chechnya: Tombstone of Russian Power* (New Haven, CT: Yale University Press, 1998) 70–73.

41. Alexandre Bennigsen, "Muslim Conservative Opposition to the Soviet Regime: The Sufi Brotherhoods in the North Caucasus," in Jeremy Azrael, ed., *Soviet Nationality Policies and Practices* (Westport, CT: Praeger, 1978) 334–49.

42. Lieven, *Chechnya*, 102–46. Thomas De Waal and Carlotta Gall, *Chechnya: Calamity in the Caucasus* (New York: NYU Press, 1999) 173–372.

43. Lieven, *Chechnya*, 96–101.

44. Emil Souleimanov. "Chechnya, Wahhabism, and the Invasion of Dagestan," *Middle Eastern Review of International Affairs*, Dec 2005, 9(4).

45. "Kadyrov Akhmad (Akhmad-khadzhi)," *Kavkazskiy uzel*, 28 May 2001, https://www.kavkaz-uzel.eu/articles/13679/

46. Jean-François Ratelle and Emil Souleimanov, "A Perfect Counterinsurgency? Making Sense of Moscow's Policy of Chechenisation," *EAS*, Sep 2016, 68(8): 1287–1314.

47. Vera Mironova and Ekaterina Sergatskova, "The Chechens of Syria: The Meaning of Their Internal Struggle," *Foreign Affairs*, 7 Sep 2017, https://www.foreignaffairs.com/articles/syria/2017-09-07/chechens-syria.

48. Joshua Yaffa, "Putin's Dragon: Is the Ruler of Chechnya Out of Control?," *New Yorker*, 31 Jan 2016, https://www.newyorker.com/magazine/2016/02/08/putins-dragon.

49. Quoted in Yaffa, "Putin's Dragon."

Chapter Three. Russia's Near Abroad and the Geopolitics of Empire

1. Dmitry Medvedev, "Interv'yu Dmitriya Medvedeva rossiyskim telekanalam," The Kremlin, 31 Aug 2008, http://www.kremlin.ru/events/president/news/1276. Dmitri Trenin, "Russia's Spheres of *Interest*, Not *Influence*," *Washington Quarterly*, Oct 2009, 32(4): 3–22.

2. Jeffrey Mankoff, *Russian Foreign Policy: The Return of Great Power Politics*, 2d ed., (Lanham, MD: Rowman & Littlefield, 2011), 219–62.

3. A. B. Chubays, "Missiya Rossii v XXI veke," *Nezavisimaya gazeta*, 1 Oct 2003, https://www.ng.ru/ideas/2003-10-01/1_mission.html.

4. "Kontseptsiya vneshney politiki Rossiyskoy Federatsii," Ministry of Foreign Affairs, 30 Nov 2016, http://www.mid.ru/ru/foreign_policy/official _documents/-/asset_publisher/CptICkB6BZ29/content/id/2542248.

5. Alexander Morrison, "Metropole, Colony, and Imperial Citizenship in the Russian Empire," *Kritika*, Spring 2012, 13(2): 345–46.

6. Felix Schnell, "Empire in Disguise: The Soviet-Russian Imperial Metamorphosis After World War I," *Journal of Modern European History*, 2015, 13(2): 203–25.

7. Jiayi Zhou, "The Muslim Battalions: Soviet Central Asians in the Soviet-Afghan War," *Journal of Slavic Military Studies*, 2012, (25): 302–28.

8. Yevgeny Primakov, "Russia in World Politics: A Lecture in Honor of Chancellor Gorchakov," *International Affairs* (Moscow), 1998, 44(3): 11.

9. "Primakovskiye chteniya 2019," Insitut mirovoy ekonomiki i mezhdunarodnykh otnosheniy (IMEMO RAN), https://www.imemo.ru/primakov -readings. "Lavrov: V nedal'yekom budushchem istoriki sformuliruyut takoye ponyatiye, kak 'doktrina Primakova,'" TASS, 28 Oct 2014, https://tass .ru/politika/1537769.

10. Alena Ledeneva, *Can Russia Modernize? Sistema, Power Networks and Informal Governance* (Cambridge: Cambridge University Press, 2013). Brian Whitmore, "Putin's Dark Ecosystem: Graft, Gangsters, and Active Measures," CEPA, 20 Sep 2018, https://www.cepa.org/putins-dark-ecosystem.

11. Jeffrey Mankoff, "'Un-Civil Society' and the Sources of Russian Influence in West Asia: The South Caucasus," in Mehran Kamrava, ed., *The Great Game in West Asia: Iran, Turkey, and the South Caucasus* (Oxford: Oxford University Press, 2017) 141–60.

12. Ronald Grigor Suny, *The Making of the Georgian Nation* (Bloomington: Indiana University Press, 1994) 58–59. Thomas DeWaal, *The Caucasus: An Introduction*, 2nd ed. (Oxford: Oxford University Press, 2018) 38–40. Muriel Atkin, "Russian Expansion in the Caucasus to 1813," in Michael Rywkin, ed., *Russian Colonial Expansion to 1917* (London: Mansell, 1988) 167–70.

13. Elton L. Daniel, "Gōlestan Treaty," *EIr*, http://www.iranicaonline.org/ articles/golestan-treaty. F. Ismail, "The Making of the Treaty of Bucharest, 1811–1812," *MES*, May 1979, 15(2): 167–68. Donald Rayfield, *Edge of Empires: A History of Georgia* (Clerkenwell: Reaktion, 2012) 265–83.

14. Firouzeh Mostashari, *On the Religious Frontier: Tsarist Russia and Islam in the Caucasus* (London: Bloomsbury, 2017) 51–56 (quote, p. 51). Nancy Shields Kollman, *The Russian Empire 1450–1801* (Oxford: Oxford University Press, 2017) 306–11.

15. De Wall, *The Caucasus*, 44.

16. Richard G. Hovannisian, "Russian Armenia: A Century of Tsarist Rule." *JfGO*, Mar 1971, 19(1): 333–35.

17. Quoted in L. Hamilton Rhinelander, "Russia's Imperial Policy: The Administration of the Caucasus in the First Half of the Nineteenth Century," *Canadian Slavonic Papers*, 1975, 17(2/3): 229.

18. Nicholas B. Breyfogle, *Heretics and Colonizers: Forging Russia's Empire in the South Caucasus* (Ithaca: Cornell University Press, 2005) 1–48.

19. Michael A. Reynolds, *Shattering Empires: The Clash and Collapse of the Ottoman and Russian Empires 1908–1918* (Cambridge: Cambridge University Press, 2011) 143–55.

20. Alex Marshall, *The Caucasus Under Soviet Rule* (London: Routledge, 2010) 231–32.

21. Ibid., 279–80.

22. DeWaal, *The Caucasus*, 79–98.

23. Dmitri Trenin, *The End of Eurasia: Russia on the Border Between Geopolitics and Globalization* (Washington, DC: Carnegie Endowment, 2002) 181–86.

24. Thornike Gordadze, "Georgian-Russian Relations in the 1990s," in Svante Cornell and Frederick Starr, eds., *The Guns of August 2008: Russia's War in Georgia* (London: M. E. Sharpe, 2009) 28–48.

25. Sergey Markedonov, "De facto Statehood in Eurasia: A Political and Security Phenomenon," *Caucasus Survey*, 2015, 3(3): 195–206.

26. R. Craig Nation, "Russia and the Caucasus," *Connections*, Spring 2015, 14(2): 3–6.

27. Joshua Kucera, "U.S. Intelligence: Russia Sabotaged BTC Pipeline Ahead of 2008 Georgia War," *EurasiaNet*, 11 Dec 2014, https://eurasianet .org/us-intelligence-russia-sabotaged-btc-pipeline-ahead-of-2008-georgia -war.

28. Daniel Brower, *Turkestan and the Fate of the Russian Empire* (London: RoutledgeCurzon, 2003) x–xi.

29. Daniel G. Prior, "High Rank and Power Among the Northern Kirghiz: Terms and Their Problems, 1845–1864," in Paolo Sartori, ed., *Explorations in the Social History of Modern Central Asia (19th–Early 20th Century)* (Leiden: Brill, 2013) 137–79.

30. Adeeb Khalid, "Culture and Power in Colonial Turkestan," *Cahiers d'Asie centrale*, 2009, (17/18): 14–17.

31. A. M. Gorchakov, "The Gorchakov Circular on Russia's Mission in Central Asia, 1864," in James A. Cracraft, ed., *Major Problems in the History of Imperial Russia* (Lexington, MA: D. C. Heath, 1993) 410–11.

32. Adeeb Khalid, "Society and Politics in Bukhara, 1868–1920," *CAS*, 2000, 19(3–4): 367–96.

33. Trenin, *End of Eurasia*, 187–90.

34. Steven Sabol, *Russian Colonization and the Genesis of Kazak National Consciousness* (London: Palgrave Macmillan, 2003) 38–48.

35. Daniel Brower, "Kyrgyz Nomads and Russian Pioneers: Colonization and Ethnic Conflict in the Turkestan Revolt of 1916," *JfGO*, 1996, 44(1): 41–53. Sabol, *Russian Colonization*, 53–72.

36. Published Central Asian casualty figures vary because of incomplete records. See Alexander Morrison, review of *The Revolt of 1916 in Russian Central Asia* by Edward Dennis Sokol, *Slavic Review*, 2017, 76(3): 772–78.

37. Jeff Sahadeo, "Progress or Peril: Migrants and Locals in Russian Tashkent, 1906–14," in Breyfogle et al., eds., *Peopling the Russian Periphery*, 148–65.

38. Marie Broxup, "The Basmachi," *CAS*, 1983, 2(1): 57–81.

39. Yuri Slezkine, "The USSR as a Communal Apartment, or How a Socialist State Promoted Ethnic Particularism," *Slavic Review*, Summer 1994, 53(2): 428–30.

40. Anita Sengupta, "Imperatives of National Territorial Delimitation and the Fate of Bukhara 1917–1924," *CAS*, 2000, 19(3–4): 394–415. Amanda Ferrant, "Mission Impossible: The Politico-geographical Engineering of Soviet Central Asia's Republican Boundaries," *CAS*, 2006, 25(1–2): 61–74.

41. Sergey Abashin et al., "Soviet Rule and the Delineation of Borders in the Ferghana Valley, 1917–1930," in S. Frederick Starr et al., eds., *Ferghana Valley: The Heart of Central Asia* (London: Routledge, 2011) 94–118.

42. Adrienne Lynn Edgar, *Tribal Nation: The Making of Soviet Turkmenistan* (Princeton, NJ: Princeton University Press, 2004) 221–60.

43. Sarah Cameron, *The Hungry Steppe: Famine, Violence, and the Making of Soviet Kazakhstan* (Ithaca: Cornell University Press, 2018).

44. Trenin, *End of Eurasia*, 189–90.

45. Viktoriya Panfilova, "Berdymukhammedov otkazalsya ot pomoshchi Rossii," *Nezavisimaya gazeta*, 2 Feb 2016, https://www.ng.ru/cis/2016-02-02/8 _turkmenia.html.

46. Gerry Shih, "In Central Asia's Forbidding Highlands, a Quiet Newcomer: Chinese Troops," *Washington Post*, 18 Feb 2019, https://www.washingtonpost .com/world/asia_pacific/in-central-asias-forbidding-highlands-a-quiet -newcomer-chinese-troops/2019/02/18/.

47. Timofey Bordachev et al., "Rossiya, Kitay, i SShA v Tsentrasl'noy Azii: Balans interesov i vozmozhnosti sotrudnichestva," Valdai Club, Sep 2016, http://ru.valdaiclub.com/files/13120/.

48. Vladimir Putin "Zayavleniye po itogam vstrechi s Almazbekom Atambayevym," The Kremlin, 24 Jun 2019, http://kremlin.ru/events/president/ news/61094.

49. "Personal Remittances, Received (% of GDP)," World Bank, 2019, https:// data.worldbank.org/indicator/BX.TRF.PWKR.DT.GD.ZS.

50. Vladimir Putin, "Zadesaniye mezhdunarodnogo diskussionogo kluba <Valdai>," The Kremlin, 19 Sep 2013, http://kremlin.ru/events/president/news/ 19243.

51. "Kontseptsiya vneshney politiki."

52. "Putin: CIS Was Created for a Civilized Divorce," *New Europe*, 3 Apr 2005, https://www.neweurope.eu/article/putin-cis-was-created-civilised-divorce/.

53. Dmitri Trenin, "Revising the Concept of Eurasia," Carnegie Moscow Center, 29 Jan 2013, https://carnegie.ru/2013/01/29/revising-concept-of-eurasia

-pub-50797. Aleksandr Lukin, "Zamysel o bol'shoy Yevrazii: Smozhet li Rossiya stat' novym mirovym tsentrom sily?," *Nezavisimaya gazeta*, 4 Mar 2019, http://www.ng.ru/ideas/2019-03-04/7_7523_ideas.html. Evgeny Vinokurov and Aleksandr Libman, *Eurasian Integration: Challenges of Transcontinental Regionalism* (London: Palgrave Macmillan, 2012) 16–29.

54. Timofey V. Bordachev and Andrei S. Skriba, "Russia's Eurasian Integration Policies," in David Cadier, ed., *The Geopolitics of Eurasian Economic Integration*, LSE, Jun 2014: 18, http://www.lse.ac.uk/ideas/Assets/Documents/reports/LSE-IDEAS-Geopolitics-of-Eurasian-Economic-Intergration.pdf.

55. Marlène Laruelle, "Eurasia, Eurasianism, Eurasian Union: Terminological Gaps and Overlaps," PONARS, Jul 2015, (336), http://www.ponarseurasia.org/memo/eurasia-eurasianism-eurasian-union-terminological-gaps-and-overlaps. Yuriy Kofner, "Obraz budushchego EAES," Russian International Affairs Council, 27 Dec 2019, https://russiancouncil.ru/blogs/GreaterEurasia/obraz-budushchego-eaes/.

56. "Deklaratsiya o formirovanii yedinogo ekonomicheskogo prostranstva Respubliki Belarus, Respubliki Kazakhstan i Rossiyskoy Federatsii," The Kremlin, 9 Dec 2010, http://kremlin.ru/supplement/802.

57. Vladimir Putin, "Novyy integratsionnyy proyekt dlya Yevrazii—budushcheye, kotoroye rozhdayetsya segodnya," *Izvestiya*, 3 Oct 2011, https://iz.ru/news/502761.

58. "K velikomu okeanu: Ot povorota na vostok k Bol'shoy Yevrazii," in S. A. Karaganov and T. V. Bordachev, eds., *K velikomu okeanu: khronika povorota na Vostok* (Moscow: Valdai, 2019) 242–303.

59. "Kontseptsiya vneshney politiki."

60. Irina Busygina, "Russia in the Eurasian Economic Union: Lack of Trust Limits the Possible," PONARS, Feb 2019, (571), http://www.ponarseurasia.org/memo/russia-eurasian-economic-union-lack-trust-russia-limits-possible.

61. Rilka Dragneva and Kataryna Wolczuk, "The Eurasian Economic Union: Deals, Rules and the Exercise of Power," Chatham House, May 2017, https://www.chathamhouse.org/sites/default/files/publications/research/2017-05-02-eurasian-economic-union-dragneva-wolczuk.pdf.

62. "Ustav Organizatsii Dogovora o kollektivnoy bezopasnosti," Article VII (amended), 26 Apr 2012, https://odkb-csto.org/documents/documents/ustav_organizatsii_dogovora_o_kollektivnoy_bezopasnosti_/

63. Nikolaus Von Twickel, "Lukashenko Plays Coy with Kremlin," *Moscow Times*, 28 Aug 2009.

64. Vladimir Putin, "Plenarnoye zasedaniye Peterburgskogo mezhdunarodnogo ekonomicheskogo foruma," The Kremlin, 17 Jun 2016, http://kremlin.ru/events/president/news/52178.

65. Dmitri Trenin, "Russia's Evolving Grand Strategy: Will It Work?," Carnegie Moscow Center, 20 Jul 2017, https://carnegie.ru/2017/07/20/russia-s-evolving-grand-eurasia-strategy-will-it-work-pub-71588. David G. Lewis, "Geopolitical Imaginaries in Russian Foreign Policy: The Evolution of 'Greater Eurasia,'" *EAS*, 2018, 70(10): 1612–37. Timofey Bordachev, "No-

voye Yevraziystvo," *Rossiya v global'noy politike*, Sep/Oct 2015, (5), https://globalaffairs.ru/articles/novoe-evrazijstvo.

66. Andrey Kortunov, "Vosem' printsipov Bol'shogo yevraziyskogo partnerstva," Russian International Affairs Council, 25 Sep 2020, https://russiancouncil.ru/analytics-and-comments/analytics/vosem-printsipov-bolshogo-evraziyskogo-partnerstva.

67. Oleg Remyga, "Linking the Eurasian Economic Union and China's Belt and Road," CSIS, 9 Nov 2018, https://reconnectingasia.csis.org/analysis/entries/linking-eurasian-economic-union-and-chinas-belt-and-road/.

68. Seçkin Köstem, "Russia's Search for a Greater Eurasia: Origins, Promises, and Prospects," Woodrow Wilson Center, 26 Feb 2019, https://www.wilsoncenter.org/publication/kennan-cable-no-40-russias-search-for-greater-eurasia-origins-promises-and-prospects.

69. Vladimir Putin, "Bol'shaya press-konferentsiya Vladimira Putina," The Kremlin, 16 Dec 2019, http://kremlin.ru/events/president/news/62366.

Turkey

1. Erik J. Zürcher, *The Young Turk Legacy and Nation Building: From the Ottoman Empire to Atatürk's Turkey* (London: I. B. Tauris, 2010) 124–50. Virginia H. Aksan, "Ottoman to Turk: Continuity and Change," *International Journal*, Winter 2005–6, 61(1): 23.

2. Kemal H. Karpat, *The Politicization of Islam: Reconstructing Identity, Faith, and Community in the Late Ottoman State* (Oxford: Oxford University Press, 2001) 313–14.

3. Metin Heper, "The Ottoman Legacy and Turkish Politics," *Journal of International Affairs*, Fall 2000, 54(1): 63–82. Aksan, "Ottoman to Turk." Şerif Mardin, "The Ottoman Empire," in Karen Barkey and Mark von Hagen, eds., *After Empire: Multiethnic Societies and Nation-Building* (Boulder, CO: Westview, 1997) 122–24.

4. Peter F. Sugar, *Southeastern Europe Under Ottoman Rule, 1354–1804* (Seattle: University of Washington Press, 1977) 3–4.

5. "Turkey's PKK Conflict: The Death Toll," International Crisis Group, 20 Jul 2016, https://www.crisisgroup.org/europe-central-asia/western-europemediterranean/turkey/turkey-s-pkk-conflict-death-toll.

6. Selim Deringil, *The Well-Protected Domains: Ideology and the Legitimation of Power in the Ottoman Empire 1876–1909* (London: I. B. Tauris, 2011) 176.

7. Ahmet Davutoğlu, *Stratejik derinlik: Türkiye'nin uluslararası konumu* (Ankara: Küre, 2001).

Chapter Four. Those Who Call Themselves Turks

1. Dorothée Schmid, "Turqie: Le syndrome du Sèvres, ou la guerre qui n'en finit pas," *Politique étrangère*, Spring 2014, 79(1): 199–213.

2. Ayşe Kadioğlu, "The Paradox of Turkish Nationalism and the Construction of Official Identity," *MES*, Apr 1996, 32(2): 191–92.

3. Michael A. Reynolds, "Buffers not Brethren: Young Turk Military Policy in the First World War and the Myth of Panturanism," *Past & Present*, May 2009, (203): 137–79.

4. Yusuf Akçura and Ismail Fehmi, "Yusuf Akçura's Üç Tarz-i Siyaset ('Three Kinds of Policy')," *Oriente moderno*, 1981, 61(1/12): 1–20.

5. Nora Fisher Onar, "Echoes of a Universalism Lost: Rival Representations of the Ottomans in Today's Turkey," *MES*, Mar 2009, 45(2): 232.

6. Gökhan Çetinsaya, "Rethinking Nationalism and Islam: Some Preliminary Notes on the Roots of the 'Turkish-Islamic Synthesis' in Modern Turkish Political Thought," *Muslim World*, Jul–Oct 1999, 89(3–4): 368.

7. Ahmet Davutoğlu, "Dışişleri Bakanı Sayın Ahmet Davutoğlu'nun Türk Ocakları'nın kuruluşunun 100. yılını kutlama etkinlikleri kapsamında düzenlenen 'Büyük Türkiye'ye Doğru' sempozyumunda yaptığı konuşma," Ministry of Foreign Affairs, 26 Mar 2011, http://www.mfa.gov.tr/disisleri-bakani-sayin-ahmet-davutoglu_nun-turk-ocaklari_nin-kurulusunun-100_-yilini-kutlama-etkinlikleri-kapsaminda-duzenlenen.tr.mfa.

8. Ahmet Davutoğlu, "Address of H.E. Prof. Ahmet Davutoğlu, Minister of Foreign Affairs, Republic of Turkey," *Osmanlı mirası ve günümüz Balkan Müsülman toplumları* (Balkanlar Medeniyet Merkezi, 2009), 17, https://cns.ba/wp-content/uploads/2014/03/osmansko-naslijede-i-musulmanske-zajednice-Balkana-danas-zbornik-radova.pdf.

9. Süleyman Demirel, "Cumhurbaşkanı Sayın Süleyman Demirel'in Türkçe konuşan ülkeler devlet başkanları VI. zirve toplantısı'nda yaptıkları konuşma," Turkish Presidency, 8 Apr 2000, https://tccb.gov.tr/konusmalari-suleyman-demirel/1718/4127/cumhurbaskani-sayin-suleyman-demirelin-turkce-konusan-ulkeler-devlet-baskanlari-vi-zirve-toplantisinda-yaptiklari-konusma.

10. Seçkin Köstem, "When Can Idea Entrepreneurs Influence Foreign Policy? The Rise of the 'Turkic World' in Turkish Foreign Policy," *Foreign Policy Analysis*, 2017, (13): 722–40.

11. İlber Ortaylı, "Türkiyelilik," *Milliyet*, 5 Apr 2015, http://www.milliyet.com.tr/turkiyelilik/ilber-ortayli/pazar/yazardetay/05.04.2015/2039097/default.htm.

12. Hakan T. Karateke, "Opium for the Subjects? Religiosity as a Legitimizing Factor for Ottoman Sultans," in Karateke and Marius Reinkowski, *Legitimizing the Order: The Ottoman Rhetoric of State Power* (Leiden: Brill, 2005) 111–29.

13. R. Tschudi, "Bektāshiyya," *EI2*, I: 1161–63. Colin Imber, "The Ottoman Dynastic Myth," *Turcica*, 1987, 19: 7–27.

14. Kemal Karpat, *The Politicization of Islam: Reconstructing Identity, State, Faith, and Community in the Late Ottoman State* (Oxford: Oxford University Press, 2001), 89–116. M. Hakan Yavuz, "Is There a Turkish Islam? The Emergence

of Convergence and Consensus," *Journal of Muslim Minority Affairs*, Oct 2004, 24(2): 213–32. Hamid Algar, "Na<u>ksh</u>bandiyya," *EI2*, VII: 936–37.

15. Daniel Goffman, "Ottoman *millets* in the Early Seventeenth Century," *New Perspectives on Turkey*, 1994, (11): 135–58. Benjamin Braude, "Foundation Myths of the *Millet* System," in Benjamin Braude and Bernard Lewis, eds., *Christians and Jews in the Ottoman Empire: The Functioning of a Plural Society* (Teaneck, NJ: Holmes & Meier, 1982) 69–90.

16. Karen Barkey and George Gavrilis, "The Ottoman Millet System: Non-Territorial Autonomy and Its Contemporary Legacy," *Ethnopolitics*, 2016, 15(1): 24.

17. Madeline C. Zilfi, "The Kadizadelis: Discordant Revivalism in Seventeenth Century Istanbul," *Journal of Near Eastern Studies*, Oct 1986, 45(4): 251–69.

18. Denise Natali, "*Kurdayetî* in the Late Ottoman and Qajar Empires," *Critique: Critical Middle Eastern Studies*, Fall 2002, 11(2): 180.

19. Brian Glyn Williams, "Hijra and Forced Migration from Nineteenth-Century Russia to the Ottoman Empire: A Critical Analysis of the Great Crimean Tatar Emigration of 1860–1861," *Cahiers du monde russe*, Jan–Mar 2000, 41(1): 81–83, 94–104. Alan W. Fisher, "Emigration of Muslims from the Russian Empire in the Years After the Crimean War," *JfGO*, 1987, 35(3): 356–57.

20. "Tanzimat Fermanı," Tarihi Olaylar, 3 Sep 1839, https://www.tarihiolaylar .com/tarihi-olaylar/tanzimat-fermani-1373.

21. Quoted in Selim Deringil, *The Well-Protected Domains: Ideology and the Legitimation of Power in the Ottoman Empire 1876–1909* (London: I. B. Tauris, 2011) 169.

22. Stefano Taglia, "Ottomanism Then and Now: Historical and Contemporary Meanings: An Introduction," *WdI*, Nov 2016, 56(3–4): 279–89 (quote, p. 284).

23. Şerif Mardin, "Turkish Islamic Exceptionalism Yesterday and Today: Continuity, Rupture and Reconstruction in Operational Codes," *Turkish Studies*, Jun 2005, 6(2): 149–52.

24. Çetinsaya, "Rethinking Nationalism and Islam."

25. Selim Deringil, "The Invention of Tradition as Public Image in the Late Ottoman Empire, 1808–1908," *Comparative Studies in Society and History*, Jan 1993, 35(1): 3–29 (quote, p. 5).

26. Deringil, *Well-Protected Domains*, 46–50 (quote, p. 47). Kemal H. Karpat, *The Politicization of Islam: Reconstructing Identity, State, Faith, and Community in the Late Ottoman State* (Oxford: Oxford University Press, 2001) 155–82.

27. Akçura and Fehmi, "Yusuf Akçura's Üç Tarz-i Siyaset," 18.

28. On Gaspıralı, see Svetlana Chervonnaya, "Pantyurkizm i panislamizm v ros-siyskoy istorii," *Otechestvennye zapiski*, 2003, 14(5), http://www.strana-oz.ru/ 2003/5/pantyurkizm-i-panislamizm-v-rossiyskoy-istorii. Alexandre Benningsen, *Ismail Gasprinski (Gaspraly) and the Origins of the Jadid Movement in Russia* (Oxford: Society for Central Asian Studies, 1985).

29. Justin McCarthy, *The Ottoman Peoples and the End of Empire* (London: Edward Arnold, 2001) 28.

30. Quoted in Jacob M. Landau, *Pan-Turkism in Turkey: A Study of Irredentism* (London: Hurst, 1981) 50.

31. Raymond Kevorkian, *The Armenian Genocide: A Complete History* (London: I. B. Tauris, 2010). Ronald Grigor Suny, *"They Can Live in the Desert but Nowhere Else": A History of the Armenian Genocide* (Princeton, NJ: Princeton University Press, 2015). Thomas de Waal, *Great Catastrophe: Armenians and Turks in the Shadow of Genocide* (Oxford: Oxford University Press, 2008).

32. "Ulusal Ant (Mısak-i Milli)," Türk Tarihi Kurumu, 28 Jan 1920, https://www.webcitation.org/6Ol8KkhHX.

33. David Kushner, *The Rise of Turkish Nationalism 1876–1908* (London: Frank Cass, 1977) 98–99. Ebru Boyar, *Ottomans, Turks and the Balkans: Empire Lost, Relations Altered* (London: I. B. Tauris, 2007) 45–54.

34. Onar, "Echoes," 232. Peter F. Sugar, *Southeastern Europe Under Ottoman Rule, 1354–1804* (Seattle: University of Washington Press, 1977) 3–4.

35. Quoted in Metin Heper, "The Ottoman Legacy and Turkish Politics," *Journal of International Affairs*, Fall 2000, 54(1): 75.

36. Şener Aktürk, "Persistence of the Islamic Millet as an Ottoman Legacy: Mono-Religious and Anti-Ethnic Definition of Turkish Nationhood," *MES*, Nov 2009, 45(6): 893–909.

37. Fatma Müge Göçek, "Turkish Historiography and the Unbearable Weight of 1915," in Richard Hovannisian, ed., *The Armenian Genocide: Cultural and Ethical Legacies* (Piscataway, NJ: Transaction, 2007) 337–68.

38. Guenter Lewy, *Armenian Massacres in Ottoman Turkey: A Disputed Genocide* (Salt Lake City: University of Utah Press, 2010) 245–50.

39. Suny, "'They Can Live in the Desert,'" xii.

40. Aktürk, "Persistence of the Islamic Millet."

41. Philip Robins, *Suits and Uniforms: Turkish Foreign Policy since the Cold War* (Seattle: University of Washington Press, 2003) 181–89.

42. "Kılıçdaroğlu: Saray kölesi olan biri, yargıç koltuğunda oturamaz," *Hürriyet*, 19 Jun 2018, https://www.hurriyet.com.tr/kilicdaroglu-saray-kolesi-olan-biri-yargic-ko-40871717.

43. Onar, "Echoes," 232–33.

44. M. Hakan Yavuz, *Islamic Political Identity in Turkey* (Oxford: Oxford University Press, 2002) 141. Also see Svante E. Cornell and M. K. Kaya, "The Naqshbandi-Khalidi Order and Political Islam in Turkey," Hudson Institute, 5 Sep 2015, http://www.eurasiareview.com/05092015-the-naqshbandi-khalidi-order-and-political-islam-in-turkey-analysis.

45. Hakan Övünç Ongur, "Identifying Ottomanisms: The Discursive Evolution of Ottoman Pasts in the Turkish Presents," *MES*, 2015, 51(3): 416–32. Erik Jan Zürcher, "Young Turks, Ottoman Muslims and Turkish Nationalists: Identity Politics 1908–1938," in Kemal H. Karpat, ed., *Ottoman Past and Today's Turkey* (Leiden: Brill, 2000) 150–79.

46. Burhanettin Duran and Cemil Aydın, "Competing Occidentalisms of Modern Islamist Thought: Necip Fazıl Kısakürek and Nurettin Topçu on Christianity, the West and Modernity," *Muslim World,* Oct 2013, 103(4): 498–90. Alessio Calabrò, "Islamist Views on Foreign Policy: Examples of Turkish Pan-Islamism in the Writings of Sezai Karakoç and Necmettin Erbakan," *Insight Turkey,* Winter 2017, 19(1): 157–84.
47. "Necip Fazıl Kısakürek Ödülleri bize bu toprağın sesini, kokusunu, nefesini taşıyacaktır," Turkish Presidency, 2 Nov 2014, https://www.tccb.gov.tr/haberler/410/1473/necip-fazil-kisakurek-odulleri-bize-bu-topragin-sesini-kokusunu-nefesini-tasiyacaktir. Cornell and Kaya, "The Naqshbandi-Khalidi Order."
48. Quoted in Ongur, "Identifying Ottomanisms," 421.
49. Fırat Taşdemir, "İslam birliği idealini savunan lider: Necmettin Erbakan," Anadolu Ajansı, 26 Feb 2020, https://www.aa.com.tr/tr/portre/-islam-birligi-idealini-savunan-lider-necmettin-erbakan/1745248.
50. Lerna K. Yanık, "Bringing the Empire Back In: The Gradual Rediscovery of the Ottoman Empire in Turkish Foreign Policy," *WdI,* 2016, 56(3–4): 480–87.
51. Ongur, "Identifying Ottomanisms," 423.
52. M. Hakan Yavuz, "The Assassination of Collective Memory: The Case of Turkey," *Muslim World,* Jul–Oct 1999, 89(3–4): 193–207.
53. Turgut Özal, "Türkiye'nin önünde hacet kapıları açılmıştır," *Türkiye günlüğü,* Summer 1992, (19): 17.
54. Recep Tayyip Erdoğan, "İslam Dünyasının umudu Türkiye'dir," Turkish Presidency, 28 Apr 2016, https://www.tccb.gov.tr/haberler/410/43789/islam-dunyasinin-umudu-turkiyedir.html.
55. Recep Tayyip Erdoğan, "Tarih bir milletin sadece mazisi değil, istikbalinin de pusulasıdır," Turkish Presidency, 10 Feb 2018, https://www.tccb.gov.tr/haberler/410/89372/tarih-bir-milletin-sadece-mazisi-degil-istikbalinin-de-pusulasidir.
56. Ahmet Davutoğlu, *Systemic Earthquake and the Struggle for World Order* (Cambridge: Cambridge University Press, 2020) 188–223.
57. İştar Gözaydın, "Ahmet Davutoğlu: Role as an Islamic Scholar Shaping Turkey's Foreign Policy," in Nassef Manabilang Adiong, ed., *Islam and International Relations: Diverse Perspectives* (Cambridge: Cambridge Scholars, 2013) 50–59.
58. Michael Reynolds, "The Key to the Future Lies in the Past: The Worldview of Erdoğan and Davutoğlu," Hudson Institute, 3 Sep 2015, https://www.hudson.org/research/11595-the-key-to-the-future-lies-in-the-past-the-worldview-of-erdo-an-and-davuto-lu.
59. Lorenzo Vidino, "Erdogan's Long Arm in Europe," *Foreign Policy,* 7 May 2019, https://foreignpolicy.com/2019/05/07/erdogans-long-arm-in-europe-germany-netherlands-milli-gorus-muslim-brotherhood-turkey-akp/.
60. Behlul Özkan, "Turkey, Davutoglu, and the Idea of Pan-Islamism," *Survival,* 2014, 56(4): 119–40.

61. "Davutoğlu: Arap barharı Türk baharıdır da," Haber7, 25 May 2011, http://www.haber7.com/siyaset/haber/747177-davutoglu-arap-bahari-turk -baharidir-da.

62. Ahmet Davutoğlu, "Dışişleri Bakanı Sayın Ahmet Davutoğlu'nun 'Arap Uyanışı ve Ortadoğu'da barış: Müslüman ve Hristiyan perspektifler,'" Ministry of Foreign Affairs, 7 Jul 2012, http://www.mfa.gov.tr/disisleri-bakani -sayin-ahmet-davutoglu_nun-_arap-bahari-ve-yeni-ortadogu_da-baris_ -musluman-ve-hritiyan-perspektifler_-konferans.tr.mfa.

63. Sultan al-Kanj, "Reviewing the Turkey-HTS Relationship," Chatham House, May 2019, https://syria.chathamhouse.org/research/reviewing-the -turkey-hts-relationship.

64. Şaban Kardaş, "Türkiye ve Arap Baharı: Türkiye'nin Orta Doğu politikasındaki değişiklikler," HASEN, Spr. 2013, https://istihbaratsahasi .files.wordpress.com/2013/06/trkiye-ve-arap-bahar-trkiyenin-orta-dou -politikasndaki-deiiklikler.pdf.

65. Akçura and Fehmi, "Yusuf Akçura's Üç Tarz-i Siyaset," 18.

66. Landau, *Pan-Turkism*, 29–30.

67. Ibid., 45–46. Reynolds, *Shattering Empires*, 149–55.

68. İlker Aytürk, "The Racist Critics of Atatürk and Kemalism, from the 1930s to the 1960s," *Journal of Contemporary History*, Apr 2011, 46(2): 308–35.

69. Landau, *Pan-Turkism*, 153–57.

70. Svante E. Cornell, "Erbakan, Kısakürek, and the Mainstreaming of Extremism in Turkey," Hudson Institute, 4 Jun 2018, https://www.hudson.org/ research/14375-erbakan-k-sak-rek-and-the-mainstreaming-of-extremism -in-turkey. Yüksel Taşkin, "Upsurge of the Extreme Right in Turkey: The Intra-Right Struggle to Redefine 'True Nationalism and Islam,'" *MES*, Jan 2008, 44(1): 131–32.

71. Landau, *Pan-Turkism*, 170.

72. "Ümit Özdağ kimdir? MHP Gaziantep milletvekili Ümit Özdağ hakkında bilinmeyenler," *Hürriyet*, 16 Nov 2016, http://www.hurriyet.com.tr/ gundem/mhpden-ihrac-edilen-umit-ozdag-kimdir-40278634.

73. Landau, *Pan-Turkism*, 187, 195–97. Aytürk, "The Racist Critics of Atatürk and Kemalism," 327–28.

74. Türk Dili Konuşan Ülkeler İşbirliği Konseyi, http://www.turkkon.org/ tr-TR/AnaSayfa. TİKA, "Hakkımızda," https://www.tika.gov.tr/tr/sayfa/ hakkimizda-14649.

75. "Cumhurbaşkanı Erdoğan: Andımız ezanı Türkçe okumak, okutmak isteyenlerin eseridir-1," *Haberler*, 3 Nov 2018, https://www.haberler.com/ cumhurbaskani-erdogan-andimiz-ezani-turkce-okumak-11399387-haberi.

76. "Sincan Uygur Özerk Bölgesi'ndeki oruç yasağı iddiaları hk," Ministry of Foreign Affairs, 30 Jun 2015, http://www.mfa.gov.tr/no_-192_-30-haziran -2015_-sincan-uygur-ozerk-bolgesi_ndeki-oruc-yasagi-iddialari-hk_.tr.mfa.

77. Mustafa Bağ, "Cumhurbaşkanı Erdoğan'ın 'Uygurlar mutlu' ifadesenin çeviri hatası olduğu iddiası," *EuroNews*, 24 Jul 2019, https://tr.euronews.com/

2019/07/24/cumhurbaskani-erdoganin-uygurlar-mutlu-ifadesinin-ceviri
-hatasi-oldugu-iddiasi.

78. Carlotta Gall, "They Built a Homeland Far from China's Grip. Now They're Afraid," *New York Times*, 21 Dec 2019, https://www.nytimes.com/2019/12/21/world/asia/xinjiang-turkey-china-muslims-fear.html. Abdullah Ayasun, "Uyghurs Wary of Turkey's Pending Extradition Deal with China," *The Diplomat*, 7 Jan 2021, https://thediplomat.com/2021/01/uyghurs-wary-of-turkeys-pending-extradition-deal-with-china/.

79. "Ukrayna'nın egemenliğine ve Kırım dâhil toprak bütünlüğüne desteğimiz sürecektir," Turkish Presidency, 3 Feb 2020, https://www.tccb.gov.tr/haberler/410/116514/-ukrayna-nin-egemenligine-ve-kirim-d-hil-toprak-butunlugune-destegimiz-surecektir-.

80. Vladimir Mukhin, "Udarnuyu moshch' Ukrainy ukrepit oruzhiye iz Turtsii," *Nezavisimaya gazeta*, 15 Dec 2020, https://www.ng.ru/armies/2020-12-15/1_8040_alliance.html.

81. Burak Tuygan, "Turkish Religious Diplomacy Raises Tensions with Bulgaria," *Ahval*, 1 Nov 2019, https://ahvalnews-com.cdn.ampproject.org/c/s/ahvalnews.com/bulgaria-turkey/turkish-religious-diplomacy-raises-tensions-bulgaria.

82. Şuhnaz Yilmaz and İpek K. Yosmaoğlu, "Fighting the Spectres of the Past: Dilemmas of Ottoman Legacy in the Balkans and the Middle East," *MES*, 2008, 44(5): 677–93.

Chapter Five. On the Margins of the Nation and the State

1. Jenna Krajeski, "The Consequences of the Battle for Kobani," *New Yorker*, 26 Feb 2015, https://www.newyorker.com/news/news-desk/the-consequences-of-the-battle-for-kobani.

2. On Turkey's Kurdish challenge, see Denise Natali, *The Kurds and the State: Evolving National Identity in Iraq, Turkey, and Iran* (Syracuse: Syracuse University Press, 2005). Mesut Yeğen, "The Turkish State Discourse and the Exclusion of Kurdish Identity," in Sylvia Kedourie, ed., *Turkey: Identity, Discourse, Politics* (London: Frank Cass, 1996). Zeynep M. Kaya, *Mapping Kurdistan: Territory, Self-Determination, and Nationalism* (Cambridge: Cambridge University Press, 2019). Aliza Marcus, *Blood and Belief: The PKK and the Kurdish Fight for Independence* (New York: NYU Press, 2007). Henri J. Barkey and Graham Fuller, *Turkey's Kurdish Question* (Lanham, MD: Rowman & Littlefield, 1998). Metin Heper, *The State and Kurds in Turkey: The Question of Assimilation* (London: Palgrave Macmillan, 2007). Ramazan Aras, *The Formation of Kurdishness in Turkey: Political Violence, Fear and Pain* (London: Routledge, 2014). Martin van Bruinessen, *Agha, Shaikh and State: The Social and Political Structures of Kurdistan* (London: Zed, 1992).

3. Ahmet Davutoğlu, "Dışişleri Bakanı Sayın Ahmet Davutoğlu'nun Türk Ocakları'nın kuruluşunun 100. yılını kutlama etkinlikleri kapsamında

düzenlenen 'Büyük Türkiye'ye Doğru' sempozyumunda yaptığı konuşma," Ministry of Foreign Affairs, 26 Mar 2011, http://www.mfa.gov.tr/disisleri -bakani-sayin-ahmet-davutoglu_nun-turk-ocaklari_nin-kurulusunun-100_ -yilini-kutlama-etkinlikleri-kapsaminda-duzenlenen.tr.mfa.

4. Hirmis Aboona, *Assyrians, Kurds, and Ottomans: Intercommunal Relations on the Periphery of the Ottoman Empire* (Amherst, NY: Cambria, 2008) 94–97.

5. John S. Guest, *The Yezidis: A Study in Survival* (London: KPI, 1987) 187–96.

6. Denise Natali, "Kurds," *Encyclopedia of Islam and the Muslim World*, 2nd ed. (London: Macmillan Reference, 2016) 625–29.

7. M. Köbach, "Amasya, Peace of," *EIr*; http://www.iranicaonline.org/articles/ amasya-peace.

8. Latif Tas, "The Myth of the Ottoman *Millet* System: Its Treatment of Kurds and a Discussion of Territorial and Non-Territorial Autonomy," *International Journal on Minority and Group Rights*, 2014, (21): 497–526.

9. Van Bruinessen, *Agha, Shaikh and State*, 133–44, 157–62. Natali, *Kurds and the State*, 1–14.

10. Gábor Ágoston, "A Flexible Empire: Authority and Its Limits on the Ottoman Frontiers," *International Journal of Turkish Studies*, 2003, 9(1–2): 15–32.

11. Michael Eppel, "The Demise of the Kurdish Emirates: The Impact of Ottoman Reforms and International Relations on Kurdistan During the First Half of the Nineteenth Century," *MES*, Mar 2008, 44(2): 249–50.

12. Frederick F. Anscombe, "Islam in the Age of Ottoman Reform," *Past & Present*, Aug 2010, 208(1): 159–89.

13. Van Bruinessen, *Agha, Shaikh and State*, 175–85.

14. Eppel, "The Demise of the Kurdish Emirates," 240, 245–57.

15. M. Hakan Yavuz, "Five Stages of the Construction of Kurdish Nationalism in Turkey," *Nationalism and Ethnic Politics*, 2001, 7(3): 6. See also Kaya, *Mapping Kurdistan*, 32–34.

16. Michael A. Reynolds, *Shattering Empires: The Clash and Collapse of the Ottoman and Russian Empires 1908–1918* (Cambridge: Cambridge University Press, 2011) 51.

17. Ronald Grigor Suny, *"They Can Live in the Desert but Nowhere Else": A History of the Armenian Genocide* (Princeton, NJ: Princeton University Press, 2015) 281–95.

18. Kaya, *Mapping Kurdistan*, 34–37.

19. Sabri Ateş, "In the Name of the Caliph and the Nation: The Sheikh Ubeidullah Rebellion of 1880–81," *IS*, 2014, 47(5): 735–98. Natali, *The Kurds and the State*, 5–14.

20. Selim Deringil, *The Well-Protected Domains: Ideology and the Legitimation of Power in the Ottoman Empire 1876–1909* (London: I. B. Tauris, 2011) 69–84.

21. Kamal Soleimani, "Islamic Revivalism and Kurdish Nationalism in Sheikh Ubeydullah's Poetic Oeuvre," *Kurdish Studies*, May 2016, 4(1): 5–24.

22. Elvan Alkaya, "Bave Kurdan (Kürtlerin Babası) Sultan Abdülhamid," *Yeni şafak*, 8 Feb 2016, https://www.yenisafak.com/yazarlar/elvanalkaya/bave -kurdan-kurtlerin-babasi-sultan-abdulhamid-2026668.

23. Janet Klein, *Margins of Empire: Kurdish Militias in the Ottoman Tribal Zone* (Stanford: Stanford University Press, 2011) 1–94. Selim Deringil, "'The Armenian Question Is Finally Closed': Mass Conversions of Armenians in Anatolia During the Hamidian Massacres of 1895–1897," *Comparative Studies in Society and History*, Apr 2009, 51(2): 344–71. Uğur Ümit Üngör, *The Making of Modern Turkey: Nation and State in Eastern Anatolia, 1913–1950* (Oxford: Oxford University Press, 2011) 55–106.

24. Van Bruinessen, *Agha, Shaikh and State*, 185–86. Maya Arakon, "Kurds at the Transition from the Ottoman Empire to the Turkish Republic," *TPQ*, Spring 2014, 13(1): 139–48.

25. Andrew Mango, "Atatürk and the Kurds," in S. Kedourie, ed., *Seventy-five Years of the Turkish Republic* (London: Frank Cass, 2006) 1–26.

26. Natali, *Kurds and the State*, 73–77.

27. Hüseyin Yayman, "Şark meselesinden demokratik açılıma Türkiye'nin Kürt sorunu hafızası," SETA, 2011: 16–17, https://file.setav.org/Files/Pdf/20130130121531_seta-turkiyenin_kurt_sorunu_hafizasi.pdf.

28. Natali, *Kurds and the State*, 77–89.

29. Heper, *The State and Kurds*, 83–85. Umut Uzer, "The Kurdish Identity of Turkish Nationalist Thinkers: Ziya Gökalp and Ahmet Arvasi Between Turkish Identity and Kurdish Ethnicity," *Turkish Studies*, 2013, 14(2): 394–409.

30. "Cumhuriyet tarihi Kürt raporları," *Al-Jazeera Türk*, http://www.aljazeera.com.tr/dosya/cumhuriyet-tarihi-kurt-raporlari.

31. Barkey and Fuller, *Turkey's Kurdish Question*, 67–70.

32. Ibid., 86–95 (quote, p. 87).

33. Ibid., 94–103.

34. Marcus, *Blood and Belief*, 85–86.

35. "PKK: The Kurdistan Workers Party," The Kurdish Project, https://thekurdishproject.org/history-and-culture/kurdish-nationalism/pkk-kurdistan-workers-party/.

36. "Turkey: IX Restrictions on the Use of the Kurdish Language," Human Rights Watch, 1999, https://www.hrw.org/reports/1999/turkey/turkey993-08.htm.

37. Barkey and Fuller, *Turkey's Kurdish Question*, 147–49.

38. Natali, *Kurds and the State*, 107–16.

39. Şener Aktürk, "One Nation Under Allah? Islamic Multiculturalism, Muslim Nationalism and Turkey's Reforms for Kurds, Alevis, and Non-Muslims," *Turkish Studies*, 2018, 19(4): 523–51. F. Stephen Larrabee, "Turkey's New Kurdish Opening," *Survival*, Oct/Nov 2013, 55(5): 133–46. Barkey and Fuller, *Turkey's Kurdish Question*, 102–7, 135–37.

40. Namık Durukan, "Erdoğan: Kürt açılımı için çalışma başlattık," *Milliyet*, 23 Jul 2009, https://www.milliyet.com.tr/siyaset/erdogan-kurt-acilimi-icin-calisma-baslattik-1120538.

41. "Report on the Human Rights Situation in South-East Turkey," United Nations High Commissioner for Human Rights, Feb 2017, https://www.ohchr

.org/Documents/Countries/TR/OHCHR_South-East_TurkeyReport
_10March2017.pdf.

42. "Erdogan Says HDP Co-leader Demirtas Is Responsible for 53 Deaths,"
     TRT World, 9 Jul 2017, https://www.trtworld.com/turkey/erdogan-says
     -hdp-co-leader-demirtas-is-responsible-for-53-deaths-8645. Zeynep M.
     Kaya and Matthew Whiting, "The HDP, the AKP, and the Battle for Turk-
     ish Democracy," *Ethnopolitics*, 2019, 18(1): 92–106.

43. "Cumhurbaşkanlığı Sözcüsü Kalın: 'PKK/PYD/YPG Kürt kardeşlerimizin
     temsilcisi olamaz,'" Turkish Presidency, 8 Jan 2019, https://www.tccb.gov.tr/
     haberler/410/100472/cumhurbaskanligi-sozcusu-kalin-pkk-pyd-ypg-kurt
     -kardeslerimizin-temsilcisi-olamaz. More generally, Aktürk, "One Nation
     Under Allah?," 538–39.

44. Senem Aslan, "Everyday Forms of State Power and the Kurds in the Early
     Turkish Republic," *IJMES*, February 2011, 43(1): 89.

45. Muhittin Ataman, "Özal [sic] Leadership and Restructuring of Turkish Eth-
     nic Policy in the 1980s," *MES*, Oct 2002, 38(4): 123–42.

46. "Turkey and the Iraqi Kurds: Conflict or Cooperation?," International Cri-
     sis Group, 13 Nov 2008, https://www.crisisgroup.org/middle-east-north
     -africa/gulf-and-arabian-peninsula/iraq/turkey-and-iraqi-kurds-conflict-or
     -cooperation.

47. Avshalom H. Rubin, "Abd al-Karim Qasim and the Kurds of Iraq: Central-
     ization Resistance, and Revolt, 1958–63," *MES*, May 2007, 43(3): 353–82.

48. Denise Natali, "Syria's Spillover on Iraq: State Resilience," *Middle East Policy*,
     Spring 2017, 24(1): 52–53.

49. Marcus, *Blood and Belief*, 79–80, 94–96.

50. "Whatever Happened to the Iraqi Kurds?," Human Rights Watch, 11 Mar
     1991, https://www.hrw.org/reports/1991/iraq/. Barkey and Fuller, *Turkey's
     Kurdish Question*, 16–17.

51. Marcus, *Blood and Belief*, 99–100.

52. Anne Sofie Schøtt, "The Kurds of Syria: From the Forgotten People to
     World Stage Actors," Royal Danish Defense College, Jun 2017, https://pure
     .fak.dk/ws/files/7248264/The_Kurds_of_Syria.pdf.

53. Chris Hedges, "Iraqis Are Arming the Rebel Kurds in Turkey's South," *New
     York Times*, 20 Oct 1991, https://www.nytimes.com/1991/10/20/world/
     iraqis-are-arming-the-rebel-kurds-in-turkey-s-south.html. Marcus, *Blood
     and Belief*, 101–3.

54. "Turks Mount Big Attack on Kurdish Rebels in Iraq," *New York Times*,
     21 Mar 1995, https://www.nytimes.com/1995/03/21/world/turks-mount
     -big-attack-on-kurdish-rebels-in-iraq.html.

55. Frank Bruni, "A Nation at War: Ankara; Turkey Sends Army Troops into
     Iraq, Report Says," *New York Times*, 22 Mar 2003, https://www.nytimes.com/
     2003/03/22/world/a-nation-at-war-ankara-turkey-sends-army-troops-into
     -iraq-report-says.html.

56. Kadir Üstün and Lesley Dudden, "Turkey–KRG Relationship: Mu-
     tual Interests, Geopolitical Challenges," SETA Foundation, 20 Sep 2017,

https://setadc.org/turkey-krg-relationship-mutual-interests-geopolitical -challenges/.

57. "Yeni Türkiye'yi inşa ediyoruz," *Hürriyet*, 17 Nov 2013, https://www.hurriyet .com.tr/gundem/yeni-turkiyeyi-insa-ediyoruz-25138414.

58. Ahmet Davutoğlu, "Sayın Bakan'ın IKB Başkanı Mesud Barzani ile yaptığı basın açıklaması," Ministry of Foreign Affairs, 3 Nov 2011, http://www .mfa.gov.tr/sayin-bakan_in-ikb-baskani-mesud-barzani-ile-yaptigi-basin -aciklamasi_-3-kasim-2011_-ciragan-sarayi_-istanbul.tr.mfa.

59. Michael R. Gordon and Kamil Kakol, "Turkish Strikes Target Allies of U.S. in Iraq and Syria," *New York Times*, 25 Apr 2017, https://www.nytimes.com/ 2017/04/25/world/middleeast/turkey-kurds-airstrikes-iraq-syria.html. "Turkey Informed Russia, U.S., Northern Iraq Before Hitting PKK, Erdogan Says," *Daily Sabah*, 25 Apr 2017, https://www.dailysabah.com/war -on-terror/2017/04/25/turkey-informed-russia-us-northern-iraq-before -hitting-pkk-erdogan-says.

60. "Davutoğlu: 'Kürt bölgesinin güvenliği Türkiye için hayati,'" *Cumhuriyet*, 22 Nov 2014, http://www.cumhuriyet.com.tr/haber/davutoglu-kurt -bolgesinin-guvenligi-turkiye-icin-hayati-146801.

61. Özlem Kayhan Pusane, "Two Years After the Independence Referendum: Are Turkey–KRG Relations Normalizing?," *TPQ*, 9 Sep 2019, http:// turkishpolicy.com/blog/38/two-years-after-the-independence-referendum -are-turkey-krg-relations-normalizing.

62. Burak Kadercan, "Making Sense of Turkey's Syria Strategy: A 'Turkish Tragedy' in the Making," *War on the Rocks*, 4 Oct 2017, https://warontherocks .com/2017/08/making-sense-of-turkeys-syria-strategy-a-turkish-tragedy-in -the-making/.

63. Faysal Itani and Aaron Stein, "Turkey's Syria Predicament," Atlantic Council of the United States, May 2016, https://www.atlanticcouncil.org/wp -content/uploads/2016/05/Turkey_s_Syria_Predicament.pdf. Aslı S. Okyay, "Turkey's Post-2011 Approach to Its Syrian Border and Its Implications for Domestic Politics," *International Affairs*, 2017, 93(4): 829–46.

64. Haid Haid, "Turkey's Efforts to Professionalize Its Syrian Allies," Carnegie Endowment, 2 Nov 2018, https://carnegieendowment.org/sada/77637.

65. Khaled al-Khateb, "Syrian Opposition Forms Force to Hold Its Army Accountable," *Al-Monitor*, 22 Mar 2018, https://www.al-monitor.com/pulse/ originals/2018/03/syria-opposition-military-police-euphrates-national -army.html.

66. Tessa Fox, "Who Exactly Is Turkey Resettling in Syria?," *Foreign Policy*, 19 Dec 2019, https://foreignpolicy.com/2019/12/19/who-exactly-is-turkey -resettling-in-syria/.

67. Madeleine Edwards, "As Syria's Proxies Converge on Idlib, What's Next for Turkey's Northern State-Within-a-State?," *Syria Direct*, 6 Aug 2018, https:// syriadirect.org/news/as-syria%e2%80%99s-proxies-converge-on-idlib -what%e2%80%99s-next-for-turkey%e2%80%99s-northern-state-within -a-state/.

68. Jeffrey Mankoff, "Don't Forget the Historical Context of Russo-Turkish Competition," *War on the Rocks*, 7 Apr 2020, https://warontherocks.com/2020/04/dont-forget-the-historical-context-of-russo-turkish-competition/.

Chapter Six. The Geopolitics of the Post-Ottoman Space

1. Ahmet Davutoğlu, "Turkey's Foreign Policy Vision: An Assessment of 2007," *Insight Turkey*, 2008, (10)1: 77–96.

2. Nicholas Danforth, "The Nonsense of Neo-Ottomanism," *War on the Rocks*, 29 May 2020, https://warontherocks.com/2020/05/the-nonsense-of-neo-ottomanism/.

3. "O tabiri kullanmadık, kullanmayacağız," *Sabah*, 18 Mar 2010, https://www.sabah.com.tr/Gundem/2010/03/18/o_tabir_kullanmadik_kullanmayacagiz.

4. İbrahim Kalın, "U.S.–Turkish Relations Under Obama: Promise, Challenge, and Opportunity in the 21st Century," *Journal of Balkan and Near Eastern Studies*, 2010, 12: 99.

5. "Erdoğan'dan dış politika yorumu: Neo Osmanlıcılık değil reel politika," *Milliyet*, 17 Jan 2011, https://www.milliyet.com.tr/siyaset/erdogandan-dis-politika-yorumu-neo-osmanlicilik-degil-reel-politika-1340373.

6. Einar Wigen, "Post-Ottoman Studies: An Area Studies That Never Was," in Evá Á. Csató et al., eds., *Building Bridges to Turkish: Essays in Honor of Bernt Brendemoen* (Wiesbaden: Hassarowitz, 2013) 313–26.

7. Umut Uzer, *Identity and Turkish Foreign Policy: The Kemalist Influence in Cyprus and the Caucasus* (London: I. B. Tauris, 2011) 97–105.

8. Zeynep Gürcanlı, "Erdoğan, Lozan dosyasını açtı! Ancak bu kez daha temkinli," *Sözcü*, 21 Oct 2019, https://www.sozcu.com.tr/2019/gundem/erdogan-lozan-dosyasini-acti-ancak-bu-kez-daha-temkinli-5402236/.

9. Cengiz Candar and Graham Fuller, "Grand Geopolitics for a New Turkey," *Mediterranean Quarterly*, 2001, 12(2). Igor Torbakov, "Neo-Ottomanism Versus Neo-Eurasianism? Nationalism and Symbolic Geography in Postimperial Turkey and Russia," *Mediterranean Quarterly*, 2017, 28(2): 135–37. İsmail Cem, *Turkey in the New Century* (Nicosia: Rustem, 2000).

10. Gabriela Özel Volfová, "Turkey's Middle Eastern Endeavors: Discourses and Practices of Neo-Ottomanism Under the AKP," *WdI*, 2016, (56): 494.

11. Ahmet Davutoğlu, *Stratejik derinlik: Türkiye'nin uluslarası konumu* (Ankara: Küre, 2001) 69.

12. Davutoğlu, "Address of H.E. Prof. Ahmet Davutoğlu," 19. Davutoğlu, *Stratejik derinlik*, 53–54. Davutoğlu, "Turkey's Mediation: Critical Reflections from the Field," *Middle East Policy*, Spring 2013, 20(1): 83–90.

13. Behlül Özcan, "Turkey, Davutoglu and the Idea of Pan-Islamism," *Survival*, Aug–Sep 2014, 56(4): 119–40.

14. Bülent Aras, "The Davutoğlu Era in Turkish Foreign Policy," *Insight Turkey*, 2009, 11(3): 131. Torbakov, "Neo-Ottomanism Versus Neo-Eurasianism," 139–40.

15. Recep Tayyip Erdoğan, "PYD ve YPG terör örgütleri PKK'nın atığıdır," Turkish Presidency, 15 Oct 2016, https://www.tccb.gov.tr/haberler/410/ 53628/pyd-ve-ypg-teror-orgutleri-pkknin-atigidir.

16. Ryan Gingeras, "Blue Homeland: The Heated Politics Behind Turkey's New Maritime Strategy," *War on the Rocks*, 2 Jun 2020, https://warontherocks .com/2020/06/blue-homeland-the-heated-politics-behind-turkeys-new -maritime-strategy/.

17. Quoted in Michael Reynolds, "The Key to the Future Lies in the Past: The Worldview of Erdoğan and Davutoğlu," Hudson Institute, 3 Sep 2015, https://www.hudson.org/research/11595-the-key-to-the-future-lies-in-the -past-the-worldview-of-erdo-an-and-davuto-lu.

18. Davutoğlu, *Stratejik derinlik*, 53–54.

19. Dimitar Bechev, "Very Long Engagement: Turkey in the Balkans," in Kerem Öktem et al., eds., *Another Empire? A Decade of Turkey's Foreign Policy Under the Justice and Development Party* (Istanbul: Bilgi University Press, 2012) 211.

20. Alan Fisher, "The Ottoman Crimea in the Sixteenth Century," in Fischer, *Between Russians, Ottomans, and Turks: Crimea and Crimean Tatars* (Istanbul: Isis Press, 1998) 35–65. Suraiya Faroqhi, *The Ottoman Empire and the World Around It* (London: I. B. Tauris, 2004) 77–78.

21. Maurus Reinkowski, "Conquests Compared: The Ottoman Expansion in the Balkans and the Mashreq in an Islamicate Context," in Oliver Jens Schmitt, ed., *The Ottoman Conquest of the Balkans: Interpretations and Research Debates* (Vienna: Österreichische Akademie der Wissenschaften, 2016) 51–55. Klaus Kreiser, "Über den 'Kernraum' des Osmanisches Reiches," in Klaus-Detlev Grothusen, ed., *Die Türkei in Europa* (Göttingen: Vandenhoeck & Ruprecht, 1979) 53. Şevket Pamuk, "The Ottoman Monetary System and Frontier Territories in Europe, 1500–1700," in Kemal Karpat and Robert Zens, eds., *Ottoman Borderlands: Issues, Personalities, and Political Change* (Madison: University of Wisconsin Press, 2003) 175–82.

22. Halil İnalcik, *An Economic and Social History of the Ottoman Empire*, Vol. 1 (Cambridge: Cambridge University Press, 1994) 132–42.

23. McCarthy, *Ottoman Peoples*, 43. Alan W. Fisher, "Emigration of Muslims from the Russian Empire in the Years After the Crimean War," *JfGO*, 1987, 35(3): 356–57.

24. Erik Sjöberg, *The Making of the Greek Genocide: Contested Memories of the Ottoman Greek Catastrophe* (London: Berghahn, 2017) 17–53.

25. Bechev, "A Very Long Engagement."

26. Tomasz Kamusella, *Ethnic Cleansing During the Cold War: The Forgotten 1989 Expulsion of Turks from Communist Bulgaria* (London: Routledge, 2018). Sylvie Gangloff, "The Impact of the Ottoman Legacy on Turkish Policy in the Balkans (1991–1999)," Sciences Po, Nov 2005, https://www.sciencespo.fr/ ceri/sites/sciencespo.fr.ceri/files/artsg.pdf.

27. Gregorios Demestichas, "Greek Security and Defense Policy in the Eastern Mediterranean," *Mediterranean Quarterly*, Summer 1997, 8(2): 215–27.

28. Helen Walasek, "Destruction of the Cultural Heritage in Bosnia-Herzegovina: An Overview," in Walasek, ed., *Bosnia and the Destruction of Cultural Heritage* (London: Routledge, 2016) 23–142.

29. Steven L. Burg and Paul S. Shoup, *The War in Bosnia-Herzegovina: Ethnic Conflict and International Intervention* (Armonk, NY: M. E. Sharpe, 1999) 307–8.

30. Chuck Sudetic, "Bosnia Neighbors Nervously Seek Pacts," *New York Times,* 18 Feb 1993, https://www.nytimes.com/1993/02/18/world/bosnia-neighbors-nervously-seek-pacts.html.

31. Birgül Demirtaş, "Turkey and the Balkans: Overcoming Prejudices, Building Bridges, and Constructing a Common Future," *Perceptions,* Summer 2013, 18(2): 163–84.

32. Asli Aydıntaşbaş, "From Myth to Reality: How to Understand Turkey's Role in the Western Balkans," ECFR, 13 Mar 2019: 9, https://www.ecfr.eu/publications/summary/from_myth_to_reality_how_to_understand_turkeys_role_in_the_western_balkans.

33. Erhan Türbedar, "Trilateral Balkan Summit in Istanbul," TEPAV, Apr 2010, https://www.tepav.org.tr/upload/files/1274094120r2517.Trilateral_Balkan_Summit_in_Istanbul.pdf.

34. "Türkiye-Bosna Hersek-Sırbistan dışişleri bakanları ortak basın toplantısı," Ministry of Foreign Affairs, 9 Feb 2010, http://www.mfa.gov.tr/turkiye-bosna-hersek-sirbistan-uclu-danisma-toplantisinin-metni.tr.mfa.

35. "Erdoğan: Kosova, Türkiye'dir . . . ," *Hürriyet,* 23 Oct 2013, https://www.hurriyet.com.tr/gundem/erdogan-kosova-turkiyedir-24968405.

36. Quoted in Zia Weise, "Turkey's Balkan Comeback," *Politico,* 17 May 2018, https://www.politico.eu/article/turkey-western-balkans-comeback-european-union-recep-tayyip-erdogan/.

37. Janusz Bugajski, "Is Turkey Destabilizing the Balkans?," CEPA, 11 Apr 2018, https://www.cepa.org/turkey-balkans.

38. "TCG Anadolu KKTC'de demirleyebilir," *Yeni şafak,* 11 Nov 2018, https://www.yenisafak.com/gundem/tcg-anadolu-kktcde-demirleyebilir-3414171.

39. Ahmet Erdi Öztürk and İştar Gözaydın, "A Frame for Turkey's Foreign Policy via the Diyanet in the Balkans," *Journal of Muslims in Europe,* Oct 2018, 7(3): 345.

40. Esin Isik, "Turkey Builds Biggest Mosque of Balkans in Albania," Anadolu Ajansı, 18 Jan 2019, https://www.aa.com.tr/en/life/turkey-builds-biggest-mosque-of-balkans-in-albania/1368253.

41. Aleksandar Vasovic, "Turkey's Erdogan Gets Warm Welcome in Mainly Muslim Serbian Town," Reuters, 11 Oct 2017, https://www.reuters.com/article/us-serbia-turkey/turkeys-erdogan-gets-warm-welcome-in-mainly-muslim-serbian-town-idUSKBN1CG24F.

42. Aydıntaşbaş, "From Myth to Reality," 15–16.

43. Hamdi Fırat Büyük and Ahmet Erdi Öztürk, "The Role of Leadership Networks in Turkey–Balkan Relations in the AKP Era," *TPQ,* 29 Nov 2019,

http://turkishpolicy.com/article/982/the-role-of-leadership-networks-in
-turkey%E2%80%93balkan-relations-in-the-akp-era.

44. "Izetbegovic Says His Father 'Bequeathed' Bosnia to Erdogan," Beta, 20 Oct
2017, https://www.b92.net/eng/news/region.php?yyyy=2017&mm=10&dd
=20&nav_id=102605.

45. Blerta Begisholli, "Kosovo 'Broke Law' When Deporting Turkish 'Gu-
lenists,'" *Balkan Insight*, 5 Feb 2019, https://balkaninsight.com/2019/02/05/
kosovo-broke-law-when-deporting-turkish-gulenists-02-05-2019/.

46. Reynolds, "Key to the Future." Recep Tayyip Erdoğan, "Müslümanlar için
mübarek beldelerimizi korumak imkân değil, iman meselesidir," Turkish Presidency, 25 Jul 2017, https://www.tccb.gov.tr/haberler/410/80036/
muslumanlar-icin-mubarek-beldelerimizi-korumak-imkn-degil-iman
-meselesidir.

47. Selcan Hacaoglu, "Mapping the Turkish Military's Expanding Footprint,"
Bloomberg, 7 Mar 2019, https://www.bloomberg.com/news/articles/2019–
03–07/mapping-the-turkish-military-s-expanding-footprint-quicktake.

48. Şaban Kardaş, "Türkiye ve Arap Baharı: Türkiye'nin Orta Doğu
politikasındaki değişiklikler," Hazar Strateji Enstitüsü, Spring 2013,
https://istihbaratsahasi.files.wordpress.com/2013/06/trkiye-ve-arap-bahar
-trkiyenin-orta-dou-politikasndaki-deiiklikler.pdf.

49. Gábor Ágoston, "A Flexible Empire: Authority and Its Limits on the Ottoman Frontiers," *International Journal of Turkish Studies*, 2003, (9): 15–31.

50. Gökhan Çetinsaya, *Ottoman Administration of Iraq, 1890–1908* (London:
Routledge, 2006) 4–23. Mesut Uyar, "Ottoman Arab Officers Between Nationalism and Loyalty During the First World War," *War in History*, 2013,
20(4): 526–44.

51. David Fromkin, *A Peace to End All Peace: The Fall of the Ottoman Empire and
the Creation of the Modern Middle East* (New York: Henry Holt, 1989) 99–103.

52. Gönül Tol, "The 'Turkish Model' in the Middle East," *Current History*, Dec
2012, 111(749): 350–56.

53. Lundgren Jörum, "Syria's 'Lost Province': The Hatay Question Returns,"
Carnegie Middle East, 28 Jan 2014, http://carnegie-mec.org/diwan/54340.

54. Kadir Üstün, "Why Does Turkey Care About Mosul?" *Al-Jazeera*, 24 Nov
2016, https://www.aljazeera.com/indepth/opinion/2016/11/turkey-care
-mosul-161123084559305.html. "Land Certificates Show Turkish Ties
to Iraq," Anadolu Ajansı, 26 Oct 2016, https://www.aa.com.tr/en/todays
-headlines/land-certificates-show-turkish-ties-to-iraq/672855. Recep Tayyip Erdoğan, "PYD ve YPG terör örgütleri PKK'nın atığıdır," Turkish
Presidency, 15 Oct 2016, https://www.tccb.gov.tr/haberler/410/53628/
pyd-ve-ypg-teror-orgutleri-pkknin-atigidir.

55. Aaron Stein, "The Origins of Turkey's Buffer Zone in Syria," *War on the
Rocks*, 11 Oct 2014, https://warontherocks.com/2014/12/the-origins-of
-turkeys-buffer-zone-in-syria/.

56. "Yeni bir Ortadoğu doğuyor!," *Milliyet*, 10 Jun 2010, https://www.milliyet
.com.tr/ekonomi/yeni-bir-ortadogu-doguyor-1249276.

57. Birol Baskan, "Turkey's Pan-Islamist Foreign Policy," *Cairo Review of Global Affairs*, Spring 2019, https://www.thecairoreview.com/essays/turkeys-pan-islamist-foreign-policy/.

58. Paul Salem, "Turkey's Image in the Arab World," TESEV, May 2011, https://www.files.ethz.ch/isn/129502/Paul_Salem_FINAL.pdf.

59. Steven A. Cook, *False Dawn: Protest, Democracy, and Violence in the New Middle East* (Oxford: Oxford University Press, 2017) 35–39.

60. İbrahim Kalın, "Turkey and the Arab Spring," MEI, 24 May 2011, https://www.mei.edu/publications/turkey-and-arab-spring.

61. Stein, "Origins of Turkey's Buffer Zone."

62. Elizabeth Tsurkov, "Who Are Turkey's Proxy Fighters in Syria?," *New York Review of Books*, 27 Nov 2019, https://www.nybooks.com/daily/2019/11/27/who-are-turkeys-proxy-fighters-in-syria/.

63. Ozkan, "Turkey, Davutoglu and the Idea of Pan-Islamism," 134.

64. Yusuf Karataş, "Halep, Musul, Trablus: 'Milli güvenlik' mi, yeni Osmanlıcı yayılmacılık mı?," *Evrensel*, 20 Nov 2019, https://www.evrensel.net/yazi/85354/halep-musul-trablus-milli-guvenlik-mi-yeni-osmanlici-yayilmacilik-mi.

65. Adel Allouche, *The Origins and Development of the Ottoman-Safavid Conflict (906–962/1500–1555)* (Berlin: Klaus Schwarz Verlag, 1983) 137–40. See also C. J. Edmonds, "The Iraqi-Persian Frontier, 1639–1938," *Asian Affairs*, Summer 1975, 6(2): 147–54.

66. Murat Yaşar, "The North Caucasus Between the Ottoman Empire and the Tsardom of Muscovy: The Beginnings, 1552–1570," *Iran and the Caucasus*, 2016, (20): 105–25.

67. Kemal A. Karpat, *Ottoman Population, 1830–1914: Demographic and Social Characteristics* (Madison: University of Wisconsin Press, 1985).

68. Michael A. Reynolds, *Shattering Empires: The Clash and Collapse of the Ottoman and Russian Empires 1908–1918* (Cambridge: Cambridge University Press, 2011) 130–33.

69. Etienne Forestier-Peyrat, "The Ottoman Occupation of Batumi, 1918: A View from Below," *Caucasus Survey*, 2016, 4(2): 165–82.

70. Reynolds, *Shattering Empires*, 255–59.

71. Mustafa Aydın, "Turkish Policy Toward the Caucasus," *Quarterly Journal*, Sep 2002, (3): 39–42.

72. Ünal Çeviköz, "Turkey in a Reconnecting Eurasia: Foreign Economic and Security Interests," CSIS, Apr 2016, https://csis-website-prod.s3.amazonaws.com/s3fs-public/publication/160429_Cevikov_TurkeyReconnectingEurasia_Web.pdf.

73. Mitat Çelikpala and Cavid Veliyev, "Azerbaijan-Georgia-Turkey: An Example of a Successful Regional Cooperation," Kadir Has University, Nov 2015, https://www.khas.edu.tr/cms/cies/dosyalar/files/CIES%20Policy%20Brief%2004.pdf.

74. Joshua Kucera, "Georgians Wary of Rising Turkish Influence in Batumi," *EurasiaNet*, 9 Mar 2017, https://eurasianet.org/georgians-wary-of-turkeys-rising-influence-in-batumi.
75. Erdoğan, "PYD ve YPG terör örgütleri PKK'nın atığıdır."
76. Ali Babacan, "Calming the Caucasus," *New York Times*, 23 Sep 2008, https://www.nytimes.com/2008/09/23/opinion/23iht-edbabacan.1.16407371.html.
77. Bülent Aliriza, "Turkey and the Crisis in the Caucasus," CSIS, 9 Sep 2008, https://www.csis.org/analysis/turkey-and-crisis-caucasus.
78. Aydın, "Turkish Policy Toward the Caucasus."
79. Jeffrey Mankoff, "The Big Caucasus: Between Fragmentation and Integration," CSIS, Mar 2012, https://csis-prod.s3.amazonaws.com/s3fs-public/legacy_files/files/publication/120326_Mankoff_BigCaucasus_Web.pdf.
80. Joshua Kucera, "U.S. Intelligence: Russia Sabotaged BTC Pipeline Ahead of 2008 Georgia War," *EurasiaNet*, 11 Dec 2014, https://eurasianet.org/us-intelligence-russia-sabotaged-btc-pipeline-ahead-of-2008-georgia-war.
81. "Turkish Foreign Minister Calls for Enlarged NATO, Georgia Membership," Reuters, 23 Jan 2020, https://www.reuters.com/article/us-davos-meeting-turkey-georgia/turkish-foreign-minister-calls-for-enlarged-nato-georgia-membership-idUSKBN1ZM1HB.
82. İlber Ortaylı, "Yeni Osmanlıcılık," *Milliyet*, 25 Jun 2011, http://www.milliyet.com.tr/yeni-osmanlicilik/ilber-ortayli/pazar/yazardetay/26.06.2011/1406764/default.htm.

Iran

1. Reza Zia-Ebrahimi, *The Emergence of Iranian Nationalism: Race and the Politics of Dislocation* (New York: Columbia University Press, 2018), 204–5. Iran's Film Board produced an official documentary of the ceremony, available at https://www.youtube.com/watch?v=TTSuN6s1jr8.
2. Abdolhossein Zarrinkoub, *Two Centuries of Silence*, trans. Paul Sprachman (Costa Mesa, CA: Mazda, 2017) 63.
3. James Mattis, quoted in Dexter Filkins, "The Warrior Monk," *New Yorker*, 29 May 2017, 43.
4. Quoted in Alam Saleh, "Iran's National Identity Problematic," *Sfera politicii*, 2012, 4(170): 55.
5. Gherardo Gnoli, *The Idea of Iran: An Essay on Its Origin* (Rome: Istituto Italiano per il Medio ed Estremo Oriente, 1989).

Chapter Seven. Iranian Identity and Iran's "Empire of the Mind"

1. Fereshteh Davaran, *Continuity in Iranian Identity: Resilience of a Cultural Heritage* (London: Routledge, 2010) 168–69. Ali Mozaffari, *Forming National Identity in Iran: The Idea of Homeland Derived from Ancient Persian and*

Islamic Imaginations of Place (London: I. B. Tauris, 2014) 1–3. Alam Saleh, *Ethnic Identity and the State in Iran* (London: Palgrave Macmillan, 2013) 45–58.

2. Firoozeh Kashani-Sabet, "Cultures of Iranianness: The Evolving Polemic of Iranian Nationalism," in Nikki R. Keddie and Rudi Matthee, eds., *Iran and the Surrounding World: Interactions in Culture and Cultural Politics* (Seattle: University of Washington Press, 2002) 162–81.

3. Juan R. I. Cole, "Iranian Culture and South Asia, 1500–1900," in Keddie and Matthee, eds., *Iran and the Surrounding World*, 15–35.

4. Michael Axworthy, *Iran: Empire of the Mind* (New York: Penguin, 2007). More skeptically, see Mostafa Vaziri, *Iran as Imagined Nation: The Construction of National Identity*, 2nd ed. (Piscataway, NJ: Gorgias, 2013) 3–12, 59–60, 72–73.

5. Kashani-Sabet, "Cultures of Iranianness," 166–67.

6. Rasmus Christian Elling and Alam Saleh, "Ethnic Minorities and the Politics of Identity in Iran," *IS*, 2016, 49(1): 164.

7. Imad Salamey and Zanoubia Othman, "Shia Revival and *Welayat Al-Faqih* in the Making of Iranian Foreign Policy," *Politics, Religion & Ideology*, Jun 2011, 12(2): 197–212. Ali Khamenei, "The Leader: Iranians Quashed Dangerous Conspiracy of Enemies," Office of the Supreme Leader, 7 Jan 2020, https://www.leader.ir/en/content/24007/The-Leader%E2%80%99s-remarks-in-meeting-with-Basij-forces.

8. Shapur Shahbazi, "Darius (iii): Darius I the Great," *EIr*, http://www.iranicaonline.org/articles/darius-iii.

9. Gherardo Gnoli, "Iranian Identity (ii): Pre-Islamic Period," *EIr*, http://www.iranicaonline.org/articles/iranian-identity-ii-pre-islamic-period.

10. Richard N. Frye, "Iranian Identity in Ancient Times," *IS*, 1993, (26): 143–46.

11. Ibid. See also Firoozeh Kashani-Sabet, "Fragile Frontiers: The Diminishing Domains of Qajar Iran," *IJMES*, May 1997, 29(2): 205–7. Abbas Amanat, "Iranian Identity Boundaries: A Historical Overview," in Farzin Vejdani and Abbas Amanat, eds., *Iran Facing Others: Identity Boundaries in Historical Perspective* (London: Palgrave Macmillan, 2012) 4, 10–12.

12. D. N. MacKenzie, "Ērān, Ērānšahr," *EIr*, http://www.iranicaonline.org/articles/eran-eransah.

13. Gherardo Gnoli, *The Idea of Iran: An Essay on Its Origin* (Rome: Istituto Italiano per il Medio ed Estremo Oriente, 1989) 136–48. Gnoli, "Iranian Identity (ii)." Touraj Daryaee, *Sasanian Persia: Rise and Fall of an Empire* (London: I. B. Tauris, 2009) 22–25.

14. Gnoli, *Idea of Iran*, 139.

15. Rudi Matthee, *Persia in Crisis: Safavid Decline and the Fall of Isfahan* (London: I. B. Tauris, 2012) 14–15.

16. Mozaffari, *Forming National Identity*, 109. Gnoli, *Idea of Iran*, 179.

17. Vaziri, *Iran as Imagined Nation*, 15.

18. Mozaffari, *Forming National Identity*, 107–9.

19. Afshin Marashi, *Nationalizing Iran: Culture, Power, and the State, 1870–1940* (Seattle: University of Washington Press, 2008) 12.

20. Vaziri, *Iran as Imagined Nation,* 102. Ahmad Ashraf, "The Crisis of National and Ethnic Identities in Contemporary Iran," *IS,* 1993, 26(1–2): 159–64. Touraj Atabaki, "Agency and Subjectivity in Iranian National Historiography," in Atabaki, ed., *Iran in the 20th Century: Historiography and Political Culture* (London: Bloomsbury, 2009) 70–73.

21. Hamid Algar, "Ākūndzāda," *EIr,* http://www.iranicaonline.org/articles/akundzada-playwright. Reza Zia-Ebrahimi, *The Emergence of Iranian Nationalism: Race and the Politics of Dislocation* (New York: Columbia University Press, 2018) 40–53.

22. Patrick Clawson and Michael Rubin, *Eternal Iran: Continuity and Chaos* (London: Palgrave Macmillan, 2005) 11. David Motadel, "Iran and the Aryan Myth," in Ali Ansari, ed., *Perceptions of Iran: History, Myths and Nationalism from Medieval Persia to the Islamic Republic* (London: I. B. Tauris, 2014) 130–35.

23. Zia-Ebrahimi, *Emergence of Iranian Nationalism,* 59. Zia-Ebrahimi, "Self-Orientalization and Dislocation: The Uses and Abuses of the 'Aryan' Discourse in Iran," *IS,* 2011, 44(4): 445–72. Motadel, "Iran and the Aryan Myth." Vaziri, *Iran as Imagined Nation,* 114–20.

24. M. Bayat, "Āqā Khan Kermānī," *EIr,* http://www.iranicaonline.org/articles/aqa-khan-kermani.

25. Zia-Ebrahimi, *Emergence of Iranian Nationalism,* 58, 99–101.

26. Kashani-Sabet, "Cultures of Iranianness," 166–67.

27. Elling and Saleh, *Minorities in Iran,* 134–35.

28. Ibid., 121–24 (quote, p. 123).

29. Firoozeh Kashani-Sabet, *Frontier Fictions: Shaping the Iranian Nation, 1804–1946* (Princeton, NJ: Princeton University Press, 1999) 217. Mohamad Tavakoli-Targhi, *Refashioning Iran: Orientalism, Occidentalism and Historiography* (London: Palgrave, 2001) 8–17.

30. Alireza Asgharzadeh, *Iran and the Challenge of Diversity: Islamic Fundamentalism, Aryanist Racism, and Democratic Struggles* (London: Palgrave Macmillan, 2007) 101–7.

31. Quoted in Alam Saleh, "Iran's National Identity Problematic," *Sfera politicii,* 2012, 4(170): 54. Mehrdad Mashayekhi, "The Politics of Nationalism and Political Culture," in Samih K. Farsoun and Mehrdad Mashayekhi, eds., *Political Culture in the Islamic Republic* (London: Routledge, 1992) 112. For the latter quote, see Mehran Kamrava, "Khomeini and the West," in Arshin Adib-Moghaddam, ed., *A Critical Introduction to Khomeini* (Cambridge: Cambridge University Press, 2014) 162.

32. Ali M. Ansari, *The Politics of Nationalism in Modern Iran* (Cambridge: Cambridge University Press, 2012), 1, 216–30.

33. Mortada Mutahhari [Morteza Motahhari], "Islam and Iran: A Historical Study of Mutual Services," trans. Wahid Akhtar, *Politics & Current Affairs,* 1989, 6(2), https://www.al-islam.org/printpdf/book/export/html/23072.

34. Saleh, *Ethnic Identity*, 33–35. Ervand Abrahamian, *Khomeinism: Essays on the Islamic Republic* (Berkeley: University of California Press, 1993) 15. Mashayekhi, "Politics of Nationalism," 112.

35. Haggay Ram, "The Immemorial Iranian Nation? School Textbooks and Historical Memory in Post-Revolutionary Iran," *Nations & Nationalism*, Jan 2000, 6(1): 67–90.

36. Tarek Osman, "Iran's Play for Middle Eastern Leadership: Where It Comes from and Why It Can't Last," *Foreign Affairs*, 20 Jan 2017, https://www.foreignaffairs.com/articles/middle-east/2017-01-20/iran-s-play-middle-eastern-leadership.

37. Ali Khamenei, "Leader's Speech at Imam Reza's Holy Shrine," Office of the Supreme Leader, 23 Mar 2015, http://leader.ir/en/speech/12975/Leader's-Speech-at-Imam-Reza's-Holy-Shrine.

38. Quoted in Kim Ghattas, "Iran's Identity Crisis," *Foreign Policy*, 5 Oct 2015, http://foreignpolicy.com/2015/10/05/irans-identity-crisis/.

39. Shahram Akbarzadeh and James Barry, "State Identity in Iranian Foreign Policy," *British Journal of Middle Eastern Studies*, 2016, 43(4): 613–29. Mahdi Mohammad Nia, "Understanding Iran's Foreign Policy: An Application of Holistic Constructivism," *Alternatives: Turkish Journal of International Relations*, 2010, 9(1): 148–80. Hossein Karimifard, "Constructivism, National Identity and the Foreign Policy of the Islamic Republic of Iran," *Asian Social Science*, Feb 2012 8(2): 239–46.

40. Beeta Baghoolizadeh, "Reconstructing a Persian Past: Contemporary Uses and Misuses of the Cyrus Cylinder in Iranian Nationalist Discourse," *Ajam Media Collective*, 6 Jun 2013, http://www.ajammc.com/2013/06/06/reconstructing-a-persian-past-contemporary-uses-and-misuses-of-the-cyrus-cylinder-in-iranian-nationalist-discourse. Zachary Keck, "Ahmadinejad and the Politics of Mahdism in Iran," *E-International Relations*, 3 Jun 2011, http://e-ir.info/2011/06/03/ahmadinejad-and-the-politics-of-mahdism-in-iran.

41. Saeid Jafari, "Cyrus the Great Enters Iranian Politics," *Al-Monitor*, 2 Nov 2016, http://www.al-monitor.com/pulse/en/originals/2016/11/iran-cyrus-day-commemoration-nouri-hamedani-protest.html. Abbas Milani, "Is Ahmadinejad Islamic Enough for Iran?" *Foreign Policy*, 29 Apr 2011, https://foreignpolicy.com/2011/04/29/is-ahmadinejad-islamic-enough-for-iran-2/.

42. Christoph Marcinkowski, *Shiite Identities: Community and Culture in Changing Social Contexts* (Münster: LIT, 2010) 92–93.

43. Quoted in Farhang Rajaee, *Islamic Values and World View: Khomeyni on Man, the State, and International Politics*, Vol. 13 (Lanham, MD: University Press of America, 1983) 82.

44. Ruhollah Khomeini letter to Ali Khamenei, quoted in "What Is Wilayat al-Faqih?," Al-Islam.org, https://www.al-islam.org/Shi'a-political-thought-ahmed-vaezi/what-wilayat-al-faqih#historical-background.

45. Mohsen M. Milani, "The Transformation of the *Velayat-e Faqih* Institution: From Khomeini to Khamenei," *Muslim World*, Jul–Oct 1992, 82(3–4): 177.

46. Hamid Dabashi, *Shi'ism: A Religion of Protest* (Cambridge, MA: Harvard University Press, 2011).

47. Farid Mirbaghari, "Shi'ism and Iran's Foreign Policy," *Muslim World*, Oct 2004, 94: 555–63.

48. Hasan Bik Rumlu, *A Chronicle of the Early Safawis: Being the Ahsanu't-tawarikh of Hasan Rumlu*, Vol. 2, ed. and trans. C. N. Seddon (Baroda: Oriental Institute, 1931) 26–27.

49. Homa Katouzian, *The Persians: Ancient, Medieval, and Modern Iran* (New Haven, CT: Yale University Press, 2010) 114–15.

50. Michael Mazzaoui, Preface, in Mazzaoui, ed., *Safavid Iran and Her Neighbors* (Salt Lake City: University of Utah Press, 2003) vii. See also Bert Fragner, "The Safavid Empire and the Sixteenth and Seventeenth Century Political and Strategic Balance of Power Within the World System," in William Floor and Edmund Herzig, eds., *Iran and the World in the Safavid Age* (London: I. B. Tauris, 2012) 28.

51. "Gōlāt," *EIr*, http://www.iranicaonline.org/articles/golat. Kathryn Babayan, *Mystics, Monarchs and Messiahs: Cultural Landscapes of Early Modern Iran* (Cambridge, MA: Harvard University Press, 2003).

52. Shahzad Bashir, "The Origins and Rhetorical Evolution of the Term Qizilbāsh in Persianate Literature," *Journal of the Economic and Social History of the Orient*, 2014, (57): 364–91.

53. Adel Allouche, *The Origins and Development of the Ottoman-Ṣafavid Conflict: (906–962/1500–1555)* (Berlin: Klaus Schwarz Verlag, 1983) 100–146. Abolala Soudavar, "The Early Safavids and Their Cultural Interactions with Surrounding States," in Keddie and Matthee, eds., *Iran and the Surrounding World*, 89–120.

54. Said Amir Arjomand, "The Clerical Estate and the Emergence of a Shi'ite Hierocracy in Safavid Iran: A Study in Historical Sociology," *Journal of the Economic and Social History of the Orient*, 1985, 28(2): 169–219.

55. Colin P. Mitchell, *The Practice of Politics in Safavid Iran: Power, Religion and Rhetoric* (London: I. B. Tauris, 2009) 102.

56. Said Amir Arjomand, *The Shadow of God and the Hidden Imam: Religion, Political Order, and Societal Change in Shi'ite Iran from the Beginning to 1890* (Chicago: University of Chicago Press, 2010) 132–44.

57. Rudi Matthee, "The Safavid-Ottoman Frontier: Iraq-i Arab as Seen by the Safavids," *International Journal of Turkish Studies*, Summer 2003, 9(1): 157–73.

58. Roy Mottahedeh, *The Mantle of the Prophet: Learning and Power in Modern Iran* (London: Chatto & Windus, 1986) 205.

59. Ed Blanche, "The Battle for Iraq's Soul—Najaf vs. Qom," *Arab Weekly*, 17 Jul 2015, https://thearabweekly.com/battle-iraqs-soul-najaf-v-qom.

60. Frederic Wehrey et al., *Dangerous But Not Omnipotent: Exploring the Reach and Limitations of Iranian Power in the Middle East* (Santa Monica, CA: RAND Corporation, 2009) 110–12.

61. Vali Nasr, "When the Shiites Rise," *Foreign Affairs*, Jul–Aug 2006, 85(4), https://www.foreignaffairs.com/articles/iran/2006-07-01/when-shiites-rise.

62. Ali Khamenei, "IRI Supports an Integrated, Stable Iraq," Office of the Supreme Leader, 30 Oct 2011, https://www.leader.ir/en/content/8834/IRI-supports-an-integrated,-stable-Iraq.

63. Guido Steinberg, "The Badr Organization: Iran's Most Important Instrument in Iraq," SWP, Jul 2017, https://www.swp-berlin.org/en/publication/the-badr-organization-irans-instrument-in-iraq/.

64. Mohammad R. Kalantari and Ali Hashem, "Washington Doesn't Understand Shiite Clerics in Iran or Iraq," *Foreign Policy*, 20 Jan 2020, https://foreignpolicy.com/2020/01/30/washington-doesnt-understand-shiite-clerics-in-iran-or-iraq/.

65. Harith Hasan al-Qarawee, "Sistani, Iran, and the Future of Shii Clerical Authority in Iraq," Brandeis University Crown Center for Middle Eastern Studies, January 2017, https://www.brandeis.edu/crown/publications/middle-east-briefs/pdfs/101-200/meb105.pdf.

66. "Iran's Networks of Influence—Chapter Four: Iraq," in *Iran's Networks of Influence in the Middle East*, IISS, Nov 2019, https://www.iiss.org/publications/strategic-dossiers/iran-dossier/iran-19-06-ch-4-iraq.

67. Jason Davison and Ahmed Rasheed, "Fractures Grow Among Iraq Militias, Spell Political Retreat," Reuters, 1 Apr 2020, https://www.reuters.com/article/us-iraq-militias/fractures-grow-among-iraq-militias-spell-political-retreat-idUSKBN21J5EZ.

68. Erin Cunningham and Mustafa Salim, "Iran's Spiritual Power Play," *Washington Post*, 5 May 2019, https://www.washingtonpost.com/world/2019/05/05/irans-spiritual-power-play/.

69. Tim Arango, "Iran Presses for Official to Be Next Leader of Shiites," *New York Times*, 11 May 2012, https://www.nytimes.com/2012/05/12/world/middleeast/iran-promotes-its-candidate-for-next-shiite-leader.html.

70. Patrick Clawson et al., Middle East FAQs, Vol. 1: "What Is the Shia Crescent?" WINEP, 17 Jan 2018, https://www.washingtoninstitute.org/policy-analysis/view/middle-east-faqs-volume-1-what-is-the-shia-crescent.

71. Shireen T. Hunter, "Iran and the Spread of Revolutionary Islam," *Third World Quarterly*, Apr 1988, 10(2): 730–49.

72. Wehrey et al., *Dangerous But Not Omnipotent*, 86–103. Adam Shatz, "In Search of Hezbollah," *New York Review of Books*, 29 Apr 2004, http://www.nybooks.com/articles/17060.

73. Ben Hubbard, "Iran Out to Remake Mideast with Arab Enforcer: Hezbollah," *New York Times*, 27 Aug 2017, https://www.nytimes.com/2017/08/27/world/middleeast/hezbollah-iran-syria-israel-lebanon.html.

74. Michael Young, "Is War Between Hezbollah and Israel Likely in the Coming Year?," Carnegie Middle East, 21 Sep 2017, http://carnegie-mec.org/diwan/73150.

75. Kate Linthicum, "Could Iran—and Hezbollah—Strike in Latin America?," *Los Angeles Times*, 10 Jan 2020, https://www.latimes.com/world-nation/story/2020-01-10/the-trump-administration-is-warning-that-hezbollah-could-strike-in-latin-america.

76. Keith A. Petty, "Veiled Impunity: Iran's Use of Non-State Armed Groups," *Denver Journal of International Law and Policy*, 2008, 36(2): 191–219. "Can Iran Create Basij-Like Forces in Pakistan?," UAE Future Center for Advanced Research & Studies, 26 Nov 2017, https://futureuae.com/book.php/Mainpage/Item/3463/can-iran-create-basij-like-forces-in-pakistan.

77. Adam Taylor, "Why Iran Is Getting the Blame for an Attack on Saudi Arabia Claimed by Yemen's Houthis," *Washington Post*, 16 Sep 2019, https://www.washingtonpost.com/world/2019/09/16/why-iran-is-getting-blame-an-attack-saudi-arabia-claimed-by-yemens-houthis/.

78. Ali M. Latifi, "How Iran Recruited Afghan Refugees to Fight Assad's War," *New York Times*, 30 Jun 2017, https://www.nytimes.com/2017/06/30/opinion/sunday/iran-afghanistan-refugees-assad-syria.html. Lars Houch, "Understanding the Fatemiyoun Division: Life through the Eyes of a Militia Member," MEI, 22 May 2019, https://www.mei.edu/publications/understanding-fatemiyoun-division-life-through-eyes-militia-member.

79. Alissa J. Rubin and Falih Hassan, "Iraq Protestors Burn Down Iranian Consulate in Night of Anger," *New York Times*, 27 Nov 2019, https://www.nytimes.com/2019/11/27/world/middleeast/iraqi-protest-najaf-iran-burn.html.

80. Ali Fathollah-Nejad, "Iranians Respond to the Regime: "Leave Syria Alone!," *Al-Jazeera*, 2 May 2018, https://www.aljazeera.com/indepth/opinion/iranians-respond-regime-leave-syria-180501081025309.html.

Chapter Eight. Iran's Borderlands

1. Farideh Farhi, "Crafting a National Identity Amidst Contentious Politics in Contemporary Iran," *IS*, Mar 2005, 38(1): 12.

2. Touraj Atabaki, "Ethnic Diversity and Territorial Integrity of Iran: Domestic Harmony and Regional Challenges," *IS*, Mar 2005, 38(1): 32.

3. Arash Khazeni, *Tribes & Empire on the Margin of Nineteenth-Century Iran* (Seattle: University of Washington Press, 2009) 8.

4. Quoted in Rasmus Christian Elling, "Matters of Authenticity: Nationalism, Islam, and Ethnic Diversity in Iran," in Negin Nabavi, ed., *Iran: From Theocracy to Green Movement* (London: Palgrave Macmillan, 2012) 92.

5. Rasmus Christian Elling, *Minorities in Iran: Nationalism and Ethnicity after Khomeini* (London: Palgrave Macmillan, 2013) 92–95.

6. *Dastur al-Moluk: A Safavid State Manual by Mohammad Rafi al-Din Ansari*, ed. and trans. Willem Floor and Mohammad H. Faghfoory (Costa Mesa, CA: Mazda, 2007): 11–5. *Tadhkirat al-Mulūk: A Manual of Safavid Administration*, ed. and trans. Vladimir Minorsky (London: Gibb Memorial Trust, 1943) 43–44, 112–13.

7. Khazeni, *Tribes & Empire*, 16.

8. Ervand Abrahamian, *Iran Between Two Revolutions* (Princeton, NJ: Princeton University Press, 1982) 41.

9. Shaul Bakhash, "The Evolution of Qajar Bureaucracy: 1779–1879," *MES*, May 1971, 7(2): 139–68.

10. Abbas Vali, *Kurds and the State in Iran: The Making of Kurdish Identity* (London: I. B. Tauris, 2011) 4.

11. George Lenczowski, "Foreign Powers' Intervention in Iran During World War I," in Edmund Bosworth and Carole Hillenbrand, eds., *Qajar Iran: Political, Social and Cultural Change, 1800–1925: Studies Presented to Professor Elwell-Sutton* (Edinburgh: Edinburgh University Press, 1984) 76–92.

12. Abbas Amanat, *Iran: A Modern History* (New Haven, CT: Yale University Press, 2017) 407–11, 441–44. Abrahamian, *Iran Between Two Revolutions*, 111–12. Elling, *Minorities in Iran*, 161–63.

13. Elling, *Minorities in Iran*, 129.

14. Quoted in Leonard M. Helfgott, "The Structural Foundations of the National Minority Problem in Revolutionary Iran," *IS*, 1980, 13(1–4): 204–5.

15. A. Stephanie Cronin, "Re-Interpreting Modern Iran: Tribe and State in the Twentieth Century," *IS*, Jun 2009, 42(3): 364. William Samii, "The Nation and Its Minorities: Ethnicity, Unity, and State Policy in Iran," *Comparative Studies of South Asia, Africa, and the Middle East*, 2000, 20(1–2): 129.

16. Cronin, "Re-Interpreting Modern Iran," 382–84.

17. The Constitution of the Islamic Republic of Iran, Introduction, Articles 11, 15, 19, https://www.wipo.int/edocs/lexdocs/laws/en/ir/ir001en.pdf.

18. Ali Khamenei, "Persian Poetry Has Always Been Virtuous," Office of the Supreme Leader, 2 Jun 2018, http://english.khamenei.ir/news/5714/Persian -poetry-has-always-been-virtuous.

19. Quoted in Elling, *Minorities in Iran*, 59.

20. Samii, "The Nation and Its Minorities," 135.

21. Emil Souleimanov, Kamil Pikal, and Josef Kraus, "The Rise of Nationalism Among Iranian Azerbaijanis: A Step Toward Iran's Disintegration?," *Middle East Review of International Affairs*, Spring 2013, 17(1): 73.

22. Marat Grebennikov, "The Puzzle of a Loyal Minority: Why Do Azerbaijanis Support the Iranian State?," *Middle East Journal*, Winter 2013, 67(1): 64–76.

23. Gilles Riaux, "The Formative Years of Azerbaijani Nationalism in Post-Revolutionary Iran," *CAS*, 2008, 27(1): 46.

24. Firuz Kazemzadeh, "Iranian Relations with Russia and the Soviet Union to 1921," *CHI*, VII: 334–40.

25. Helfgott, "Structural Foundations," 206.

26. Brenda R. Shaffer, *Borders and Brethren: Iran and the Challenge of Azerbaijani Identity* (Cambridge, MA: MIT Press, 2002) 22–32.

27. Nikki R. Keddie, "The Iranian Power Structure and Social Change, 1800–1969: An Overview," *IJMES*, Jan 1971, 2(1): 3–20.

28. Nikki R. Keddie, *Qajar Iran and the Rise of Reza Khan 1796–1925* (Costa Mesa, CA: Mazda, 2012) 59–60. Amanat, *Iran*, 330–85. Mangol Bayat, *Iran's First Revolution: Shi'ism and the Constitutional Revolution of 1905–1909* (Oxford: Oxford University Press, 1991) 232–60.

29. Touraj Atabaki, "Ethnic Diversity and Territorial Integrity of Iran: Domestic Harmony and Regional Challenges," *IS*, Mar 2005, 38(1): 23–44. "Azerbaijan iv: Islamic History to 1941," *EIr*, http://www.iranicaonline.org/articles/azerbaijan-iv.

30. Quoted in Eric Hooglund and William Royce, "The Shi'i Clergy of Iran and the Conception of an Islamic State," *State, Culture, and Society*, Spring 1985, 1(3): 111.

31. Brenda Shaffer, "The Formation of Azerbaijani Collective Identity in Iran," *Nationalities Papers*, 2000, 28(3): 454–60. Atabaki, "Ethnic Diversity and Territorial Integrity," 39–40. Alam Saleh, *Ethnic Identity and the State in Iran* (London: Palgrave Macmillan, 2013) 66–67.

32. Emil Souleimanov and Ondrej Ditrych, "Iran and Azerbaijan: A Contested Neighborhood," *Middle East Policy*, Summer 2007, 14(2): 104.

33. Shaffer, "Formation of Azerbaijani Collective Identity," 466–67.

34. Jean-Christophe Peuch, "Iran: Cartoon Protests Point to Growing Frustration Among Azerbaijanis," RFE/RL, 31 May 2006, https://www.rferl.org/a/1068797.html.

35. Amanat, *Iran*, 441.

36. Elling, *Minorities in Iran*, 36–38. Amanat, *Iran*, 441–44.

37. Christopher T. Fisher, "'Moral Purpose Is the Important Thing': David Lilienthal, Iran, and the Meaning of Development in the U.S., 1956–63," *International History Review*, Sep 2011, 33(3): 433.

38. Juan R. I. Cole, "Shi'i Clerics in Iraq and Iran, 1722–1780: The Akhbari-Usuli Conflict Reconsidered," *IS*, Winter 1985, 18(1): 3–34.

39. Roy Mottahedeh, *The Mantle of the Prophet: Learning and Power in Modern Iran* (London: Chatto & Windus, 1986) 210–15. Moojan Momen, "Usuli, Akhbari, Shaykhi, Babi: The Tribulations of a Qazvin Family," *IS*, Sep 2003, 36(3): 317–37.

40. Anthony H. Cordesman, *The Gulf and the Search for Strategic Stability: Saudi Arabia, the Military Balance in the Gulf, and Trends in the Arab-Israeli Military Balance* (London: Routledge, 1984) 648–49.

41. "Rebel Music," *The Economist*, 19 Jan 2019: 48. Golnaz Esfandiari, "Poverty, Separatism, and Bloody Memories of War: Why Iran's Khuzestan Matters," RFE/RL, 28 Sep 2018, https://www.rferl.org/a/iran-khuzestan-poverty-separatism-bloody-war-memories/29515269.html.

42. Mehdi Khalaji, "The Shia Arabs of Khuzestan," WINEP, 25 Sep 2018, https://www.washingtoninstitute.org/policy-analysis/view/the-shia-arabs-of-khuzestan.

43. C. J. Edmonds, "Kurdish Nationalism," *Journal of Contemporary History*, 1971, 6(1): 87–88. Rudi Matthee, *Persia in Crisis: Safavid Decline and the Fall of Isfahan* (London: I.B. Tauris, 2011), 125–27. Michael Eppel, "The Kurdish Emirates: Obstacles or Precursors to Kurdish Nationalism?," in Michael M. Gunter, ed., *Routledge Handbook on the Kurds* (London: Routledge, 2018) 37–47.

44. Mehmet Firat Kilic, "Between Empires: The Movement of Sheikh Ubeydullah," *International Journal of Kurdish Studies*, 2006, 20(1/2): 57–121.

45. Vali, *Kurds and State*, 9–13.

46. Martin van Bruinessen, "A Kurdish Warlord on the Turkish-Persian Frontier in the Early 20th Century: Isma'il Aqa Simko," in Touraj Atabaki, ed., *Iran and the First World War: Battleground of the Great Powers* (London: I. B Tauris, 2006) 69–93. Edmonds, "Kurdish Nationalism," 96.

47. Cronin, "Re-Interpreting Modern Iran," 379.

48. Denise Natali, *The Kurds and the State: Evolving National Identity in Iraq, Turkey, and Iran* (Syracuse: Syracuse University Press, 2005), 120–25 (quote, p. 121).

49. Edmonds, "Kurdish Nationalism," 99.

50. Ibid. Vali, *Kurds and the State*, 1–2, 28–82.

51. Saleh, *Ethnic Identity*, 68–70.

52. "Son dakika: Türkiye ve İran'dan toplantı sonrası ortak bildiri," *Sabah*, 8 Sep 2020, https://www.sabah.com.tr/gundem/2020/09/08/turkiye-ve-iran-arasindaki-yuksek-duzeyli-isbirligi-konseyi-altinci-toplantisinin-ardindan-ortak-bildiri-yayimlandi.

53. Jeff Eden, *Slavery and Empire in Central Asia* (Cambridge: Cambridge University Press, 2018) 37–47.

54. Khazeni, *Tribes & Empire*, 197–98.

55. Abdurrahman Deveci, "İran Türkmenleri: Türkmensahra," ORSAM, 1 Oct 2009, https://orsam.org.tr/tr/iran-turkmenleri-turkmensahra/.

56. Adrienne Lynn Edgar, *Tribal Nation: The Making of Soviet Turkmenistan* (Princeton, NJ: Princeton University Press, 2004) 43.

57. Türel Yılmaz, "İran'da unutulmuş bir toplum: Türkmen Sahra Türkmenleri," Akademi Ortadoğu, Mar 2007, 201–11.

58. Ibid.

59. Ali Temizel, "İran Türkmenlerinde sosyal ve kültürel hayat," in Kamil Aydın, ed., *Düşünce dünyasında Türkiz*, Nov–Dec 2015, 6(36): 33–46. Faisal Alahwazi, "A Brief Human Rights Report About South Turkmenistan," Ahwazi Center for Human Rights, 8 Apr 2015, http://acfh.info/en/?p=1653.

60. Kaan Dilek, "İran'ın Orta Asya politikaları," Ahmet Yesevi Üniversitesi, Sep 2011: 59–62, http://www.ayu.edu.tr/static/kitaplar/iran_ortaasya_raporu.pdf.

61. Zahid Ali Khan, "Balochistan Factor in Pak-Iran Relations: Opportunities and Constraints," *South Asian Studies*, 2012, 27(1): 132–33.

62. Martin Axmann, *Back to the Future: The Khanate of Kalat and the Genesis of Baloch Nationalism 1915–1955* (Oxford: Oxford University Press, 2008). "Baluchistan (i). Geography, History and Ethnography (cont.)," *EIr*; http://www.iranicaonline.org/articles/baluchistan-ia.

63. Pirouz Mojtahed-Zadeh, *Boundary Politics and International Borders of Iran: A Study of the Origin, Evolution, and Implications of the Boundaries of Modern Iran with Its 15 Neighbors* (Boca Raton, FL: Universal, 2006) 200–203.

64. "Baluchistan (i). Geography, History and Ethnography (cont.)."

65. Ahmad Reza Taheri, "The Sociopolitical Culture of Iranian Baloch Elites," *IS*, 2013, 46(6): 973–94.

66. Vahe S. Boyajian, "Is There an Ethno-Religious Aspect in Balochi Identity?," *Iran and the Caucasus*, 2016, 20(3–4): 397–405.

67. Lubna Adid Ali, "Pak-Iran Relations in the Post-Imperial World," *Journal of Political Studies*, Winter 2009, 16(1): 6.

68. Umar Farooq, "The Battle for Sistan-Baluchistan," *Wall Street Journal*, 5 Dec 2013, https://blogs.wsj.com/indiarealtime/2013/12/05/the-battle-for-sistan-baluchistan/.

69. Arif Rafiq, "Border Violence in Baluchistan Tests Iran-Pakistan Relations," *World Politics Review*, 4 Nov 2014, http://www.worldpoliticsreview.com/articles/14342/border-violence-in-baluchistan-tests-iran-pakistan-relations.

70. Thomas Erdbrink, "Insurgents in Pakistan Stepping Up Iran Strikes," *New York Times*, 9 Oct 2014, https://www.nytimes.com/2014/10/10/world/asia/pakistan-sunni-insurgents-step-up-attacks-in-iran.html. Muhammad Naveed Qaisar and Amjad Abbas Khan, "Pakistan–Iran Relations in a Regional Context," *South Asian Studies*, 2017, 32(1): 256.

71. Elling, *Minorities in Iran*, 198.

Chapter Nine. Greater Iran (*Iranzamin*) and Iran's Imperial Imagination

1. Robert Kaplan, *The Revenge of Geography: What the Map Tells Us About Coming Conflicts and the Battle Against Fate* (New York: Random House, 2012) 267.

2. Firoozeh Kashani-Sabet, *Frontier Fictions: Shaping the Iranian Nation, 1804–1946* (Princeton, NJ: Princeton University Press, 1999) 19.

3. Ibid., 46.

4. Mohsen Milani, "Iran in a Reconnecting Eurasia: Foreign Economic and Security Interests," CSIS, Apr 2016, https://www.csis.org/analysis/iran-reconnecting-eurasia.

5. "Iran's Networks of Influence—Chapter Four: Iraq," in *Iran's Networks of Influence in the Middle East*, IISS, Nov 2019, https://www.iiss.org/publications/strategic-dossiers/iran-dossier/iran-19-06-ch-4-iraq.

6. Abbas Amanat, "Iranian Identity Boundaries: A Historical Overview," in Farzin Vejdani and Abbas Amanat, eds., *Iran Facing Others: Identity Boundaries in Historical Perspective* (London: Palgrave Macmillan, 2012) 4, 10–12.

7. Gherardo Gnoli, "Iranian Identity (ii): Pre-Islamic Period," *EIr*, http://www.iranicaonline.org/articles/iranian-identity-ii-pre-islamic-period. Ahmad Ashraf, "Iranian Identity (iii): Medieval Islamic Period," *EIr*, https://www.iranicaonline.org/articles/iranian-identity-iii-medieval-islamic-period. Kashani-Sabet, "Fragile Frontiers," 205–7.

8. Christine Noelle-Karimi, *The Pearl in Its Midst: Herat and the Mapping of Khurasan (15th–19th Centuries)* (Vienna: Österreichische Akademie der Wissenschaften, 2014) 6–7.

9.   Gherardo Gnoli, *The Idea of Iran: An Essay on Its Origin* (Rome: Istituto Italiano per il Medio ed Estremo Oriente, 1989) 47–53. Michael Witzel, "The Home of the Aryans," in A. Hinze and E. Tichy, eds., *Anusantatyi: Festschrift für Johana Narten zum 70. Gebürtstag* (Dettelbach: J. H. Röll, 2000) 283–338. Gherardo Gnoli., "Avestan Geography," *EIr,* http://www.iranicaonline.org/articles/avestan-geography.

10.   D. N. MacKenzie, "Ērān, Ērānšahr," *EIr,* http://www.iranicaonline.org/articles/eran-eransah.

11.   Daryaee, *Sasanian Persia,* 4–6. See also Ph. Gignoux, "Anērān," *EIr,* http://www.iranicaonline.org/articles/aneran.

12.   Henning Börm, "Das Königtum der Sasaniden—Strukturen und Probleme. Bemerkungen aus althistorischer Sicht," *Klio,* 2008, 90(2): 437–38. Touraj Daryaee, "The Changing 'Image of the World': Geography and Imperial Propaganda in Ancient Persia," *Electrum,* 2006, (6): 99–109.

13.   Shabnam J. Hollday, *Defining Iran: Politics of Resistance* (London: Routledge, 2011) 48–49.

14.   Dick Davis, "Iran and *Aniran:* Shaping a Legend," in Vejdani and Amanat, eds., *Iran Facing Others,* 37–48.

15.   Hamd-Allāh Mustawfi, *The Geographical Part of the* Nuzhat-al-Qulub, trans. G. Le Strange (Leiden, 1919) 23. Kashani-Sabet, *Frontier Fictions,* 15–19. Kashani-Sabet, "Fragile Frontiers: The Diminishing Domains of Qajar Iran," *IJMES,* May 1997, 29(2): 206.

16.   Alex Vatanka, *Iran and Pakistan: Security, Diplomacy, and American Influence* (London: I. B. Tauris, 2015) 171.

17.   Ali Khamenei, "Iran's Military Authority: From Lacking Barbed Wire to Destroying Al-Assad," Office of the Supreme Leader, 10 Feb 2020, https://english.khamenei.ir/news/7358/Iran-s-military-authority-from-lacking-barbed-wire-to-destroying. Mana Kia, "Imagining Iran Before Nationalism: Geocultural Meanings of Land in Azar's *Atashkadeh,*" in Kamran Scot Aghaie and Afshin Marashi, eds., *Rethinking Iranian Nationalism and Modernity* (Austin: University of Texas Press, 2014) 89–112. Michael Rubin, "Strategies Underlying Iranian Soft Power," AEI, 7 Mar 2017, https://www.aei.org/research-products/journal-publication/strategies-underlying-iranian-soft-power/.

18.   Andrew C. Kuchins and Jeffrey Mankoff, "Turkey, Russia, and Iran in the Caucasus," in Samuel J. Brannen, ed., *The Turkey, Russia, Iran Nexus,* CSIS, Nov 2013: 12–22, https://csis-website-prod.s3.amazonaws.com/s3fs-public/legacy_files/files/publication/131112_Brannen_TurkeyRussiaIranNexus_Web.pdf.

19.   Abbas Maliki, "Iran's Northeastern Borders: From Sarakhs to Khazar (The Caspian Sea)," in Keith McLachlan, ed., *The Boundaries of Modern Iran* (New York: St. Martin's, 1994) 21–22. Charles van der Leeuw, *Azerbaijan: A Quest for Identity* (New York: St. Martin's, 2000) 37–47. Touraj Atabaki, *Azerbaijan: Ethnicity and the Struggle for Power in Iran* (London: I. B. Tauris,

2000) 7–9, 24–26. "Azerbaijan (iv): Islamic History to 1941," *EIr*, http://www
.iranicaonline.org/articles/azerbaijan-iv.

20. Donald Rayfield, *Edge of Empires: A History of Georgia* (Clerkenwell: Reaktion, 2012) 187–201.

21. Eskandar Beg Monshi, *History of Shah 'Abbas the Great*, Vol. 1, trans. Roger
M. Savory (Boulder, CO: Westview Press, 1978) 140–41.

22. A. L. Narochnitskiy, ed., *Istoriya narodov severnogo Kavkaza* (Moscow: Aka-
demiya Nauk SSSR, 1958) 323–25.

23. Rudi Matthee, *Persia in Crisis: Safavid Decline and the Fall of Isfahan* (London:
I. B. Tauris, 2011) 28.

24. Valerian N. Gabashvili, "The Undiladze Feudal House in the [sic] Sixteenth
to Seventeenth-Century Iran According to the Georgian Sources," *IS*, Feb
2007, 40(1): 37–58.

25. Narochnitskiy, ed., *Istoriya narodov severnogo Kavkaza*, 311–19.

26. Walter Posch, *Der Fall Alkâs Mîrzâ: Osmanisch-safavidische Beziehungen
1545–1550*, Vol. 1 (Vienna: Österreichische Akademie der Wissenschaften,
2013) 63–78. Willem Floor, "Who Were the Shamkhal and the Usmi?,"
Zeitschrift der Deutschen Morgenländischen Gesellschaft, 2010, 160(2): 341–81.

27. Narochnitskiy, ed., *Istoriya narodov severnogo Kavkaza*, 323–25.

28. Farrokh, *Iran at War*, 81–82. "Russia (i): Russo-Iranian Relations up to the
Bolshevik Revolution," *EIr*, http://www.iranicaonline.org/articles/russia-i
-relations. Lockhart, *Fall of the Safavī Dynasty*, 233–35.

29. Touraj Atabaki, "Ethnic Diversity and Territorial Integrity of Iran: Domestic
Harmony and Regional Challenges," *IS*, Mar 2005, 38(1): 26–27.

30. Charles King, *Ghost of Freedom: A History of the Caucasus* (Oxford: Oxford
University Press, 2008) 27–30.

31. "Gōlestan Treaty," *EIr*, http://www.iranicaonline.org/articles/golestan
-treaty. Muriel Atkin, *Russia and Iran, 1780–1828* (Minneapolis: University
of Minnesota Press, 1980) 99–122.

32. Guillaume Riaux, "The Formative Years of Azerbaijani Nationalism in Post-
Revolutionary Iran," *CAS*, 2008, 27(1): 48–50.

33. Shahin Abbasov, "Azerbaijan: Arrest of Islamic Party Leader Puts Religion
in the Political Spotlight," EurasiaNet, 11 Jan 2011, http://www.eurasianet
.org/node/62692.

34. Emil Aslan Souleimanov, "Azerbaijan, Islamism, and Unrest in Nardaran,"
CACI Analyst, 27 Dec 2015, https://www.cacianalyst.org/publications/
analytical-articles/item/13316-azerbaijan-islamism-and-unrest-in-nardaran
.html.

35. Milani, "Iran in a Reconnecting Eurasia," 12.

36. Jon Alterman and Jonathan Hillman, "Iran's Railway Revolution Aims at Expanded Trade, Investment," *Nikkei Asian Review*, 10 May 2017, http://asia
.nikkei.com/Viewpoints/Jon-B.-Alterman-and-Jonathan-Hillman/Iran-s
-railway-revolution-aims-at-expanded-trade-investment.

37. Milani, "Iran in a Reconnecting Eurasia," 15–16. Kuchins and Mankoff,
"Turkey, Russia, and Iran in the Caucasus."

38.   Timur Erpeli, "Polzucheye vkhozhdeniye," *Kavkaz.Realii*, RFE/RL, 20 Dec 2016, http://www.kavkazr.com/a/polzhuchee_vkhozhdeniye/28178481.html.

39.   Jeffrey Mankoff, "Turkey, Russia, and Iran in Afghanistan and Central Asia," in Brannen, ed., *The Turkey, Russia, Iran Nexus*, 23–33.

40.   Noelle-Karimi, *The Pearl in Its Midst*, 6–7.

41.   Roger Savory, *Iran Under the Safavids* (Cambridge: Cambridge University Press, 1980) 36.

42.   Rudi Matthee, "Relations Between the Center and the Periphery in Safavid Iran: The Western Borderlands v. the Eastern Frontier Zone," *The Historian*, Fall 2015, 77(3): 455–56.

43.   Matthee, "Center and the Periphery."

44.   Noelle-Karimi, *The Pearl in Its Midst*, 48–49, 59–60. Jean Aubin, "L'avènement des Safavides reconsidéré: Études safavides III," *Moyen Orient et Océan Indien*, 1988, (5): 26–27.

45.   Monshi, *History of Shah Abbas*, Vol. 1, 95. Audrey Burton, "The Fall of Herat to the Uzbegs in 1588," *Iran*, 1988, 26: 119–23.

46.   Pirouz Mojtahed-Zadeh, *The Small Players of the Great Game* (London: Routledge, 2007) 126–28.

47.   Quoted in Peter John Brobst, "Sir Frederic Goldsmid and the Containment of Persia, 1863–73," *MES*, 1997, 33(2): 197–215.

48.   "The Persian Treaty," http://marxengels.public-archive.net/en/ME1014en .html. See also Kashani-Sabet, *Frontier Fictions*, 31–32. Mojtahed-Zadeh, *Small Players*, 144–49. Amanat, *Pivot of the Universe*, 277–309.

49.   Mojtahed-Zadeh, *Small Players*, 149.

50.   Ibid., 122–25.

51.   Mohsen M. Milani, "Iran's Policy Towards Afghanistan," *Middle East Journal*, Spring 2006, 60(2): 236–37.

52.   "Afghanistan-Iran: Mehdi, 'My Hands Were Hurting Because the Handcuffs Were Too Tight,'" RAWA News, 27 Feb 2012, http://www.rawa.org/ temp/runews/2012/02/27/afghanistan-iran-mehdi-my-hands-were-hurting -because-the-handcuffs-were-too-tight.html. Sumitha Narayanan Kutty, "Iran's Continuing Interests in Afghanistan," *Washington Quarterly*, 2014, 37(2): 140–41, 145.

53.   Ali A. Jalali, "A Historical Perspective on Iran–Afghan Relations," in Ali Mohammadi and Anoushirvan Ehteshami, eds., *Iran and Eurasia* (London: Ithaca Press, 2000) 125–36.

54.   Milani, "Iran's Policy Towards Afghanistan," 240–41.

55.   Nushin Arabzadah, "Afghanistan's Turbulent Cleric," *The Guardian*, 18 Apr 2009, https://www.theguardian.com/commentisfree/2009/apr/18/ afghanistan-Shi'a-law-women. Kutty, "Iran's Continuing Interests in Afghanistan," 149–50.

56.   Shahram Akbarzadeh and Niamatullah Ibrahimi, "The Taliban: A New Proxy for Iran in Afghanistan?," *Third World Quarterly*, 2020, 41(5): 764–82.

57.   Kutty, "Iran's Continuing Interests in Afghanistan," 144–49. Neil Padukone, "All Silk Roads Lead to Tehran," *Foreign Policy*, 23 Jan 2012, http://

foreignpolicy.com/2012/01/23/all-silk-roads-lead-to-tehran/. Kayhan Bar-zegar, "Iran's Foreign Policy in Post-Taliban Afghanistan," *Washington Quarterly*, Summer 2014, 37(2): 119–37.

58. Kutty, "Iran's Continuing Interests in Afghanistan," 143–44. James Dobbins and James Shinn, "Afghan Peace Talks: A Primer," RAND Corporation, 2011: 58, http://www.rand.org/pubs/monographs/mg1131.html.

59. Alireza Nader et al., *Iran's Influence in Afghanistan: Implications for the U.S. Drawdown* (Santa Monica, CA: RAND Corporation, 2014) 6–10, 13–17. Shah Mahmoud Hanifi, "Making Space for Shi'ism in Afghanistan's Public Sphere and State Structure," *Perspectives on History*, Jul 2015, https://www.historians.org/publications-and-directories/perspectives-on-history/summer-2015/making-space-for-Shi'ism-in-afghanistans-public-sphere-and-state-structure.

60. Ali Khamenei, "Tajikistan, Inseparable Part of Iranian Culture," Office of the Supreme Leader, 8 May 2007, http://leader.ir/en/content/3607/Tajikistan,-inseparable-part-of-Iranian-culture.

61. Mark Vinson, "Iranian Soft Power in Tajikistan: Beyond Cultural and Economic Ties," Jamestown Foundation Eurasia Daily Monitor, 14 Mar 2012, https://jamestown.org/program/iranian-soft-power-in-tajikistan-beyond-cultural-and-economic-ties/.

China

1. "President Xi Jinping Delivers Important Speech and Proposes to Build a Silk Road Economic Belt with Central Asian Countries," Ministry of Foreign Affairs, 7 Sep 2013, https://www.fmprc.gov.cn/mfa_eng/topics_665678/xjpfwzysiesgjtfhshzzfh_665686/t1076334.shtml.

2. "Full Text of President Xi's Speech at Opening of Belt and Road Forum," Xinhua, 14 May 2017, http://www.xinhuanet.com/english/2017-05/14/c_136282982.htm.

3. A. F. P. Hulsewé, *China in Central Asia: The Early Stage: 125 B.C.–A.D. 23; An Annotated Translation of Chapters 61 and 96 of the History of the Former Han Dynasty* (Leiden: Brill, 1979) 211.

4. Wang Hui, *China from Empire to Nation-State*, trans. Michael Gibbs Hill, (Cambridge, MA: Harvard University Press, 2014) 101–3.

5. Thomas S. Mullaney, *Coming to Terms with the Nation: Ethnic Classification in Modern China* (Berkeley: University of California Press, 2011) 14.

6. Dru C. Gladney, "Representing Nationality in China: Refiguring Majority/Minority Identities," *Journal of Asian Studies*, Feb 1994, 53(1): 92–123.

7. Justin M. Jacobs, *Xinjiang and the Modern Chinese State* (Seattle: University of Washington Press, 2016) 236.

8. William A. Callahan, "National Insecurities: Humiliation, Salvation, and Chinese Nationalism," *Alternatives*, Mar–May 2004, 29(2): 199–218.

9. *The Li Ki (The Book of Rites)*, Part 1, trans. James Legge, Sacred Books of the East, 27 (London, 1885 [1967]), http://www.sacred-texts.com/cfu/liki.

Chapter Ten. Civilization and Imperial Identity in China

1. Chi-shen Chang, "The Idea of Chineseness and Ethnic Thought of Wang Fuzhi," in Cheng-tian Kuo, *Religion and Nationalism in Chinese Societies* (Amsterdam: Amsterdam University Press, 2017) 55–88.

2. Arif Dilik, "Culture in Contemporary IR Theory: The Chinese Provocation," in Robbie Shilliam, ed., *International Relations and Non-Western Thought: Imperialism, Colonialism, and Investigations of Global Modernity* (London: Routledge, 2010) 139–56. Ren Xiao, "Traditional Chinese Theory and Practice of Foreign Relations: A Reassessment," in Zheng Yongnian, ed., *China and International Relations: The Chinese View and the Contribution of Wang Gungwu* (London: Routledge, 2012) 112. Liu Junping, "The Evolution of *Tianxia* Cosmology and Its Philosophical Implications," *Frontiers of Philosophy on China*, Dec 2006, 1(4): 517–38.

3. Suisheng Zhao, *A Nation State by Construction: Dynamics of Modern Chinese Nationalism* (Stanford: Stanford University Press, 2004) 49.

4. Chenchen Zhang, "Situated Interpretations of Nationalism, Imperialism, and Cosmopolitanism: Revisiting the Writings of Liang in the Encounter Between Worlds," *Journal of Historical Sociology*, Sep 2014, 27(3): 350–54.

5. Joseph R. Levenson, *Confucian China and Its Modern Fate* (Berkeley: University of California Press, 1968).

6. Justin M. Jacobs, *Xinjiang and the Modern Chinese State* (Seattle: University of Washington Press, 2016) 34–37.

7. Dru C. Gladney, "Representing Nationality in China: Refiguring Majority/Minority Identities," *Journal of Asian Studies*, Feb 1994, 53(1): 92–123.

8. Wong Yew Leong, "*Li* and Change," Paper presented at the Twentieth World Congress of Philosophy, Aug 1998, http://www.bu.edu/wcp/Papers/Asia/AsiaWong.htm.

9. Heather A. Peters, "Ethnicity Along China's Southwestern Frontier," *Journal of East Asian Archaeology*, 2001, 3(1): 75–102.

10. Allen Chun, "Fuck Chineseness: On the Ambiguities of Ethnicity as Culture as Identity," *Boundary*, Summer 1996, 23(2): 113.

11. Pan Yihong, "Integration of the Northern Ethnic Frontiers in Tang China," *Chinese Historical Review*, May 2012, 19(1): 3–26.

12. Ibid., 6. Peter Perdue, "Erasing the Empire, Re-Racing the Nation: Racialism and Culturalism in Imperial China," in Ann Laura Stoler et al, eds., *Imperial Formations* (Santa Fe, NM: School for Advanced Research, 2007) 149–51.

13. Yuri Pines, "Beasts or Humans: Pre-Imperial Origins of the 'Sino-Barbarian' Dichotomy," in R. Amitai and M. Biran, eds., *Mongols, Turks, and Others* (Leiden: Brill, 2004) 59–102. Stevan Harrell, "Introduction: Civilizing Projects and the Reaction to Them," in Harrell, ed., *Cultural Encounters on China's Ethnic Frontiers* (Seattle: University of Washington Press, 1995) 3–36.

14. Pan Yihong, "Integration of the Northern Ethnic Frontiers," 6–7.

15. Prasenjit Duara, "The Legacy of Empires and Nations in East Asia," in Pal Nyiri and Joana Breidenbach, eds., *China Inside Out: Contemporary Chinese Nationalism and Transnationalism* (Budapest: CEU, 2005) 39.

16. Mark C. Elliott, *The Manchu Way: The Eight Banners and Ethnic Identity in Late Imperial China* (Stanford: Stanford University Press, 2001) 340–50.

17. Mark C. Elliott, "La Chine moderne: Les Mandchous et la définition de la nation," *Annales-HHS*, Nov–Dec 2006, (6): 1462–63.

18. Peter Zarrow, *After Empire: The Conceptual Transformation of the Chinese State, 1885–1924* (Stanford: Stanford University Press, 2012) 24–88.

19. Quoted in Hao Chang, *Liang Ch'i-ch'ao and Intellectual Transition in China* (Cambridge, MA: Harvard University Press, 1971) 164.

20. Quoted in Zarrow, *After Empire*, 70.

21. Bill Hayton, *The Invention of China* (New Haven, CT: Yale University Press, 2020) 106–16.

22. Pankaj Mishra, *From the Ruins of Empire: The Revolt Against the West and the Re-Making of Asia* (New York: Farrar, Straus and Giroux, 2012) 171. Luke Cooper, "The International Relations of the 'Imagined Community': Explaining the Late Nineteenth-Century Genesis of the *Chinese* Nation," *Review of International Studies*, 2015, (41): 490–92.

23. Quoted in Joshua A. Fogel, "Race and Class in Chinese Historiography: Divergent Interpretations of Zhang Bing-Lin and Anti-Manchuism in the 1911 Revolution," *Modern China*, Jul 1977, 3(3): 364.

24. Robert D. Weatherly and Qiang Zhang, "History and Legitimacy in Contemporary China Towards Competing Nationalisms," in Cheng-tian Kuo, ed., *Religion and Nationalism in Chinese Societies* (Amsterdam: Amsterdam University Press, 2017) 146–48. Chow, "Narrating Race," 56–63, 75 (quote).

25. Quoted in Julia Schneider, "Early Chinese Nationalism: The Origins Under Manchu Rule," in *Interpreting China as a Regional and Global Power*, ed. Bart Dessein (London: Palgrave Macmillan, 2014) 19.

26. Jacobs, *Xinjiang*, 34–37. Frank Dikötter, "Culture, 'Race,' and Nation: The Formation of National Identity in Twentieth-Century China," *Journal of International Affairs*, Winter 1996, 49(2): 596–97.

27. Hayton, *Invention of China*, 106–16, 132–35.

28. Constitution of the People's Republic of China, Preamble, http://www .npc.gov.cn/englishnpc/Constitution/2007–11/15/content_1372962.htm. Christopher P. Atwood, "National Questions and National Answers in the Chinese Revolution; Or, How Do You Say *Minzu* in Mongolian?," Indiana East Asian Working Paper, Jul 1994, (5): 36–38.

29. Quoted in Joseph W. Esherick, "How the Qing Became China," in Esherick, Hasan Kayalı, and Eric van Young, eds., *Empire to Nation: Historical Perspectives on the Making of the Modern World* (Lanham, MD: Rowman & Littlefield, 2006) 245. Shao Dan, *Remote Homeland, Recovered Borderland: Manchus, Manchukuo, and Manchuria, 1907–1985* (Honolulu: University of Hawai'i Press, 2011) 90–92.

30. Hayton, *Invention of China*, 141–44.

31. Sun Yat-sen "The Three Principles of the People [*San-min chu-i*]," in Julie Lee Wei et al., eds., *Prescriptions for Saving China: Selected Writings of Sun Yat-sen* (Stanford, CA: Hoover Institution Press, 1994) 225.

32. Chiang Kai-shek, *China's Destiny & Chinese Economic Theory*, ed. Philip J. Jaffe (New York: Roy, 1947) 40.

33. Thomas C. Mullaney, *Coming to Terms with the Nation: Ethnic Classification in Modern China* (Berkeley: University of California Press, 2011) 27–28.

34. Mao Zedong, "On Coalition Government," 24 Apr 1945, https://www .marxists.org/reference/archive/mao/selected-works/volume-3/mswv3_25 .htm#p21.

35. Dru C. Gladney, "China's National Insecurity: Old Challenges at the Dawn of the New Millennium," in *Asian Perspectives on the Challenge of China*, Institute for National Strategic Studies, 2004, https://pdfs.semanticscholar.org/ 4188/f4a9c5ee6af43c6a6247489ae27ef4bf4bdf.pdf.

36. "Constitution of the Chinese Soviet Republic," 1931, Articles 4 and 13, https://www.worldstatesmen.org/Chinese-Soviet-Republic-Const1931.pdf. Magnus Fiskesjö, "Rescuing the Empire: Chinese Nation-Building in the Twentieth Century," *European Journal of East Asian Studies*, 2006, 5(1): 26–27.

37. Michael H. Hunt, "Chinese National Identity and the Strong State: The Late Qing-Republican Crisis," in Lowell Dittmer and Samuel S. Kim, eds., *China's Quest for National Identity* (Ithaca: Cornell University Press, 1993) 62–79. James Leibold, *Reconfiguring Chinese Nationalism: How the Qing Frontier and Its Indigenes Became Chinese* (London: Palgrave Macmillan, 2007) 81–112, 147–76.

38. Quoted in Fiskesjö, "Rescuing the Empire," 27.

39. Zhao, *A Nation State by Construction*, 179–80.

40. June Dreyer, "China's Minority Nationalities in the Cultural Revolution," *China Quarterly*, 1968, (35): 97.

41. Constitution of the People's Republic of China, 20 Sep 1954, Article 3, https://web.archive.org/web/20140328031523/http://www.hkpolitics.net/ database/chicon/1954/1954ae.pdf.

42. Leo K. Shin, *The Making of the Chinese State: Ethnicity and Expansion on the Ming Borderlands* (Cambridge: Cambridge University Press, 2006) 11–18.

43. Zhao, *A Nation State by Construction*, 180–81.

44. Mullaney, *Coming to Terms with the Nation*, 10–11.

45. Hongyi Harry Lai, "China's Western Development Program: Its Rationale, Implementation and Prospects," *Modern China*, 2002, 28(4): 445–46.

46. Shin, *Making of the Chinese State*, 201–6.

47. "China's Ethnic Policy and Common Prosperity and Development of All Ethnic Groups: Consolidating and Developing the Great Unity of All Ethnic Groups," State Council, 27 Sep 2009, http://www.china.org.cn/ government/whitepaper/node_7078073.htm.

48. "Religious Extremism Notably Curbed in Xinjiang: Senior Chinese Official," Xinhua, 14 Apr 2014, http://www.xinhuanet.com/english/2018–04/14/c_137111356_2.htm.

49. "Xinjiang Authorities Sentence Uyghur Philanthropist to Death for Unsanctioned Hajj," RFA, 21 Nov 2018, https://www.rfa.org/english/news/uyghur/philanthropist-11212018131511.html.

50. Dikötter, "Culture, 'Race' and Nation," 98.

51. Zhao, *A Nation State by Construction*, 182–87, 194–98.

52. James Leibold, "The *Minzu* Net: China's Fragmented National Form," *Nations and Nationalism*, 2016, 22(3): 426. Frank Dikötter, *The Discourse of Race in Modern China* (London: Hurst, 1992) 118. Shin, *Making of the Chinese State*, 184–85.

53. Dryer, "China's Minority Nationalities," 96–109. Leibold, *Reconfiguring Chinese Nationalism*, 147–76.

54. James DeShaw Rae and Xiaodan Wang, "Placing Race, Culture, and the State in Chinese National Identity: Han, Hua, or Zhongguo?," *Asian Politics and Policy*, Jul 2016, 8(3): 481.

55. Thomas Christensen, "Chinese Realpolitik: Reading Beijing's World-View," *Foreign Affairs*, Sep–Oct 1996, 75(5): 37–52 (quote, p. 46).

56. Suisheng Zhao, "A State-Led Nationalism: The Patriotic Education Campaign in Post-Tiananmen China," *Communist and Post-Communist Studies*, 1998, 31(3): 287–302 (quote, p. 289).

57. Hayton, *Invention of China*, 128–32, 151–53.

58. Mark Elliott, "The Case of the Missing Indigene: Debate Over a 'Second-Generation' Ethnic Policy," *China Journal*, January 2015, (73): 193–94.

59. Constitution of the Communist Party of China, 24 Oct 2017, http://www.xinhuanet.com//english/download/Constitution_of_the_Communist_Party_of_China.pdf. "Ceremony Held in Hunan to Pay Homage to Legendary Ancestor of Chinese Nation," Xinhua, 13 Oct 2019, http://www.xinhuanet.com/english/2019–10/13/c_138468879.htm.

60. Nimrod Baranovitch, "Others No More: The Changing Representation of Non-Han Peoples in Chinese History Textbooks, 1951–2003," *Journal of Asian Studies*, 2010, 69(1): 85–122.

61. Daniel Goodkind, "The Chinese Diaspora: Historical Legacies and Contemporary Trends," U.S. Census Bureau, Aug 2019, https://www.census.gov/content/dam/Census/library/working-papers/2019/demo/Chinese_Diaspora.pdf.

62. Prasenjit Duara, "Transnationalism in the Era of Nation-States: China, 1900–1945," *Development and Change*, Oct 1998, 29(4): 661.

63. Hayton, *Invention of China*, 77–78.

64. Shao Dan, "Chinese by Definition: Nationality Law, *Jus Sanguinis*, and State Succession, 1909–1980," *Twentieth-Century China*, 2009, 35(1): 4–28 (quote, p. 18).

65. Paul J. Bolt, *China and Southeast Asia's Ethnic Chinese: State and Diaspora in Contemporary Asia* (Westport, CT: Praeger, 2000) 38–40.

66. Mette Thunø, "Reaching Out and Incorporating Chinese Overseas: The Trans-territorial Scope of the PRC by the End of the 20th Century," *China Quarterly*, Dec 2001, (168): 910–29.

67. Harry Harding, "The Concept of 'Greater China': Themes, Variations and Reservations," *China Quarterly*, Dec 1993, (136): 660–86.

68. Qiu Yuanping, "Overseas Chinese and the Chinese Dream," *Qiushi Journal*, Jul 2014, 6(4), http://english.qstheory.cn/2014-11/15/c_1113079613.htm.

69. Xi Jinping, "Secure a Decisive Victory in Building a Moderately Prosperous Society in All Respects and Strive for the Great Success of Socialism with Chinese Characteristics for a New Era," State Council, 18 Oct 2017, http://www.xinhuanet.com/english/download/Xi_Jinping's_report_at_19th_CPC _National_Congress.pdf.

70. Takashi Suzuki, "China's United Front Work in the Xi Jinping Era—Institutional Developments and Activities," *Journal of Contemporary East Asia Studies*, 2019, 8(1): 83–98.

71. Joshua Kurlantzick, *Charm Offensive: How China's Soft Power Is Transforming the World* (New Haven, CT: Yale University Press, 2007) 77–80.

72. "Overseas Chinese Encouraged to Contribute to Tibet, Xinjiang Development," Xinhua, 7 May 2010, http://www.china-embassy.org/eng/xw/ t693047.htm.

73. "Xi Meets Representatives of Overseas Chinese," *People's Daily*, 28 May 2019, http://www.chinadaily.com.cn/a/201905/28/WS5ced49c9a31048422 60be51f.html.

74. Elena Barabantseva, "Who Are 'Overseas Ethnic Chinese Minorities'? China's Search for Transnational Ethnic Unity," *Modern China*, Jan 2012, 38(1): 78–109.

75. John O'Neill, "China's President Ends U.S. Visit with Yale Speech," *New York Times*, 21 Apr 2006, https://www.nytimes.com/2006/04/21/nyregion/ chinas-president-ends-us-visit-with-yale-speech.html.

76. Devin Stewart, "China's Influence in Japan: Everywhere Yet Nowhere in Particular," CSIS, 23 Jul 2020, https://www.csis.org/analysis/chinas-influence -japan-everywhere-yet-nowhere-particular.

Chapter Eleven. China's Inner Asian Borderlands

1. Austin Ramzy and Chris Buckley, eds., "The Xinjiang Papers; 'Absolutely No Mercy': Leaked Files Expose How China Organized Mass Detentions of Muslims," *New York Times*, 16 Nov 2019, https://www.nytimes.com/ interactive/2019/11/16/world/asia/china-xinjiang-documents.html.

2. Dominic Lieven, *Empire: The Russian Empire and Its Rivals* (New Haven, CT: Yale University Press, 2002) 82–83. Bill Hayton, *The Invention of China* (New Haven, CT: Yale University Press, 2020) 184–214.

3. Peter C. Perdue, "From Turfan to Taiwan: Trade and War on Two Chinese Frontiers," in *Untaming the Frontier in Anthropology, Archaeology, and History*,

ed. Bradley J. Parker and Lars Rodseth (Tempe: University of Arizona Press, 2005) 27–51.

4. Liu Xiaoyuan, "Rediscovery of the Frontier in Recent Chinese History," in William C. Kirby, ed., *The People's Republic of China at 60: An International Assessment* (Cambridge, MA: Harvard Asia Center, 2011) 307.

5. Quoted Joseph W. Esherick, "How the Qing Became China," in Esherick, Hasan Kayalı, and Eric van Young, eds., *Empire to Nation: Historical Perspectives on the Making of the Modern World* (Lanham, MD: Rowman & Littlefield, 2006) 232–33.

6. Michael Clarke, "The Problematic Progress of 'Integration' in the Chinese State's Approach to Xinjiang, 1759–2005," *Asian Ethnicity*, Oct 2007, 8(3): 265–66. Ning Chia, "The Lifanyuan and the Inner Asian Rituals in the Early Qing (1644–1795)," *Late Imperial China*, Jun 1993, 14(1): 60–92. Nicola Di Cosmo, "Qing Colonial Administration in Inner Asia," *International History Review*, Jun 1998, 20(2): 294–95.

7. Esherick, "How the Qing Became China," 229–59. James A. Millward, *Beyond the Pass: Economy, Ethnicity, and Empire in Qing Central Asia, 1759–1864* (Stanford: Stanford University Press, 1998) 233–35, 241–52. C. Patterson Giersch, "'Grieving for Tibet': Conceiving the Modern State in Late-Qing Inner Asia," *China Perspectives*, 2008, 3(75): 4–18. Huhbator Borjigin, "The History and the Political Character of the Name of 'Nei Menggu' (Inner Mongolia)," *Inner Asia*, 2004, (6): 66–68. Cecily McCaffery, "From Chaos to New Order: Rebellion and Ethnic Regulation in Late Qing Inner Mongolia," *Modern China*, 2011, 37(5): 528–61. Mark C. Elliott, "The Limits of Tatary: Manchuria in Imperial and National Geographies," *JAS*, Aug 2000, 59(3): 603–46. Elliott, *The Manchu Way: The Eight Banners and Ethnic Identity in Late Imperial China* (Stanford: Stanford University Press, 2001) 355, 358–59.

8. Thomas S. Mullaney, *Coming to Terms with the Nation: Ethnic Classification in Modern China* (Berkeley: University of California Press, 2011) 25.

9. Esherick, "How the Qing Became China," 243–48. Hayton, *Invention of China*, 187–93.

10. Young-tsu Wong, *Beyond Confucian China: The Rival Discourses of Kang Youwei and Zhang Binglin* (London: Routledge, 2010) 58–59.

11. Constitution of the People's Republic of China, Article 116, http://www.npc.gov.cn/zgrdw/englishnpc/Constitution/2007-11/15/content_1372990.htm.

12. David L. Phillips, "China's Regional Ethnic Autonomy Law: Does It Protect Minority Rights?," Statement to Congressional-Executive Committee on China, 11 Apr 2005, https://www.cecc.gov/sites/chinacommission.house.gov/files/documents/roundtables/2005/CECC%20Roundtable%20Testimony%20-%20David%20Phillips%20-%204.11.05.pdf.

13. Haiting Zhang, "The Laws on the Ethnic Minority Autonomous Regions in China: Legal Norms and Practices," *Loyola University of Chicago International Law Review*, Spring–Summer 2012, 9(2): 249–64.

14. Elliott, "Limits of Tatary," 604–5.

15. Elliott, *The Manchu Way*, 340–50.

16. Elliott, "Limits of Tatary," 617–19. Shelley Rigger, "Voices of Manchu Identity, 1635–1935," in Stevan Harrell, ed., *Cultural Encounters on China's Ethnic Frontiers* (Seattle: University of Washington Press, 1995) 197–98.

17. Prasenjit Duara, "The Imperialism of 'Free Nations': Japan, Manchukuo, and the History of the Present," in Ann Laura Stoler et al., eds., *Imperial Formations* (Santa Fe, NM: School for Advanced Research, 2007) 211–39.

18. Yamamuro Shin'ichi, *Manchuria Under Japanese Domination*, trans. Joshua A. Fogel (Philadelphia: University of Pennsylvania Press, 2006) 235–36.

19. Shao Dan, *Remote Homeland, Recovered Borderland: Manchus, Manchukuo, and Manchuria, 1907–1985* (Honolulu: University of Hawai'i Press, 2011) 210–18, 291–94.

20. Daniel Kane, "Language Death and Language Revivalism: The Case of Manchu," *Central Asiatic Journal*, 1997, 41(2): 231–49.

21. Quoted in Gertrude Roth Li, "State Building Before 1644," *CHC*, IX: 31.

22. Charles R. Bawden, *The Modern History of Mongolia*, 2nd ed. (London: Routledge, 2009) 47.

23. Borjigin, "The History and the Political Character of the Name of 'Nei Menggu,'" 63–64. Liping Wang, "From Masterly Brokers to Compliant Protégés: The Frontier Governance System and the Rise of Ethnic Confrontation in China—Inner Mongolia, 1900–1930," *American Journal of Sociology*, 2015, 120(6): 1641–42.

24. Wang, "From Masterly Brokers," 1650–53.

25. Ibid., 1672–76.

26. Enze Han, "The Dog That Hasn't Barked: Assimilation and Resistance in Inner Mongolia, China," *Asian Ethnicity*, Feb 2011, 12(1): 67–68.

27. Joakim Enwall, "Inter-ethnic Relations in Mongolia and Inner Mongolia," *Asian Ethnicity*, Jun 2010, 11(2): 243.

28. Uradyn Bulag, "Mongolian Ethnicity and Linguistic Anxiety in China," *American Anthropologist*, Dec 2003, 105(4): 754–59.

29. "Herding Mentality: Chinese Mongolians Have Become a Model for Assimilation," *The Economist*, 3 Jun 2017: 35–36.

30. Nasan Bayar, "A Discourse of Civilization/Culture and Nation/Ethnicity from the Perspective of Inner Mongolia, China," *Asian Ethnicity*, 2014, 15(4): 439–57.

31. Anran Wang, "Ethnic Identity, Modern Nationhood, and the Sino-Mongolian Contention Over the Legacy of Chinggis Khan," *Studies in Ethnicity and Nationalism*, 2016, 16(3): 357–77.

32. Han, "The Dog That Hasn't Barked," 70–73.

33. Enze Han, "From Domestic to International: The Politics of Ethnic Identity in Xinjiang and Inner Mongolia," *Nationalities Papers*, Nov 2011, 39(6): 941–62.

34. Bayar, "A Discourse of Civilization/Culture," 449.

35. Han, "The Dog That Hasn't Barked," 67–69.
36. "Successful Practice of Regional Autonomy in Tibet," State Council, Sep 2015, http://english.gov.cn/archive/white_paper/2015/09/06/content_2814 75183815861.htm.
37. Timothy Brook, "Tibet and the Chinese World Empire," in William D. Coleman et al., eds., *Empires and Autonomy Movements in the History of Globalization* (Vancouver: University of British Columbia Press, 2009) 30.
38. Quoted in Pan Yihong, "The Sino-Tibetan Treaties in the Tang Dynasty," *T'uong Pao*, 1992, (78): 146.
39. Timothy Brook, "Chinggisid Rule and the Mongol Great State," in Timothy Brook et al., eds., *Sacred Mandates: Asian International Relations since Chinggis Khan* (Chicago: University of Chicago Press, 2018) 28.
40. George N. Patterson, "China and Tibet: Background to the Revolt," *China Quarterly*, Jan–Mar 1960, (1): 87–102.
41. Zahiruddin Ahmad, *Sino-Tibetan Relations in the Seventeenth Century* (Rome: Istituto Italiano per il Medio ed Estremo Oriente, 1970) 154–58.
42. Brook, "Tibet and the Chinese World Empire," 27–28.
43. Quoted in Tsepon W. D. Shakabpa, *Tibet: A Political History* (New Haven, CT: Yale University Press, 1973) 138.
44. Peter Schwieger, *The Dalai Lama and the Emperor of China: A Political History of the Tibetan Institution of Reincarnation* (New York: Columbia University Press, 2015) 112–45.
45. Luciano Petech, *China and Tibet in the Early 18th Century: History of the Establishment of Chinese Protectorate in Tibet* (Leiden: Brill, 1950) 222–23, 230–39.
46. Peter Hopkirk, *Trespassers on the Roof of the World: The Secret Exploration of Tibet* (New York: Kodansha America, 1995) 159–83.
47. Dahpon David Ho, "The Men Who Would Not Be Amban and the One Who Would: Four Frontline Officials and Qing Tibet Policy, 1905–1911," *Modern China*, Apr 2008 34(2): 225–42.
48. "Convention Between Great Britain, China, and Tibet, Simla (1914)," http://www.tibetjustice.org/materials/treaties/treaties16.html.
49. Alexander Andreyev, *Soviet Russia and Tibet: The Debacle of Secret Diplomacy, 1918–1930s* (Leiden: Brill, 2003) 239–92.
50. Melvyn C. Goldstein, "Tibet and China in the Twentieth Century," in Morris Rossabi, ed., *Governing China's Multiethnic Frontiers* (Seattle: University of Washington Press, 2004) 192–94.
51. Liu Xiaoyuan, *Recast All Under Heaven: Revolution, War, Diplomacy, and Frontier China in the 20th Century* (New York: Continuum, 2010) 156–58.
52. Sulmaan Wasif Khan, *Muslim, Trader, Nomad, Spy: China's Cold War and the People of the Tibetan Borderlands* (Chapel Hill: University of North Carolina Press, 2016) 2, 135.
53. Ma Rong and Jean E. DeBernardi, *Population and Society in Contemporary Tibet* (Hong Kong: HKU, 2011) 55–56.
54. Khan, *Muslim, Trader, Nomad, Spy*, 119–26.

55. Liu Xiaoyuan, *Recast All Under Heaven*, 161–63.
56. Matthew T. Kapstein, "A Thorn in the Dragon's Side: Tibetan Buddhist Culture in China," in Rossabi, ed., *Governing China's Multiethnic Frontiers*, 243–45. Melvyn C. Goldstein, *The Snow Lion and the Dragon: China, Tibet, and the Dalai Lama* (Berkeley: University of California Press, 1997) 102–9.
57. Ma Rong and DeBernardi, *Population and Society*, 43–44.
58. Shale Horowitz and Peng Yu, "Holding China's West: Explaining CCP Strategies of Rule in Tibet and Xinjiang," *Journal of Chinese Political Science*, 2015, (20): 463.
59. Goldstein, "Tibet and China," 207–11.
60. "Historical Witness to Ethnic Equality, Unity and Development in Xinjiang: Implementing the System of Ethnic Regional Autonomy," State Council, 24 Sep 2015, http://www.china.org.cn/government/whitepaper/node_7230328.htm.
61. "Development and Progress in Xinjiang: Foreword," State Council, 21 Sep 2009, http://www.china.org.cn/government/whitepaper/node_7077515 .htm. "Historical Witness to Ethnic Equality, Unity, and Development in Xinjiang," State Council, 24 Sep 2015, http://www.china.org.cn/ government/whitepaper/node_7230328.htm.
62. Dru C. Gladney, "La question Ouïgour: Entre islamisation et ethnicisation," *Annales HSS*, Sep–Dec 2004, (5–6): 1176.
63. Wang Zhenping, "Ideas Concerning Diplomacy and Foreign Policy Under the Tang Emperors Gaozu and Taizong," *Asia Major*, 3rd Series, 2009, 22(1): 257.
64. Bawden, *Modern History of Mongolia*, 1–5, 81–134. James Millward, *Eurasian Crossroads: A History of Xinjiang* (New York: Columbia University Press, 2009) 91–92. Peter C. Perdue, *China Marches West: The Qing Conquest of Central Eurasia* (Cambridge, MA: Harvard University Press, 2010).
65. Quoted in Perdue, *China Marches West*, 283.
66. Laura J. Newby, "The Begs of Xinjiang: Between Two Worlds," *Bulletin of the School of Oriental and African Studies*, 1998, 61(2): 278–81.
67. Joseph F. Fletcher, "Ch'ing Inner Asia ca. 1800," *CHC*, X: 35–106.
68. Millward, *Eurasian Crossroads*, 169–70. Ildikó Bellér-Hann, "Feudal Villains or Just Rulers? The Contestation of Historical Narratives in Eastern Xinjiang," *CAS*, Sep 2012, 31(3): 313–14.
69. Linda Benson, *The Ili Rebellion: The Moslem Challenge to Chinese Authority in Xinjiang, 1944–1949* (Armonk, NY: M. E. Sharpe, 1990) 25–26.
70. Millward, *Eurasian Crossroads*, 180.
71. Benson, *Ili Rebellion*, 39–41.
72. Ibid., 45–46. Millward, *Eurasian Crossroads*, 217–30.
73. "Ethnic Groups in Xinjiang Are Part of Chinese Nation: White Paper," Xinhua, 21 Jul 2019, http://www.xinhuanet.com/english/2019-07/21/c _138244717.htm.

74. "Xinjiang," *The China Story*, Australian Centre on China in the World, 2 Aug 2012, https://www.thechinastory.org/keyword/xinjiang/.

75. Yuchao Zhu and Dongyan Blachford, "'Old Bottle, New Wine'? Xinjiang *Bingtuan* and China's Ethnic Frontier Governance," *Journal of Contemporary China*, 2016, 25(97): 25–40. James Seymour, "Xinjiang's Production and Construction Corps and the Sinification of Eastern Turkestan," *Inner Asia*, 2000, (2).

76. Gardner Bovingdon, "Heteronomy and Its Discontents: 'Minzu Regional Autonomy' in Xinjiang," in Rossabi, ed., *Governing China's Multiethnic Frontiers*, 117–21, 129.

77. Barry Sautman, "Is Xinjiang an Internal Colony?," *Inner Asia*, 2000, (2): 241.

78. Hongyi Harry Lai, "China's Western Development Program: Its Rationale, Implementation, and Prospects," *Modern China*, Oct 2002, 28(4): 432–66. Yueyao Zhao, "Pivot or Periphery? Xinjiang's Regional Development," *Asian Ethnicity*, Sep 2001, 2(2): 203–4.

79. Tsukasa Hadano, "Ten Years After Xinjiang Riots, China Pushes Growth Story," *Nikkei Asian Review*, 5 Jul 2019, https://asia.nikkei.com/Politics/Ten-years-after-Xinjiang-riots-China-pushes-growth-story.

80. Austin Ramzy and Chris Buckley, eds., "The Xinjiang Papers; 'Absolutely No Mercy': Leaked Files Expose How China Organized Mass Detentions of Muslims," *New York Times*, 16 Nov 2019, https://www.nytimes.com/interactive/2019/11/16/world/asia/china-xinjiang-documents.html.

Chapter Twelve. Sinocentrism and the Geopolitics of *Tianxia*

1. "Full text of President Xi's Speech at Opening of Belt and Road Forum," Xinhua, 14 May 2017, http://www.xinhuanet.com/english/2017-05/14/c_136282982.htm. Denghua Zhang, "The Concept of 'Community of Common Destiny' in China's Diplomacy: Meaning, Motives and Implications," *Asia & the Pacific Policy Studies*, 2018, 5(2): 196–207.

2. Nadège Rolland, "China's Vision for a New World Order," NBR, 27 Jan 2020: 49, https://www.nbr.org/publication/chinas-vision-for-a-new-world-order/.

3. Ian Johnson, "How Does China's Imperial Past Shape Its Foreign Policy Today?," *China File*, 15 Mar 2017, http://www.chinafile.com/conversation/how-does-chinas-imperial-past-shape-its-foreign-policy-today.

4. Zhao Tingyang, "A Political Philosophy in Terms of All-Under-Heaven (Tian-xia)," *Diogenes*, Feb 2009, 56(1): 5–18. Feng Zhang, "The Tianxia System: World Order in a Chinese Utopia," *Global Asia*, 2010, 4(4): 108–12.

5. M. Taylor Fravel, *Strong Border, Secure Nation: Cooperation and Conflict in China's Territorial Disputes* (Princeton, NJ: Princeton University Press, 2008) 10–69.

6. Liu Qing, "Liberalism in Contemporary China: Potential and Predicaments," trans. Matthew Galway and Lu Hua, Reading the Chinese Dream, https://

www.readingthechinadream.com/liu-qing-liberalism-in-contemporary
-china.html.

7. Wang Mingming, "All Under Heaven (*Tianxia*): Cosmological Perspectives
and Political Ontologies in Pre-modern China," *HAU Journal of Ethnographic Theory*, 2012, 2(1): 341–43.

8. Ren Xiao, "Traditional Chinese Theory and Practice of Foreign Relations:
A Reassessment," in Zheng Yongnian, ed., *China and International Relations:
The Chinese View and the Contribution of Wang Gungwu* (London: Routledge,
2012) 112. Liu Junping, "The Evolution of *Tianxia* Cosmology and Its
Philosophical Implications," *Frontiers of Philosophy on China*, Dec 2006, 1(4):
517–38.

9. Zhao Tingyang, "Rethinking Empire from a Chinese Concept 'All-Under-
Heaven' (Tian-xia)," *Journal for the Study of Race, Nation and Culture*, 2006,
12(1): 31.

10. Quoted in Howard W. French, *Everything Under the Heavens: How the Past
Helps Shape China's Push for Global Power* (New York: Alfred A. Knopf, 2017),
frontispiece.

11. Qin Yaqing, "Why Is There No Chinese International Relations Theory?,"
International Relations of the Asia-Pacific, Aug 2007, (7): 322.

12. June Teufel Dreyer, "China's Tianxia: Do All Under Heaven Need One Arbiter?," *YaleGlobal Online*, 30 Oct 2014, https://yaleglobal.yale.edu/content/
chinas-tianxia-do-all-under-heaven-need-one-arbiter. John King Fairbank,
"A Preliminary Framework," in Fairbank, ed., *The Chinese World Order: Traditional China's Foreign Relations* (Cambridge, MA: Harvard University Press,
1968) 1–19. More critically, see Zhang Feng, "Re-Thinking the 'Tribute
System': Broadening the Conceptual Horizon of East Asian Politics," *Chinese Journal of International Politics*, Winter 2009, 2(4): 545–74.

13. James A. Millward, *Beyond the Pass: Economy, Ethnicity, and Empire in Qing
Central Asia, 1759–1864* (Stanford, CA: Stanford University Press, 1998)
6–10, 48–49.

14. Thomas J. Barfield, *Perilous Frontier: Nomadic Empires and China, 221 BC
to AD 1757* (London: Basil Blackwell, 1989) 52. See also Peter C. Perdue,
"Nature and Nurture on Imperial China's Frontiers," *Modern Asian Studies*,
2009, 43(1): 257.

15. Liu Xiaoyuan, *Recast All Under Heaven: Revolution, War, Diplomacy, and Frontier China in the 20th Century* (New York: Continuum, 2010) 11.

16. Ibid.

17. Rolland, "China's Vision," 32–33.

18. Joseph Y. S. Cheng, "Convincing the World of China's Tradition to Pursue
Universal Harmony," *Journal of Chinese Political Science*, Jun 2012, 17(2): 165–
85. Xi Jinping, "Carry On the Enduring Spirit of Mao Zedong Thought,"
26 Dec 2013, in Xi Jinping, *The Governance of China*, Vol. 1 (Beijing: Foreign
Languages Press, 2014) 27–37.

19. June Teufel Dreyer, "The 'Tianxia Trope': Will China Change the International System?," *Journal of Contemporary China*, 2015, 24(96): 1016–17.

20. Zhao Tingyang, "A Political Philosophy," 6.

21. Zhao Tingyang, "All-Under-Heaven and Methodological Relationism: An Old Story and New World Peace," in Fred Dallmayr and Zhao Tingyang, eds., *Contemporary Chinese Political Thought: Debates and Perspectives* (Lexington: University of Kentucky Press, 2012) 60. William A. Callahan, "Chinese Visions of World Order: Post-hegemonic or a New Hegemony?," *International Studies Review*, 2008, (10): 752–53.

22. Yan Xuetong, "Xun Zi's Thoughts on International Politics and Their Implications," *Chinese Journal of International Politics*, 2008, (2): 159.

23. Yan Xuetong, "The Shift of the World Centre and Its Impact on the Change of the International System," *East Asia*, 2013, (30): 233.

24. Yan Xuetong, "Xun Zi's Thoughts," 156, 163–65.

25. Callahan, "Chinese Visions of World Order," 750.

26. French, *Everything Under the Heavens*, 263.

27. Rolland, "China's Vision," 36.

28. "Xi Urges Breaking New Ground in Major Country Diplomacy with Chinese Characteristics," Xinhua, 24 Jun 2018, http://www.xinhuanet.com/english/2018-06/24/c_137276269.htm.

29. Wang Yi, "Peaceful Development and the Chinese Dream of National Rejuvenation," *China International Studies*, Jan–Feb 2014, (4): 30.

30. Kristine Lee and Alexander Sullivan, "People's Republic of the United Nations: China's Emerging Revisionism in International Organizations," CNAS, May 2019, https://www.cnas.org/publications/reports/peoples-republic-of-the-united-nations.

31. Philippa Hetherington and Glenda Sluga, "Liberal and Illiberal Internationalisms," *Journal of World History*, Mar 2020, 31(1): 1–9.

32. "RATS ShOS v bor'be s 'tremya zlami,'" Shanghai Cooperation Organization, 11 Feb 2011, http://infoshos.ru/ru/?idn=7678. Michael Clarke, "Xinjiang and the Trans-nationalization of Uyghur Terrorism: Cracks in the 'New Silk Road'?," *Asan Forum*, Feb 2017, http://www.theasanforum.org/xinjiang-and-the-trans-nationalization-of-uyghur-terrorism-cracks-in-the-new-silk-road/

33. Zhao Huasheng, "China's Views and Expectations from the Shanghai Cooperation Organization," *Asian Affairs*, May–Jun 2013, 53(3): 440. Flemming Splidsboel Hansen, "The Shanghai Cooperation Organization," *Asian Survey*, Jul 2008, 39(2): 217–32.

34. Xi Jinping, "Work Together to Build the Silk Road Economic Belt and the 21st-Century Maritime Silk Road," Ministry of Foreign Affairs, 15 May 2017, https://www.fmprc.gov.cn/mfa_eng/wjdt_665385/zyjh_665391/t1465819.shtml.

35. Rolland, "China's Vision," 41–42. Wang Yi, "Creating New Prospects for Advancing China's Major Country Diplomacy Under the Guidance of Xi Jinping Thought on Diplomacy," *Qiushi Journal*, 2019, 11(1), http://english.qstheory.cn/2019-07/09/c_1124517815.htm. "Quick Guide to China's

Diplomatic Levels," *South China Morning Post*, 20 Jan 2016, https://www
.scmp.com/news/china/diplomacy-defence/article/1903455/quick-guide
-chinas-diplomatic-levels.

36. Fravel, *Strong Border*, 126–219.

37. J. J. Singh, *The McMahon Line: A Century of Discord* (New Delhi: Harper-
Collins India, 2019), chapters 17–19. Jin Wu and Steven Lee Myers, "Battle
in the Himalayas," *New York Times*, 18 Jul 2020, https://www.nytimes.com/
interactive/2020/07/18/world/asia/china-india-border-conflict.html.

38. S. C. M. Paine, *Imperial Rivals: China, Russia, and Their Disputed Frontier* (Armonk, NY: M. E. Sharpe, 1996) 9–10.

39. Perdue, *China Marches West*, 161–73. Benjamin Elman, "Ming-Qing Border
Defense, the Inward Turn of Chinese Cartography, and Qing Expansion
in Central Asia in the Eighteenth Century," in Diana Lary, ed., *The Chinese
State at the Borders* (Seattle: University of Washington Press, 2007) 29–56.

40. "Traité d'amitié et de limites entre la Russie et la Chine" (Aigun) and "Traité
additionnel conclu le 2/14 Novembre, 1860, à Pékin, entre Sa Majesté
l'Empereur de Toutes les Russies et Sa Majesté le Bogdo-Khan de Chine"
(Beijing), in *Treaties Between the Empire of China and Foreign Powers: Together
with Regulations for the Conduct of Foreign Trade, Conventions, Agreements, Regulations, etc.* (Shanghai: North China Herald, 1906) 100, 105–12.

41. Ian W. Campbell, "'Our Friendly Rivals': Rethinking the Great Game in
Ya'qub Beg's Kashgaria, 1867–77," *CAS*, 2014, 33(2): 199–214.

42. Thomas E. Ewing, "Revolution on the Chinese Frontier: Outer Mongolia in
1911," *Journal of Asian History*, 1978, 12(2): 102–5.

43. Liu Xiaoyuan, *Reins of Liberation: An Entangled History of Mongolian Independence, Chinese Territoriality, and Great Power Hegemony, 1911–1950* (Washington, DC: Woodrow Wilson Center, 2006) 4–17, 36–44.

44. Ewing, "Revolution on the Chinese Frontier," 111–12.

45. James Palmer, *The Bloody White Baron: The Extraordinary Story of the Russian
Nobleman Who Became the Last Khan of Mongolia* (New York: Basic Books,
2009) 196–209.

46. Liu Xiaoyuan, *Reins of Liberation*, 45–77.

47. William A. Callahan, "National Insecurities: Humiliation, Salvation, and
Chinese Nationalism," *Alternatives*, 2004, 29(2): 209–10.

48. Quoted in Zhihua Shen and Julia Lovell, "Undesired Outcomes: China's
Approach to Border Disputes During the Early Cold War," *Cold War History*, 2015, 15(1): 96.

49. Shen and Lovell, "Undesired Outcomes," 101–8.

50. Fravel, *Strong Border*, 201–17.

51. Neville Maxwell, "How the Sino-Russian Boundary Conflict Was Finally
Settled: From Nerchinsk 1689 to Vladivostok 2005 via Zhenbao Island
1969," *Critical Asian Studies*, 2007, 39(2): 248.

52. Dong Wang, "The Discourse of Unequal Treaties in Modern China," *Pacific
Affairs*, Fall 2003, 76(3): 399–425.

53. "V MID Kitaya otsenili slova Lavrova o mife o 'kitayskoy ugroze,'" RIA-Novosti, 7 Jul 2019, https://ria.ru/20190717/1556603999.html.

54. Assel Bitabarova, "Contested Views of Contested Territories: How Tajik Society Views the Tajik-Chinese Border Settlement," *Eurasia Border Review*, 2015, 6(1): 63–81.

55. Bruce Pannier, "Central Asian Land and China," RFE/RL, 2 May 2016, https://www.rferl.org/a/central-asian-land-and-china/27711366.html.

56. Carla Freeman and Drew Thompson, "China on the Edge: China's Border Provinces and Chinese Security Policy," CFTNI/Johns Hopkins University, Apr 2011: 16.

57. Mingjiang Li, "From Look-West to Act-West: Xinjiang's Role in China-Central Asian Relations," *Journal of Contemporary China*, 2016, 25(100): 523–24.

58. Roman Vakulchuk and Indra Overland, "China's Belt and Road Initiative through the Lens of Central Asia," in Fanny M. Cheung and Ying-yi Hong, eds., *Regional Connection Under the Belt and Road Initiative: The Prospects for Economic and Financial Cooperation* (London: Routledge, 2019) 115–33.

59. Steven Parham, "The Bridge That Divides: Local Perceptions of the Connected State in the Kyrgyzstan-Tajikistan-China Borderlands," *CAS*, 2016, 35(3): 351–68.

60. Wang Jisi, "'Marching Westwards': The Rebalancing of China's Geostrategy," in Shao Binhong, ed., *The World in 2020 According to China: Chinese Foreign Policy Elites Discuss Emerging Trends in International Politics* (Leiden: Brill, 2014) 129–36.

61. Peter Hartcher, "China's Global Ambitions: Are There Lessons to Be Learnt from Tibet?," *Sydney Morning Herald*, 21 Aug 2017.

62. Sébastien Peyrouse, "Discussing China: Sinophilia and Sinophobia in Central Asia," *Journal of Eurasian Studies*, 2016, (7): 14–23.

63. Jonathan Hillman, *The Emperor's New Road: China and the Project of the Century* (New Haven, CT: Yale University Press, 2020) 17–38.

64. Ibid., 209–10.

65. "Competing Visions," CSIS Reconnecting Asia, https://reconnectingasia .csis.org/analysis/competing-visions/.

66. Hillman, *Emperor's New Road*, 7. Nadège Rolland, "China's Eurasian Century? Political and Strategic Implications of the Belt and Road Initiative," NBR, 23 May 2017, https://www.nbr.org/publication/chinas-eurasian -century-political-and-strategic-implications-of-the-belt-and-road -initiative/. Rafaello Pantucci and Sarah Lain, "China's Eurasian Pivot: The Silk Road Economic Belt," *Whitehall Papers*, 2016, 88(1): 1–98. William A. Callahan, "China's 'Asia Dream': The Belt and Road Initiative and the New Regional Order," *Asian Journal of Comparative Politics*, 2016: 1–18.

67. "President Xi Jinping Delivers Important Speech."

68. "Vision and Actions on Jointly Building Silk Road Economic Belt and 21st-Century Maritime Silk Road," Ministry of Foreign Affairs and Ministry of

Commerce, 28 Mar 2015, https://reconasia-production.s3.amazonaws.com/media/filer_public/e0/22/e0228017-7463-46fc-9094-0465a6f1ca23/vision_and_actions_on_jointly_building_silk_road_economic_belt_and_21st-century_maritime_silk_road.pdf.

69. Hillman, *Emperor's New Road*, 209–11.

70. Ruan Zongze, "What Kind of Neighborhood Will China Build?," *China International Studies*, Mar–Apr 2014, (45): 27. Xi Jinping, "Work Together."

71. Jacob Stokes, "China's Periphery Diplomacy: Implications for Peace and Security in Asia," USIP, May 2020, https://www.usip.org/sites/default/files/2020-05/20200520-sr_467-chinas_periphery_diplomacy_implications_for_peace_and_security_in_asia-sr.pdf.

72. "Visions and Actions."

73. Andrea Brinza, "China's Continent-Spanning Trains Are Running Half-Empty," *Foreign Policy*, 5 Jun 2017, http://foreignpolicy.com/2017/06/05/chinas-continent-spanning-trains-are-running-half-empty-one-belt-one-road-bri/.

74. Maximillian Hess, "Central Asian Gas Exports to China: Beijing's Latest Bargaining Chip?," FPRI, 16 Jun 2020, https://www.fpri.org/article/2020/06/central-asian-gas-exports-to-china-beijings-latest-bargaining-chip/.

75. Deborah Brautigam and Meg Rithmire, "The Chinese 'Debt Trap' Is a Myth," *The Atlantic*, 6 Feb 2021, https://www.theatlantic.com/international/archive/2021/02/china-debt-trap-diplomacy/617953/.

76. Joel Wuthnow, "Chinese Perspectives on the Belt and Road Initiative: Strategic Rationales, Risks, and Implications," Institute for National Strategic Studies, Oct 2017, https://inss.ndu.edu/Portals/68/Documents/stratperspective/china/ChinaPerspectives-12.pdf.

77. Bradley Jardine, "Why Are There Anti-China Protests in Central Asia?," *Washington Post*, 16 Oct 2019, https://www.washingtonpost.com/politics/2019/10/16/why-are-there-anti-china-protests-central-asia/.

78. Gerry Shih, "In Central Asia's Forbidding Highlands, a Quiet Newcomer: Chinese Troops," *Washington Post*, 18 Feb 2019, https://www.washingtonpost.com/world/asia_pacific/in-central-asias-forbidding-highlands-a-quiet-newcomer-chinese-troops/2019/02/18/. Nadège Rolland, ed., "Securing the Belt and Road Initiative: China's Evolving Military Engagement Along the Silk Roads," NBR, Sep 2019, https://www.nbr.org/wp-content/uploads/pdfs/publications/sr80_securing_the_belt_and_road_sep2019.pdf.

79. Liu Zhenmin, "Insisting on Win-Win Cooperation and Forging the Asian Community of Common Destiny Together," *China International Studies*, Mar–Apr 2014, (45): 19.

80. Umida Hashimova, "Before and Beyond 5G: Central Asia's Huawei Connections," *The Diplomat*, 19 Feb 2020, https://thediplomat.com/2020/02/before-and-beyond-5g-central-asias-huawei-connections/.

81. Nadège Rolland, "Mapping the Footprint of Belt and Road Influence Operations," *Sinopsis*, 12 Aug 2019, https://sinopsis.cz/en/rolland-bri-influence-operations/.

82. Sergey Markedonov, "Ne tol'ko Poyas i Put.' Chego zhdut drug ot druga Kitay i Yuzhnyy Kavkaz?," 31 Oct 2019, Carnegie Moscow Center, https://carnegie.ru/commentary/80239.

83. Jane Nakano and William Li, "China Launches the Polar Silk Road," CSIS, 2 Feb 2018, https://www.csis.org/analysis/china-launches-polar-silk-road.

84. James Kynge and Jonathan Wheatley, "China Pulls Back from the World: Rethinking Xi's 'Project of the Century,'" *Financial Times*, 11 Dec 2020, https://www.ft.com/content/d9bd8059-d05c-4e6f-968b-1672241ec1f6.

Conclusion: A World Safe for Empire?

1. Heather A. Conley, Jonathan Hillman, and Matthew Melino, "The Western Balkans with Chinese Characteristics," CSIS, 30 Jul 2019, https://www.csis.org/analysis/western-balkans-chinese-characteristics.

2. Farnaz Fassihi and Steven Lee Myers, "Defying U.S., China and Iran Near Trade and Military Partnership," *New York Times*, 11 Jul 2020, https://www.nytimes.com/2020/07/11/world/asia/china-iran-trade-military-deal.html. Bill Hayton, "China's Pressure Costs Vietnam $1 Billion in the South China Sea," *The Diplomat*, 22 Jul 2020, https://thediplomat.com/2020/07/chinas-pressure-costs-vietnam-1-billion-in-the-south-china-sea/.

3. Jeffrey Mankoff, "Don't Forget the Historical Context of Russo-Turkish Competition," *War on the Rocks*, 7 Apr 2020, https://warontherocks.com/2020/04/dont-forget-the-historical-context-of-russo-turkish-competition/.

4. Wang Xiyue, "China Won't Rescue Iran," *Foreign Policy*, 18 Dec 2020, https://foreignpolicy.com/2020/12/18/china-wont-rescue-iran/. Strobe Talbott and Maggie Tennis, "The Only Winner of the US-Iran Showdown Is Russia," Brookings, 9 Jan 2020, https://www.brookings.edu/blog/order-from-chaos/2020/01/09/the-only-winner-of-the-us-iran-showdown-is-russia/.

5. Ruth Deyremond, "The Uses of Sovereignty in Twenty-First-Century Russian Foreign Policy," *EAS*, 2016, 68(6): 957–84.

6. Stephen M. Walt, *The Hell of Good Intentions: America's Foreign Policy Elite and the Decline of U.S. Primacy* (New York: Farrar, Straus and Giroux, 2018) 21–52.

7. Fiona Hill and Omer Taspinar, "Turkey and Russia: Axis of the Excluded?," *Survival*, 2006, 48(1): 81–92. See also Jamsheed K. Choksy and Carol E. B. Choksy, "China and Russia Have Iran's Back," *Foreign Affairs*, 17 Nov 2020, https://www.foreignaffairs.com/articles/united-states/2020-11-17/china-and-russia-have-irans-back.

8. Ishaan Tharoor, "The Execution of a Former Turkish Leader That Still Haunts Erdogan," *Washington Post*, 30 Jul 2016, https://www.washingtonpost.com/world/the-execution-of-a-former-turkish-leader-that-still-haunts-erdogan/2016/07/29/4772c256-54b4-11e6-994c-4e3140414f34_story.html.

9. Timothy Frye et al., "Is Putin's Popularity Real?," *Post-Soviet Affairs*, 2017, 33(1): 1–15.

10. Hans-Ulrich Wehler, "Bismarck's Imperialism 1862–1890," *Past and Present*, Aug 1970, (48): 119–55.
11. Miriam Berger, "The Divisive Legacy of Iran's Royal Family," *Washington Post*, 16 Jan 2020, https://www.washingtonpost.com/world/2020/01/16/divisive-legacy-irans-royal-family.

Index

Page numbers followed by letter m *refer to maps.*

Abbas I (Safavid ruler), 171, 195, 196
Abdali Pashtuns, rebellion of, 163
Abdülhamid II (Ottoman Sultan), 82, 86, 94, 95, 112–13; and Sunni caliphate, 133, 134
Abdullah, Abdullah, 203
Abdülmecid I (Ottoman Sultan), 111, 112
Abkhazia: Russian occupation of, 19, 40; struggle for independence from Georgia, 66, 67, 68; Turkey's approach to conflict in, 97; after World War I, 65
Absolute Guardianship, doctrine of, 161, 163; opposition to, 176–77, 179
Achaemenid dynasty: legacy of, Mohammad Reza Shah's appeal to, 146, 147; and origins of Iran, 155
Adygea, Republic of, 17m, 45, 52, 57
Aegean islands, Turkish claims on, 126, 127
Afghanistan: British policies in, 201; and China, security mechanism with, 266; Greater Iran concept and, 192, 200; imperial rivalries in, 9, 270; Iranian imperial heritage and, 194; Iran's involvement in, 149, 155, 191, 199,

200–204, 205; Persian component of identity of, 158, 160, 202; Shi'as in, 168; Soviet-backed government in, 202; Soviet invasion of, 191, 199; Taliban in, 203; U.S.-led invasion of, and opportunities for Iran, 191; U.S. presence in, opposition to, 203
Afsharid dynasty: capital of, 170; and Persianate world, 150
Ahmadinejad, Mahmoud, 160, 204
Ahund, Osman, 183–84
Aigun, Treaty of, 259, 261
Ajaria: special status after World War I, 65; Turkey's claims regarding, 126, 138
Akçura, Yusuf, 90, 94, 101, 103
Akhbari school of Shi'ism, 179
Akhondzadeh (Akhundov), Mirza Fath Ali, 157
AKP (Justice and Development Party), Turkey: antimigrant backlash and, 100; emergence of, 99; foreign policy vision of, 123–28, 133, 135–36; and imperial articulation of nation, 91, 92; Islam and nationalism embraced by, 91–92, 105; and Kurdish borderlands, strategy for integrating, 86, 109, 113,

AKP (*continued*)
  115, 116–17, 122; Middle East policies of, 133, 135–37; minority policies
  of, 96; Naqshbandi Sufi order and,
  97; and new Turkic-centric order,
  vision of, 137, 142, 143; and Ottoman
  revivalism, 82, 85–86, 90–91, 113,
  123, 124, 142, 143; post-Ottoman vision of, dilemma in, 101, 142; protests
  against, 82; and Turkic organizations
  in Eurasia and Middle East, 103–4;
  on Turkish identity, 85, 90; uneasy
  balance of democracy and Islamism
  in, 142; uniform of, 132
Albania: in Ottoman Empire, 128; Turkey's relations with, 131–32
Aleksandra Fedorovna (Empress of Russia), 28
Aleksey Mikhailovich (Tsar of Muscovy),
  33
Aleppo: in Ottoman Empire, 133; Turkish claims on, 126, 135
Alevis, Turkish, 93, 101, 110, 117; Soviet
  influence among, 115
Alexander I (Emperor of Russia), 1, 64
Alexander III (Emperor of Russia), 24,
  27, 65
Alexandretta (Hatay), Turkish claims on,
  126, 135
Aliyev, Heydar, 104
Allahverdi Khan (Safavid governor),
  196
All Under Heaven. See *tianxia*, concept
  of
Alqas Mirza, 196
Altai, Republic of, 45
Altishahr ("six cities"), 245, 246
Amanat, Abbas, 178
Amasya, Peace of, 110, 138, 195
Anatolia, eastern: Armenian minor-
  ity in, 112; ethnic cleansing in, 65,
  102, 112, 113, 121; in Greater Iran,
  189; interimperial "shatter zone" in,
  9; Islamization in, 92; Kurds of, 84,

  110; "politics of difference" in, 111,
  114–15; as postimperial borderland,
  84, 121; Russian objectives in, 62; in
  Turkish Republic, efforts to integrate,
  121–22. See also Caucasus; Kurds
Anderson, Benedict, 10
Andrussovo, Peace of, 32, 33
Aneran (Aneranshahr), concept of, 193
Anglo-Persian Oil Company, 178
Aqa Mohammad Shah (Qajar ruler), 175,
  195, 197, 200
Aq Qoyunlu dynasty, 175
Arabestan. See Khuzestan
Arabian Peninsula: Iran's borderlands in,
  178–80; Islam in, vs. Turkish Islam,
  105; Ottoman legacy in, 124, 133,
  134. See also specific countries
Arab Spring: in Syria, suppression of,
  120; Turkey's response to, 86, 100,
  124, 136–37
Aral Sea, 71
Ardashir I Papagan (Sasanian ruler), 156
ariya (term), 155–56
Armenia: in CSTO, 76; in EAEU, 74;
  Iran's support for, 177, 194, 195, 197;
  Nagorno-Karabakh conflict and, 66,
  67, 76, 138; in Ottoman Empire, 138;
  revolution of 2018 in, 63; in Russian
  Empire, 64, 197; Russia's support for,
  67, 140, 142; territorial expansion of,
  Soviet policies on, 62; territorialization of ethnicity in, 64, 66; Turkey's
  relations with, 140; after World War
  I, 65–66
Armenians: and Kurds, conflicts between, 111, 112; massacres of, 65, 94,
  96, 112, 113, 138; in Turkey, 96
Asian Infrastructure Investment Bank
  (AIIB), 256
al-Assad, Bashar, 109; Hezbollah's support for, 166; Russian support for,
  137; suppression of Arab Spring
  uprisings by, 120
al-Assad, Hafez, 118

Astrakhan khanate, Russian conquest of, 25, 46
Atabaki, Touraj, 177
Atabat, Shi'ite center in, 163, 179, 273
Atatürk (Mustafa Kemal), 82–83; adoption of one-party rule, 13, 102; civic nation envisioned by, 89; conservative opposition to, 91, 97–98, 106; foreign policy of, 84; and Kurdish tribal elites, 113, 115; vs. pan-Turkic organizations, 102; secularization under, 83, 85, 97; and territorial integrity of Republic, 124, 125, 138–39; threat of Kurdish separatism and, 13, 108, 113–14, 181; on Turkish identity, 83, 89, 95–96
Atsız, Nihal, 102, 103
Austria-Hungary, imperial legacy and, 11
authoritarianism: postimperial states and, 5, 275; struggle to assimilate borderlands and, 13–14, 45
Avesta, 156, 157, 192
Axworthy, Michael, 154
Azerbaijan, Iranian, 174–78; historical importance of, 170, 174–75; opposition to Doctrine of Absolute Guardianship, 176–77; Qajar rule in, 172, 175; and Republic of Azerbaijan, 175, 176, 177, 187, 195, 198–99; Russian and Ottoman influences in, 175; Soviet claims on, 61, 66, 176; volatility in, 169–70, 171, 176–77; during World War I, 172, 180
Azerbaijan, Republic of: closure of Soviet-Iranian border and, 197; cross-border linkages with Iranian Azerbaijan, 175, 176, 177, 187, 195, 198–99; Iran's relations with, 195, 197–99; Israel's relations with, 177; Nagorno-Karabakh conflict and, 66, 67, 76, 138; Persian language in, 158; in Russian Empire, 64, 197; Russian influence in, 55, 66, 142; Turkey's relations with, 12, 103, 104, 137,

138, 139, 140, 142; Western energy companies in, 67
Azeris: in Iran's ruling elite, 9, 170, 174; Islamic Revolution and, 154, 174; separatist movements of, 10, 138, 149, 174, 175
al-Azm family (Damascus), 133

Babacan, Ali, 140
Badr Organization (Iraq), 164, 168
Bahrain: Greater Iran concept and, 189, 192; Hezbollah-style militias in, 166
Bakhtiyaris, in Iran, 171, 173, 174, 178
Bakiyev, Kurmanbek, 75
Baku-Tbilisi-Ceyhan (BTC) oil pipeline, 67, 139, 141
Baku-Tbilisi-Erzurum gas pipeline, 67
Balkans: Chinese investment in, 267, 270; Christian nationalist movements in, 39, 93, 94, 96, 129; imperial rivalries in, 9, 270; Islamization of, 92; Muslim refugees from, 93, 96–97, 129; in Ottoman Empire, 39, 92, 128–29; post-Ottoman, nation-building projects in, 106; Russian expansion in, 38–39, 61; Russo-Turkish tensions over, 270; strategic competition between EU/NATO and Russia in, 132, 141; Turkey's interests/influence in, 85, 91, 99, 105–6, 128–32, 141–42. *See also specific countries*
Balkan Wars (1912–13), 95, 96
Balkh, Iranian control over, 200, 202
Balochistan, Pakistan, 185
Baltic states: in Russian Empire, 61; separatist movements in, 29, 36
Baluch: in Iranian borderlands, 170, 173, 174, 185, 200; Islamic Revolution and, 154
Baluchistan, Iran, 185–87; nationalist movement in, 173; in Qajar era, 185–86, 201; volatility in, 169, 171, 185–86, 187
Bandera, Stepan, 35

Banner system, in Qing China, 217, 221, 236

Banu K'ab tribal confederacy, 178, 179

Banu Tarf tribal confederacy, 178, 179

Barkey, Karen, 7

Barzani, Masoud, 118, 119, 120

Barzani, Mustafa, 117, 118, 182

Basayev, Shamil, 55, 56

Bashkir revolts, 47

Bashkortostan, 45, 51

Bashneft oil company, 51

Basmachi rebellion, 70

Basra province, Iraq, 179

Batumi, Turkish claims on, 126, 138, 139–40

Beijing, Treaty of, 259, 261

Bektashis, 92, 97

Belarus: contested identity of, 19, 36; in CSTO, 76; in EAEU, 74; East Slav unity and, 19, 31, 36; Polish-Lithuanian partitions and, 33; in Russian Empire, 33, 34; in Soviet Union, 34, 35–36; statehood of, 36; as successor state to Kyivan Rus, 31–32; ties with Russia, 24–25, 36–37, 61

Belarusian language, restrictions on use of, 36

Belt and Road Initiative (BRI), China, 14, 68, 78, 208, 251, 263–68; constraints on, 268; EAEU compared to, 75; Greater Eurasia initiative and, 76, 79; investments associated with, 265–66; lack of democratic accountability in, 266, 267; and new regional order, pursuit of, 211–12, 252–53, 263–64, 267–68, 272; security role of, 266, 267; *tianxia* paradigm and, 253, 267–68; UN's Millennium Development Goals and, 256

Bender, Moldova, 1–2; Russian peacekeeping force in, 1, 2, 4; as transition zone, 15

Bhutan, China's territorial disputes with, 258, 263

Bismarck, Otto von, 11

Bitlisi, Idris-i, 111

Blue Homeland, Turkey's concept of, 127

Bolsheviks, minority policies of, 28, 47. *See also* Soviet Union

borderlands: Chinese, 210–11, 231–50; Iranian, 150, 167, 169–88; Russian, 34, 44–52, 58–59; Turkish, 84, 86, 107–22; volatility of, 11, 13–14. *See also specific regions*

Bosnia, Turkey's relations with, 131, 132

Bosnian War: refugees from, 127, 129; Turkey's involvement in, 106, 129, 130–31

Brest, Union of, 32

Brezhnev, Leonid, 35

Britain: departure from EU, 11; Eurasian postimperial states compared to, 3–4, 11; and Hong Kong, 4, 213; and Inner Asia, 233; and Khorasan, 200–201; and Khuzestan, 178

British India, Tibet and, 242–43

Brook, Timothy, 241

Bukhara, Emirate of, 69, 70, 183, 194, 201

Bulgaria: independence movement in, 38–39; Muslim refugees from, 129; in Ottoman Empire, 128; Turkey's policies in, 105

Burbank, Jane, 8

Burma, relations with China, 261

Bush, George W., 37

Çakmak, Fevzi, 114

Candar, Cengiz, 126

Catherine II (Empress of Russia): policies in Georgia, 64, 197; policies in Ukraine, 33

Caucasus: China's engagement in, 76, 267; elites in, post-Soviet heritage and, 63, 77–78; imperial rivalries in, 9, 63, 64, 77, 138, 191, 270; Iranian cultural influence in, 200; Iranic languages spoken in, 158; Iran's engagement in, 150, 170, 190, 194–99, 205; Kurdish population in, 110; Ottoman Empire and, 93, 96–97, 137, 138, 196–97; pan-Turkic propaganda in, 102; during Russian Civil War, 54; Russian conquests in, 196, 197, 201; Russo-Iranian cooperation in, 205; Russo-Turkish competition in, 138–41, 270; Safavid rule in, 171, 195–96; Turkey's interests/influence in, 91, 98, 99, 103, 105, 137–41. *See also* Anatolia, eastern; North Caucasus; South Caucasus; *specific countries*

Caucasus Cooperation and Stability Pact, 140

Caucasus Emirate, 56

Çavuşoğlu, Mevlut, 141

CCP. *See* Chinese Communist Party

Cem, İsmail, 126

Central Asia: China's dominant economic position in, 68, 72, 76, 78–79, 250, 263, 266, 270; China's engagement in, 78, 208, 211, 252, 262, 265, 266, 270; cotton production in, 69, 71; elites in, Soviet heritage and, 63, 77–78; Eurasian integration schemes and, 73–76; Greater Iran and, 189; imperial rivalries in, 9, 63, 77, 246, 270; Iran's involvement in, 150, 190, 191, 199–204, 205; post-Soviet states in, 71–72; in Russian Empire, 47, 61, 68–70, 183, 201, 259; Russia's interests/influence in, 20–21, 46, 60, 72–73, 77–78, 270; Soviet rule in, 70–71; Turkey's interests/influence in, 78, 91, 98, 99, 103, 106, 139; U.S. forces deployed in, 72, 75–76. *See also specific countries*

Cevdet Paşa, Ahmed, 93

Chabahar port, Iran, 186; connection to Afghanistan, 203, 204

Charles XII (King of Sweden), 1

Chechnya, 17*m*, 45, 52; declaration of independence, 55–56; imperial forms of rule in, 20; Iran's relations with, 199; Islamist influences in, 56, 57; in North Caucasus Imamate, 53; and Putin's rise and legitimation of power, 13, 56; refugees from, in Turkey, 127; resistance to Russian rule, 45, 51, 52; in Russian Empire, 197; Russia's policies regarding, 8, 20, 45, 56, 57–58, 59, 275; subsidies for reconstruction of, 56, 57; Turkey's approach to conflict in, 97, 140–41; wars in, 13, 20, 45, 55–56, 66

Chiang Kai-shek, 221

China: autonomous regions in, 234–35; Belt and Road Initiative (BRI) of, 14, 68, 78, 208, 211–12, 251, 252–53, 263–68; "century of humiliation" narrative, 209, 211; civilizational distinctiveness of, belief in, 6, 213; classic imperial model and, 263; and Community of Common Destiny, 212, 251, 256, 257, 265, 267; Cultural Revolution in, frontier regions during, 224, 238, 244, 248, 250; exclusion from current world order, 5; foreign policy of, 251–52; as global power, emergence of, 252–53, 268; Greater Eurasia initiative and, 76–77; growing economic and military might of, 270–71; imperial legacy and, 2, 3, 8, 208–9, 267, 269–75; Inner Asian borderlands of, 210–11, 231–50; and international cooperation, alternative vision of, 212, 215, 251–52, 255, 256–57; Japanese invasion of, 236; nation-building in, 214, 215, 219–20; and new regional order, aspirations regarding, 123, 205, 211–12, 220, 252–53, 257, 263–64, 267–68; and overseas Chinese *(huaqiao huaren)*, mobilization of, 12–13, 215, 226–30; Persian language in, 158;

China (*continued*)
and "politics of difference," 214,
221; revisionism of, 5–6; and Russia,
boundary negotiations with, 211,
258–59, 261, 262; and Russia, changing power balance between, 262;
and Russia, strategic rapprochement
with, 72, 78, 261, 272; security forces
in neighboring states, 72, 266; as
territorially bounded state, 252, 258;
tianxia concept and, 212, 213, 214,
251, 253–57; and Turkey, strategic
cooperation with, 104; and U.S.,
competition with, 274; and "win-win"
cooperation, rhetoric of, 209, 212,
264; in World Trade Organization,
5. *See also* People's Republic of China
(PRC); Republic of China (ROC);
specific dynasties and regions
Chinese Communist Party (CCP): challenges to, and outward pressures, 274;
Confucian ideals embraced by, 212,
220, 224, 252, 274; Han-centrism of,
222, 224, 225, 235; minority policies
of, 221–25, 234; post-Tiananmen
nationalism of, 224; Qing legacy
embraced by, 10–11
Chinese identity: ambiguous framing of,
227; concept of *zhonghua minzu* and,
12, 214, 219, 225, 226–27; Confucian
culture and, 213–14, 215, 220; Han-
centric dimension of, 210, 214–15,
218, 220, 225; imperial elements in,
215, 226, 230, 249; state as arbiter
of, 225; territorial conception of,
231; *xuetong zhuyi* (principle of blood
lineage) and, 227–28
Chinggis Khan, 238; in Chinese national
history, 239
CHP (Republican People's Party),
Turkey, 97, 102; threat of Kurdish
separatism and, 113–14
Christians: in Islamic Republic of Iran,
174; in Ottoman Empire, nationalist

movements of, 39, 93, 94, 96, 129;
Ottoman levy of children (*devşirme*),
92
Chubais, Anatoly, 61
CIS (Commonwealth of Independent
States), 73
civilizational distinctiveness: of China, 6,
213; of Iran, 6, 148, 160; of postimpe-
rial Eurasian states, claims regarding,
6, 271, 275; of Russia, 6, 40, 41–42; of
Turkey, 6, 99
Cold War: imperial legacies disguised by,
269–70; Soviet domination of Eastern
Europe in, 39; Turkey during, 134
Collective Security Treaty Organization
(CSTO), 72, 75–76
Committee of Union and Progress,
Turkey. *See* CUP
Commonwealth of Independent States
(CIS), 73
Community of Common Destiny, China
and, 212, 251, 256, 257, 265, 267
compatriots: concept of, imperial legacy
and, 25, 40, 42; Russian irredentism
and claims of supporting, 12, 40;
Russia's demands for loyalty of, 19;
Turkish references to idea of,
90–91
Confucian culture/ideals: and ap-
proaches to "barbarians," 215–16,
219; as basis for unification, 214;
CCP's/PRC's embrace of, 212, 215,
220, 224, 252, 255, 274; and Chinese
identity, 213–14, 215, 220; and new
international norms, calls for, 256;
and political legitimacy, 213–14;
spread in Central Asia, 78; and *tianxia*
concept, 213, 214, 251, 255
Cooper, Frederick, 8
Cooperation Council of Turkic-
Speaking States (*Türkkon*), 103
Cossacks: Don, 34; Pugachev uprising,
47; during Russian Civil War, 54;
Zaporozhian, 32

Covid-19 pandemic, 104, 268

Crimean Peninsula: as ethnic republic, 44; ethnic Russian majority in, 37; Muslim refugees from, 93; pan-Turkic propaganda in, 102; Russian conquest in 1780s, 138

Crimean Peninsula, Russia's annexation of, 18; justifications used for, 18, 31, 37, 40; popular support for, 273–74; Putin's popularity boost following, 43; Turkey's response to, 104

Crimean Tatars: diaspora of, 104; Turkish solidarity with, 106

Crimean War, 18, 27

CSTO (Collective Security Treaty Organization), 72, 75–76

Cultural Revolution, China's, frontier regions during, 224, 238, 244, 248, 250

CUP (Committee of Union and Progress), Turkey, 82; and massacre of Ottoman Armenians, 138; and pan-Turkic propaganda, 102, 134; and Turkish nationalism, 95

Cyprus: northern, Turkish invasion of, 135; Turkey's territorial disputes with, 126, 131; Turkish ethnonationalism and crisis over, 103

Cyrus the Great (Achaemenid ruler), 146, 147, 160

Dagestan, 17m, 45, 52; Chechen invasion of, 56; Iranian policies regarding, 199; in North Caucasus Imamate, 53; purges of local elites in, 51; in Russian Empire, 64, 197; Safavid influence in, 196

Dalai Lama, 240; flight to India, 243, 261; Panchen Lama as alternative to, 244; Qing dynasty and, 241, 242; as Tibet's spiritual leader, 229, 240

Damad, Mir, 163

Damansky (Zhenbao) Island, 261

Danilevsky, Nikolay, 38

Darius I (Achaemenid ruler), 155

Davutoğlu, Ahmet, 86; on Arab Spring, 100; Balkan pivot of, 130–31; foreign policy vision of, 123, 124, 125, 126–28, 130–31, 135–36; on Islam and Turkish identity, 99–100; on Kurdish-Turkish relations, 109, 119, 122; Middle East policies of, 133, 137; post-Ottoman vision of, 101, 142; speech in Sarajevo, 91, 106; on *tarihdaşlık*, 90; on Turkey's civilizational identity, 99

Dawa Party (Iraq), 164

Demirel, Süleyman, 91, 103

Demirtaş, Selahattin, 116

Democratic Union Party (PYD), in northern Syria, 120–21

Democrat Party (DP), Turkey, 115

Deng Xiaoping: and geopolitics of *tianxia*, 255; and Gorbachev, border agreements with, 261, 262; and Han-centrism, 224

dervish orders: in Iran, 162; in Ottoman Empire, 92. *See also* Sufi orders

Dink, Hrant, 96

Diyanet (Directorate of Spiritual Affairs), Turkey, 97; outreach using, 130, 131

Diyarbakır: Kurdistan *eyalet* centered on, 112; in Ottoman Empire, 110–11

Dodon, Igor, 132

Donbas, Ukraine, 34, 38

Don Cossacks, 34

DP (Democrat Party), Turkey, 115

Dreyer, June, 224

Dudayev, Dzhokhar, 55

Dugin, Aleksandr, 36, 39, 42, 74

Dungans (Hui), in Xinjiang, 245, 246

Durrani, Ahmad Shah, 200

EAEU. *See* Eurasian Economic Union (EAEU)

East Slavs: belief in unity of, 19, 31, 36, 41; religion and identity of, 25, 32; in Russian Empire, 23

East Turkestan: Ili Revolt in, 247, 248;
imperial legacy and, 13; Kashgar-
based Islamic emirate in, 246; Turkey's interest in, 85. *See also* Xinjiang
East Turkestan Republic (ETR), efforts
to create, 247
education: and Chinese influence in
Central Asia, 78; and Iranian influence in Afghanistan and Tajikistan,
204; and Russification, 26, 27, 29, 51
Eisenstein, Sergey, 29
Elchibey, Abulfaz, 55, 177, 198
Elliott, Mark, 225
empire: as category of analysis, 6–7;
nation-building within, challenges
of, 10; and "politics of difference," 8;
teleological view of, 6. *See also* imperial legacy
empires, Eurasian: boundaries of, 9;
collapse of, communal violence accompanying, 10; minority groups in,
9–10; new age of, 2, 15; ruling dynasties in, 9. *See also* postimperial states,
Eurasian
Enver Paşa, İsmail, 95, 138, 184
Erbakan, Necmettin, 98, 99, 134
Erdoğan, Recep Tayyip: Balkan policies
of, 131, 132; Caucasus policies of,
139, 140; foreign policy under, 86,
104, 123–25, 126, 127–28; imperial
nostalgia mobilized by, 3, 15, 270,
273; on Islamic identity of Turkey,
85, 99–100; Islamist influences on,
98; Kurdish policies of, 116, 119;
Middle East policies of, 133, 135,
137; and national identity, contending discourses of, 91; and Ottoman
heritage, efforts to reclaim, 3, 15, 82,
85, 99, 106, 123; post-Ottoman vision
of, central dilemma in, 101; protests
against, 82; on Turkism *(Türkçülük)*,
103; Xinjiang crackdown and, 104,
271
Erekle II (King of Kartli-Kakheti), 64

Eskandar Beg Monshi, 195, 200
ethnic fusion *(sliyaniye)*, concept of, 29
ethnic republics: imperial legacies and,
46–47; as liminal space, 44; nationalist movements in, 51–52; nativization
(korenizatsiya) policy in, 34–35, 48,
49; "politics of difference" in, 8, 20,
45, 57–58; Russian efforts to tighten
authority over, 58, 59; in Russian
Federation, 20, 44–45, 50–52; after
Soviet collapse, 20, 66; in Soviet
Union, 20, 34–35, 37, 47–52, 54–55,
70–71; Yeltsin's efforts to separate
Russia from, 20, 24, 62. *See also specific
republics*
ethnonationalism: Chinese, 219; emergence of, impact on Eurasian empires, 10, 24; and hostility to empire,
29, 30, 38; Iranian, 158, 181; Russian,
24, 27–31, 38; Turkish, 91, 101–3;
Turkmen, 183–84; undercurrent
of, in postimperial Eurasian states,
12
Eurasia: as geographic pivot of history, 9;
multipolar, emergence of, 21; Russian
use of term, 73. *See also* empires, Eurasian; postimperial states, Eurasian;
specific countries and regions
Eurasian Economic Union (EAEU), 14,
74–75, 78, 272; and Belt and Road
Initiative (BRI), 79; and Greater Eurasia initiative, 76; and Iran, 205
Eurasian identity, promotion of, 39
Eurasian integration, Russian schemes
for, 73–77
Eurasianism, 39
European imperialism, Eurasian empires
compared to, 9–10
European Union (EU): Balkan states
and, 131, 132; Britain's departure
from, 11; Greater Eurasia initiative
and, 76; Russia in relation to, 5, 62,
132; Turkish membership in, elusive
quest for, 5, 130

Far East, Russian: agricultural colonization of, 47; China's relations with, 252, 258; imperial legacies in, 46

Far North, Russian, 46. *See also* Siberia

Fars, Iran, 172, 196

Fatemiyoun Division, Syria, 168

Faulkner, William, 15

Ferdowsi, Abolqasem, 154, 156, 193

Ferghana Valley: resistance to Russian rule, 70; Soviet republics in, 71

Filofey (Russian monk), 38

Finland, Grand Duchy of, separatist movement in, 27–28

Finland, NATO membership of, Russian position on, 61

France, imperial legacy of, 3–4

Gamsakhurdia, Zviad, 55

Gaspıralı (Gasprinsky), İsmail, 94–95

Georgia: breakaway regions in, 66, 67, 68; Iranian influence in, efforts to reestablish, 199; NATO membership of, calls for, 67, 141; Orthodox Church of, 64; in Ottoman Empire, 138; Rose Revolution in, 63, 67, 199, 273; Russian annexation of (1801), 65, 138, 197; Russian influence in, 55, 62, 64, 67; Russian invasion of (2008), 40, 68, 140, 141, 199; Safavid rule in, 171, 195; after Soviet collapse, 66; Turkey's relations with, 139–40, 141; U.S. influence in, concerns about, 67–68

Ghaznavid dynasty, 193

Gizel, Innokenty, 32–33

global economic crisis of 2008: and push for Eurasian integration, 74; Turkey after, 141

global order, Westphalian: alternative visions of, 272, 275; Chinese alternative to, 212, 251–52, 255, 256–57, 266; Eurasian postimperial states and challenges to, 4, 5, 7, 11, 15, 270, 271–72, 275; Islamic Republic's rejection of, 161; U.S. and, 4, 5, 271

Gobineau, Joseph Arthur de, 157

Gökalp, Ziya, 95, 101, 103, 114

Goldsmid, Sir Frederic, 200–201

Gorbachev, Mikhail: and China, strategic rapprochement with, 261, 262; and ethnic republics, 49, 55

Gorchakov, Aleksandr, 69

Greater China *(Da Zhongguo)*, vs. China proper *(Benbu Zhongguo)*, 234

Greater East Asian Coprosperity Sphere, Japan and, 236

Greater Eurasia initiative, 76–77, 79

Greater Iran *(Iranzamin)*, idea of, 150, 189–94, 205–6

Greater Khorasan. *See* Khorasan

Greater Turkey, idea of, 90; challenges to, 105–6; in Kurdish borderlands, 109

Greater Turkic World, 91, 92

Great Leap Forward, and Han colonization, 248

Great Qing *(Da Qing)*, 210, 249; territory of, ca. 1800, 207m

Great Russians, 19

Great Unity *(datong)*, concept of, 212

Great Wall, China, 216, 237

Great Western Development program (China), 249, 262

Greece: in Ottoman Empire, 128; population exchange with Turkey, 129; Turkey's territorial disputes with, 126, 131

Greek Catholic Church, creation of, 32

Green Movement (Iran), 188

Guangxi, China, 234

Gülen, Fethullah, 103

Gülen schools: in Balkans, 130, 132; in Caucasus, 139

Gulf War (1991), 118

Gumilev, Lev, 39, 74

Guomindang, 209, 221; and Inner Asian borderlands, 233; minority policies of, 221, 222; position on Mongolia, 260

Halveti order, 92
Halych-Volyn (Galicia-Volhynia), 32
Hamas, Iran's support for, 149, 155
Hamidiye Light Cavalry Regiments,
    113, 115
Han, Enze, 240
Hanafi *madhab*, and Turkish Islam, 105,
    110, 112
Hanbali *madhab*, 105
Han dynasty (China), relations with
    "barbarians," 215, 216, 220, 245
Han identity/culture, in China: CCP
    and, 222, 224; centrality of, 210,
    214–15, 218, 220, 225; state based on,
    218–19
Han population: in Inner Mongolia,
    237, 238–39, 240; resettlement of,
    as tool for integration, 250; in Tibet,
    235, 244–45; in Xinjiang, 235, 248,
    249
Hatay (Alexandretta), Turkish claims on,
    126, 135
Hawaii, Chinese émigrés in, 227
Hayat Tahrir al-Sham, Turkey's support
    for, 101
Hazaras, in Afghanistan, 203, 204
HDP (Peoples' Democratic Party),
    Turkey, 116, 117, 122
Helali (Safavid poet), 200
Herat: Imam Khomeini Relief Commit-
    tee in, 204; Iranian influence in, 200,
    201, 202; in Persian world, 194
Hezb-e Wadhat (Party of Unity), Af-
    ghanistan, 202, 203
Hezbollah, 165–66; Iran's support for,
    155, 165, 168
Hillman, Jonathan, 264
Hobson, J. A., 9
Holodomor, 35
Holy Rus, concept of, 41; imperial
    legacy and, 25
Hong Kong: Britain and, 4, 213; Chinese
    claims to, 226, 252
Hong Taiji, 238

Hosayn Khan, 185
Hosking, Geoffrey, 3, 23
Houthis, 167
huaxia (civilization), concept of, 213; *li*
    (ritual) and, 216; vs. *tianxia*, 253; and
    zhonghua minzu (all-Chinese nation),
    214
Hui (Dungans), in Xinjiang, 245, 246
Hu Jintao, 251, 265
Hungary, in Ottoman Empire, 128
Huntington, Samuel, 6
Hussein, Saddam. *See* Saddam Hussein

Ichkeria, Chechen Republic of, 55–56
identity, culturally focused approaches
    to, 12. *See also* national identity
Ili Revolt, East Turkestan, 247, 248, 261
Ilkhanate, 156
Ilyin, Ivan, 28, 31, 36
imperial legacy: as category of analysis,
    6–7; of China, 2, 3, 8, 208–9, 267,
    269–75; Cold War rivalry disguising,
    269–70; combined with nationalism,
    paradox of, 10–11; and concept of
    compatriots, 25, 40, 42; elites and ap-
    peal to, 3, 4, 8, 11, 14–15; of Eurasian
    postimperial states, 2–4, 8, 15, 269–75;
    impact on peripheries, 8; of Iran, 2,
    3, 8, 269–75; persistence of, 269–70;
    rejected by Turkish Republic, 83–84,
    85; of Russia, 2, 3, 8, 18–21, 43, 78–79,
    269–75; factors undermining, 43, 78–
    79; salience for contemporary politics,
    2, 11, 15; of Turkey, 2, 3, 8, 90–92,
    101–6, 123–28, 141–42, 269–75. *See
    also* postimperial states, Eurasian
India: and China, relations with, 243,
    255, 258; Dalai Lama in, 243, 261;
    Greater Eurasia initiative and, 76, 77;
    and Tibet, 242–43, 244
Ingushetia, 17*m*, 45, 52; Iranian interests
    in, 199; resistance to Russian rule
    in, 54; Soviet administrative reforms
    and, 55

Inner Asia: assimilationist policies in, 224–25, 232, 235–37, 244–45, 250; Chinese policies in, 216, 231–50; history of de facto sovereignty in, 233; imperial rivalry in, 233, 234; Qing dynasty and, 232–34, 241–42, 245–47; regions composing, 232; Soviet intervention in, 234, 245, 247. *See also specific regions*

Inner Mongolia, 210, 232, 237–40; assimilation of, 239–40; as autonomous region, 234, 238

İnönü, İsmet, 109

interimperial "shatter zone(s)", 9, 63, 64, 77, 138, 246, 270; managed competition over, 272–73

International Monetary Fund, Chinese development assistance compared to, 266

International North-South Transit Corridor, 198

international order. *See* global order, Westphalian

Iran: 2,500th anniversary of founding of, 146; adoption of Shi'ism in, 148, 162; and Afghanistan, 149, 155, 191, 192, 199, 200–204, 205; and anti-ISIS resistance in Iraq, 164; borderlands of, 150, 167, 169–88; claims to exceptionalism, 6, 148, 160; competition between U.S. and Russia/China and, 275; as "empire of the mind," 154, 192; entanglement with peripheries of, 14; exclusion from current world order, 5; Greater Eurasia initiative and, 76, 77; imperial legacy of, 2, 3, 8, 146–48, 150, 159, 160, 205–6, 269–75; and Iraqi Shi'a, 164–65; Kurds in, 117, 180–83; minority groups in, 149, 154, 169–88; nation-building in, 156–58; origins of name, 155–56; Persianate cultural realm and, 148, 158, 192; and "politics of difference," 149–50; pre-Islamic past

of, as lost golden age, 157; revisionism of, explanations for, 5–6; Soviet occupation during World War II, 176, 181–82; supraethnic/suprareligious idea of, durability of, 275; as territorially bound nation, efforts to reimagine, 149, 153, 154; territory of, ca. 1740, 145*m*; victimization narrative of, 150, 201; vulnerability to exploitation by Russia and China, 271; during World War I, 169, 170, 172, 176, 180; during World War II, 169, 170, 176, 181–82. *See also* Islamic Republic of Iran; *specific dynasties and regions*

Iranian identity: contested and plural nature of, 153, 274; ethnic component of, 157; Islamic and imperial strands of, tension between, 274; Islam/Shi'ism and, 153, 159, 167–68, 177; Persian and Islamic strands of, synthesis of, 154, 159–60; Persianate culture and, 148, 153–54, 158; sectarian approach to, 167; supranational, Islamic Republic's appeal to, 171

Iran-Iraq War: Afghan refugees during, 202; imperial symbols invoked in, 148, 274; Iranian Kurdistan during, 182; Iraqi Shi'as during, 159; Khuzestan during, 179; sectarianism in, 149

Iranzamin (Greater Iran), idea of, 150, 189–94, 205–6

Iraq: anti-Iranian protests among Shi'as in, 168; anti-ISIS resistance in, 164; artificial borders of, 135; Greater Iran concept and, 192; Hezbollah-style militias in, 166, 168; as imperial periphery, 9; Iran's ambitions toward, 191; Kurds in, massacres of, 109, 118; Kurds in, Turkey's policies regarding, 86, 107, 108, 109, 117, 118–20, 122; in Ottoman Empire, 133; and PKK, 84, 118, 119; refugees from, in Turkey, 127; separation from Ottoman

Iraq (*continued*)
  Empire, 134; Shi'ite parties/move-
  ments in, 163–65; Talabani as president of, 161; ties with Iran, adoption
  of Shi'ism and, 148; Turkey's interest
  in, 124, 133, 135; Turkmen militias
  in, 103; U.S.-led invasion of, and
  opportunities for Iran, 191; U.S.-led
  invasion of, Turkey's response to, 119,
  133, 135; war in, Iran's involvement
  in, 155
IRGC. *See* Islamic Revolutionary Guard
  Corps
Isfahan: Afghans' conquest of, 163, 196,
  200; in Safavid empire, 196
Islam: and Iranian identity, 153, 159,
  167–68, 177, 274; and nationalism, in
  Turkey, 91–92, 98, 105; vs. nationality,
  Khomeini on, 159; Ottoman, model
  of, 98, 99, 127; in Ottoman Empire,
  92; and Ottoman identity, 85, 93, 94;
  political, rise in Turkey, 129; and Russia's borderlands/peripheries, 56, 57,
  68, 72; territorially bounded form of,
  Kemalist project of, 97; in Turkey's
  vision of new regional order, 127–28,
  142; Turkish (democratic), model
  of, 105, 123; and Turkish identity,
  conceptions of, 85, 90, 91, 99–100,
  105. *See also* Shi'as/Shi'ism; Sunnis/
  Sunnism
Islamic Party of Azerbaijan, 198
Islamic Republic of Iran, 147, 153; and
  Azerbaijan, 197–99; backlash against
  foreign adventures of, 168; borderlands of, administration of, 150, 186,
  187; and China, 205; democratic
  rule in, imperfect history of, 161,
  273; ethnic unrest in, potential for,
  188; foreign policy of, 149, 150, 159,
  190; Greater Iran (*Iranzamin*) idea
  and, 190, 194; haphazard borders of,
  148; as hybrid state, 161; imperial
  legacy and, 147–48, 150, 159, 160,

205–6, 274; and Middle East's sectarian geopolitics, 154–55; nationality
  subsumed by Islam in, 159; and new
  regional order, aspirations regarding,
  155, 165–66, 168, 190–91; non-
  Persian and non-Shi'ite periphery of,
  policies in, 173–74, 187–88; and permanent revolution, 161; and Russia,
  194, 199, 205; sectarian movements
  promoted by, 154–55, 165, 168;
  Shi'ism and foreign policy of, 148–49,
  154–55, 161–68; and supranational
  Iranian identity, appeal to, 170–71;
  synthesis of Islam and Persian-Iranian
  nationalism in, 149, 154, 159–61; U.S.
  and, campaign of resistance against,
  147, 150–51, 155, 161
Islamic Revolution (1979), Iran: efforts
  to spread, 154, 165; Iranian Kurdistan
  during, 182; Iranian Turkmen during,
  184; minorities' support for, 149, 154;
  trauma accompanying loss of empire
  and, 151
Islamic Revolutionary Guard Corps
  (IRGC), 161; and Badr Organization,
  164; and Hezbollah, 165; minority
  groups represented in, 174
Islamic State of Iraq and Syria (ISIS):
  Central Asians in ranks of, 72; siege
  of Kobani, Syria, 107, 110, 116, 119,
  120; Sistani's *fatwa* against, 164;
  Syrian Democratic Forces in fight
  against, 120
Islamist movements/Islamism: in
  Chechnya, 56, 57; in Turkey, 97–98;
  Turkey's support for, 100
Ismail I (Safavid ruler), 148, 161, 162, 196
Israel: Azerbaijan and, 177; EAEU and,
  75; Hezbollah as military check on,
  166; invasion of southern Lebanon,
  165; Iran's campaign of resistance
  against, 161; Turkey's relations with,
  133, 134, 136. *See also* Palestine
Ivan III (Grand Prince of Muscovy), 32

Ivan IV (Tsar of Russia), 25, 29, 46
Izetbegović, Alija, 132
Izetbegović, Bakir, 132

Jaish al-Adl (Baluch group), 187
al-Jalili family (Mosul), 133
Jamiat-e Islami, 202
Jangalis, uprising of, 172
Japan: and Inner Asia, 233, 234, 236, 259; invasion of China, 236
Jebtsundamba Khutukhtu, 259
Jewish Autonomous Oblast, Russian Federation, 51
Jews: in Islamic Republic of Iran, 174; in Russian Empire, 27; in Turkey, 96; in Ukraine, 35
Jia Yi, 254
Jordan: separation from Ottoman Empire, 134; Turkey's relations with, 135
Jundullah (Baluch group), 187
Jurchen, 235. *See also* Manchus
Justice and Development Party (Turkey). *See* AKP

Kabardino-Balkaria, 17*m*, 52, 56
Kadeer, Rebiya, 229
Kadyrov, Akhmad, 56, 57
Kadyrov, Ramzan, 8, 20, 57–58, 59
Kai-wing Chow, 218
Kalat, Khanate of, 185
Kalın, İbrahim, 124, 136
Kandahar, Iranian control of, 200
Kangxi Emperor (Qing ruler), 242
Kang Youwei, 214, 218, 219, 227, 255
Karachaevo-Cherkessia, 17*m*, 52
al-Karaki al-Amili, Ali al-Muhaqqiq, 163
Karakoç, Sezai, 119
Kartli-Kakheti, Kingdom of, 64, 195, 197
Karzai, Hamid, 203
Kashani-Sabet, Firoozeh, 157, 189
Kata'ib Hezbollah militia (Iraq), 164
Katkov, Mikhail N., 27

Kazakhs: along PRC's borders, 223; in Xinjiang, 245, 248
Kazakhstan: Belt and Road Initiative (BRI) announced in, 208, 264; China's relations with, 211, 252, 257, 258, 262; denomadization of, 71; in EAEU, 74; ethnic Russian minority in, 63; Eurasian integration plans and, 74; Nagorno-Karabakh conflict and, 76; nuclear testing in, 71; Russia's engagement with, 61, 70, 71, 72, 259; Soviet republic of, 70–71; uprising during World War I, 70; Uyghur diaspora organizations in, 257
Kazakh steppe, Russian settlement in, 69–70
Kazan khanate, Russian conquest of, 25, 46
KDPI (Kurdish Democratic Party of Iran), 181, 182
Kemal, Mustafa. *See* Atatürk
Kemal, Namık, 94
Kermani, Mirza Aqa Khan, 157
Kerman-Sistan, Qajar rule in, 172
Khakassia, Republic of, 45
Khalka Mongols, 259
Khamenei, Ayatollah Ali: on cultural ties with Tajikistan, 204; elevation to rank of ayatollah, 164; Greater Iran (*Iran-zamin*) idea and, 194; and Hezbollah, 166; imperial past invoked by, 3, 160; on Persian language and culture, 174; and Sistani, 164
Khan, Ismail, 203
Khan, Sulmaan Wasif, 243
Khatami, Mohammad, 174
al-Khattab, Ibn, 56
Khazal of Mohammareh, Sheykh, 178
Khiabani, Mohammad, 176, 177
Khiva, Khanate of, 69, 70, 183, 201
Khmelnitskiy, Bohdan, 32, 35
Khomeini, Ayatollah Ruhollah, 147–48, 161; in *Atabat*, 163; and denigration of nationality, 159; and Doctrine of

Khomeini, Ayatollah Ruhollah (*continued*)
 Absolute Guardianship, 161, 163; and
 Iranian identity, 167–68, 171; opposition to, 176–77, 179; and permanent
 revolution, 161
Khoqand, Khanate of, 69, 71, 201, 246
Khorasan (Greater Khorasan), 191, 192,
 199; etymology of name, 200; imperial rivalries in, 200–201; Iran's objectives in, 199, 201–4; major figures of,
 194; northern, nomadic Turkmen of,
 172, 183, 184; Persianization of, 184,
 202; Qajar rule in, 172, 200; Safavid rule in, 170, 171, 172, 196, 200;
 volatility of Iran's borderlands in, 170,
 172, 183, 193, 200
al-Khorasani, Abu Muslim, 159
Khorgos special economic zone, China
 and, 263
Khrushchev, Nikita, 29, 35, 49, 54
Khuzestan (Arabestan), Iranian, 178–80;
 Islamic Republic's policies in, 174;
 Saddam Hussein's plans to annex,
 179; Safavid rule in, 171; during
 World War I, 172
Kirill (Russian Patriarch), 41
Kısakürek, Necip Fazıl, 98
Kobani, Syria, ISIS siege of, 107, 110,
 116, 119, 120
Komi, protests in, 51
Korea, *tianxia* concept and, 252
Koreans, along PRC's borders, 223
korenizatsiya (nativization) policy, Soviet,
 34–35, 48, 49
Kosovo: refugees from, 127; Turkish
 policies in, 130, 131, 132
Kotku, Mehmed Zahid, 97
KRG (Kurdistan Regional Govern-
 ment), Iraq, 118; *peshmerga* fighters
 loyal to, 107, 119; Turkey's relations
 with, 86, 107, 108, 109, 119–20,
 122
Kumar, Krishan, 8, 12
Kurbsky, Andrey, 41

Kurdish Democratic Party of Iran
 (KDPI), 181, 182
Kurdish languages, 110; Turkey's ban
 on, 114
Kurdish tribal emirates, in Ottoman
 Empire, 84, 111; abolition of, 112
Kurdistan, Iranian, 171, 180–83; cross-
 border ties with Kurdish populations,
 180; Islamic Republic policies in, 174;
 nationalist movements in, 173, 176,
 181–83; Safavid rule in, 171; during
 World War I, 180; during World War
 II, 176, 181–82
Kurdistan, Ottoman, partition of, 107–8.
 See also Kurds, Turkish
Kurdistan Regional Government (Iraq).
 See KRG
Kurdistan Workers Party (Turkey). *See*
 PKK
Kurds: and Armenians, conflicts of,
 111, 112, 113; divisions among, 110,
 116–17; in Iran, 117, 180–83; in Iraq,
 86, 107, 108, 109, 117, 118–20, 122;
 Islamic Revolution in Iran and, 154;
 nationalist movement of, 112; in
 Ottoman Empire, 110–13; Ottoman
 partition and, 107–8, 113, 117; in
 Perso-Iranic world, 154; in Syria, 107,
 109, 117, 120–21, 122. *See also* Kurdistan; Kurds, Turkish
Kurds, Turkish, 107–22; AKP's strategy
 for integrating, 86, 109, 113, 115–17,
 122; in early Republic, 113–14;
 left-wing activism among, 115; opportunities for, 108–9; "politics of
 difference" regarding, 111, 114–15;
 separatism among, Atatürk's response
 to, 13, 108, 113–14; tribal elites
 of, relations with state, 113, 115;
 violence against, 84; during War of
 Independence, 113. *See also* PKK
Kuwait, formation of, 178
Kyivan Rus: successor states to, 31–32;
 and unity of East Slavs, 31, 36, 42

Kyrgyz, in Xinjiang, 245, 248

Kyrgyzstan: China's relations with, 211, 252, 257, 258, 262; in CSTO, 75; in EAEU, 75; ethnic Russian minority in, 63; labor migrants from, in Russia, 73; Persian language in, 158; revolutions in, 63, 68; Russian involvement in, 72, 259; Soviet republic of, 71; uprising during World War I, 70; U.S. forces deployed in, 72, 75–76; Uyghur diaspora organizations in, 257

Landau, Jacob, 103

Lausanne, Treaty of, 83, 126, 129, 135

Lebanon: Hezbollah in, 165–66; Iran's relations with, 148, 149, 163, 165–66; separation from Ottoman Empire, 134; Turkey's relations with, 135

LeDonne, John, 33

Lenin, Vladimir: and ethnoterritorial federalism, 48; on European imperialism, 9; on Great Russian chauvinism, 28

li (ritual), and Chinese cultural space, 215–16

Liang Qichao, 214, 217–18, 219, 221, 227

liberal democracies, postimperial Eurasian states' failure to become, 4, 5

Liberal Democratic Party of Russia (LDPR), 30, 62

Libya: Russo-Turkish tensions over, 270, 271; Turkey's intervention in, 86, 124, 133, 137

Lieven, Dominic, 7, 15

Little Russians, 19, 32–33, 34

Liu Qing, 253

Liu Xiaoyuan, 232, 243, 254

Liu Zhenmin, 266

Lorestan, Safavid rule in, 171

Lukashenko, Aleksandr, 36, 37

Luxemburg, Rosa, 48

Luzhkov, Yury, 40

Macao: Chinese claims to, 226; *tianxia* concept and, 252

Mackinder, Halford John, 9

Mahabad, Kurdish Republic based in, 181–82

Mahmud II (Ottoman Sultan), 111–12

Malkum Khan, 157

Mamluks, Ottoman conquest of, 92

Manchukuo, 236

Manchuria (Northeastern China), 210, 235–37; assimilation and deterritorialization of, 232, 235–37; imperial rivalry in, 235, 236, 259

Manchus, 235; anger directed against, 217; as distinct *minzu* in China, 237; in Qing dynasty, 9, 217

Mansur, Sheykh (Chechen leader), 53, 55

Mao Zedong: campaign against Soviet revisionism, 261; and minority policies, 221–22, 243; on *tianxia*, 255

Martin, Terry, 48

Mashhad, Khorasan: Iranian control of, 170, 200; as Shi'ite center, 163

Masoud, Ahmed Shah, 202–3

al-Masri, Aziz Ali, 134

Matthee, Rudi, 200

Mazeppa, Ivan, 1

Mazzaoui, Michael, 162

Medvedev, Dmitry, 40, 60, 74

Mehmed VI (Ottoman Sultan), 82

MEK (Mojahedin-e Khalq), 179

mellat, concept of, 156, 157

Menderes, Adnan, 115, 273

Merv, 183; Iranian control over, 200, 201

Mesopotamia: in Greater Iran, 189; imperial rivalries in, 9, 270; Iran's borderlands in, 170; Ottoman legacy in, 124, 134

Mevlevi order, 92

MHP (Nationalist Movement Party), Turkey, 86, 91; accommodation with Islamist parties, 103; solidarity with Crimean Tatars and Uyghurs, 106; on Turkish identity, 102

Middle East: Iranic languages spoken in, 158; Iran's ambitions regarding, 168, 190; Islamist movements in, Turkey's support for, 100, 136; in Ottoman Empire, 133–34; post-Ottoman, nation-building projects in, 106; sectarian geopolitics of, Islamic Republic of Iran and, 12, 154–55, 168; Turkey's interests in, 99, 127, 133–37; Turkish-Iranian tensions over, 270. *See also specific countries*

*millet*s: in Ottoman Empire, 92–93, 111, 114; and Turkey's vision of new regional order, 128

Milli Görüş (National Vision), Turkey, 97, 98, 99; and AKP, origins of, 99; influence among Turkish migrants in Europe, 100

Ming dynasty (China), 222, 237; approach to Inner Asia, 216

minzu (nationality/ethnic groups): in People's Republic of China (PRC), 209–10, 214–15, 222; illegitimacy of secession based on, 220; non-Han, 222–23, 237

Mısak-i Milli (National Oath), Turkey, 95, 125–26, 134–35, 138

Mohammad Reza Shah. *See* Pahlavi, Mohammad Reza Shah

Mohseni, Ayatollah Asif, 203, 204

Mojahedin-e Khalq (MEK), 179

Moldova, Republic of: Russian peacekeeping force in, 1, 2, 4; unrecognized statelet of Transnistria within, 1–2, 15

Mongolia: China's Inner Asian periphery and, 211, 232, 237; China's relations with, 239, 252, 258, 261; independence of, 211, 237, 259–60. *See also* Inner Mongolia; Outer Mongolia

Monroe Doctrine, 61

Mosaddeq, Mohammad, 150

Mosul: ISIS occupation of, 119; in Ottoman Empire, 110–11, 133; Turkey's claims on, 126, 135

Motahhari, Morteza, 159

Motherland Party (Russia), 31

Mozaffar al-Din Shah (Qajar ruler), 185

Muhammad Ali Paşa, 111, 112, 133, 180

al-Muhandis, Abu Mahdi, 165

Muscovy: as successor state to Kyivan Rus, 31–32. *See also* Russia

Muslim Brotherhood, Turkey's support for, 101, 136

Muslim Unity Party (Iran), 186

Nader Shah (Afsharid ruler), 170, 175, 195, 197

Nagorno-Karabakh, after World War I, 65

Nagorno-Karabakh conflict, 66, 67; Iran's position on, 177, 197; refugees from, 127; Turkey's position on, 103, 104, 138, 139, 141, 142

Najaf, Iraq: Iranian consulate in, attack on, 168; as Shi'ite center, 163–64, 165

Najibullah, Muhammad, 202, 203

Nakhjavan (Nakhichevan): khanate of, 64; after World War I, 65

Naqshbandiyya order: common religious framework of, and Kurdish-Turkish reconciliation, 115–16; in North Caucasus, 53–54; in Ottoman Empire, 92; in Turkey, 97

Naser al-Din Shah (Qajar ruler), 183, 185, 201

Nashi (Russian youth movement), 31

Natali, Denise, 181

national identity: ambiguity of, in postimperial Eurasian states, 11–13. *See also* supraethnic national identity; *specific national identities*

nationalism: imperialism and, in Eurasian states, 10–11; Islam and, in Iran, 149, 154, 159–61; Islam and, in Turkey, 91–92, 98, 105. *See also* ethnonationalism

Nationalist Movement Party (Turkey). *See* MHP

Nationalist Party (China). See *Guomindang*

National Oath (Turkey). See *Mısak-ı Milli*

National Vision (Turkey). See *Milli Görüş*

NATO: Balkan states and, 132, 141; Georgia's membership in, calls for, 67, 141; Moldova's membership in, Russian objections to, 2; Russia in relation to, 5, 62, 132, 273; Turkey's accession to, 84

Navalny, Aleksey, 30, 273

Nazism, Ukrainian nationalism associated with, 35, 38

"near abroad": of Iran, 164; of postimperial Eurasian states, 11, 14–15; of Russian Federation, 60; Russian term for, 14, 60

Nehru, Jawaharlal, 255

Nemtsov, Boris, 57, 58

neo-Eurasianism, 39

neo-Ottomanism, 123, 125

Nepal, China's territorial disputes with, 258, 261, 263

Nerchinsk, Treaty of, 259

Nevsky, Aleksandr, 29

Nicholas I (Emperor of Russia), 26, 27, 65

Nicholas II (Emperor of Russia), 24, 27, 28

Ningxia, China, 234

Nonaligned Movement, 255

North Africa, Ottoman legacy in, 124, 133, 134

North Caucasus, 52–58; agricultural colonization of, 47; ethnic cleansing under Stalin, 54; ethnic republics in, 44, 52; imperial legacy and, 13, 45, 46; incorporation in Russian Empire, 53; Iranian engagement in, 199; liminal status of, 44, 53; Putin's policies in, 56–58; resistance to Russian rule in, 53–54, 55; after Soviet Union's

collapse, 20; Sufi orders in, 53–54, 55; system of indirect rule in, 56–57. *See also specific countries*

North Caucasus Imamate, 53

Northern Alliance, in Afghanistan, 203

North Korea, territorial demands from China, 261

North Macedonia, Turkish policies in, 131

North Ossetia, 17*m*, 45, 52, 55

Novorossiya *guberniya*, in Russian Empire, 33, 37

Nurhaci (Qing founder), 237

Öcalan, Abdullah, 109, 118, 120, 122

OCAO (Overseas Chinese Affairs Office), 228, 229

Opium Wars, 217, 259

Organization of Ukrainian Nationalists (OUN), 35

Orthodox Church: and East Slavs, unity of, 25, 32; Georgian, Russian policies regarding, 64; and Russian identity, 23, 25; and Russian World, concept of, 41

Ottoman Empire: Balkans in, 39, 92, 128–29; Caucasus and, 137, 138; Christian nationalist movements in, 39, 93, 94, 96, 129; ethnic violence in, 65, 93–96, 105, 112, 113; former, nation-building in, 125; fragmentation of, 89, 134; heritage of, AKP and revival of, 82, 85–86, 90–91, 113, 123, 124; Islam in, 92; Kurds in, 110–13; legacy of, and Turkey's geopolitical ambitions, 3, 12, 90–92, 101–6, 123–28, 141–42; legal successor of, 83; Middle East in, 133–34; *millet*s in, 92–93, 111, 114; Moldavia in, 1, 2; and "politics of difference," 142; religious minorities in, 92, 93; territory of, ca. 1689, 81*m*; in World War I, 82, 95, 138

Ottoman identity, Islam and, 85, 93, 94

Ottomanism/Ottoman nationalism,
    93–94; Turkish language and, 10, 12
OUN (Organization of Ukrainian Na-
    tionalists), 35
"Outer Manchuria," 258
Outer Mongolia: anti-Qing revolts in,
    210; China's loss of, 237, 259–60. *See
    also* Mongolia
overseas Chinese *(huaqiao huaren):*
    China's mobilization of, 12–13, 215,
    226–30; concept of *zhonghua minzu*
    and, 226–27
Overseas Chinese Affairs Office
    (OCAO), 228, 229
overseas Russians, in Russian World
    concept, 41
Özal, Turgut, 98–99, 103; foreign policy
    of, 126, 130, 134, 139; Iraqi Kurdish
    factions and, 117; Kurdish ancestry
    of, 109, 115–16; rise of political Islam
    under, 129
Özdağ, Ümit, 102

Pahlavi, Mohammad Reza Shah:
    ceremony at Persepolis, 146–47;
    and Greatoer Iran *(Iranzamin)* idea,
    194; and imperial nostalgia, 274; on
    Khuzestan, importance of, 178–79;
    Kurdish independence efforts and,
    181–82; overthrow of, 147; and Per-
    sianization of Iranian identity, 158;
    and suppression of ethnic minorities,
    117, 158, 181–82; U.S. support for,
    150; and western Afghanistan, 202;
    wife of, 173
Pahlavi, Reza Shah, 149, 153, 154, 158;
    consolidation of power by, 172, 178;
    nationalist framework established
    by, 173; and non-Persian border-
    lands, 178, 181, 184, 186; ouster of,
    173
Pahlavi dynasty, Iran: and idea of
    Greater Iran *(Iranzamin)*, 190; and
    Kurdish population, 181; minority

policies of, 173, 181, 186; nation-
    building project of, 158, 181; and
    Persian-centric conception of Iranian
    identity, 154, 158, 188
Pakistan: Baluch minority in, 185, 187;
    and China, security mechanism with,
    266; Greater Eurasia initiative and,
    76, 77; Greater Iran concept and,
    192; Hezbollah-style militias in, 166;
    and Iranian Baluch, 186; Iran's rela-
    tions with, 205; and Pashtun groups
    in Afghanistan, 202; Persian language
    in, 158
Palestine: separation from Ottoman
    Empire, 134; Turkey's involvement
    in, 133, 136–37
Palestinian Islamic Jihad, Iran's support
    for, 155
Panchen Lama, 244
pan-Slavism, 38–39
pan-Turkism, 101–2. *See also* Turkism
    (Türkçülük)
Pan Yihong, 216
Party for a Free Life in Kurdistan
    (PJAK), 182, 183
Pashtuns: in Afghan civil war, 202, 203;
    fall of Isfahan to, 163, 196, 200; in
    Perso-Iranic world, 154; in Taliban,
    203
Paskevich, Ivan, 65
Pavlovsky, Gleb, 41, 58
Peaceful Coexistence, policy of, 255
Peoples' Democratic Party (Turkey). *See*
    HDP
People's Protection Units (Syria). *See*
    YPG
People's Republic of China (PRC):
    Confucian symbolism embraced by,
    212, 215, 220, 255, 274; as hybrid
    state, 210; imperial view of frontiers
    as transition zones, 260–61; and In-
    ner Asian borderlands, 233, 236–37;
    minority policies in, 221–25; *minzu*
    (ethnic groups) within, 209–10,

214–15, 222; name of, *zhonghua* in, 219; nationality law in, 228; nation-building in, 214, 215, 219–20; and overseas Chinese *(huaqiao huaren)*, policies toward, 12–13, 215, 227, 228–30; Qing territorial legacy and, 209, 237, 249, 258–59; and territorial accommodation, strategy of, 261; as territorially bounded state, 258. *See also* China

Pereyaslav, Peace of, 32, 33

peripheries: Eurasian postimperial states' entanglement with, 4, 9, 10, 14–15; imperial legacies in, 8. *See also* borderlands

Persianate culture/world: and Iranian identity, 148, 153–54, 158, 174, 275; and Islam, in Islamic Republic of Iran, 149, 154, 159–61; unity of, Iranian politicians' emphasis on, 160

Persian Gulf, Iran's foreign policy and, 190

Persian language: countries/regions using, 153, 158, 202; Islamic Republic of Iran and, 159, 174

peshmerga fighters, Turkey and, 107, 119

Peter I the Great (Emperor of Russia), 1; administrative reforms under, 46; conquests in Caucasus, 196; and idea of common Russian identity, 23, 26

Pishevari, Jafar, 176, 177, 181

PJAK (Party for a Free Life in Kurdistan), 182, 183

PKK (Kurdistan Workers Party), Turkey: AKP's strategy for reconciliation with, 86, 109; foreign powers using, 108; idea of trans-boundary Kurdish identity and, 183; insurgency waged by, 84, 108, 115; Iranian offshoot of, 182; Iraqi Kurdish factions as allies against, 117, 119; permeability of Turkish borders and, 118; resumption of conflict with, 116, 122; Russian ties

to, 140–41; and YPG/PYD in Syria, 107, 120

PMF (Popular Mobilization Forces), Iraq, 164–65

Poland: deployment of U.S. forces in, Russia's position on, 61; and south-western Rus, 32; Soviet projection of power in, 18, 28. *See also* Poles

Poland-Lithuania: Orthodox believers in, 32; refugees from, resettlement in Ukraine, 33

Polar Silk Road, 268

Poles: massacres of, in Ukraine, 35; in Russian Empire, 10, 27, 28, 33

"politics of difference": China and, 214, 221; empires and, 8, 10, 11; Iran and, 149–50; Russia and, 8, 20, 45, 52, 56, 57–58, 59; Turkey and, 111, 114–15, 142

Politkovskaya, Anna, 57

Popular Mobilization Forces (PMF), Iraq, 164–65

postimperial states, Eurasian: border-lands of, volatility of, 11, 13–14; challenges facing, 11–15; claims to special status, 271, 275; enduring imperial legacies of, 2–4, 8, 15, 269–75; global order threatened by, 4, 5, 7, 11, 15, 270, 271–72, 275; increasing alignment among, 4, 272–73; national identity in, ambiguity of, 11–13; "near abroads" of, 11, 14–15; peripheries of, entanglement with, 4, 9, 10, 14–15; political systems in, 5, 275; power disparities among, 270–71; revisionism of, 4–6; synthesis of nationalism and imperialism in, 10–11; unstable boundaries of, 10; Western empires compared to, 3–4, 11. *See also specific countries*

PRC. *See* People's Republic of China

Primakov, Yevgeny, 62

Prosperous Borders Wealthy Minorities program (China), 262

Pugachev, Yemelyan, 47
Putin, Vladimir: and annexation of
    Crimean Peninsula, 18, 31, 40, 43;
    approach to ethnic autonomies, 50–
    52; borderland policies of, 45, 58–59;
    and China, relations with, 261; and
    civic basis of Russian identity, 30; eth-
    nonationalist movements and, 30–31;
    on Eurasian integration, 73–74, 76;
    imperial nostalgia mobilized by, 3, 15,
    18, 23, 270, 273; on national iden-
    tity, 24; North Caucasus policies of,
    56–58; popularity among far-right
    movements in U.S. and Europe, 42;
    and "power vertical," aspiration to
    create, 45; Primakov and, 62; rise and
    legitimation of, centrality of Chech-
    nya to, 13, 56; and Russian World
    Foundation, 41; Solzhenitsyn's influ-
    ence on, 36, 37; on Soviet Union's
    collapse, 18, 40; succession question
    regarding, 59; on Ukraine, 37
Puyi (former Qing emperor), 236
PYD (Democratic Union Party), in
    northern Syria, 120–21

Qadiriyya order, in North Caucasus,
    54
al-Qaeda, in North Caucasus, 56
Qajar, Aqa Mohammad, 175, 195, 197,
    200
Qajar, Fath Ali Shah, 200
Qajar, Mohammed Ali Shah, 175–76
Qajar, Mohammed Shah, 201
Qajar Iran, 9; Baluchistan in, 185–86;
    borderlands of, indirect rule in, 171,
    172; capital of, 170; emergence of
    ethnonationalism and, 10; interests
    in Caucasus, 64, 195, 197; Khorasan
    in, 172, 200; and Kurdish emirates,
    180; nation-building in, 156–57; and
    Persianate world, claims on, 150;
    and Russian Empire, contention
    with, 175; territorial losses of, 169,

170, 201; and Turkmens of northern
    Khorasan, 183
Qara Qoyunlu dynasty, 175
Qashqa'is, in Iran, 171, 173, 174
Qatar: formation of, 178; Turkish mili-
    tary footprint in, 124
Qazi Muhammad (Kurdish leader), 181,
    182
Qazvini, Hamdallah Mostawfi, 193
Qianlong Emperor (Qing ruler), 217,
    244, 245, 249
Qing dynasty (China), 9, 210, 217; at-
    tempts to Sinicize, 225; and Banner
    system, 217, 221; CCP claims regard-
    ing, 10–11; colonial encroachment
    and, 213; emergence of ethnon-
    ationalism and, 10; and Inner Asian
    borderlands, 232–34, 237–38, 241–42,
    245–47; and national imperialism,
    214; nationalist movement and,
    217–18; nationality law adopted by,
    227–28; policies in Manchuria, 235,
    236; and "politics of difference," 221;
    relations with "barbarians," 216; and
    Russia, border disputes with, 259;
    social and institutional basis of, 217;
    stable administration established by,
    213–14; territorial legacy of, claims
    regarding, 209, 237, 249, 258–59; ter-
    ritorial losses of, 211, 252; territory
    of, ca. 1800, 207m
Qin Yaqing, 254
Qizilbash, 93, 110, 162, 195, 196
Qubilai Khan (Yuan ruler), 241

Rabbani, Burhanuddin, 202, 203
Rakhmon(ov), Emomali, 72, 204
Rama, Edi, 132
Raqqa, in Ottoman Empire, 110–11
Regional Anti-Terrorism Center
    (RATS), 257
regional order, new, 272; China's vision
    of, 123, 205, 211–12, 220, 252–53,
    257, 263–64, 267–68; Iran's vision of,

155, 165–66, 168, 190–91; Russia's vision of, 73–77, 79, 123, 205; Turkey's vision of, 99–100, 123–28, 133, 135–36, 137, 140, 141–43

Renan, Ernest, 157

Republican People's Party (Turkey). *See* CHP

Republic of China (ROC): claims to Qing territorial legacy, 209; and Inner Asian borderlands, 233, 234; loss of Mongolia and, 260; Manchukuo and, 236; minority policies in, 221–25; name of, *zhonghua* in, 219; nationality law in, 228; nation-building in, 214, 219–20; tension between diversity and assimilation in, 220–21. See also *Guomindang;* Taiwan

revisionism, of Eurasian postimperial states: civilizational explanations for, 6; ideological/political explanations for, 4–5; imperial legacies and, 4; structural explanations for, 5

Reynolds, Michael, 100, 127

Richmond, Walter, 53

Rieber, Alfred, 48

ROC. *See* Republic of China

Rojava, self-proclaimed state of, 120

Rolland, Nadège, 264

Roman Danilovich (Prince of Halych-Volyn), 32

Romania: in Ottoman Empire, 128; Turkish refugees from, 129

Rossiyskiy (term): revival under Yeltsin, 29, 42, 62; as supraethnic national identity, 12, 24, 38, 42

RSFSR. *See* Russian Soviet Federative Socialist Republic

Rumlu, Hasan Beg, 162

Rus': and *Rossiya*, tension between, 25. See also Kyivan Rus

Russia (Russian Federation): annexation of Crimean Peninsula by, 18, 31, 37, 40, 43, 273–74; borderlands of, 44–45; and China, boundary negotiations with, 211, 252, 258–59, 261, 262; and China, changing power balance between, 262; and China, strategic rapprochement with, 72, 78, 261, 272; civilizational distinctiveness of, arguments for, 6, 40, 41–42; claim to great power status, 21; costs of empire-building by, 43; democratic rule in, imperfect history of, 273; economic disparities between center and periphery in, 58–59; entanglement with peripheries of, 14; ethnic republics in, 20, 44–45, 50–52; and EU/NATO, strategic competition with, 5, 62, 132; and Eurasian Economic Union, 14; exclusion from current world order, 5; foreign policy of, 25, 40; imperial legacy and, 2, 3, 8, 18–21, 43, 78–79, 269–75; intervention in affairs of smaller neighbors, 1, 2, 18–19, 43; and Iran, 194, 199, 205; and new regional order, aspirations regarding, 73–77, 79, 123; non-Western governance norms promoted by, 76; occupation of eastern Ukraine, 14, 18, 31; and "politics of difference," 8, 20, 45, 52, 56, 57–58, 59; post-Putin, questions regarding, 59; revisionism of, explanations for, 5–6; shifting boundaries of, 19; southern borders of, instability of, 20; Syrian conflict and, 137; ties with former Soviet states, 24–25, 63; and Turkey, competition with, 138–41; and Turkey, strategic cooperation with, 78, 104, 272; and Ukraine, entanglement with, 14, 24–25; and West, strategic competition with, 21, 39, 78. *See also* Russian Empire; Soviet Union; *specific regions*

Russian Agency for International Cooperation, 40

Russian Civil War: Caucasus during, 54; ethnic autonomies emerging after, 47; separatist movements during, 34

Russian Empire: collapse of, Ottoman forces after, 138; efforts to nationalize, 26–28; ethnic Russians' claims for special status in, 26–27; expansion and consolidation of, 46–47, 53; heterogeneity of, 23, 25–26; incorporation of Central Asia in, 68–70; incorporation of South Caucasus in, 197; and Inner Asia, 233; loyalty as criterion for inclusion in, 25–26; origins of, 1, 26; rise of ethnonationalism and, 27–28; territory of, ca. 1900, 16*m*–17*m*; unity of, elites' perspective on, 23–24

Russian identity: ambiguity of, 37–38; civic basis of, 25–26, 29–30; cultural-national vs. imperial conceptions of, 19, 23–24, 30, 42–43; Eurasianist views on, 39; imperial articulations of, 38–43; pan-Slavist views on, 38–39; religion and, 23, 25; top-down attempt to redefine, 31; transcending borders, claims regarding, 19, 38–43

Russian language: *korenizatsiya* (nativization) policy and use of, 49; Russian World Foundation and promotion of, 41; and Russification policies of Russian Empire, 26, 27; and Russification policies of Soviet Union, 29, 49; as state language of Russian Federation, 30, 51, 59; use in Caucasus and Central Asia, decline in, 78; use in Ukraine, 37

Russian Orthodox Church. *See* Orthodox Church

Russians, ethnic: agricultural colonization by, 46–47; claim for special status of, 24, 26–27, 28–29, 30; Soviet ethnoterritorial federalism and, 48; in successor states to Soviet Union, 62–63

Russian Soviet Federative Socialist Republic (RSFSR), 24, 47, 48; lower-level autonomies within, 48, 49

Russian World, concept of, 41; Greater Turkey idea compared to, 105; imperial legacy and, 25

Russian World Foundation, 40, 41

Russification: in Belarus and Ukraine, 35; cultural, 27; Russian Empire and policies of, 26, 27; Russian Federation and policies of, 51; Soviet Union and policies of, 29, 49

Russo-Ottoman wars, 65, 94, 111

Saakashvili, Mikheil, 67, 68

Saddam Hussein, 109; *al-Anfal* campaign of, 118; appeal to pan-Arab sentiments, 179; fall of, and opportunities for Iran/Shi'ism, 163–64; and PKK, 118; U.S.-led campaign to oust, 119

al-Sadr, Muqtada, 164

Safavid Iran, 9; Azerbaijan's position in, 175; borderlands of, indirect rule in, 171; collapse of, 163; conversion to Shi'ism in, 148, 162; empire of, term used for, 156; first capital of, 170; imperial expansion of, justification for, 162; Khorasan in, 170, 171, 172, 196, 200; and Kurdish emirates, 180; Ottoman frontier with, 133; and Persianate world, claims on, 150; revolutionary dynamic associated with, 161; Selim I's campaign against, 110; slave system in, 196

Safawiyya dervish order, 162

Safi I (Safavid ruler), 196

Said-bek (Chechen leader), 54

Said of Piran, Sheykh, 12, 113

Sakha (Yakutia), 45, 52

Salafism: vs. Islamic nationalism, 98; vs. Turkish/Ottoman Islam, 105, 127

Samanid dynasty, 193

Sasanian Empire, 154; idealized vision of, 189–90, 192–93; and idea of Khorasan, 200; and origins of Iran, 156

Saudi Arabia: and Iranian Baluch, 186; Iran's views on, 160; and Pashtun groups in Afghanistan, 202. *See also* Salafism

Savitsky, Petr, 39

Sazonov, Sergey, 34

SCO. *See* Shanghai Cooperation Organization

Selim I (Ottoman Sultan), 92, 110, 111

Serbia: EAEU and, 75; nationalist groups in, Russian support for, 39; Turkey's relations with, 130–31, 132; U.S.-led bombing of, and imperial nostalgia, 273

Serbs: attacks on Muslims, 106, 129; campaign for independence from Ottoman Empire, 38–39

Sèvres, Treaty of, 89, 113

Shaf'i *madhab*: Kurds and, 110; vs. Turkish Islam, 105

Shahnahmeh (Ferdowsi), 154, 157; and Greater Iran *(Iranzamin)* concept, 192, 193

Shahroudi, Ayatollah Mahmoud Hashemi, 165

Shakak, Ismail Aqa (Simko), 180–81

Shamil, Imam (North Caucasian leader), 53, 54, 55

Shanghai Cooperation Organization (SCO), 256, 272; Greater Eurasia initiative and, 76; Iran and, 205; Regional Anti-Terrorism Center (RATS) of, 257

Shanghai Five, 257, 262

Shapur I (Sasanian ruler), 156, 192

Shariatmadari, Ayatollah Kazem, 176–77

Shaymiyev, Mintimer, 50, 51

Shchedrovitsky, Petr, 41

Sheng Shicai, 247

Shi'as/Shi'ism: Akhbari school of, 179; *Atabat* as center of, 163; and imperial expansion, 162; and Iranian identity, 153, 159, 167–68, 177; Iran's adoption of, 148, 162; Iran's appeal to loyalty of, 12; in Iraq, 163–65; and Islamic Republic's foreign policy, 148–49,

154–55, 161; revolutionary dynamic associated with, 161–62; Saddam's fall and opportunities for, 163–64; *ulema* as independent political force in Iran, 161–63; Usuli school of, 179. *See also* Sufi orders; *ulema*

Shimun XIX (Assyrian Catholicos), 180–81

Shunzhi Emperor (Qing ruler), 241

Siberia: agricultural colonization of, 47, 61; ethnic republics in, 44; imperial legacies in, 46

Silk Road: China's invocations of, 267; in Xinjiang, 245

Silk Road Economic Belt, 208. *See also* Belt and Road Initiative (BRI)

Simko (Ismail Aqa Shakak), 180–81

Simla Convention, 242–43, 258

Sistan and Baluchistan, Iran, 185, 186. *See also* Baluchistan

Sistani, Ayatollah Ali, 164, 165

Slavic Union (Russia), 31

Slavophilism, 26–27

Soleimani, Qassem, 164, 165

Solovyev, Sergey, 46

Solzhenitsyn, Aleksandr, 29, 36, 37, 41

Somalia, 124

South Asia: Greater Iran and, 189; Iranic languages spoken in, 158; Iran's engagement in, 150, 190. *See also specific countries*

South Caucasus, 63–68; agricultural colonization of, 47; as buffer zone for Russia, 20–21; China's engagement in, 267; colonial aspects of Russian rule in, 61; ethnoterritorial conflicts in, 66–67; Eurasian integration and, 73; Greater Iran concept and, 189, 192; imperial legacy in, 46, 68; imperial rivalries in, 63, 64, 67; Iranian Qajar interests in, 64, 195, 197; Iran's engagement in, 190, 194; Russian involvement in, 20–21, 60, 64–65, 197; Soviet collapse and, 29, 36, 66;

South Caucasus (*continued*)
Turkey's intervention in, 86, 124; during World War I, 65. *See also specific countries*

South China Sea: China's claims in, 252, 257, 258; Russian state companies expelled from, 271

Southeast Asia, Chinese émigrés in, 226–27

Southern Song dynasty (China), 216

South Ossetia: ethnic tensions in, 66; Russian occupation of, 19, 40; struggle for independence from Georgia, 66, 67, 68

Soviet Union: and China, territorial disputes of, 261; collectivization and famine in, 35; ethnic minorities in, cultural and political autonomy of, 24; ethnic republics of, 20, 34–35, 37, 47–52, 54–55, 70–71; ethnic Russians in, foundational role of, 28–29; and Inner Asia, 234, 245, 247; *korenizatsiya* (nativization) policy in, 34–35, 48, 49; and Kurds, support for, 118; Russification policies in, 29, 49; southern borderlands of, 61–62; successor states to, 60, 62, 63; successor states to, Chinese trade and investment in, 68, 72, 76; and Turkey, 102; union republics of, 47, 48, 49, 70

Soviet Union, collapse of: ethnic republics after, 20, 66; and idea of "compatriots," 40; and Russia's geopolitical marginalization, 18, 40; schemes for regional integration after, 73; Turkish policies after, 91, 103, 126; Yeltsin's policies and, 62

Stalin, Josef: borderlands policies of, 48, 58, 61; claims on Iranian Azerbaijan, 61, 66; and ethnic cleansing in North Caucasus, 54, 55; on ethnic Russians, privileged status of, 28, 29; terror campaign of, 35

Stolypin, Petr, 28

Sufi orders: in North Caucasus, 53–54, 55; in Ottoman Empire, 92; in Turkey, 97–98; and Turkish Islam, influences on, 105. *See also specific orders*

Süleyman I the Magnificent (Ottoman ruler), 1, 2

Sunnis/Sunnism: Hanafi school of, 105, 110, 112; Hanbali school of, 105; in Iran's borderlands, 171, 178–87; Iran's foreign policy and, 155; in North Caucasus, 54; Ottoman sultan as preeminent ruler of, 92, 134; Shaf'i school of, 105, 110; Turkey's ambition regarding, 12, 92, 100–101, 168; and Turkish-Kurdish relations, 109. *See also* Salafism

Suny, Ronald Grigor, 8, 96

Sun Yat-sen, 220, 227

supraethnic national identity: Persianate world as, 148, 153–54, 158, 174, 275; postimperial Eurasian states and, 12; *Rossiyskiy* as, 12, 24, 38, 42; *Türkiyeli* as, 12, 91; *zhonghua minzu* as, 12, 214, 219

Syria: Arab Spring and, 136, 137; artificial borders of, 135; Astana peace process for, 272; fighters from, in Nagorno-Karabakh conflict, 141; Hezbollah's role in, 166; ISIS in, 107; Kobani siege in, 107, 110, 116, 119; Kurds in, Turkish policies regarding, 107, 109, 117, 120–21, 122; PKK and, 84, 120; pursuit of postimperial influence in, 2, 141, 270, 271; PYD/YPG in, 107, 109, 120; refugees from, in Turkey, 100, 121, 142; Russo-Turkish tensions over, 141, 270, 271; separation from Ottoman Empire, 134; Turkey's interests in, 133, 141; Turkey's intervention in, 4, 14, 86, 101, 121, 122, 124, 135, 137, 142; Turkmen militias in, 103; war in,

Iran's involvement in, 155, 166, 168, 198, 204
Syrian Democratic Forces, 120

Tabriz: as capital of Iran, 170; conversion to Shi'ism in, 162; Khiabani's revolt in, 176; Safavid conquest of, 195
Tahmasp I (Safavid ruler), 162–63, 195, 196
Taiping Rebellion, 217, 259
Taiwan: PRC's claims to, 226, 229, 252; *tianxia* concept and, 252. See also *Guomindang;* Republic of China (ROC)
Tajikistan: China's relations with, 211, 252, 258, 262; Chinese security presence in, 72, 266; in CSTO, 75; Greater Iran concept and, 192, 202; independence of, 202; Iranian imperial heritage and, 194; Iran's engagement with, 202, 204; labor migrants from, in Russia, 73; Persian component of identity of, 158, 160; post-Soviet civil war in, 72; Soviet republic of, 71
Tajiks: in Afghanistan, 203–4; in Perso-Iranic world, 154; in Safavid empire, 196
Talabani, Jalal, 118, 161
Taliban, Iran and, 203
Tang dynasty (China), relations with "barbarians," 215, 220, 241, 245
Tannu-Uriankhai, 258, 260
Taranchis, in Xinjiang, 246
Tarbaghatai, Treaty of, 259, 261
Tarim Basin, oasis cities in, 245, 246
Tatar-Bashkir Republic, 47
Tatars: in Crimea, 104, 106; in Russian Empire, 25–26
Tatarstan, 45; bilateral treaty with Russia, 50, 51; nationalist movement in, 51, 52
Thaçi, Hashim, 132

Tiananmen Square protests: centralization after, 235; embrace of Confucian culture in wake of, 252; suppression of, 224
tianxia, concept of, 212, 213, 253–57; Belt and Road Initiative (BRI) and, 253, 267–68; China's central position in, 213, 214, 251; Confucianism and, 213, 214, 251, 255; in contemporary Chinese foreign policy, 215, 251–52; and pursuit of regional influence, 253; and *zhonghua minzu*, 214
Tibet, 210, 240–45; anti-Qing revolts in, 210; assimilationist policies in, 224–25, 235, 244–45; as autonomous region, recognition of, 234, 243; Buddhist government of, abolition of, 243–44; China's efforts to integrate, 224–25, 233; Chinese claims on, 232, 240, 252; Dalai Lama as spiritual leader of, 229, 240; Han settlers in, 235, 244–45; imperial rivalries in, 241, 242–43; infrastructure projects in, 258, 263; legacy of foreign intervention and separatism in, 211; overseas Chinese investment in, 229; Panchen Lama and, 244; periods without Chinese control in, 234; Qing rule in, 241–42; reconquest of, 211; repression under Mao, 243, 250; Simla Convention and claims to sovereignty of, 242–43; Yuan rule in, 241
TİKA (Turkish Cooperation and Coordination Agency), 103, 130
Tilly, Charles, 3
Tishkov, Valery, 29, 50
Torkamanchay (Türkmenchay), Treaty of, 64, 197
Transnistrian Moldavian People's Republic, 1–2
Transoxiana: cotton production in, 69; Persian-speaking dynasties in, 159–60; settlement and administrative consolidation of, 70

Trubetskoy, Nikolay, 39

True Path Party (Turkey), 130

Tunisia, Arab Spring in, 136

Türkeş, Alparslan, 102

Turkestan, 246; Russian settlement in, 69–70. *See also* East Turkestan

Turkey (Turkish Republic): Arab Spring and, 86, 100, 124, 136–37; under Atatürk, 13, 83–84, 95–96; Balkan policies of, 85, 99, 105–6, 128–32, 141–42; Blue Homeland claims of, 127; borders with Iraq and Syria, permeability of, 117–18; and Caucasus, 98, 99, 103, 105, 137–41; and Central Asia, 78, 98, 99, 103, 106, 139; and China, strategic cooperation with, 104; as civilizational state, vision of, 6, 99; competition between U.S. and Russia/China and, 275; democratic rule in, imperfect history of, 273; entanglement with peripheries of, 14; under Erbakan, 98; under Erdoğan, 86, 99–101, 123–25; exclusion from current world order, 5, 130; failed July 2016 coup in, 116; in Greater Turkic World, 91, 92; imperial legacy and, 2, 3, 8, 83–84, 85, 90–92, 101–6, 123–28, 141–42, 269–75; instability around periphery of, 143; intervention in Syria, 4, 14, 86, 101, 121, 122, 135, 137, 142; Iranian cooperation with, 182; and Iranian Turkmen, 184; Islamist movements in, 97–98; Kurdish borderland of, 84, 107–22, 181; Middle East policies of, 99, 127, 133–37; military's involvement in politics in, 108; minority groups in, 96; nation-building in, 124, 125; NATO accession of, 84; and new regional order, aspirations regarding, 99–100, 123–28, 133, 135–36, 137, 140, 141–43; origins of, 82–83, 134; Ottoman heritage of, efforts to reclaim, 82, 85–86, 99, 113; under Özal, 98–99; and "politics of difference,"

111, 114–15, 142; popular culture of, growing reach of, 136; and postimperial rivals, 4, 104; and post-Ottoman states, 99–100, 105–6; refugees in, influence of, 96–97, 125; revisionism of, explanations for, 5–6; risks of imperial overstretch for, 87; and Russia, competition in Caucasus, 138–41; and Russia, strategic cooperation with, 78, 104, 272; subnational identities in, 96–97; and Sunni world, ambition regarding, 92, 100–101, 168; and Turkmen tribes, 184; and U.S., relations with, 4, 105; use of military and proxy forces to project power, 137; Uyghur exiles in, 104. *See also* Ottoman Empire

Turkic identity, among Azeris, 175

Turkic language, common, call for, 95

Turkic unity, campaign for, 94–95, 184

Turkic World, 90, 91

Turkish Cooperation and Coordination Agency (TİKA), 103, 130

Turkish identity: Atatürk on, 83, 89, 95–96; civic-territorial version of, 95–96; contending discourses of, 90–92; Islam and, 85, 90, 91, 99–100, 105; Kurds and, 114; National Oath (*Mısak-ı Milli*) and, 95; Ottoman-Islamic core of, 85, 86, 93; Turkism (*Türkçülük*) and, 91, 101–3

Turkish-Islamic Synthesis, 91–92, 103

Turkish language, and Ottomanism, 10, 12

Turkish Republic of Northern Cyprus, 126

Turkism (*Türkçülük*), 91, 101–3; irredentist undertones of, 103

Türkiyeli, as supraethnic national identity, 12, 91

Türkkon (Cooperation Council of Turkic-Speaking States), 103

Turkmen, in Iranian borderlands, 170, 174, 183–85, 200, 201

Turkmenistan: gas exports to China, 265; Greater Iran concept and, 192; and Iranian Turkmen, 184–85; Russian policies in, 72

Türkmen Sahra, Iran, 171, 183–85

Turkmen SSR, 184

Tuva, Republic of, 45, 258, 260

Ubeydullah of Nehri, Sheykh, 112, 180

Ukraine: civic nationalism in, development of, 37; collectivization and famine in, 35; contested identity of, 36, 37–38; eastern, Russian occupation of, 14, 18, 31; East Slav unity and, 19, 31, 36; embrace of European identity, 73; historical ties with Russia, 24–25, 31–33; as imperial periphery, 9, 61; Orange Revolution in, 63, 68; Russian World Foundation activities in, 41; Russia's annexation of Crimean Peninsula from, 18, 31, 37, 40, 43, 273–74; Russia's claims of supporting "compatriots" in, 12; Russo-Turkish tensions over, 270; separatist movements in, 29, 37–38, 42–43; in Soviet Union, 34–36, 37; as successor state to Kyivan Rus, 31–32; Turkey's relations with, 104, 270; during World War II, 35, 38

Ukrainian Insurgent Army (UPA), 35

ulema, Shi'ite: as independent political force in Iran, 161–63; nation-building efforts and, 156, 157; in Safavid Iran, provenance of, 148, 162

Ungern-Sternberg, Roman von, 260

Union of Russian People, 27

United Arab Emirates, 136, 178; Iran's views on, 160

United Nations: China's ambitions regarding, 256; Mongolia's admission to, 260

United Russia Party: on Russian ethnonationalism, 31; and system of indirect rule, 56

United States: competition with Russia and China, 274, 275; and current world order, 4, 5, 271; and Eurasian postimperial states, relations with, 4; forces deployed in Central Asia, 72, 75–76; international bodies backed by, Chinese institutions compared to, 257; invasion of Iraq, 119, 191; Iran's campaign of resistance against, 147, 150–51, 155, 161; military presence in Afghanistan, opposition to, 203; Monroe Doctrine of, Russian policies compared to, 61; as product of empire, 7; and Russia's postimperial periphery, 67–68; Turkey's relations with, 4, 105

USSR. *See* Soviet Union

Ustryalov, Nikolay, 33

Usuli school of Shi'ism, 179

Uvarov, Sergey, 26

Uyghurs, 223; China's crackdown on, 13, 215, 231, 249–50, 257; Chinese policies regarding, 223, 229–30; creation of XUAR and, 248; diaspora in Turkey, 104; overseas, China's outreach to, 229; in Qing empire, 214; terrorist attacks by, 231; Turkish solidarity with, 106; in Xinjiang, 245, 248

Uzbekistan: cotton monoculture in, 71; Greater Iran concept and, 192; Persian language in, 158; Soviet republic of, 71; U.S. bases in, 72

Valdai Discussion Club, 76

Valuyev, Petr, 33

Vietnam: China's political system compared to, 5; EAEU and, 75

Vladimir (Grand Prince of Kyiv), 18

Volga region: ethnic republics in, 44, 47; imperial legacies in, 46

Vučić, Aleksandar, 132

Wang Jisi, 263

Wang Yi, 257

Warsaw Pact, 61

Wehler, Hans-Ulrich, 274

Wei Yuan, 232

West: development assistance from, China's BRI as alternative to, 266, 267; Eurasian integration as counterweight to, 73, 74, 76; Russia's strategic competition with, 21, 39, 78. *See also* global order, Westphalian; United States

Western Thrace, Turkish claims on, 126

White émigrés, and Russian ethnonationalism, 28, 31

White (Belarusian) Russians, 19

World Trade Organization, China in, 5

World Uyghur Congress, 229

World War I: Anglo-German rivalry leading to, 274; ethnic cleansing during, 102, 112, 113; Iran during, 169, 170, 172, 176, 180; Kazakh and Kyrgyz uprisings during, 70; and nationalization of Russian Empire, 28; Ottoman Empire during, 82, 95, 138; Russo-Ottoman conflict in, 65; South Caucasus during, 65

World War II: Iran during, 169, 170, 176, 181–82; Japanese invasion of China during, 236; North Caucasus rebellions during, 54; Ukrainians in, 35, 38

Xi Jinping: alliance relations under, 257; and Belt and Road Initiative (BRI), 208, 251, 264, 266, 268; on Community of Common Destiny, 212, 251, 256; and concept of "Chinese Dream," 228; elevation to "core leader," 13; imperial past invoked by, 3; minority policies under, 223; *tianxia* model and, 256; Xinjiang policies of, 231, 249; on *zhonghua minzu*, 225

Xinhai Revolution, 233, 234, 258

Xinjiang, 210, 245–49; assimilationist policies in, 224–25, 235, 248, 249; as

autonomous region, recognition of, 234; China's commitment to maintaining control in, 252, 275; China's crackdown in, 13, 231, 233, 249–50, 257, 265; China's efforts to integrate, 224–25, 233, 249, 258, 263; demographic profile of, 248; development strategy for, 249, 258, 262; Han settlers in, 235, 248, 249; legacy of foreign intervention and separatism in, 211; overseas Chinese investment in, 229; periods without Chinese control in, 234; as postimperial borderland, 233; Qing rule in, 245–47; social and political experiment in, 231; Soviet influence in, 245, 247, 261; Turkey's response to crackdown in, 104, 271; Turkic-speakers in, AKP's interest in, 85. *See also* East Turkestan; Uyghurs

Xinjiang Uyghur Autonomous Region (XUAR), 245, 248

xuetong zhuyi (principle of blood lineage), 227–28

Xunzi (Chinese Han-era thinker), 255, 256

Yakutia (Sakha), 45, 52

Yan Xuetong, 255–56

Yaqub Beg, rebellion of, 246, 259

Yazidis, 109, 110, 117, 121

Yellow Emperor, and Han identity, 218, 219, 225

Yeltsin, Boris: anti-imperial nationalism of, 20, 24, 62; Chechen declaration of independence and, 55–56; and civic *rossiyskiy* nation, efforts to build, 29, 42, 62; and ethnic republics, 49, 50, 55; "red-brown" coalition opposing, 61; Russian nationalism mobilized by, 29–30

Yemen: Hezbollah-style militias in, 166; Iran's policies regarding, 165; Shi'ite political movement in, 167

Yerevan khanate, 64

Yermolov, Mikhail, 64
Yongzheng Emperor (Qing ruler), 254–55
Younghusband, Francis, 242
Young Ottomans, 94
Young Turks, 82, 95. *See also* CUP (Committee of Union and Progress)
YPG (People's Protection Units), in northern Syria, 107, 109, 120–21, 122
Yuan dynasty (China), 210; attempts to Sinicize, 225, 239; and Inner Asian borderlands, 232–33, 237, 241; relations with "barbarians," 216
Yuan Shikai, 220–21
Yugoslavia: territory of, in Ottoman Empire, 128; wars of succession in, 129–30. *See also* Bosnia; Kosovo; Serbia
Yunus Emre Institute, 130

Zahir Shah, Muhammad, 202
Zand dynasty, and Persianate world, 150
Zaporozhian Cossacks, revolt of, 32
Zarrinkoub, Abdolhossein, 147
Zhang Binglin (Zhang Taiyan), 218, 219, 221, 227, 234

Zhang Qian, 208, 209, 267
Zhao Tingyang, 255, 256
Zhenbao (Damansky) Island, 261
Zhirinovsky, Vladimir, 30, 62
Zhivkov, Todor, 129
zhongguo, concept of, 210, 213, 219; and Greater China *(Da Zhongguo)* vs. China proper *(Benbu Zhongguo)*, 234; vs. *tianxia*, 253
zhonghua minzu, concept of: assimilationist policies based on, 225; and nation-building efforts in post-Qing era, 219–20; and overseas Chinese, 226–27; as supraethnic national identity, 12, 214, 219
Zhou dynasty (China), 213
Zhou dynasty (China), *huaxia* and *tianxia* under, 253
Zhou Enlai, 255, 261
Zhuang ethnic group, in China, 222
Zoroastrianism, 153, 156, 174
Zou Rong, 218, 227
Zuhab, Peace of, 133
Zungharia, 146, 245
Zunghars, 241, 242, 245–46, 259
Zyuganov, Gennady, 62